NEW DIRECTIONS
IN
PIAGETIAN THEORY
AND PRACTICE

List of Contributors

Harry Beilin, Graduate School and University Center, CUNY

David M. Brodzinsky, Douglass College, Rutgers University

Rodney R. Cocking, Educational Testing Service

Eleanor Duckworth, Massachusetts Institute of Technology

David Elkind, Eliot-Pearson Department of Child Study, Tufts University

George E. Forman, University of Massachusetts, Amherst

Jeanette McCarthy Gallagher, Temple University

Herbert P. Ginsburg, University of Rochester

Joseph Glick, Graduate School and University Center, CUNY

Roberta M. Golinkoff, University of Delaware

Constance Kamii, University of Illinois at Chicago Circle and University of Geneva

Robert Karplus, Group in Science and Mathematics Education and Lawrence Hall of Science, University of California, Berkeley

Deanna Kuhn, Laboratory of Human Development, Graduate School of Education Harvard University

Lewis Lipsitt, Brown University

Pierre Mounoud, Université de Genève

Frank B. Murray, University of Delaware

Edith D. Neimark, Douglass College, Rutgers University

D. Kim Reid, The University of Texas at Dallas

Irving E. Sigel, Educational Testing Service

Charles D. Smock, University of Georgia

Ernst von Glasersfeld, University of Georgia

James Youniss, Boys Town Center, Catholic University of America

Herbert Zimiles, Bank Street College of Education

Barry J. Zimmerman, The Graduate School and University Center, CUNY

NEW DIRECTIONS IN PIAGETIAN THEORY AND PRACTICE

Edited by

IRVING E. SIGEL
Educational Testing Service
Princeton, New Jersey

DAVID M. BRODZINSKY
Douglass College
Rutgers University

ROBERTA M. GOLINKOFF
University of Delaware

LEA LAWRENCE ERLBAUM ASSOCIATES, PUBLISHERS
1981   Hillsdale, New Jersey

Lawrence Erlbaum Associates, Inc., Publishers
365 Broadway
Hillsdale, New Jersey 07642

Library of Congress Cataloging in Publication Data
Main entry under title:

New directions in Piagetian theory and practice.

Includes bibliographical references and indexes.
1. Learning—Addresses, essays, lectures. 2. Cognition
in children—Addresses, essays, lectures. 3. Thought and
thinking—Addresses, essays, lectures. 4. Piaget, Jean,
1896–   —Addresses, essays, lectures. I. Sigel,
Irving E. II. Brodzinsky, David. III. Golinkoff,
Roberta M.
LB1060.N48   370.15'23   81-3160
ISBN 0-89859-072-8   AACR2

Printed in the United States of America

Contents

III THEORY

Preface

Ever since the late 1950's and early 1960's Piaget's writings have been the source of two strands of activity: (1) testing Piagetian ideas through laboratory and other types of research, and (2) inspiring practitioners, especially educators, to shape their programmatic efforts in directions derived from Piaget's work. These two trends have had a variety of consequences, for research and for application. A burgeoning research literature has resulted, testing various positions espoused by Piaget, as well as providing data which confirmed or disconfirmed Piaget's theory and research. Concurrently, practitioners, often educators, were more concerned with the perceived value of Piaget's ideas for formulating educational programs virtually at every academic level up to and including college age individuals.

The interesting phenomenon is that in spite of the fact that some empirical research casts doubts about various Piagetian notions, e.g., stages of cognitive development, etc., practitioners often continue to accept the validity of Piaget's empirical research. Essentially, the researcher and the practitioner were operating independently with little mutual influence. How often do researchers address problems brought to them by practitioners and vice versa? Each professional group comes out of different professional orientations with different reference groups and different perspectives resulting in minimal reciprocal influence.

The papers in this volume reflect the Piaget Society's interest in helping bridge the gap and increase communication between research workers and practitioners in education and allied fields by providing the context for an active dialogue. I feel this volume represents just such an effort since the papers in this book provide extensions of Piagetian theory as well as demonstrations of its applicability. The papers were presented in two symposia sponsored by the Piaget Society.

The aims of the symposia were two: (1) to create a dialogue among researchers interested in psychological development but with diversity of theoretical perspectives, ranging from those with a fundamental disagreement with the Piagetian perspective to those who are working within a Piagetian framework; and (2) to examine the relevance and appropriateness of Piagetian theory and research to education. What is particularly noteworthy about this set of papers is that they generate controversy relative to epistemological, theoretical and applicability issues. Some of the authors can be said to represent a viewpoint diametrically opposed to that of Piaget, whereas others accept the Piagetian perspective but work to elaborate and/or fill in gaps by their empirical work. Other writers seek to find commonality between Piagetian theory and other learning models. Similarly, controversy is present among the authors interested in application of Piagetian theory to education. For some, Piaget's work while generally relevant is too difficult to apply, whereas for others the system can be the basis of an educational program especially for preschool children.

Whether the authors are dealing with epistemological, theoretical or applicability issues and questions, their papers are cogent and clear presentations of a point of view. It is their inherent rationality evidenced in their well-reasoned arguments, often supported by data, that contribute to the excitement of the discussion.

The editors provide an integrative thematic presentation in the opening chapter providing the reader with a framework within which to identify similarities and differences among all the papers. Of course, the reader may generate his/her own organizational scheme, but the editors' introduction will facilitate that effort. Their analysis of the array of papers reflects the multilayered nature of Piaget's work. The diversity of opinion expressed in this volume is testimonial to Piaget's genius, for even those who disagree with him find it necessary to clarify their own position relative to his. He has generated excitement and interest even among scholars who disagree with him. The diversity of viewpoints expressed in this book provide provocative challenges to the epistemological, theoretical and applicability issues inherent in the Piagetian perspective. The editors point out that the issues raised in the discussions, such as the question of stages or the universality of the developmental progression or the relationship between development and learning or the value of a structural approach to cognitive development are not trivial but vital questions which require clarification if not resolution. These and other issues are brought out in these papers, wherein each author addresses questions from his point of view. This confrontation will also occur in the mind of the reader, since the discrepancies and contradictions among the writers will, if Piaget is correct, activate cognitive conflicts for each reader. Such cognitive conflicts can induce cognitive structural changes among adults just as they have been reported for children. From the Piagetian point of view, it is the active engagement of the individual that creates some type of resolution to cognitive conflicts.

Should not this same cognitive conflict concept also contribute to the development of Piagetian theory? Scientific theories like humans are dynamic organic systems that must grow and change as new information and new insights arise. Unless this happens, the entropic principle begins to work and the system will die. If Piagetian theory is to grow and develop it too must come to terms with new ideas, new contradicting data and new conceptions. This volume provides some of the substance for this experience to happen. The success of such happening, of course, depends on the readers' willingness to engage in the growth-producing process of discrepancy resolution.

Unfortunately, the amount of space available in a single volume did not allow for adequate treatment of all the important issues. The planners of the symposia organized the program along the Piagetian developmental stages, i.e., sensorimotor, preoperational, and concrete and formal operational levels. Within each of these stages, particular topics were selected which highlight some central questions within that age period, e.g., among elementary school children reading is a central issue. Thus, the volume is not comprehensive, but is selective, with a range of papers which highlight some of the critical issues that face Piagetian theory; but perhaps more important than the substance is the form, wherein dialogues set a process in motion which should benefit all concerned.

I write this preface not in my role of editor of the volume, but as a past president of the Piaget Society and one who was involved in the planning of these symposia. The Society by accepting this volume acknowledges the value of disagreement, discussion and actual ideological confrontation, which in my opinion is a healthy approach to the intellectual and scientific endeavor. I would like to acknowledge the cooperation of David Brodzinsky and Roberta Golinkoff, who by their thoughtful analyses helped create a coherent volume. As in all such compilations of papers, much behind the scenes activity went on such as working out the symposia schedule, typing and editing the manuscripts where necessary, as well as preparing the index. Much of this work was done by Linda Kozelski and Sheila Kraft, who by their conscientious and skillful handling of the details, helped bring this volume to a successful completion.

Irving Sigel
Princeton, New Jersey

To Jean Piaget, in memoriam

INTRODUCTION

1 New Directions in Piagetian Theory and Research: An Integrative Perspective

David M. Brodzinsky
Douglass College,
Rutgers University

Irving E. Sigel
Educational Testing Service

Roberta M. Golinkoff
University of Delaware

Piaget and his coworkers have produced a vast body of knowledge that has influenced large segments of Western and even non-Western theory and research in psychology and education. The growth and influence of this conceptual framework over the past two decades is all the more remarkable when viewed in relation to the behavioristically oriented psychology that previously dominated Western schools of thought. Not only was Piagetian theory and methodology conceptually alien to behaviorism, but its cultural impact was considerably broader. Piaget inspired research by such diverse groups as Indian, Japanese, Nigerian, and Zambian behavioral scientists (Dasen, 1977). This is a most remarkable phenomenon.

We are still too close to grasp the full significance of this Piagetian explosion. For some, it was timely and appropriate because of the vacuousness in American science education in the mid-1950s, when Russia launched Sputnik 1. For others, it may have been the growing interest in cognitive development, and the awareness that existent developmental theory had little to say about this domain. Perhaps these were factors, but why Piagetian theory? Was it because it seemed to focus on scientifically relevant concepts: e.g., number, time, space, classifica-

3

tion? In addition, and perhaps most critical, Piaget focused on thought *about* scientific problems—logical thinking. On first blush, it looked as though Piaget and his colleagues had the answers to how children develop their thinking and reasoning about all the physical concepts. Such information, it was believed, would provide a framework for understanding children's acquisition of knowledge, as well as developing science and mathematics curricula.

This increasing interest in Piagetian theory has generated a set of new issues for psychologists and educators in the areas of epistemology, developmental theory, and application. Those scholars who have addressed these issues have been of four types: (1) those working close to Piaget's original formulations, (2) those who stay within the framework but see the need for revision, (3) those who see flaws in the theory and attempt to challenge its basic assumptions, and (4) those who reject the theory *in toto*.

Our position would seem to fit the second category because we argue that no theory is sacrosanct, and beyond change. Rather, since psychological theories are products of their era and since change is intrinsic to all living forms, change in the theory is inevitable. Change comes not only from those working within the theory, but even from the originator himself. Piaget as a scientist has become his own change agent because ''the sciences by their use of methods of experimentation and deduction solve some problems and constantly give rise to new ones . . . [Piaget, 1971, p. 232].''

Basically, what Piaget is interested in is the construction of knowledge. Kuhn (Chapter 19d) has cogently defined the foundations of Piaget's developmental psychology as ''the constructivist concept—the idea that more advanced forms of cognition are constructed anew by each individual through a process of self-directed or self-regulated activity [p. 353].'' Piaget continues to build an elaborated edifice to explicate by deduction how advanced forms of cognition are constructed and how the process of self-regulation functions. The empirical test of the deductions produces the data base which serve to provide the basis for acceptance or rejection of deductions, and in so doing, is the means of theory revision.

No theoretical system is complete or necessarily eternally valid. Scientific inquiry by its very nature is an open system. For our purpose, the critical issue is the way in which scientific inquiry has influenced Piaget's theory. After some early efforts at replicating Piaget's ideas, his theoretical formulations became increasingly pervasive among developmental psychologists. Although the theory is still pervasive, a number of current attempts are being made to revise the theory, in light of a body of empirical disconfirmations which have appeared in the last decade. The revisionist efforts are being made in at least three areas: the epistemology of the theory, the theory, itself, and the applicability of the theory to ''real world'' problems—e.g., education. This division is mirrored in the organization of this volume. This chapter highlights many of the key assumptions of Piaget's theory, and provides an integrative perspective on the issues raised by the authors in this book.

EPISTEMOLOGICAL PERSPECTIVE

The primary epistemological question addressed by the developmental psychologist is, "How do we come to know?" Psychologists, from whatever persuasion, explicitly or implicitly, adhere to a particular epistemological position. One's epistemology defines the definition of knowledge and influences the methods of studying its acquisition.

Reviewing current conceptualizations of development, one can discern at least two clearly defined systematic perspectives which result in fundamentally different epistemologies (Reese & Overton, 1970). On the one hand, the organismic model of human development provides us with a basis for a *constructivistic* epistemology, while on the other hand, the mechanistic perspective provides the basis for a *naive realist* epistemology.

It is our belief that the major impetus for interest in epistemological issues among developmental psychologists stems from Piaget's assertion that an understanding of the process of cognitive growth can best be understood within a genetic epistemological framework. Piaget has stated that knowledge is acquired through a constructivist process, which is defined in terms of the individual's organizing, structuring, and restructuring of experience—an ongoing lifelong process—in accordance with existing schemes of thought. In turn, these very schemes become modified and enriched in the course of interaction with the physical and social world. Thus, from Piaget's constructivist position, knowledge is never a direct copy of reality. In sum, "the main function of genetic epistemology is this discovery that the only way in which we get knowledge is through continual construction, and that we can have no enduring knowledge without actively maintaining this process [Gruber & Voneche, 1977, p. xxii]."

Inspired to some extent by Piaget's work, a number of developmental psychologists have addressed issues of knowledge acquisition from a constructivist orientation. However, within this group there exists a variety of perspectives as to the nature of the constructivist process. Further, there are many individuals who similarly are interested in the acquisition of knowledge, but who adopt a nonconstructivist position. In the present volume this range of orientations is represented; on the one hand, traditional behaviorism with its logical positivistic epistemology, and on the other hand, a diametrically opposed radical constructivist position. Between these two poles reside perspectives which, while not eclectic, do represent divergence.

To begin with, let us examine Lipsitt's chapter, "Sensorimotor development: What infants do and what we think about what they do." For Lipsitt (Chapter 2), the Piagetian structuralist-constructivist model is replete with constructs such as "stages," "organizations," and the like, which can "delude" the investigator into "believing" he has an explanation for a phenomenon he cannot actually observe. Hence, Lipsitt, consistent with the behaviorist paradigm, opts for descriptions and manipulations of behavior that are identifiable, eschewing hypothetical constructs. Lipsitt emphasizes a learning model of development, where transitions in developmental level are redefined as accumulations of new knowledge, acquired in a continuous, incremental fashion.

The central message of Lipsitt's chapter is exemplified in his report of an object permanence-type study (Schuberth, Werner, & Lipsitt, 1978), a replication of a study by Evans and Gratch (1972). The details of the experiment are provided enabling the reader to get a clear picture of the experimental approach. The important point for us is that where Evans and Gratch interpret infant behaviors as reflecting a new stage, Lipsitt rejects the "stage" concept as nonparsimonious and as clouding the issue. For Lipsitt, "stages represent gaps in our information as scientists, not necessarily gaps in the behavior of our subjects [Lipsitt, Chapter 2, p. 31]." He contends that change is gradual and not a sudden emergence of new behavior. Thus, for Lipsitt, the Piagetian conceptualization of behavioral outcomes can be interpreted more prudently from a traditional learning process model.

Lipsitt's epistemology calls for an antecedent-consequent analysis of change. He uses data from infant research as exemplars for his argument. Although Lipsitt's analysis of the object concept paradigm is instructive, a more convincing case possibly could have been built if he presented the issue of stage in the context of more complex developmental phenomena; e.g., children's acquisition of conservation or propositional logic. The question still remains as to whether the transitions claimed to occur with older children by some researchers can be explained as neatly in a behavioristic model as the results of the Schuberth et al. (1978) study.

Whereas Lipsitt works from a traditional behavioristic model, rejecting such terms as constructivism, and the like, as superfluous, Zimmerman (Chapter 3), an exponent of social learning theory sees some commonality between his behavioristic position and the constructivism of Piaget and his followers. In fact, Zimmerman notes that social learning theory can be construed as a cognitive theory encompassing a constructivistic perspective. For Zimmerman, constructions of knowledge can be explained within the context of reciprocal behaviorism (Bandura, 1978). From this position, the way a person constructs a situation is simultaneously controlled by previous cognitive rules and by stimulation from the environment. Zimmerman believes that cognitive constructivistic positions have placed too much emphasis on mental activity and too little on the significance of the environment. He also believes that traditional approaches to constructivism have underplayed the relationship between mental and behavioral constructivism. Zimmerman suggests that people construct environments that support their concepts, as well as constructing the concepts themselves. He argues that cognitive constructivism can, and should be, facilitated, especially by means of social learning techniques (e.g., modeling).

The superficial similarity between Zimmerman and Piaget, however, should not beguile the reader into thinking that, in fact, a paradigmatic commonality has emerged. Rather, what has been demonstrated by Zimmerman is that there are common touchstones which, although facilitating communication, still distinguish social learning theory from the constructivism of Piaget. Although it is argued by some that mixed paradigms are not workable (Reese & Overton, 1970), it may be that in this case we see a move toward rapprochement, at least at the level of description of some central cognitive processes; e.g., rule learning, imitation, etc.

It is Smock's chapter (Chapter 4) that provides the clearest picture of Piagetian constructivism, thereby serving as a pivot in our discussion. By defining key Piagetian constructs of knowledge acquisition and change (e.g., structure, equilibration, etc.), and their relevance to social contexts, Smock allows the reader the opportunity to compare two highly divergent perspectives—on the one hand, logical positivism, and on the other, radical constructivism.

What Smock has done is to organize coherently the central constructs of Piaget's theory. This organizational model (see Smock, Fig. 4.1) enables the reader to grasp clearly a Piagetian explanation of how knowledge is acquired and utilized, and the role the social milieu plays in this process. Although for Lipsitt, the more extreme behaviorist exponent in this volume, these constructs are quasi-fictional *descriptions,* useful primarily for heuristic purposes, for Piaget (and Smock), they have an *explanatory* potential. The resolution of this difference resides in the paradigmatic preference of the reader. What we have done here is to distill the issues.

Although Smock notes that Piaget is both a structuralist and a constructivist, the question arises as to whether the two necessarily go hand in hand. Can one be a structuralist without also adopting a constructivist perspective? Further, does constructivism necessarily imply a focus on structure? It is these questions that form the heart of Cocking'a chapter (Chapter 5).

In an attempt to examine the continuities and discontinuities between structuralism and constructivism, Cocking presents a thoughtful analysis of the defining features of these two constructs. He notes that within assimilative theories, such as Piaget's, the two constructs are not only compatible, but in fact, are inextricably linked. For example, Piaget argues that knowledge is derived, and never simply a direct reflection of some ontological real world. Further, knowledge is seen as being limited by the existing schemes or structures that characterize the individual's mental world. Yet, these structures are not static; on the contrary, they are dynamic, and are constantly being transformed both qualitatively and quantitatively, through the active and constructivistic processes of assimilation and accomodation. Thus, for Piaget, meaning or knowledge involves derived forms—structures, which are constructed through the active interchanges between the individual and the environment.

In formal structuralism, however, as Cocking notes, meaning is conveyed by structure or *a priori* forms, not derived forms. In addition, these structures are characterized by specific principles—wholeness, transformation, and self-regulation—which allow for "good form," while precluding "bad form." Yet,

Cocking points out, through examples in the area of language comprehension, that these principles run counter to much developmental data—particularly the diachronic aspects of development. Both "good form" and "bad form" are characteristics of the child's development, and it is only through a constructivistic perspective, argues Cocking, that one can resolve this apparent discrepancy of structuralist principles.

We have seen various reactions to Piaget's constructivist perspective, from outright rejection (Lipsitt, Chapter 2), to qualified acceptance (Zimmerman, Chapter 3), to acceptance of the essentials with some minor revisions (Cocking, Chapter 5; Smock, Chapter 4). Von Glasersfeld (Chapter 6), in contrast, in rejecting the copy theory of knowledge, adopts what he calls a "radical" constructivist perspective, a position which borders on being phenomenological. He argues that traditional conceptions of epistemology have been misleading in their characterization of human cognitive adaptation. Von Glasersfeld reinterprets that evolutionary metaphor of adaptation in terms of the concept of "viability." The former, he proposes, is too often misinterpreted in terms of environmentally induced change in the organism. Organismic change results, not from the environment *selecting* certain organisms, while *rejecting* others, but from the organism's actions, which allow it to "get by" the constraints of the environment. If the means or actions (whatever their form) are successful in allowing the organism to "get by" environmental constraints, then they are considered *viable,* and will remain in the organism's repertoire as long as they serve their purpose. Likewise, argues Von Glasersfeld, human knowledge is not a function of matching some external real world, but results from organismic activity or constructions. Constructions remain unchanged as long as they are viable—as long as they allow the human organism to "get by" environmental constraints. When constructions are no longer viable—when they are unsuccesful in allowing the organism to understand and adapt to his surroundings— new constructions emerge.

Von Glasersfeld also confronts the issue of the origin of the "constraints in experience." He suggests that these constraints should not necessarily be thought of as constraints in the "real world." On the contrary, environmental constraints are also the product of the organism's own constructions. Thus, the organism's constructivistic activity provides the basis for those experienced constraints which determine viability of the organism's knowledge. As such, organisms are their own change agents.

THEORETICAL PERSPECTIVE

In the previous section, we dealt with Piaget's metatheory and with the assumptions underlying his epistemology. In this section, we shall address the goals and issues of the theory itself.

Piaget has developed a stage dependent theory of the origins and development of intelligence. At the core of the theory is the distinction and relationship among three central concepts: *structure, function,* and *content.* Cognitive structure refers to the inferred organizational properties that underlie the child's thought and behavior. These properties change with increasing age and experience, not only quantitatively, but more importantly, in a qualitative fashion as well. In fact, qualitative change is the essence of Piaget's stage theory of intelligence.

Although cognitive structures change with age, cognitive functions do not. The latter represent the characteristics of mental activity—organization and adaptation—that are invariant throughout development. Cognitive functions are the very essence of intelligent behavior. They are the processes that account for development, refinement, and transformation of cognitive structures. As such, they are means whereby the organism strives for the goal or end state of development—namely, equilibration.

Finally, content represents substantive knowledge of the world; e.g., space, time, social rules, etc. Actions, physical and/or mental, performed on these contents form the empirical base of Piaget's theory, the base from which cognitive structures are inferred. Like structures, and unlike functions, substantive knowledge changes with age and experience, and thus is manifested in different forms at different stages of development.

Ever since Piaget's theory received serious consideration by Western behavioral scientists, it has been the focus of numerous theoretical controversies. Researchers working both outside, as well as inside, Piaget's theoretical framework have raised questions concerning the validity and/or utility of certain structural, functional, and content components of the theory. Some of the issues dealt with in this volume strike at the very heart of the theory; for example, the role of biological versus experiential factors in development (Mounoud, Chapter 7), the utility, characteristics, and universality of structures or stages (Glick, Chapter 14; Murray, Chapter 10; Neimark, Chapter 11), and the relation between language and thought. (Beilin, Chapter 8). Other issues, although not as closely linked to core components of Piaget's theory, nevertheless are extremely important, for they deal with reinterpretations (Youniss, Chapter 12), refinements (Sigel, Chapter 13), and extensions (Golinkoff, Chapter 9) of the theory. Although the issues raised within this volume certainly are not exhaustive of the problems and questions surrounding Piaget's theory, they are representative of current attempts at reconceptualizing the theory in light of recent developmental data.

Mounoud's contribution (Chapter 7) reflects an emphasis on preformations of logical structures which evolve in the course of maturation, and as such is a departure from the traditional Piagetian position. According to Mounoud, the preformed structures provide the basis for the organization of experience. Experience, itself, does not influence maturing structure, but rather provides only the content upon which the structure operates. Mounoud argues that preformed structures determine if and how the child solves a given problem. Using tasks that allow for analysis of actions—a strategy which Mounoud emphasizes—he identifies three types of internal organization, all observable within the first five years of life: (1) the sensorimotor level, defined by reflex activity, (2) the perceptive-motor level, corresponding to gestalt notions of configuration and mnemonic traces, and (3) the conceptuo-motor level, related to the ability to deal with symbols and signs.

In emphasizing the maturational basis of these internal organizations, Mounoud reiterates a classic and unresolved issue in developmental psychology; namely, the validity of preformism. Mounoud's evidence for his position is presented in studies that focus on analysis of children's actions in problem-solving contexts. Yet, whether psychological data can lay to rest the preformation question is moot. Mounoud does, of course, force us to rethink the issue by providing a rational and empirical base for his assertions. Offering levels of analysis of internal organization provides a categorization that may help in conceptualization of the issue.

The issue of preformism is not restricted to discussions about sensorimotor development, but also is relevant to discussions of cognitive competencies which emerge at later developmental levels. One area that has received particular attention with respect to the preformism issue is language, and its unique relationship to thought. In Beilin's chapter (Chapter 8), we see the preformism issue raised in the context of the controversy between the nativism of Chomsky and the constructivism of Piaget.

Chomsky (1976) argues that language competence is innately given, and represented in the form of a universal grammar. Further, he forcefully rejects the empiricist's claim that linguistic development can be accounted for by reinforcement contingencies or imitative processes. The Genevan position, on the other hand, although rejecting the empiricist explanation of language development, argues that language is tied not to a genetically programmed structure, as Chomsky suggests, but to preverbal cognitive structures that are constructed by the child during the sensorimotor period (Sinclair, 1976)—a notion that Chomsky questions. For Piaget, language becomes a vehicle for thought, a means by which cognitive structures are expressed, and not the basis of cognition. This position places Piagetian theory in direct contrast to most theories dealing with higher order mental functioning (e.g., Beilin, 1975; Bruner & Anglin, 1973; Vygotsky, 1962).

Beilin suggests that the research findings support neither Chomsky nor the traditional Piagetian position. He argues that "the theoretical relation between cognition and language is one of partial autonomy for each system [Beilin, Chapter 8, p. 120]." In other words, language neither derives wholly from cognition, nor vice versa. Instead, each system shares certain commonalities with the other, and feeds into the other's development. Although noting that recent Genevan writings have given greater emphasis to language as a source of knowledge,

Beilin argues convincingly that they have not gone far enough. He cites research that indicates that operational structures can be induced by linguistic activity—a finding that seriously threatens the tenability of the Genevan position. Beilin concludes that it is time for the Genevans to rethink their position on the relation between language and thought. He emphasizes that language is not only a vehicle for the expression of cognition, but in fact is also a dynamic force that promotes further development in intellectual and social domains.

Golinkoff (Chapter 9) extends the discussion of the relation between language and thought by focusing on the infant's transition from unintentional to intentional preverbal communication. She points out that although Piaget did not specifically emphasize the development of communication during the sensorimotor period his writings on infancy have been most heuristic for researchers in the area. Golinkoff's chapter is essentially a review of the research in the area of early communication development with emphasis on the role that Piaget's theorizing has played.

Golinkoff begins her argument by proposing that cognitive precursors for linguistic categories are constructed during the sensorimotor period, consonant with the Piagetian position. Furthermore, she notes that some communicative functions of language are probably constructed prelinguistically as well. One of these communicative functions is a preverbal form of the directive where the child purposely attempts to contact the adult and use him or her as an agent in achieving some end. Building on Piaget's description of the development of causality, Golinkoff presents an analysis of what the infant needs to know to be successful at communicating nonlinguistic messages intentionally. She argues that Stage 5 in the development of causality is at least necessary for the infant to use intentional communication—a contention that is supported by the empirical research she reviews. Thus, although Golinkoff does not work within Piaget's theory per se, she uses the theory to link perverbal cognitive constructions in the area of causality to the transition from unintentional to intentional communication.

Our previous discussion focused on issues in sensorimotor and preoperational periods of development. There are also new directions and issues around the development of concrete and formal operations. One of the central issues that investigators have addressed in the past two decades in the period of concrete operations is the nature and development of conservation.

Few, if any, concepts in developmental psychology have received as much attention as the concept of conservation. This attention is a result of the importance placed upon the concept by the Genevan researchers, themselves. For example, Inhelder and Sinclair (1969) note that the various forms of conservation are "the main symptoms of a budding system of operational structures [p. 3]."

The conservation concept has come to represent a number of things to psychologists and educators. On the one hand, it represents an experimental paradigm or a series of research procedures that are used to study specific areas of behavior and thought. For other individuals, however, conservation has become a reified construct representing a fundamental characteristic of logical reasoning. As such, conservation is said to represent an "ability" which eventually characterizes children are they mature cognitively. Because it is construed as an ability, and therefore, trainable, it is not surprising that conservation, and related concepts, have become the focus of curriculum development and instruction (Lavatelli, 1970).

In addition to the attention it has engendered, the conservation concept has become the focus of considerable controversy. In fact, some of the major criticisms leveled against Piaget's theory have centered on the development and explanation of conservation (Brainerd, 1978a). It is this issue, in fact, that forms the basis of the chapter by Murray (Chapter 10).

Murray begins by examining some of the limitations of the Genevan model of concrete operations—most notably the grouping model, which is the logical framework underlying the child's operative system of thought. At the heart of the problem is the absence of synchronous development for concrete operational abilities, thought to share a common logico-mathematical structural base. Murray pinpoints the problem when he states that "the central theoretical issue is the degree of asynchrony a structural stage theory can tolerate before the nonstructural components vitiate completely any clarity and explanatory power the stage construct confers on the phenomena [p. 144]."

Asynchrony may stem from a number of sources. Some of these are unrelated to the structural base of the concept in question (in this case, conservation). One of the most important sources is the set of criteria used to determine the presence or absence of specific cognitive skills. Researchers have debated extensively the appropriateness of various criteria and procedures for establishing the existence of conservation, and related concepts (Brainerd, 1973; Flavell, 1977; Miller, 1976; Reese & Schack, 1974). As Murray points out, however, the appropriateness of different criteria is not an empirical question that can be resolved by research, but must be understood as a corollary model or paradigm issue (Reese & Overton, 1970). He raises the question of how to establish evidence of conservation competence. He notes that the mere presence of a nonconservation response is not necessarily proof that the child is a nonconserver, anymore than a conservation response guarantees that he is a conserver. The reason for the skepticism resides in the fact that a number of nonstructural factors, including task characteristics (e.g., type of stimulus material, degree of stimulus abstractness, type of stimulus transformation, etc.) and organismic characteristics (e.g., attentional factors, cognitive style, etc.), have been shown to influence the child's performance in the conservation paradigm. What Murray does is to provide us with a clear, comprehensive, and valuable analysis of the nonstructural factors in the conservation problem, and to cast it into a broader theoretical perspective. There is need for such close task analysis if the relationship between task and performance is to be understood in developmental terms. Perhaps even more important is that Murray's chapter is an excellent paradigmatic example for creating the type of relationship between Piagetian theory and education that so desperately is needed. Although we discuss this in more detail later, it should be pointed out that Murray's chapter is rare, in that he deals not only with the specifics of a research paradigm, but with the implications of the paradigm for educational application. Unfortunately, this could not be an extensive treatment, but the prototype is there.

Another important theoretical issue dealt with in this volume concerns the universality of the fourth and final stage of Piaget's theory—formal operations. Accumulating evidence suggests that most adult samples show relatively low levels of formal operational thought (Blasi & Hoeffel, 1974; Neimark, 1975a), a finding that contradicts the assertion that formal operations are universal. As a result, Piaget (1972), himself, has begun to rethink his position regarding the development and manifestation of formal operations.

Neimark (Chapter 11), however, cautions against premature rejection or modification of the theory. Instead, she presents a unique and somewhat controversial explanation for the apparent nonuniversal nature of formal operations. Her basic thesis is that the low incidence of formal operations found among adults may be due to an artifact of the measurement process. Adults may have the competence to solve formal operational problems, but may fail to do so because of the way in which the problems are structured and/or presented. In adopting the competence-performance distinction, Neimark's analysis of formal operations bears considerable similarity to the analysis of conservation theory presented by Murray (Chapter 10). Yet Neimark offers a very specific explanation of the source of performance variability with respect to formal operations—namely, cognitive style factors.

Neimark argues that most tasks used to assess formal operations are unstructured and ambiguously presented. Further, she notes that it is under such procedural conditions that cognitive style dimensions such as field-dependence/ field-independence are most likely to become operative. For example, field-dependent individuals, although possessing the competence to solve formal operational tasks, may fail to do so because of their difficulty in disembedding relevant stimulus information in the context of unstructured tasks and ambiguous instructions.

The issue raised by Neimark is not only important with respect to the formal operational period, but, in fact, is relevant for all stages of cognitive development. Yet Piaget has not concerned himself with cognitive style variables or other individual difference dimensions at any stage of development. From Piaget's epistemological perspective, individual differences are not central because the primary topic of concern is how the generic human being acquires knowledge, not the ways in which knowledge is acquired by individuals. Still, an interest in human variability, irrespective of the ability in question, is an important research approach, because it is truly a psychological problem. We know that variability is intrinsic to development in general, and we are aware of some of the sources for such variation (Sigel & Brodzinsky, 1977). Further, it is becoming increasingly clear to psychologists that the development and utilization of cognitive structures are tied very closely to such individual difference dimensions as cognitive styles (see Brodzinsky, 1980; Case, 1974; Neimark, 1975b; Pascual-Leone, 1970). In this context, Neimark's paper is not only timely, but along with Murray's chapter, is an important contribution to our understanding of the interaction between structural and nonstructural factors in cognitive development.

Although the previous theoretical papers have tended to emphasize intraindividual characteristics interacting with task variables, they have paid little or no attention to the role of experience in a broader social and cultural sense. These papers are consonant with the prevailing approach of many Piagetian oriented researchers. Ironically, Piaget himself, as far back as 1932 in his work on morality addressed the relevance of social and personal experience, a fact which many current investigators have tended to overlook.

In his chapter, Youniss (Chapter 12) asks for a modern reading of Piaget's volume on moral judgment, which he believes will result in a revision of the current and prevalent assumption that Piaget relegates the role of the child's social experience to an insignificant place. The Youniss chapter casts a new light on the significance of Piaget's seminal ideas, creating a link between cognition of the physical and social world. Piaget is currently interpreted by many as a cognitive theorist, minimizing affect and the role of interpersonal relations. Youniss' interpretation virtually demands a revision of our current understanding of Piaget. He argues that Piaget lays the basis for a relational theory of the development of self, social conscience, and sense of justice. Why Piaget himself did not fully develop these ideas is beyond the scope of Youniss' chapter. Unfortunately, he only touches on this point. Although detailed study of such psychological concepts as self, interpersonal relationships, and the like, was not central for Piaget's subsequent work, what he did contribute, Youniss argues, must not be overlooked. The significance rests, not in Piaget's identification of these social concepts, nor in the fact that he, as an acute observer of human nature and society, acknowledges them, but that he can place them within his epistemological and conceptual scheme. This is Youniss' significant interpretation. Thus, relational theory should not be viewed as a fragment disassociated from the mainstream of Piagetian thought.

Although Youniss' reinterpretation of Piagetian thinking points to Piaget's awareness of the social context as significant for development of self and social adaptation generally, the relationship between these social experiences and cognitive functioning is not spelled out. By focusing exclusively on Piaget's (1948/

1932) book, *The Moral Judgment of the Child,* Youniss does not address the implication of his reinterpretation to other substantive areas of cognition.

Coincidently, Sigel (Chapter 13) does extend, directly and indirectly, some of the implications of Youniss's discussion of the social realm. Although neither Piaget nor Youniss identify the specific interactional behaviors involved in adult-child interchanges, Sigel addresses this issue by proposing that a particular class of social acts activates and thereby influences the development of representational thought. He refers to these social acts as *distancing strategies* because they create temporal and spatial distance between the individual and the immediate social context. Sigel, following Piaget's lead, contends that there is a close relationship between those experiences which generate cognitive conflict and cognitive growth. Interpreting cognitive conflict as "discrepancy," Sigel argues that distancing strategies generate discrepancy, and may contribute to its resolution. In this way, distancing strategies stimulate cognitive growth. Sigel presents evidence supporting his "distancing theory." Drawing on research studies with preschool children and their teachers or parents, he shows that the frequency and quality of distancing strategies does indeed make a difference in the child's capacity to deal with tasks requiring, for example, predictions, articulation of cause–effect relationships, and sequential memory.

Thus, the Youniss and Sigel chapters, although having different initial objectives, demonstrate for us quite convincingly the comprehensiveness of Piagetian theory. Perhaps more important, they do set the record straight; to wit, Piaget does not eschew the significance of social experience, rather, social engagement is a critical condition for cognitive growth.

The role of social experience in cognitive development is also addressed in the chapter by Glick (Chapter 14), but in a broader sociocultural framework. Glick notes that cross-cultural data cast serious doubt on Piaget's assumption of the universality of operational structures, at least at the deployment or performance level. The central question for Glick is the reason for variation in cognitive performance across cultures. His answer to this question is both intriguing and highly controversial.

Glick suggests that deployment or utilization of rational thought does not reflect simply the competence of the individual. To understand the meaning of cognitive performance, it must be examined within the context of the individual's sociocultural support systems. He further argues that there is not just a single form of rationality, such as Piaget's logico-mathematical system, but multiple forms of rationality, each of which is differentiately elicited and maintained by particular sociocultural conditions. Glick sees little reason to label one form of rationality as necessarily more primitive or more advanced than any other form of rationality. To the extent that certain forms of rationality lead to effective adaptation—the goal of development—they are valued, built into the cultural system, and hence are maintained. Other forms of rationality, which are not as readily linked to the values of the culture, either are suppressed, ignored, or simply are not in the awareness of cultural members. Because cultures vary in their value systems, they are likely to promote different forms of rational thought. The result is cross-cultural variation in cognitive behavior.

In examining the issue of the deployment of operational structures, Glick adopts a functional or pragmatic approach to rationality, a perspective that certainly diverges from a traditional Piagetian analysis of thought. Yet, divergence should not necessarily be interpreted as incompatability. We argue that Glick's approach is not only compatable with Piaget's theory, but in fact augments the theory by providing a framework from which to examine why variability in the deployment of cognitive operations is evident among cultures. Glick's chapter is a valuable contribution to the growing corpus of cross-cultural research in Piagetian psychology (Dasen, 1977).

APPLIED PERSPECTIVE

Regardless of whether one adopts a Piagetian perspective or not, it cannot be denied that Piaget has had a most significant impact on developmental psychology. His theory has forced researchers to reconsider earlier, and somewhat simplistic, conceptions of the developing child. But from the perspective of utility and social good, one may ask legitimately, to what end are such theoretical contributions? Of what practical use is such a comprehensive and complex construction of the human mind? After all, the criterion of applicability is not a necessary, nor well articulated requirement of science. Nevertheless, applications of Piagetian theory, particularly for the educational process, have captured the attention and imagination of educators throughout the world. The reasons for this interest reside in the intrinsic attractiveness of the theory to the educational enterprise. As we noted earlier, Piaget describes how the human intellect develops stage by stage not only in general terms, but specific to substantive content areas—e.g., number, space, time,—many of which are relevant to education. In addition, Piaget also emphasizes a model of thought based upon the "rational-scientist"—i.e., logico-mathematical reasoning. When one considers Piaget's focus on substance (space, time, etc.) in conjunction with process (logical reasoning), it is not only understandable, but almost inevitable, that Piagetian theory would arouse the interest of the imaginative and innovative educator struggling to cope with the social needs of the time.

A major impetus for application of Piaget's idea to education was the advent of compensatory education, beginning with the Head Start program. There was a need to create educational programs that would prepare "disadvantaged" youngsters for elementary school. Piaget was the only investigator of note who reported on the cognitive status of children during the preschool years. More important, he described the transition to the period at which children entered elementary school. Thus, Piaget's discussions of the development of the content and the process of cognitive growth paralleled the educational institution's age graded system. No doubt other reasons for the attractiveness of Piaget's theory to educators exist, but analysis of these reasons is beyond the scope of the volume. The fact of the matter is that it happened. The question now is how to apply so complex a theory to the educational enterprise.

The traditional educational effort can be conceptualized as involving three basic elements: *teacher preparation, curriculum development,* and *classroom organization.* As we shall see, the remaining chapters in this volume demonstrate how Piagetian theory contributes to each of these components. Of interest, however, is that while each of the authors pays homage to Piaget for his contribution to their educational efforts, they vary in the way in which Piagetian theory is interpreted and used.

Kamii (Chapter 15), a most consistent advocate of the applicability of Piagetian theory to education, demonstrates how Piaget's epistemology, his theory, and his research findings can undergird and even define a preschool program. Contending that Piagetian theory represents a revolutionary paradigm shift (Kuhn, 1970) in that it is a "constructivism by equilibration" model, Kamii proceeds to compare existent child development approaches in preschool education with a Piagetian approach. For Kamii, the child development approach refers to those efforts, which in her view, emphasize socioemotional features of development, and which have paid too little attention to cognitive growth. Her strategy is to incorporate the child development approach within the Piagetian perspective in order to achieve a proper balance between cognitive and socioemotional factors. This integration is reflected in her statements about preschool objectives: enhanced autonomy, peer relations, and the acquisition of knowledge of the social and physical world. All of these objectives "were derived from Piaget's constructivism" (Kamii, Chapter 15, p. 241).

Given the creation of the school program, the next step facing the educator is its implementation. A problem in this area may arise, however, when a program runs counter to prevailing community beliefs and values—a situation which Kamii discusses relevant to Piagetian educational programming. Such a counter-force is consistent with Kuhn's (1970) analysis of community reactions to revolutionary paradigms.

Kamii asserts that there is no direct linkage between Piaget's constructivist model and applications to the classroom. Consequently, the educator must derive relevant principles and procedures as bases for programming. Yet the complexity of the theory, its lack of specificity, and its everchanging nature, contribute to individual differences in interpretation. This clearly is apparent in the variation in educational programming, each of which claims to be "Piagetian-based" (e.g., Copple, Sigel, & Saunders, 1979; Kamii, Chapter 15; Lavatelli, 1970; Smock, Chapter 4; Weikart, Rogers, Adcock, & McClelland, 1970.)

Heretofore we were addressing the question of applying Piagetian theory to preschool children. Kamii provides a rather detailed set of suggestions for educating the young child. Her approach, like most applications of Piagetian theory to preschool education, is concerned less with subject matter than with exploration of materials, and the discovery of relationships among objects and the like.

Upon entering elementary school, however, children begin a more formal process of education. A new and more structured set of activities and curricula are encountered by the child—e.g., the critical skills of reading, writing, and arithmetic. As the child progresses in school, additional curricula also are included—science, social studies, foreign languages, etc.

The child's entrance into school raises a number of interesting questions for Piaget's theory. For example, can the theory help us to understand the child's mastery of traditional school subjects? Does Piagetian theory offer any instructional insights that are relevant for the teaching of reading, science, social studies, etc.?

Certainly Piaget's theory is not wholly unrelated to school curricula. He has dealt directly with such questions as the child's development of number concepts and geometrical reasoning. On the other hand, he has had little, if anything, to say about such fundamental skills as reading or writing. Does the theory offer insights into these subject matters? In his chapter, Elkind (Chapter 16) argues that it does, at least for reading. He makes his case with a lesson Piaget has been trying to teach; to wit, "it is only by observing children's struggles to learn that the underlying structure of the task and its particular mode of presentation are revealed" (Elkind, Chapter 16, p. 270). Following this dictum, Elkind proceeds to analyze the logical substructure of the reading process. He argues that stages of reading can be identified and understood within the context of cognitive development, in general. He suggests that reading requires a number of decoding processes. At first, the child learns to transform single letters into specific sounds. Later he or she comes to realize that the same letter can have more than one sound, and that different combinations of letters may yield sounds that are unrelated to the sounds of the individual letters. This shift in decoding, he says, is analogous to the shift from identity conservation to equivalence conservation. Identity decoding is where the sound of a single letter or combination of letters remain the same, and is recognized, regardless of context, whereas equivalence decoding is a more complex transformation involving the child's realization that the same letter or combination of letters may be associated with different sounds in different contexts. Essentially, Elkind is mapping his model of conservation onto reading.

Zimilies (Chapter 16), in his commentary, takes issue with a key aspect of Elkind's chapter; namely, the assumed isomorphism between Piagetian theoretical constructs and reading decoding processes. He suggests that there is only superficial similarity between such constructs as conservation, seriation, multiplicative classification, and the decoding processes of reading, as described by Elkind. Zimilies is skeptical about the direct applicability of Piagetian theory to reading. Instead, he asks for greater accomodation of the theory to the diverse phenomena of cognitive development, in general, and the educational setting, in particular.

The difference in viewpoint between Elkind and Zimilies on this issue indicates the kind of difference in orientation and strategy that exists among individuals identified with the Piagetian structural perspective. This difference of opinion is of more than passing interest, however, for it touches on the same fundamental issue raised in the theoretical section of this chapter, and in many of the theoretical chapters in this volume—namely, do we continue to make efforts to fit phenomena to the theory, or do we try to refine or revise the theory as new data come in? This remains a core issue for Piagetian theorists.

Although the previous chapters in this section tended to accept Piaget's basic concepts as they apply to education, Karplus (Chapter 17) questions the utility of one of Piaget's central theses; namely, the stage construct. For Piaget, each stage represents a unique and qualitatively distinct organization of the individual's mental structures. With increasing age and experience these structures change from being bound by motor action in infancy, to being dominated by perceptual and intuitive processes in the preschool years, and finally, by concrete and then formal operational processes during middle childhood and adolescence, respectively.

The construct of stage has come under attack from a number of sources (Brainerd, 1978b; Flavell, 1977). Karplus also reveals his concern with stages, not so much in terms of their validity, but as a heuristic for educational purposes. He suggests that the behavior of the student in the classroom does not show the consistency predicted by stage theory. Consequently, the teacher is hard pressed to categorize students according to Piagetian stages, and to devise stage-related curricula to meet specific instructional needs. In the place of stage, Karplus offers an alternative construct, *reasoning pattern,* which he believes not only has greater face validity with respect to actual student behavior, but also is more useful for curriculum development. Karplus defines reasoning patterns as identifiable and reproducible thought processes directed toward specific types of tasks. Although he acknowledges a degree of similarity between stages and reasoning patterns, the latter are seen as providing a more sensitive means of understanding student behavior, primarily because they are tied more closely to specific academic requirements, task content, and actual task behavior of the individual, than are stage-related structures. Thus, whereas Piaget provides a perspective describing the structure and functions of mental operations independent of content, Karplus focuses on both cognitive activity and task content. Herein lies the difference between the two perspectives.

Karplus goes on to examine the possibility of promoting more effective reasoning patterns among students within the context of a teaching strategy he labels the *Learning Cycle*. The latter, which is comprised of three phases (exploration, concept introduction, and concept application), "combines autonomous student activities and conceptual teacher input in a form of inquiry teaching...." (Karplus, Chapter 17, p. 304). Karplus concludes that the learning cycle approach, which he sees as compatible with a number of educational learning theories, offers greater potential than does Piaget's theory for making a meaningful contribution to educational theory and practice.

We have noted already the natural bond between Piaget's theory and the goals of educators—namely, the socialization of intelligence. Indeed, the interest shown in adapting Piaget's theory and research to the practice of education has been particularly intense in the past decade or so. Yet, inevitably with such a complex theory there are bound to be problems in the "translation" process. The hope of some psychologists and educators for a rather direct link between the theory and classroom practice and curriculum development seems to have been unrealized. This is not to say, however, that Piagetian theory has nothing to offer the educator. On the contrary, much can be gained by the educational theorist and practitioner through a careful and thorough reading of Piaget's work. But in doing so, educaters must be aware not only of the potential contributions, but also of the limitations of the theory, if they are to avoid pedagogical misapplications. An important step in elucidating both the benefits and drawbacks of Piaget's theory for education is provided by Ginsberg (Chapter 18).

Ginsberg is also skeptical about the direct relevance of Piaget's theory for education, certainly more so than he was in earlier writings (Ginsberg & Opper, 1969). In his chapter, Ginsberg reviews some of the commonly held assumptions concerning the application of the theory for educational practice. He notes both the contributions and potential (and actual) misapplications related to the theory. For example, Piaget has emphasized repeatedly that knowledge must be constructed; that it is never simply a direct copy of the external world. Translated to the classroom, this implies that the child must be guided through a discovery and rediscovery process in the course of mastering the subject matter in question. As valuable as this suggestion is, Ginsberg notes that it is a very general principle that is not readily translated into instructional practice. Further, this approach, and Piaget's theory in general, does not easily account for the more passive, receptive, or rote type of learning that is a common and legitimate component of school learning. Ginsberg observes that Piaget's emphasis on active learning too frequently has been misinterpreted to imply physical activity. He points out, in fact, that the more sophisticated or mature forms of active learning occur on the level of reflective abstraction—that is, children's active and conscious awareness of their own thought processes.

These are but two examples of the implications of Piaget's theory for education that Ginsberg deals with. He concludes by arguing that Piaget's theory, although offering general pedagogical guidelines, has little to contribute in the way of specific recommendations that would directly affect classroom teaching.

Mechanisms of Learning and Development

The papers by Gallagher, Reid, Forman, Kuhn, and Duckworth (Chapter 19)[1] form a subset held together by a common theme—how knowledge is acquired in an educational context. Although each paper focuses on a different population of children in terms of age and psychological characteristics, these investigators are striving to understand the basic problem of knowledge acquisition. Gallagher and Reid suggest that engaging children in situations involving contradictions—a procedure reminiscent of Piaget's method clinique and Sigel's inquiry strategies—stimulates cognitive growth. Yet in spite of some consensus that the use of contradictions is a proper educational stimulant, there is still need to explain how this process works. What are the mechanics, the processes which are activated, and how does the child acquire the "stuff" with which to engage in the process of interaction? For Gallagher, the assimilative-accomodative model suffices, and this perspective is elaborated by Kuhn who takes a strong constructivist position. Forman actually seems to be describing the same phenomenon but defines the engagement as a "negation of a negation." Duckworth's discussion also lends support to the general theme, holding that surprises are the grist of life. Whatever type of definition is offered, the same question arises: Just why does contradiction and consequently reflective abstraction work? Kuhn's argument about the significance of the anticipatory schema points to a relevant process, but again the mechanisms are identified only in a vague sense. Essentially, the model under discussion seems to be a tension reduction one, where imbalance is generated and the individual must resolve the contradiction. Such a resolution creates harmony. Yet the dialecticians argue that there is never any harmony—there is only temporary stability and "off the individual goes again."

Thus, we are left with assertions but no explanations. Still, such observations should not be rejected simply because the mechanisms are undefined. The present situation is analogous to earlier models of electricity or even aspirin. For many years electricity and aspirin were used for many important functions—electricity to power machines and aspirin to control many bodily aches and pains. Yet the mechanisms or the essences of these elements were not known. It was only recently that the reason for aspirin's effectiveness in reducing fevers was identified. But the effectiveness of electricity or of aspirin was in no way reduced or enhanced. The same principle can be applied to the use of contradiction as a powerful tool in the service of educational practice. To help children become active problem solvers and active thinkers, employment of contradictions and surprises may well be advocated, even though the mechanics of the process are not well understood.

---

[1]These papers comprised a symposium on the "Mechanisms of Learning" organized by George Forman and Jeanette Gallagher.

This brings us to the second major concern of these chapters; namely, the constructive process. Although all the authors hold to a constructivist view of learning, none of them clearly defines just how this process works. Yet we have a sense that the metaphor is one of a builder, transforming raw experience to a coherent and organized product. The child experiences, and this experience becomes part of his or her repertoire that is built into some kind of organization. Again, the process is only vaguely described, in this case even by Piaget. What does become evident from Reid's chapter, however, is that the emotional state of the child can play a significant role in the constructive process. Reid points out that whereas children who are retarded or emotionally disturbed go through similar constructive processes as normal children, they are likely to do so in a more fragmented and hence less efficient way. This poses an interesting problem in methodology, because if the child is too disturbed to properly function in a testing situation, one does not know if the underlying cognitive processes are affected or if the child is not able to relate to that particular situation. In any event, pointing out the role of emotional distress in the course of cognitive functioning calls attention to the study of the relationship between affect and cognition, an area already too much neglected.

CONCLUSIONS

For nearly 60 years, Piaget has been studying issues in genetic epistemology. In this time, he has constructed an elaborate and impressive theory of the origin and determinants of knowledge. Yet, Piaget's work has been the center of controversy for many years. Critics have attacked his epistemology, his theory, and his methodology. At first, and to a great extent, these criticisms arose because of the radically different perspective that Piaget adopted in his approach to intelligence, at least in comparison to the behavioristically oriented perspective that previously had dominated American psychology. These criticisms were to be expected for they were based upon a paradigm that was quite different than the one underlying Piaget's theory.

Other criticisms, however, particularly more recent ones, have come from individuals who either support the basic tenets of the theory, or at least are sympathetic to the major goals of the theory. These criticisms have been in response to perceived inconsistencies within the theory, or to discrepancies between theory predictions and research findings. Many of the chapters in this volume have called for revisions in Piaget's theory, and if not revisions, at least clarifications of tenets of the theory that were formerly held unquestioningly. A key example is the concept of activity. Several of the authors in this volume (Kuhn, Ginsberg, Smock, Kamii) have begun to examine the use of this concept in Piagetian theory. Although we can accept the proposition that the concept of activity is essential to descriptions of how the child's cognitive development advances, its theoretical and empirical characterization has been much too vague.

Another thread that weaves in a zigzag fashion through these chapters is the issue of the relationship between the cognitive and the social domains (Youniss, Sigel, Golinkoff, Glick). Whereas some have criticized Piaget for his failure to attend to the social context in which knowledge is constructed, others have rediscovered in Piaget an acknowledgment of the general influence of the social sphere. Unfortunately, as several authors in this volume have noted (Youniss, Sigel), Piaget fails to discuss the details of the linkage between social and cognitive development.

The Genevan response to the criticisms of the theory, such as those raised in this volume, as well as elsewhere, has varied. On the one hand, attempts have been made, however, limited, to bring the theory in line with the general findings of accumulated research—e.g., the controversy over the development and deployment of formal operations (Piaget, 1972). Some criticisms, however, essentially have been ignored, or at least downplayed—e.g., the controversy concerning the common grouping structure assumed to underlie all aspects of concrete operational thought.

Whether Piaget and his coworkers will be able to respond sufficiently to the criticisms and problems that have arisen in the literature is something that cannot be answered at the present time. There is no question, however, that Piaget's theory is changing. Piagetian theory of the 1980s certainly is not the same theory that existed in the 1930s; nor is it likely that the former will remain the same in the decades to come. All theories, if they are to remain viable, must be dynamic and open to change. Piaget's theory is no exception. The important question, as we noted in an earlier section of this chapter, is the direction and form of the change.

We argue that theoretical change is a dialectical process, in the sense described by Riegel (1979). This process is evident in the chapters of this volume. Change has occurred within Piagetian theory as a function of the Piagetian oriented researcher's response to both internal and external criticism. This is reflected in the increased attention paid to the role of nonstructural factors in cognitive development (e.g., task characteristics, individual difference factors such as cognitive styles, social and cultural experience, etc), the place of language in the development of thought, and the problems of direct application of the theory to educational settings. Yet, advances in Piaget's theory have also stimulated change in other theoretical systems. We note particularly the efforts of social learning theorists to incorporate within their theories such Piagetian notions as constructivism (Zimmerman, Chapter 3). Perhaps these changes reflect an implicit move toward increasing mutual influence among theoretical systems, leading to an eventual synthesis. Certainly, the dialectical process is ongoing. This volume, in its own unique way, although not considering all the pertinent issues, is a step toward the rapprochement.

REFERENCES

Bandura, A. The self-system in reciprocal determinism. *American Psychologist,* 1978, *33,* 344–358.

Beilin, H. *Studies in the cognitive basis of language development.* New York: Academic Press, 1975.

Blasi, A., & Hoeffel, E. C. Adolescence and formal operations. *Human Development,* 1974, *17,* 344–363.

Brainerd, C. J. Judgments and explanations as criteria for the presence of cognitive structures. *Psychological Bulletin,* 1973, *79,* 172–179.

Brainerd, C. J. *Piaget's theory of intelligence.* Englewood Cliffs, New Jersey: Prentice-Hall, 1978. (a)

Brainerd, C. J. The stage question in cognitive-developmental theory. *Behavioral and Brain Sciences,* 1978, *2,* 173–182. (b)

Brodzinsky, D. M. Cognitive style differences in children's spatial perspective taking. *Developmental Psychology,* 1980, *16,* 151–152.

Bruner, J. B., & Anglin, J. M. *Beyond the information given.* New York: Norton, 1973.

Case, R. Structures and strictures: Some functional limitations on the course of cognitive growth. *Cognitive Psychology,* 1974, *6,* 544–573.

Chomsky, N. On the biological basis of language capacities. In R. W. Rieber (Ed.), *The neuropsychology of language: Essays in honor of Eric Lenneberg.* New York: Plenum, 1976.

Copple, C., Sigel, I. E., & Saunders, R. *Educating the young thinker.* New York: Van Nostrand, 1979.

Dasen, P. (Ed.). *Piagetian psychology: Cross-cultural contributions.* New York: Gardner Press, 1977.

Evans, W. F., & Gratch, G. The stage IV error in Piaget's theory of object concept development: Difficulties in object conceptualization or spatial localization. *Child Development,* 1972, *43,* 682–688.

Flavell, J. H. *Cognitive development.* Englewood Cliffs, N.J.: Prentice-Hall, 1977.

Ginsberg, H., & Opper, S. *Piaget's theory of intellectual development: An introduction.* (1st ed.) Englewood Cliffs, N.J.: Prentice-Hall, 1969.

Gruber, H. E., & Voneche, J. J. (Eds.). *The essential Piaget.* New York: Basic Books, 1977.

Inhelder, B., & Sinclair, H. Learning cognitive structures. In P. Mussen, J. Langer, & M. Covington (Eds.), *Trends and issues in developmental psychology.* New York: Holt, Rinehart, & Winston, 1969.

Kuhn, T. S. *The structure of scientific revolutions.* (2nd ed.) Chicago: University of Chicago Press, 1970.

Lavatelli, C. *Early childhood curriculum: A Piagetian program.* Boston: American Service & Engineering, 1970.

Miller, S. A. Nonverbal assessment of Piagetian concepts. *Psychological Bulletin,* 1976, *83,* 405–430.

Neimark, E. D. Intellectual development in adolescence. In F. D. Horowitz (Ed.), *Review of child development research.* Vol 4. Chicago: University of Chicago Press, 1975. (a)

Neimark, E. D. Longitudinal development of formal operations thought. *Genetic Psychology Monographs,* 1975, *91,* 171–225. (b)

Pascual-Leone, J. A mathematical model for the transition in Piaget's developmental stages. *Acta Psychologica,* 1970, *63,* 301–345.

Piaget, J. *The moral judgment of the child.* Glencoe, Ill: The Free Press, 1948. (Originally published, London: Kegan Paul, 1932.)

Piaget, J. *Insight and illusion of philosophy.* New York: World Publishing Company, 1971.

Piaget, J. Intellectual evolution from adolescence to adulthood. *Human Development*, 1972, *15*, 1-12.

Reese, H. W., & Shack, M. L. Comment on Brainerd's criteria for cognitive structures. *Psychological Bulletin*, 1974, *81*, 67-69.

Reese, H. W., & Overton, W. F. Models of development and theories of development. In L. R. Goulet & P. B. Baltes (Eds.), *Lifespan developmental psychology: Research and theory*. New York: Academic Press, 1970.

Riegel, K. F. *Foundations of dialectical psychology*. New York: Academic Press, 1979.

Schuberth, R. E., Werner, J. S., & Lipsitt, L. P. The stage IV error in Piaget's theory of object concept development: A reconsideration of the spatial localization hypothesis. *Child Development*, 1978, *49*, 744-748.

Sigel, I. E., & Brodzinsky, D. M. Individual differences: a perspective for understanding intellectual development. In H. L. Hom & P. A. Robinson (Eds.), *Psychological processes in early education*. New York: Academic Press, 1977.

Sigel, I. E., & Saunders, R. An inquiry into inquiry: Question-asking as an instructional model. In L. G. Katz (Ed.), *Current topics in early education*. Vol 2. Norwood, N.J.: Ablex Publishing Corp., 1979.

Sinclair, H. Epistemology and the study of language. In B. Inhelder & H. H. Chipman (Eds.), *Piaget and his school*. New York: Springer-Verlag, 1976.

Vygotsky, L. *Thought and language*. Cambridge, Mass.: Massachusetts Institute of Technology, 1962.

Weikart, D. P., Rogers, L., Adcock, C., & McClelland, J. *The cognitively oriented curriculum: A framework for preschool teachers*. Washington, D.C.: National Association for the Education of Young Children, 1970.

II EPISTEMOLOGY

2

Sensorimotor Development: What Infants Do and How We Think About What They Do

Lewis P. Lipsitt
Brown University

> *The interaction between the subject and his environment is a complex organization at every level of development and particularly at birth . . . At birth the exchange between the child and the environment is defined by a reflex organization that we will call* internal *sensorimotor organization (or internal sensorimotor model). The sensorimotor organization is responsible for all the movements of the infant (sucking, arm, hand, eye movements, etc). In other words, it specifies the movements in relation to the information given by the sensory receptors. This organization contains a formal structure (processing center or general coordination center).*
> —Pierre Mounoud (This Volume)

The attribution of "organizations" to mental processes, which presume underlying "structures" that are "responsible" for behavior, is an act of the scientist quite far removed from the behavior of the person whom we seek to understand. The postulation of "coordination centers" as explanatory concepts bears considerable similarity with the assumption of reified "stages" that are also assumed by some developmental theorists to explain behavior, particularly transitions in behavior that we are accustomed to observe in children as they grow older. Age and growth are directly measurable. Similarly, changes in behavior with increasing experience or the passage of time can be directly observed, and the observed behavioral changes can in fact be attributed to specific experiences (such as learning trials) through the use of appropriately controlled observations. "Organizations," "structures," "stages," and "coordination centers," on the other hand, cannot be directly observed. They are postulations. The advantage they provide must be weighed against the disadvantageous influence they can have, by deluding us into believing we have explained a behavioral phenomenon when we have only substituted one unknown for another.

STAGES AND STRUCTURES IN DEVELOPMENT

Concepts of stages and structures in developmental psychology have served an important purpose in facilitating speculation and theorizing. Such postulations, however, have also tended to mask underlying processes that might otherwise have yielded to behavioral (antecedent-consequent) analysis if the posited structure or stage had been interpreted as a mere metaphor, manner of speaking, or heuristic device.

Structural concepts, of which stages are one type, do help to organize data and do help us communicate about observed behavior in an abbreviatory way. One psychologist usually knows what another psychologist means, in general and in a fairly noncontroversial way, when it is said that a child is still in the sensorimotor stage, or even by the term "preoedipal child." In either instance, one conjures a child who is still behaving in certain ways, and not behaving yet in others.

It is admittedly very useful for communication purposes, if not for the eventual understanding of the underlying behavior processes, to think in terms of the preverbal versus the verbal child, the nonwalker versus the walking child, the preoperational and the concrete operations child. There are hazards, however. Take for example, the following pronouncement: "The first period of development is called the Sensorimotor because the child solves problems using his sensory systems and motoric activity rather than the symbolic processes that characterize the other three major periods" (Ault, 1977). In buying the descriptive abbreviation, "the sensorimotor period," there is an implicit purchase of a white elephant. While such dichotomizations and categorizations are useful for descriptive and communication ease, they tend to obfuscate the real nature of development, particularly the importance of transitional periods, which are seldom sudden. Transitions are themselves, after all, important foci of study, especially for those of us interested in learning processes. It is an interesting fact that babies generally creep before they crawl, and crawl before they walk. The mere documentation, however, of the characteristic sequencing of such behaviors with increasing age does not tell us much, if anything, about the antecedents for the achievement of walking behavior. We cannot *explain* walking behavior by asserting that the child is in "the walking stage."

The age-and-stage orientation to understanding child development tends to emphasize constitutional-maturational determinants, and to belittle learning antecedents (Brainerd, 1978). The deprecation or oversight of learning processes has not been the only consequence of developmentalists' predilections for stage concepts, however. Certain important transitional biological processes are also often slighted by the age-and-stage orientation to human development. Hormonal changes occurring in the course of human development and which give rise to descriptions of human behavior in terms such as "pre-sexual," "adolescent," "adult," or "mature," do not typically take place in a stepwise fashion. We run the risk of overlooking important transitional phenomena, both behavioral and physiological, by adhering to a language which ascribes jump-wise changes in such functioning. While, as admitted, there is descriptive and abbreviatory value to stage concepts in human development, they place verbal constraints on us and thus limit our conceptualizations. Stage concepts tend to force our thinking into a certain rather rigid mold with respect to the influence of cumulative experience on the development of human behavior.

Stage concepts often inhibit optimism about the potentialities of humans, especially the educational potential of children (Lipsitt, 1966). In the area of infant learning, for example, numerous references of 40 years or so ago suggested that the cortical immaturity of the newborn human was such as to forbid learning. The cerebral innervation of the child under three months of age was just too immature. The reasoning was usually circular and based upon non-morphological observations: A feeble attempt at conditioning had been made, no learning was observed, and the conclusion was drawn that poorly developed physiological structures precluded a positive finding.

Another case in point is that of what the educators call "reading-readiness." For some time it has been quite blatantly assumed that reading readiness, which after all is merely a statement as to whether it is possible to *teach* a given child a certain behavior at a certain time, is either present or absent in a child. Now, it is unquestionably true that most children below a certain age (e.g., one year) probably cannot be taught to read and that most children beyond a certain age (e.g., eight years) probably can be taught to read. It does not follow therefore that children pass a certain momentary point in the life span beyond which reading is suddenly easy whereas earlier it was very difficult or impossible. We now know a great deal more about the techniques necessary to facilitate reading in young children than we did even a decade ago, and children can probably be taught to read earlier than previously, if one wishes to take the trouble. Readiness to do *anything* depends not only on age but also on the particular methods, procedures, or techniques that we employ in facilitating the transition.

As we gain more information about the specific processes involved in going from one "stage" to another, our understanding of such processes tends, or should tend, to eliminate the concepts of stages from our thinking. Stages do have an heuristic value in the history of our understanding of human development, but when stage explanations are superceded by *process* explanations, we ourselves have finally come of age. The more we learn about development, seemingly the more stages do we require and the smaller do the steps become. Stages represent gaps in our information as scientists, not necessarily gaps in the behavior of our subjects.

A more serious objection to concepts of stages is in our tendency to *reify* these stages. The empirical hazard is that we come to regard those stages as real conditions of the organism rather than as artifacts of our observational procedures and methodologies. Conceptualizations of development in terms of stages are usually followed closely by the adoption of a structural view of the mind. The postulation of structures is usually based upon behavioral observations, to be sure, but the language quickly becomes metaphorical. The special words, initially devised merely to abbreviate complex behavioral patterns, now become taskmasters and slaves.

The argument here is against psychological typologies, particularly when the use of typological vocabularies tends to stifle further search for underlying processes and transitional attributes. Contrary to some views, the learning-process psychologist has not entirely escaped the lure of the typological lingo. We have our anxious and nonanxious children, we have our conditioned subjects and those who failed to condition, and we have a peculiar sort of stage-concept in our use of the terms "performance criterion" or "learning criterion." Arbitrary adoption of such designations of subject attributes or behavioral characteristics builds into the organism's behavior a step or stage that is not really there, but is there only in our thinking *about* his or her behavior. The organism has not *really* become a learner at the point where we decreed him to be, by verbal agreement, a learner. Nor have his mental structures been at all affected by our verbal agreements! Some psychological theorists seem more aware of and self-conscious about the fictional and heuristic character of their hypothetical constructs than others.

TRANSITIONS AND LEARNING PROCESSES

A stage theory of development necessitates the introduction of some notion of transition from one stage to another. In Piagetian theory, the mechanism of transition usually involves some sort of perturbation in which the old schemas or rules will not work for new, or more complex, input. There is a sense in Piaget's theory about stages and transitions that the child has a kind of disturbance of consciousness, or disequilibrium, when confronted with dissonant messages from the environment, on the one hand, and his prior appreciation of the way things are, on the other.

Some recent attempts have been made to discover the antecedents for the shift in infants' behavior when they achieve the level of object permanence. The so-called Stage IV error in Piaget's theory of object permanence has been of particular fascination to behaviorally oriented child developmentalists, perhaps because the actions of infants prior to their achievement of object permanence are so incongruous, even for a 12 month old. In the typical Stage IV task, the child is shown an interesting object and is encouraged to look at it while the examiner hides it under one of two cloths, usually in a well of some sort. Once the object is hidden, the child is encouraged to seek and find it. He does, and may do so several times. Then, again with the child watching closely, the object is hidden in the alternate well. The "prepermanence" child continues to seek the object in the old place, often to the amusement and amazement of adults. He even looks stunned when upon removing the cloth, he does not find the object in the first location. The child's perturbation is clearly over not finding the object in the first hiding spot. Somewhere along the way, however, that "silly" kind of perturbation must yield to another kind. In this next "step," the child must become perturbed enough over the failure to find the object that he must now seek elsewhere. Perplexity must give impetus to, through frustration, anger, or whatever, a search in other logically possible locations. One most logical possibility, based upon stimulus generalization if nothing else, would be the second well which looks like and is *nearly* in the same location as the well that is dry. Perturbation-mediated search will ultimately yield the correct answer. Yet there are no studies of this process whereby prepermanence infants become "transformed" through a process involving (1) error-production, (2) perturbation, (3) continued search, (4) discovery of the alternate location and the pleasure involved in that discovery, and, eventually, (5) learning that the object is sometimes in the first hiding place, sometimes in the other, and always in the one where the experimenter is seen to have been last hiding it.

Not long ago, Schuberth, Werner, and Lipsitt (1978) took up the task of trying to understand the mechanisms and processes of object permanence behavior, particularly the interesting Stage IV error. Evans and Gratch (1972) had conducted an experiment to determine whether the error reflects difficulties in spatial localization or object conceptualization. They allowed two groups of infants to recover a toy twice in succession at location A. Five hiding trials at B were then administered. One group was tested on the B trials with the same toy as had been used on A trials. For the other group, a different toy was used. They reasoned that if the errors occur because of a limited understanding of space (the spatial localization error), the infant can conceive of places only in terms of prior actions, and without regard to the object's identity; hiding a new toy at B should have no different effect than hiding the same toy. However, if the infant errs because he has knowledge of the object only in terms of the context in which he previously acted upon it (the object conceptualization hypothesis) then the introduction and hiding of a new toy should reduce errors.

Actually, a reduction in errors with the new toy could also be attributed to increased distinctiveness of a new testing situation, and its concomitantly reduced transfer of training from the A trials to the B. trials. Anything which enhances the discriminability of the B trials from the A trials, or the novelty of the situation, should promote "object-permanence" behavior. Gratch and Evans reported that there were no differences between the two groups with respect to errors; an equivalent number erred on the first B trial, and the two groups generated comparable error strings on successive trials. Confirmation of the null hypothesis led Gratch and Evans to conclude that Stage IV errors are essentially place-going errors. Their data did not support Piaget's presumption as to the basis of Stage IV errors. They could as well have concluded that their data did not endorse a learning interpretation.

In a replication of the Gratch and Evans design, Schuberth et al. (1978) carried out a study on 24 infants aged about 9 months. The procedure was identical to that of Gratch and Evans, with one exception. In the Gratch and Evans study, the same-toy and different-toy infants were treated differently during the interval between the last hiding trial at A and the first at B. For the same-toy infants, the toy was taken away from the child, his attention was maintained, and the toy was moved slowly to the B well. For the different-toy infants, the experimenter took the old toy away and, maintaining the child's attention, slowly moved the old toy out of sight, returning with the new toy. The new toy was held in front of the child and, as the child looked on, it was moved slowly to the B well. This procedure should indeed have enhanced the distinctiveness of the B condition from the A condition, and should have thus promoted break-up of the response error pattern. There is no indication that this was the intent of Gratch and Evans in treating the two groups differently, but the fact that the extra effort favoring a learning interpretation did *not* have the expected effect attests to the robustness of the Stage IV error.

In Schuberth et al (1978), the test-procedure confound was removed by using the same procedure for both groups. For both groups, the previous toy was moved out of sight after the last A trial, and either the same or the new toy was then introduced at B for the first time. In our version of the procedure, the toy in the well was visible to the child before the well was covered. A 3 second interval was allowed before the tray containing wells A and B was pushed toward the child for the attempt at recovery. If the toy was found, play with it for five seconds was permitted before the toy was taken away in preparation for the next trial. The A trials were discontinued after the child had searched and recovered the toy on two consecutive trials. None of the children made errors on the first trial, and only one on the second.

The same procedure was followed for the B trials. When an infant searched mistakenly at well A, the tray was pulled away to prevent search at B. Trials continued until a correct search was made, but if a child mistakenly searched at A for five trials, the following trials were run on an error-correction basis; that is, after making the wrong response, the tray was left in place to allow another attempt.

In this study, 11 same-toy children searched at A on the first B trial, but only 4 different-toy children did so. This was a reliable difference between the groups. The same-toy group made more consecutive errors than the different-toy group, and this effect was also reliable. The only errors made by the different-toy children occurred on the first B trial, and successful recoveries were made on all subsequent trials.

Thus, different-toy children made fewer errors in the "transfer of training" situation involving the B trials. My thinking about this effect is that any condition that tends to enhance the distinctiveness of the transfer task relative to the original training task, such as by introducing a new toy for the B trials, should reduce the "negative transfer" to the second task. In the Schuberth et al. study this is indeed what happened. The wonder is that the same effect was not obtained by Gratch and Evans, especially since their procedures during the transition interval between the A trials and the B trials were such as to promote the distinctiveness of the changed conditions. (They moved the B toy into place in a distinctive way relative to the way in which they had been presenting the A toy.)

The significant decrease in B errors when a new toy was hidden is consistent with Piaget's object concept hypothesis. However, the results are problematic for Piaget's account in that one third of the infants in the different-toy condition searched at A on the first B trial. It appears that the subjects made a "smooth" transition to correct B trial performance rather than a sudden transition invited by the Piaget explanation. The gradualization of changed behavior, from A to B trials, is more suggestive of a learning process, in which transfer errors are at first made (at least by a fair number of children), whereupon attention of the child is directed to the error, and a correction is thereupon made in succeeding trials. Indeed the different-toy children made no errors whatever following the first B trial.

Butterworth (1977) has argued that the B errors do not reflect conceptualizations as postulated by Piaget. Contrary to Piaget's assumption that infants code the location of a hidden object in terms of their own activity (i.e., the child goes on subsequent occasions to the location at which the behavior has previously occurred and been successful), Butterworth contends that object location is coded in terms of a "duality of relations between a self-referent body-centered space, i.e., an egocentric spatial code (Paillard, 1974), and the visual field, i.e., an allocentric spatial code (Merleau-Ponty, 1962)." Moving a toy from location A to B is believed by Butterworth to generate conflict between these equiprobable frames of reference subserving the perception of space. The developmental problem for the infant is thus one of coordinating the frames of reference that define the location of an object in space.

The reason I am dwelling so on this experimental model and these findings is that, to a person trained like myself in the "old" learning theory postulates or principles (such as the law of effect, the proposition that experience improves behavior in the direction of the reinforcement, the notion of transfer of training, the idea that generalization plays an important role in the behavioral performance, or the phenomena of acquired distinctiveness and equivalence), it just seems more prudent and parsimonious to suppose that identifiable parameters affecting B trial behavior can be isolated, manipulated, and evaluated as to their relevance in the Stage IV error situation.

A simple learning interpretation of the fascinating A-cum-B error aberration in sensorimotor level children would hold that the experience of searching successfully for the object at A intensifies the tendency to return to A on subsequent occasions when the object is hidden. When the object is placed at B, the infant errs because the habit strength established for search at A overrides the yet-to-be established response of searching at B. (There is negative transfer.)

Learning theory has not, as yet, been wildly successful in accounting for qualitative changes in behavior that define Piaget's sequence (Lipsitt & Reese, 1977). It is admitted that these qualitative shifts are of special fascination. Viewers of our videotapes from the aforementioned Schuberth et al. study, including the experimenters themselves, never cease to be amazed at the apparent "stupidity" of the preobject-concept child in his persistent search for the toy at the A well, when the toy has been so clearly (to us postobject-concept individuals) placed in the B well, Nonetheless, increasing the distinctiveness of the B well from the A well placement *does* attenuate the effect, and that's the point. Indeed, the introduction of a delay between hiding the object at B and allowing retrieval enhances the probability of errors (Gratch, Appel, Evans, LeCompte, & Wright, 1974; Harris, 1973). Gratch et al. argue that the effect of delay is to disrupt the overt bodily orientation adopted by the child to direct his search to location B (much as W. S. Hunter [1913] found that children who positioned their bodies during a delay interval in a delayed reaction task did better when later allowed to proceed to the hidden goal), causing a return to the older, successful A-response. One can as easily invoke an explanation involving temporal dissolution of memory traces, more so for recent, fewer, and less effective B trials than for the older, greater number of, and more effective A trials.

The Gratch et al. (1974) explanation is in fact consistent with the theorizing of Piaget (1954), when he asserts that the infant through his own motor activity constructs increasingly complex notions or ideas about the permanence and stability of objects in time and space. The infant in Stage IV conceives of an object as "a reality at disposal in a certain context, itself related to a certain action [p. 45]." The infant in this stage of development, the Piaget supposition goes, has a concept of object which is inextricably bound to the context in which the object has been previously acted upon. Finding a toy at location A, then, in the standard task effectively marks it as a toy *for that place*. The subsequent errors at B are therefore attributed by Piaget to difficulties in object localization, an explanation which is collapsible with the acquired equivalence or "failure of acquired distinctiveness" explanation presented here (Dollard & Miller, 1950, p. 104).

The point is perhaps obvious that, in my view, the positing of hypothetical structures to account for behaviors which accrue and which are in a continuous state of change is at best gratuitous, particularly when the structures are essentially response-defined rather than tied to specific antecedents or manipulable stimulation.

ACKNOWLEDGMENTS

Final work was done on this manuscript while the author was a Fellow at the Center for Advanced Study in the Behavioral Sciences, Stanford University. Support of the Spencer Foundation and the Harris Foundation is gratefully acknowledged.

REFERENCES

Ault, R. L. Children's cognitive development: *Piaget's theory and the process approach*. New York: Oxford University Press, 1977.

Brainerd, C. *Piaget's theory of intelligence*. Englewood Cliffs, N.J.: Prentice-Hall, 1978.

Butterworth, G. Object disappearance and error in Piaget's Stage IV task. *Journal of Experimental Child Psychology*, 1977, 23, 391–401.

Dollard, J. & Miller, N. E. *Personality and psychotherapy*. New York: McGraw-Hill, 1950.

Evans, W. F., & Gratch, G. The Stage IV error in Piaget's theory of object concept development: Difficulties in object conceptualization or spatial localization? *Child Development*, 1972, 43, 682–688.

Gratch, G., Appel, K. J., Evans, W. F., LeCompte, G. K., & Wright, N. A. Piaget's Stage IV object concept error: Evidence of forgetting or object conception? *Child Development*, 1974, 45, 71–77.

Harris, P. L. Perseverative errors in search by young children, *Child Development*, 1973, 44, 28–33.

Hunter, W. S. Delayed reaction in animals and children. *Behavior Monographs*, 1913, 2, No. 6. p. 45.

Lipsitt, L. P. Learning processes of human newborns. *Merrill-Palmer Quarterly of Behavior and Development*, 1966, 12, 1.

Lipsitt, L. P., & Reese, H. W. Lifespan developmental psychology. In P. G. Zimbardo & F. L. Ruch (Eds.), *Psychology and life*. (Diamond Printing, brief 9th ed.). Glenview, Ill.: Scott, Foresman, 1977.

Merleau-Ponty, M. *Phenomenology of perception*. London: Routledge and Kegan Paul, 1962.

Paillard, J. Le traitement des informations spatiales. In *De l'espace corporel a l'espace ecologique*. Symposium de l'association de psychologie scientifique de langue francaise. Paris: Presses Universitaries de France, 1974. Pp. 7–54.

Piaget, J. *The construction of reality in the child*. New York: Basic Books, 1954.

Schuberth, R. E., Werner, J. S., & Lipsitt, L. P. The Stage IV error in Piaget's theory of object concept development: A reconsideration of the spatial localization hypothesis. *Child Development*, 1978, 49, 744–748.

3 Social Learning Theory and Cognitive Constructivism

Barry J. Zimmerman
The Graduate School and University Center
The City University of New York

Many Piagetians might be surprised to find a social learning psychologist participating in a discussion of cognitive constructivism. It is often assumed that such terminology is an anathema to a theoretical position which is behavioral and deterministic. Doesn't cognitive constructivism imply: (1) that human psychological functioning is active rather than passive in nature? (2) that psychological functioning is unique to each person rather than being lawful? (3) that inner states rather than external stimuli control behavior? and (4) that the phenomenon of learning is mental rather than behavioral?

In this chapter, it will be suggested that the phenomena of cognitive constructivism is not foreign to behavioral-deterministic accounts. In fact, it has been extensively studied within this tradition; some of the classic studies which support conclusions of constructivism have emerged from research conducted from deterministic paradigms (Rosenthal & Zimmerman, 1978). Finally it will be suggested that behavioral-deterministic accounts in general and social learning theory in particular have some unique advantages for explaining and predicting people's constructive cognitive activity.

The terminology "cognitive constructivism" requires precise definition. The term "cognitive" means that learning is not a peripheral process, i.e., treatable solely in terms of overt stimuli and responses. It suggests that learning occurs centrally and can be best treated as knowledge or information that is distinct from, but not independent of, overt stimuli and responses. It will be argued throughout this chapter that recognizing the existence of cognitive activity in no way precludes it from being explained lawfully and deterministically. In fact, there are distinct advantages for doing so, and they will be enumerated later.

39

The term "constructivism" is more ambiguous. It has distinct meanings for different people. In general it suggests that humans act upon their environment rather than react to it. Information does not simply happen to a person, it requires self-generated mental activity by the person to make sense of his environment. Constructivism implies that learning is an interpretive activity and that rather abrupt changes in behavior might be expected, such as when a person achieves what Gestalt psychologists called "insight." Although many behavioral-deterministic theories have not given much emphasis to the role of a person's mental activity during learning, its presence does not pose any particular explanatory difficulty to most behavioral accounts. Deterministic approaches treat personal activity such as transforming a word to read it upside-down simply as a previously learned response or rule. However, evidence that behavior changes abruptly and that such changes are not well predicted by prior response strength did conflict with older associationistic behavioral theories prominent during the first half of this century. Yet today even Skinner's (1953) model has avoided most assumptions of simple associationism. Although evidence of constructive activity by people during learning can be explained in behavioral-deterministic accounts, cognitive psychologists were quite right in stressing the importance of this activity during learning and the need to treat it more comprehensively. Social learning psychologists have made an extensive effort to rectify this situation through research on "self-control" (e.g., Bandura & Kupers, 1964; Thoresen & Mahoney, 1974). These efforts will be discussed in greater detail later.

Many cognitive psychologists have concluded that evidence of constructivism in psychological functioning obviates deterministic accounts. They generally reason along the following lines: If each person perceives and interprets stimuli in a unique manner, then accounts which attempt to establish linkages between external stimuli and people's reactions are ruled out. Instead they suggest that researchers should change their emphasis and study each person's unique cognitive style in as stimulus-free a manner as possible. Then those *individual differences* in cognitive functioning, once assessed, can be used to make predictions for that person. Each person's uniqueness is stressed in these accounts. Individual differences are usually treated as *qualitatively* distinct cognitive styles or traits such as a field-dependent person, a child in the preoperational stage, or a cognitively impulsive youngster. These accounts can be viewed as being nondeterministic in the sense that the question of *how* each person's cognitive style arises is seldom given much attention. Users of this approach are asked to accept each person's individual differences in cognitive functioning as a given and to confine themselves to finding out what works for that type of person.

In trait approaches, cognitive functioning is seen as being relatively independent of the environment. People's constructive activities are primarily determined by their own cognitive traits rather than by environmental information, and people are generally ascribed great personal latitude to selectively apply their cognitive traits in overt behavior.

In recent years this *personalistic* or trait approach to cognitive functioning has been heavily criticized particularly in the area of personality. Mischel (1968) has been a key social learning figure who has criticized person-centered trait notions. There has been a continuing series of critical articles and rebuttals on this topic (Bem & Allen, 1974; Bowers, 1973; Hogan, DeSoto, & Solano, 1977; Mischel, 1973, 1977). This debate is relevant for psychologists interested in conceptual behaviors as well as those interested in social and emotional functioning. In essence, Mischel has questioned the trans-situational validity of personalistic approaches for predicting behavior. He has also pointed out that trait-like notions tend to be logically circular. Cognitive styles are inferred from responses regularities. For example "impulsivity" is inferred if a child performs quickly on a discrimination task and makes a lot of errors. Then, this impulsivity trait is in turn used to "explain" a child's error-prone rapid performance. It is circular because behaviors are renamed as traits. These traits then are used to explain the same behaviors from which they were inferred. The charge that trait-like theories engage in nominalism is serious and bears directly on their predictive power. However, it is not the purpose of this chapter to discuss limitations of trait approaches to cognitive functioning. Instead the purpose is to suggest how the phenomena of cognitive constructivism is treated from a deterministic posture and to indicate some of the advantages of doing so.

Personalistic approaches to cognitive functioning also stress the *generative* or *creative* aspect of human behavior. The fact that a child may produce sentences that he never heard before, or can invent a new mousetrap are often cited as indicating the hopelessness of deterministic accounts in explaining cognitive functioning. Such accomplishments, it is suggested, are beyond the reach of experiential approaches to psychological functioning since by definition the response was not available for learning from other people or from the environment. Adherents of personalistic theories have concluded that such findings require a taxonomic approach for studying psychological functioning, for example, comparing creative and uncreative people.

Social learning theory as proposed by Bandura (1977) is cognitive, constructivistic, and deterministic. It is cognitive since learning is viewed as the acquisition of knowledge rather than acquiring responses in any peripheral sense. It is constructivistic in that previously acquired cognitive rules are considered during responding in reciprocal conjunction with environmental sources of information. (The details of Bandura's notion of reciprocal causation will be discussed later.) It is deterministic in that cognitive functioning is treated as being linked to present or previous experiences rather than as a quasi-independent state as do personalistic approaches.

Bandura (1977) treats human functioning in terms of four subprocesses: attention, retention, motoric factors, and motivation. Basically this theory is a synthesis of information processing and behavioristic models. Bandura devised this theory because he felt that information processing models didn't explain how knowledge affects behavior and that behavioristic accounts didn't explain cognitive functioning. His first two subprocesses, attention and retention, are drawn from the information processing literature. The latter two processes, motivation and motoric factors, are drawn from behavioral theories. Bandura's model attempts to explain not only the perception and interpretation of information, but also *how* knowledge is translated into behavior and under what conditions a person will exhibit the responses. The complexities of how these subprocesses interact during human functioning will not be discussed in this chapter. This issue has been treated in great length in most of Bandura's recent books (e.g., 1969, 1977).

The exciting aspect of Bandura's model concerning constructivism is his notion of reciprocal determinism. Bandura (1978) has suggested that a person's behavior jointly controls and is controlled by the environment and cognitive processes (see Fig. 31). Social learning psychologists agree with Skinner (1953) that behavior is caused by the environment. But they also recognize that a person's behavior simultaneously changes that environment. Traditional cognitive theories have stressed mainly how people have controlled their environment. Social learning theory assumes that both behavioral and cognitive theories are partially correct. Thus, the cat in Thorndike's puzzle-box has certain escape behaviors reinforced by door-opening, but the cat then changes his environment once it emerges from the box. The new environment no longer prompts nor reinforces escape responses. Although the environment directly affects people's behavior, they can usually do something about it—particularly if they have formed accurate conceptual rules about functional relationships between behavior and environmental outcomes. This paradigm has spawned a great deal of helpful and creative research on *self-control* of problem behaviors (e.g., Goldfried & Merbaum, 1973; Thoresen & Mahoney, 1974). For example, obese people can be taught to determine which stimuli provoked them to overeat such

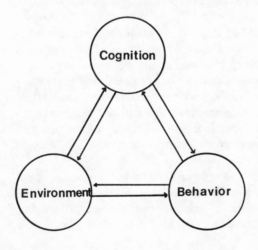

FIG. 3.1.   A schematic representation of a social learning conception of reciprocal determinism.

as putting fattening food in front of their cupboards. Once critical stimuli have been isolated, then an obese person can be taught to control these stimuli, such as putting these same foods in the back of the cabinet.

Social learning psychologists believe that the phenomena of constructivism can be usefully viewed from a reciprocal determinism vantage. The way people construct concepts about stimulus is assumed to be jointly influenced by previously acquired cognitive rules and by experiences with the stimulus which occur prior to, during, and after responding. For social learning psychologists, constructivism not only refers to abstractions that people form but also to their *actions* and their interpretation of the subsequent results. Assume that an infant boy has played with a red ball since birth and has formed the rule that BALLS ARE THINGS THAT BOUNCE. Then his mother gives him a new billiard-type ball and labels it as BALL. The boy will be unable to bounce this type of ball, and this feedback will compel him to change him conceptual rule about balls. Thus, the boy's initial attempts to manipulate the ball were determined by his mother's labeling of the stimulus, the resemblance of the new stimulus to his own red ball, and by his prior conceptual rule about balls. But the discrepant information produced by his attempts to manipulate the stimulus reciprocally required him to alter his conceptual rule about balls. Undoubtedly, the boy's subsequent interactions with ball-like stimuli will be changed as well. Thus, cognitive rules lead to actions that affect the environment and in turn are influenced by those environmental outcomes. This is what social learning psychologists mean by "reciprocal determination of behavior."

From a social learning point of view, constructive mental activity is not seen as a *fixed* process determined inflexibly by states, traits, or stages. Instead it is viewed as a *fluid* process that is highly sensitive to experience, particularly that of a social nature. Social learning psychologists believe that the way a person interprets or constructs stimuli depends on interpretations modeled by others, the reactions of other people and events to his or her conceptually directed behavior as well as cognitive structures.

The cognitive basis for mental constructivism is treated as a *rule*. A child can learn a MORE OR LESS rule by watching other people model judgments of relative amount and by receiving affirmative feedback for imitating this judgment rule. This rule once acquired can be used by the child to react to novel stimuli. This *transfer* of a rule to new stimuli is what personalistic theories call creative or generative responses. That is to say, once a relative size rule is acquired, a child can use the rule to draw a unique picture; or once a child learns a plural morpheme rule, he or she can form plurals of words that were never heard in that form. It is suggested that the creative-generative aspects of human conceptual functioning can be easily explained on the basis of transfer of rules.

Social learning research on rule learning was carried out to demonstrate this process: that children can induce rules embedded in a model's performance such as a conservation rule, and that they can then generalize this rule to other conceptually-related stimuli. There is now extensive evidence that a wide variety of conceptual rules ranging from Piagetian concepts to language syntax can be acquired socially and generalized appropriately (Rosenthal & Zimmerman, 1978; Zimmerman & Rosenthal, 1974).

Thus, social learning theorists treat mental activity as determined by prior rules as well as by information gathered from the environment during responding. The expressed beliefs of other people, their actions, and their responses to the learner are considered to be very important sources of information. Social learning theory differs from Piaget's theory in that it sees constructive activity as less determined by ages and stages than by information gleaned from social sources. Therefore precocious learning of concepts and developmental reversals in conceptual functioning are predicted by social learning psychologists under appropriate circumstances. These predictions conflict with Piaget's theory. No attempt will be made to compare Piaget's theory and a social learning account. This is a vast topic which has been discussed at some length elsewhere (Bandura, 1977; Zimmerman, 1978).

It is suggested that the social learning notion of reciprocal determinism includes constructivism at a physical as well as a mental level. Physical constructivism implies that people can to a degree create or select environments for themselves based on their preexisting concepts. A clinician once told a story about a paranoid man who feared Sears Roebuck. The paranoid lived in the West just after World War II, and he kept moving from town to town just as soon as Sears would open a new branch store in each community. His moving was effective in preventing alterations in his delusion for many years. He never had to endure Sears long enough to find out that his fear was baseless. Eventually he was surrounded by Sears, and he had to confront his fears. To the degree that the paranoid could control his environment, he could sustain his fear; but, his ability to keep Sears at a distance was limited. Thus, reciprocal determinism implies that no one of the three major elements in human functioning (behavior, cognitive activity, or the environment) is totally determinent but that each's influence is circumscribed by the other elements in a complex, interdependent manner. Changing people's beliefs will not help them function more effectively if they lack the requisite behavioral competencies or live in an environment that is unsupportive of new responses. At the same time, for people who have a potentially supportive environment and the behavioral competence to control it, the acquisition of a belief can lead to selffulfilling outcomes. To social learning psychologists, the construct of constructivism must encompass phenomena outside people's minds to be viable. It must include consideration of their environment and their behavioral competence to control that environment as well. The social learning formulation can account for children's acquisition of concepts just as it can explain the formation and maintenance of phobias. For example, in order to fully understand why a young boy thinks his teddy bear is alive, one must know how he plays with his doll and the reactions he receives from the doll (e.g., does it walk, talk, or wet) and from the people who watch his doll play.

There is one final issue on which social learning theory differs from most other constructive theories. This involves the type of experiences that develop or facilitate the use of constructive processes, particularly in children. Social learning psychologists treat these processes as rules or coding schemes which can be learned through observation, imitation, and reinforcement. This formulation undoubtedly seems implausible to people adhering to other constructive theories. They usually ask, "How can a learning process which is essentially passive and reproductive lead to cognitive outcomes which are active and creative?"

Unlike social learning theory, many cognitive approaches assume that discovery learning is the optimal process for learning concepts. This assumption was advanced because overt discovery learning and covert constructive processes seem to share the properties of activity and creativity. During discovery learning it is reasoned, the youngster must mentally "construct" each concept as it is acquired because not all relevant information is presented. Thus concepts learned by discovery are assumed to be inherently better because of the process by which they were acquired. It is not fully clear how such concepts are assumed to be superior. Adherents usually believe that concepts learned through discovery are retained better, transferred better, and the learning process is perhaps assumed to be more satisfying.

This difference in instructional emphasis boils down to the old argument between the relative advantages of discovery and more directive approaches such as modeling and instruction. Many psychologists would conclude that once constructive aspects of cognitive processes are accepted as real, that discovery approaches would necessarily be optimal fof teaching children concepts. There is reason to question this seemingly obvious conclusion.

If one reexamines the research on discovery learning (e.g., Gagne & Brown, 1961; Wittrock, 1966), one finds little evidence supporting the superiority of discovery approaches. Concepts evolved through discovery aren't more stable in time or more generalizable than those acquired in a more direct fashion. In addition, discovery approaches have the disadvantage of being inefficient and sometimes even ineffective with relatively naive (to the concept) subjects, such as young children (Glaser, 1966).

People who have used modeling procedures to teach concepts to children have found that overt activity is usually not necessary for forming concepts. Instead evidence indicates that retention and transfer of concepts is more related to other parameters of learning such as the types of examples and the quality of information children are exposed to rather than their degree of overt personal activity (Rosenthal & Zimmerman, 1973; Zimmerman & Jaffe, 1977).

There is research support for the suggestion that constructive activity can be learned through demonstration or instruction and that this learning can be equal to or superior to that produced by discovery approaches. Zimmerman and Rosenthal (1972) found that watching another person demonstrate and explain a concept created not only better learning than response-contingent discovery approaches, but it also created better transfer.

Recent evidence supports the general conclusion that overt experience is not necessary for concept acquisition for older children and adults, but indicates that this conclusion may not apply to very young children. Wolff and Levin (1972) found that motoric involvement with toys aided recall of paired toys by kindergartners but not by third graders. Although motoric contact with stimuli appears helpful for these young children, is it necessary for an optimal learning procedure? Can modeled interactions produce equal or better outcomes? The answers to these questions are not yet clear. Wolff, Levin, and Longobardi (1974) studied this issue using a yoking procedure in which one kindergartner was asked to manipulate two paired toys to "do something together" while a second kindergartner observed. No differences in recall were evident between the two groups of children in immediate posttesting, but the manipulation group displayed superior recall after one day. The authors concluded that direct motoric involvement was necessary for image formation in kindergarten-aged children.

In recent research, Brody, Mattson, and Zuckerwise (1978) found that watching an adult model manipulate two toys together assisted kindergartners learn to associate the toys significantly more than if the children directly manipulated the toys themselves. These authors concluded that the imagery elicited through modeling was superior in promoting learning and recall to that created by the children themselves based on their own constructive reactions.

How can these apparently contradictory results be explained? It appears that the *quality* of the model's demonstration may have been the critical factor determining image formation. In the second study by Wolff and associates, no attempt was made to control the quality of modeled motoric interactions as in the Brody et al. study, nor to determine their vicarious effectiveness. Given the age of these children and the lack of directions to the first child to make his or her interactions meaningful to the second child in the dyad, it seems likely that these modeled interactions were of lower quality than the experimentally devised procedures of the Brody et al. study. Although there is considerable evidence (e.g., Rosenthal, Alford, & Rasp, 1972; Zimmerman & Jaffe, 1977) of the importance of the information qualities of modeling experiences in determining observational learning generally, a definitive answer to this issue regarding imagery production must await further research. It is clear from the present data that even young kindergartners can, at least under some conditions, use the vicarious constructions of other people to produce more durable representation than they could produce themselves. It is also true that haptic information appears to assist learning and recall for young children.

Advocates of discovery approaches to instruction usually deprecate vicarious learning methods because they appear to be passive and reproductive in nature. Although observers are *overtly* passive during modeling, this doesn't mean they are *mentally* passive. On the contrary, both Piaget's research as well as social learning research indicates that vicarious learning requires active constructive activity on the part of the observer. Piaget (1962) concluded that sophisticated forms of imitation such as delayed imitation and imitation of novel response did not occur until the latter stages of sensory-motor development. His data indicated that considerable general cognitive development was necessary before such imitation could occur. Bandura and Jeffery (1973) found that imitation particularly after a delay, was related to an observer's degree of cognitive activity. So the critical question is whether overt activity during learning is *necessary* to promote mental constructive activity? The aforementioned data suggests it is not.

Social learning psychologists accept the conclusion that learning involves constructive or interpretive activity. However, they prefer instructional procedures which make learning or constructive activity *easier* rather than more difficult, particularly in the initial stages of concept formation. Later after the concept is fairly well abstracted, greater complexity can be included in generalization to impoverished stimulus environments if desired. However, the goal is to *facilitate* constructive activity rather than impede it. Since modeling procedures generally convey much information, they make constructive activity relatively easy. Advocates of discovery methods appear to believe that the *effort* expended in constructing concepts will produce dividends. This notion is remarkably close to the stance of nineteenth century faculty psychologists. These psychologists and philosophers believed that strenuous mental exercise, such as studying Greek or Latin, enhanced a person's reasoning skills. Thorndike's (e.g., Thorndike & Woodworth, 1901) famous studies examining the transfer of skill from such academic disciplines to other courses discredited this mind-as-a-muscle notion.

It is suggested that the phenomena of constructivism can be explained within a deterministic-behavioral theory. Constructivism is neither foreign to this tradition, nor does it create explanatory problems to most contemporary behavioral theories unless cognitive processes are denied. It is possible to recognize that the substance of learning is representational rather than behavioral, and yet to treat these representations as causally linked to the environment. It was suggested that active human functioning can be recognized as an integral part of learning and yet a deterministic account is possible based on Bandura's reciprocal dependency concept. This notion implies also that people construct environments which support their concepts as well as the concepts themselves. It also suggests a person's self-created environments may do much to preserve concepts even if these concepts are inaccurate. Finally an assumption made by many cognitive psychologists interested in constructivism that discovery approaches are the most effective way of teaching concepts to children was questioned. There is considerable evidence to suggest that rules underlying constructive activity can be and are commonly induced from social model's performance. It was cautioned that the overtly passive posture of observers during vicarious learning should not be assumed to indicate an absence of covert constructive activity. In fact most evidence indicates that vicarious learning cannot occur without considerable mental constructive activity.

In conclusion, it is suggested that treating constructivism as a lawful activity does not detract from its unique qualities, and it doesn't reduce people to being mere automatons. Social learning psychologists suggest that by adopting a reciprocal determinism stance people can be viewed as both consciously acting upon their environment, and yet forming constructions that are lawful and predictable.

REFERENCES

Bandura, A. *Principles of behavior modification.* New York: Holt Rinehart & Winston, 1969.

Bandura, A. *Social learning theory.* Englewood Cliffs, New Jersey: Prentice Hall, 1977.

Bandura, A. The self system in reciprocal determinism. *American Psychologist,* 1978, *33,* 344–358.

Bandura, A., & Jeffery, R. W. Role of symbolic coding and rehearsal processes in observational learning. *Journal of Personality and Social Psychology,* 1973, *26,* 122–130.

Bandura, A., & Kupers, C. J. The transmission of patterns of self-reinforcement through modeling. *Journal of Abnormal and Social Psychology,* 1964, *69,* 1–9.

Bem, D. J., & Allen, A. On predicting some of the people some of the time. *Psychological Review,* 1974, *81,* 506–520.

Brody, G. H., Mattson, S. L., & Zukerwise, B. L. Imagery induction in preschool children: An examination of subject and experimenter generated interactions. *Journal of Genetic Psychology,* 1978, *132,* 307–311.

Bowers, K. S. Situationism in psychology: Analysis and critique. *Psychological Review,* 1973, *80,* 307–336.

Gagne, R. M., & Brown, L. T. Some factors in the programming of conceptual learning. *Journal of Experimental Psychology,* 1961, *62,* 313–321.

Glaser, R. Variables in discovery learning. In L. S. Shulman & E. R. Keisler (Eds.), *Learning by discovery.* Chicago: Rand McNally, 1966.

Goldfried, M. R., & Merbaum, M. *Behavioral change through self-control.* New York: Holt, Rinehart and Winston, 1973.

Hogan, R., DeSoto, C. B., & Solano, C. Traits, tests, and personality research. *American Psychologist,* 1977, *32,* 255–264.

Mischel, W. *Personality and assessment.* New York: Wiley, 1968.

Mischel, W. Toward a cognitive social learning reconceptualization of personality. *Psychological Review,* 1973, *80,* 252–283.

Mischel, W. On the future of personality measurement. *American Psychologist,* 1977, *32,* 246–254.

Piaget, J. *Play, dreams, and imitation in childhood.* New York: Norton, 1962.

Rosenthal, T. L., Alford, G. S., & Rasp, L. M. Concept attainment, generalization, and retention through observation and verbal coding. *Journal of Experimental Child Psychology,* 1972, *13,* 183–194.

Rosenthal, T. L., & Zimmerman, B. J. Organization, observation, and guided practice in concept attainment and generalization. *Child Development,* 1973, *44,* 606–613.

Rosenthal, T. L., & Zimmerman, B. J. *Social learning and cognition.* New York: Academic Press, 1978.

Skinner, B. F. *Science and human behavior.* New York: Macmillan, 1953.

Thoresen, C. J., & Mahoney, M. *Behavioral self control.* New York: Holt, Rinehart & Winston, 1974.

Thorndike, E. L., & Woodworth, R. S. The influence of improvement in one mental function upon the efficiency of other functions. *Psychological Review,* 1901, *1,* 247–61, 284–95, 553–64.

Wittrock, M. C. The learning by discovery hypothesis. In L. S. Shulman and E. R. Keisler (Eds.), *Learning by discovery.* Chicago: Rand McNally, 1966.

Wolff, P., & Levin, J. R. The role of overt activity in children's imagery production, *Child Development,* 1972, *43,* 537–543.

Wolff, P., Levin, J. R., & Longobardi, E. T. Activity and children's learning. Child Development, 1974, 45, 221-223.

Zimmerman, B. J. A social learning explanation for age-related changes in children's conceptual behavior. Contemporary Educational Psychology, 1978, 3, 11-19.

Zimmerman, B. J., & Jaffee, A. Teaching through demonstration: the effects of structuring imitation and age. Journal of Educational Psychology, 1977, 69, 773-778.

Zimmerman, B. J., & Rosenthal, T. L. Observation, repetition, and ethnic background in concept attainment and generalization. Child Development, 1972, 43, 605-613.

Zimmerman, B. J., & Rosenthal, T. L. Observational learning of rule-governed behavior by children. Psychological Bulletin, 1974, 81, 29-42.

4 Constructivism and Educational Practices

Charles D. Smock
University of Georgia[1]

INTRODUCTION

Until recently "constructivism" has played a minor role in both epistemology and science, though the fundamental notions were known and debated among the early Greek philosophers (von Glasersfeld, 1974). Relegated to being critics and, at times, petulant naggers, the constructivists found modern physical science setting the stage for a "return of the repressed." Mack, in 1886, recognized the tenuous base of any form of positivism in science: "We are accustomed to regarding the object as existing unconditionally, although there is *no such thing* as unconditional existence. To extrapolate this experience beyond the limits of experience and *to assume the existence* of 'thing in itself' has no intelligible meaning. We have become accustomed (only) to regarding an object as existing permanently [Toulmin, 1970, p. 30]." Einstein also recognized a form of constructivism when he said: "Science is not just a collection of laws, a catalog of unrelated facts. It is a creation of the human mind, with its *freely invented* ideas and concepts. The only justification for our mental structures is whether and in what way our theories form a link with the world of sense impression [Einstein & Infeld, 1952, p. 310]." And, finally, the father of operationalism, stated, "When we say that we see a thing out there in space, we are exploiting correlations built, by experience and repetition, into the structure and functioning of our

[1]The project presented or reported herein was performed pursuant to a Grant from the U.S. Office of Education, Department of Health, Education, and Welfare. However, the opinions expressed herein do not necessarily reflect the position or policy of the U.S. Office of Education, and no official endorsement by the U.S. Office of Education should be inferred.

brains [Bridgeman, 1961, p. 46].'' Thus, some early Greeks and modern physicists agree that the existence of objects depends on our personal constructive coordination of experiential data and the subsequent projection of these structures into the "outside" world.

Piaget made the analysis of this process of coordination of experiential data the foundation of his theory of knowledge and knowledge acquisition. His analysis offers substantial evidence that "object permanence" is the result of the subjects' coordinations of patterns of experiential data. In the process of his analysis, Piaget constructed both an epistemology and a theory of the development of knowledge that constitute fundamental contributions to theory construction, research and practice for psychology and education.

Piaget came upon the scientific and philosophical scene at a time (1920s) when a scientific revolution was apparent though not completely accepted. The history of the physical sciences contains many examples of such paradigm shifts (or broken images if you will) but only later will we be able to determine whether or not Piaget has exacted such a revolution in the behavioral sciences. In any case, Piaget was apparently well suited to the task. We most often recognize his epistemology or psychology, but Piaget's methodological creativeness should not be ignored. His revival and particular conception of natural genetic epistemology required a bold, independent, as well as capable mind. It is easy to forget that only 20 years ago his idea of building a theory of knowledge, let alone a cognitive psychology on the basis of naturalistic, genetic, structural, and operational bases, seemed absurd to most psychologists.

My purpose in this chapter is to first, review the essentials of Piaget's epistemology and of his cognitive developmental theory. Second, I will describe one application of his theory to education; specifically, a model for developmental change that applies to any system whether it be a child, a teacher, or a community educational system. Piaget has clearly recognized the impossibility of direct application of his theory to educational practices. Two good reasons are immediately apparent. First, the complex theoretical structure has to be operationalized, a task that is impossible without construction of a "model" containing a coherent set of "essential" principles to guide practices. Second, Piaget (1971c) warns that we must clearly differentiate pedagogy from psychology. Experimental pedagogy is concerned less with the general and spontaneous characteristics of the child than with their modification through the teaching-learning process. Thus, Piaget rejects the notion of inflexible stages characterized by invariant age limits and fixed thought content as a necessary, or valuable, consequence of the concept of developmental stage. Cognitive structural changes that come about through maturation and those that derive from the child's individual experience can, and often need be, considered as separate factors in intellectual development. For example, available research suggests that mathematical structures can be learned if the structures of interest are supported by more elementary structures. Where the work of the Genevan group has dealt with the development of the child independent of particular subject matter curricula, *experimental* pedagogy is a *necessary* compliment of cognitive developmental psychology. Theoretical and empirical analysis of the degree of correspondence between mathematical (or social science) *and* psycho-logical operational structures clearly illustrates the potential of this position (Steffe, 1975).

PIAGET'S CONSTRUCTIVE EPISTEMOLOGY

Piaget's constructivist theory of knowledge and knowledge acquisition is complex and I have no intention of trying to add new insights into the many epistemological issues that have and can be raised about *that* Piagetian theory. Here, the essentials of his position will be sufficient to indicate the necessity for consistency among the epistemological assumptions, the theory of cognitive development and a proposed model for educational change.

Piaget's primary assumption is one of *subject-object unity*. Knowledge does not arise from the object nor from the subject, but from their interactions; that is, between the subject and the perceived object. To know objects the subject must act upon, and transform, them. These transformations consist of actions that connect, displace, combine, take apart, and reassemble, etc. To know an object (reality), then, means to construct systems of transformations that can be carried out with objects (Piaget, 1971b). Such transformational systems constitute knowledge but are *not copies* of a reality—only possible isomorphic models of reality from which we may choose.

Knowledge acquisition is a biologically oriented process in which a subject evolves *his own objective sense of* reality. That evolution or *construction* of knowledge is assumed to proceed through two types of activities: the coordination of actions and coordinations related to "objects." The structures of actions (knowledge) are constructed in that they are not in the objects (they are dependent on the action) nor a "given" in the subject (the subject must generate coordination of the actions). Thus, the notion of action (or operation) as a transformation is central to Piaget's constructionistic epistemology. He emphasizes over and over that knowledge is a continuous construction and in each act of understanding, some degree of invention is involved (Piaget, 1973). And, in development, the transformation from one stage to the next is characterized by formation of new structures which previously were neither in the external world nor in the minds of the subject.

The construction of knowledge, as indicated above, involves two types of action structure that give rise to two types of knowledge: physical and logical-mathematical. Physical knowledge is derived from activities related to the subject's abstractions from objects themselves. Generally, physical knowledge relates to the figurative aspects (Furth, 1969) of knowing because the subject attempts to represent reality as it appears without transforming it. Logical-mathematical knowledge, on the other hand, is derived (abstracted) from activities and operations themselves. That is, logical-mathematical knowledge emerges from the subject's reflection on his own coordinating activity which yields an expanded internal structure of logical-mathematical relations. The notion of reflective abstraction, and the conditions for generation of logical-mathematical knowledge, is one of the revolutionary aspects of Piaget's epistemological position for education. The implication that logical-mathematical knowledge is not directly teachable—but rather consists of invention by the subject himself—has been more than disconcerting to many psychologists and educators. The tenability and/or limits to the generalization is, as yet, empirically unknown and, in my view, does require a new perspective on the teaching-learning processes. However, it *does not prohibit* the development of instructional practices designed to facilitate *reconstruction* of existing (social) knowledge consistent with Piaget's theory of cognitive development (Kaufman and Banet, 1976).

The final aspect of Piaget's epistemology that educators must consider is that the processes of construction of logical-mathematical and figurative knowledge are functionally different than the symbolic processes by which the subject *represents* actions. An object or event within the subject-object interaction that provides some knowledge to the subject about another object or event is a "signifier." An *index* representation involves a direct relationship between an object and a representation of that object; e.g., a cry is an *index* of a baby's presence. A *symbol* is differentiated from an object but retains a degree of similarity to objects; e.g., a child represents a car with a block of wood. Finally, the third type of signifier is a *sign* which is differentiated from the significant but is conventional and often arbitrary; e.g., linguistic or other socially agreed upon representations are considered signs.

These epistemological assumptions did not appear full-blown, but were the product of both theoretical and empirical analysis over a period of years. Piaget's biological background and early commitment to a *natural genetic* methodology inevitably, it now seems, directed him toward an *operational* and *structural* analysis of knowledge acquisition. The operational theory of intellectual development that emerged is characterized by a complexity that does not allow for quick or easy understanding, appears inherently ambiguous at certain parts, and has an openness that permits gradual (or partial) modification without serious implication for the theory as a whole.[2] During the past 10 years, however, the major aspects of the theory of cognitive development have become much clearer. Both psychologists and educators are utilizing Piaget's conceptualizations for

---

[2]For example, Piaget's recent recognition of the significance of advances in "category theory" as requiring analytic attention to "correspondence" as well as "transformation" in his theory of knowledge and knowledge acquisition (Abeles, 1976).

research and for practice (and malpractice!). In the next section, I will discuss what, in my opinion, is the minimum set of assumptions in the operational theory of intelligence necessary to generate models for educational practices. The reader should be cautioned that *consistency* among the epistemology/cognitive development theory and any "model" for research and/or practice derived from the theory must be evaluated, but it is the theory, and not the epistemology, that is of primary concern to the psychologist and educator.

OPERATIONAL THEORY OF INTELLIGENCE

Much of the earlier misunderstanding of Piaget's theory of cognitive development, and its application, arose from a natural tendency to assimilate the meanings of words to our own conceptual structures. To avoid these errors requires considerable effort including conscious attention to certain theoretical relations that are the fundamental starting points for the theory. Firstly, knowledge is defined as an *invariance under transformation;* thus, the notions of object permanence and conservation concepts. Secondly, intelligence (knowledge acquisition) refers to those *activities,* at all levels of organismic functioning, which involve the *construction* of invariances in organism-environment relations. An understanding of intelligence, and intellectual development, requires analysis of both the patterning or structure of the critical activities (organization) and the associated functional processes (adaptation).

Adaptation consists of the operation of two complimentary biological processes and the internal self-regulating mechanism of equilibration. One of the two processes (assimilation) concerns the application of prior formed cognitive structures to the interpretation of sensory data. New data or events are incorporated into existing structures through ongoing *physical* and *mental* activity. Such events and the products of new experience can be incorporated into the cognitive structures only to the extent they are consistent with existing functional structures. Accommodative activity, on the other hand, is the process whereby adaptation occurs through modification of existing structures to fit newly assimilated sensory data. Activities such as play, practical or symbolic, represent assimilative activity, whereas memory, in the sense of involving past experience, and imitation are accommodative since only prior formed structures are transformed for a new use or application.

The second aspect of intelligence concerns the organization of activities (practical or mental operations) necessary for *maintaining invariance under transformation.* Piaget recently (1970b) elaborated his position that all human beings possess the same biological structures and functions that, in "exchange" with the common features (elements) of the natural world, generate structures (scheme) supporting the behavioral functions characteristic of each stage of development. Logical thought, in the Piagetian sense, is universal and of fundamental importance to an understanding of development and learning. The notion that complex cognitive structures (e.g., language) are "programmed" at birth is rejected. Rather, Piaget (1968) accounts for the universality and stability of structures across cultures in terms of the self-regulating mechanism of equilibration. Thus, the mind at any point in development is the unfinished product of continual self-construction (Piaget, 1971a). "Logical" processes are generative and not fixed. Structures are not preformed, but self-regulatory, transformational systems with the functional factors in that constructions involve the processes of assimilation and accommodation. It follows from these considerations that there is an "inherent logic" to development.

Operational systems consist of elements and laws of combination of those elements that form a "logical" closed system. These mental structures are observable in the actions of the organism in its environment. They are describable in terms of formal or logical-mathematical structures. Genetic psychological analyses of these structures are a necessary prerequisite to an understanding of thought processes since there is "no structure without genesis, no genesis without structure."

During the sensorimotor period of development, action structures of the individual are revealed in "practical" groups, i.e., the coordinated action patterns of the individual (Forman, 1973). During the preoperational period, the child constructs representations called figurative structures which do not have the operational property of reversibility. Piaget was able to identify operational structures with mathematical system properties in children between ages five and seven. The discovery of a resemblance between the structure of the mental action system (reasoning or thought) and mathematical structures (i.e., mathematical groups and lattices) had a profound effect on Piaget's thinking. Thought, it would appear, has the same or similar properties, as mathematical group structures and both are governed by the same internal logic.

Piaget (1957a, 1957b) has taken maximum advantage of the possibility that mathematical group and lattice theories might well describe the nature of reasoning or operational thought. To review the fundamentals: a mathematical group is a system consisting of a set of elements, together with an operation (law of combination), which yields the following system properties:

1. when applied to the elements of the set, the combinatorial operation will yield only elements of the set; no elements external to the set can be produced;
2. each set contains a neutral (or identity) element that, when combined with another element of the set, yields the same element set;
3. each element of the set has an inverse belonging to the set which, in combination with any other element, yields the neutral or identity element;
4. the combinatory operation is associative; i.e., $[(n + m) + p = n + (m + p)]$.

Piaget found it necessary to generate a "grouping" model with additional properties (i.e., both group and lattice properties) to describe the concrete operational structures. Most importantly, the properties of these *psychological groupings* are not derived from the properties of things, but from action *patterns in relation to things*. Thus, the elements of psychological groups are themselves transformations that characterize the individual's operations as he acts upon sense data.

The interrelation of these fundamental concepts of Piaget's cognitive developmental theory is presented in Fig. 4.1. It should be obvious by now that an understanding of both the organizational (structural) and adaptive (process) components of the theory, as well as the complimentary and reciprocal nature of their relationship, is necessary for the development of adequate models for educational practices at all levels.

The educational researcher attempting to gain empirical evidence concerning the validity of this theory for instructional practice must, at some point, be

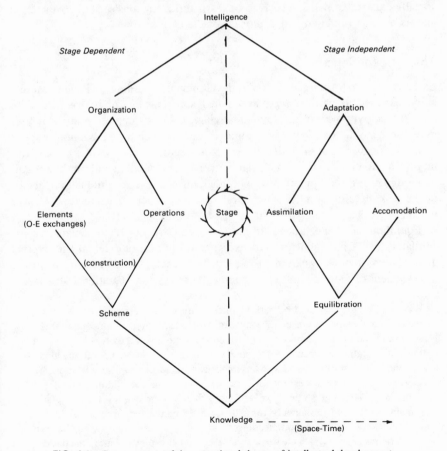

FIG. 4.1   Core concepts of the operational theory of intellectual development.

concerned with the fundamental issues that differentiate pedagogy from psychology. Specifically, if we are to go beyond the superficial "truisms" (e.g., development precedes learning) of the theory, then serious attention must be given to analysis of the correspondence, and contradictions, of the characteristics of psycho-logic systems and those conceptual structures inherent in the relevant subject matter area (e.g., mathematics, science, language, etc). To focus exclusively on the process of acquisition (i.e., the stage independent or dynamics of the theory) at best provides teachers with new understanding of children, and at the worst, deludes us to think that education and schooling are synonomous. Remember Dewey?!

Three aspects of the theory, seem then to require special consideration by educational theorists: (1) the role of experience in cognitive development; (2) the distinction between operative (logical-mathematical experience) and figurative (physical experience) thought processes; and (3) the conceptual structure of socially existent knowledge basis to be learned (i.e., reconstructed) *by* the child and its relation to the cognitive process of the child.

Role of Experience

Experience is not a unique factor in development according to Piaget. Merely being exposed to particular environmental situations is conducive neither to cognitive activity nor to developmental change. For example, children may or may not make discoveries in the course of play. Watching a laboratory experiment (or conducting one), and/or listening to a lecture, only provides an opportunity for a child to acquire a particular concept. An essential condition for cognitive progress is disequilibraiton which, inherently, means the child is "engaged" in the task. Equilibration is the central factor in conceptual structural change whether that change refers to "stage" or to "concept" learning.

Equilibration is the process of intrinsic (self) regulation that balances assimilatory and accommodatory processes, compensates for external and internal disturbances (internal or external to a particular structure) and makes possible the development of more complex, hierarchically integrated operational structures.

> Rhythms, regulations, and operations, these are the three essential procedures of the self-regulation and self-conservation of structures; anyone is, of course, free to see in this the "real" composition of structures, or to invert the order by considering the operative mechanisms the source of origin, in an atemporal and quasi-Platonic form, and by deriving everything from these mechanisms. In any case, however, it will be necessary, at least with regard to the building up of new structures, to distinguish two levels of regulation. On the one level the regulation remains internal to the already formed or nearly completed structure and, thus, constitutes its self-regulation, leading to a state of equilibrium when this self-regulation is achieved. On the other level, the regulation plays a part in the building

up of new structures and integrating them as substructures into larger ones [Piaget, 1968, p. 16; Ernst von Glasersfeld, translator].[1]

Disequilibrium occurs as the child assimilates data from immediate experience into existing mental structures. As cognitive structures change to accommodate to the new experiential data, equilibrium is restored. The equilibration process is one of auto-regulation—both of the transformations of data based on existing cognitive structures and of changes through accommodation. Thus, the child must be exposed to situations that are likely to "engage" the functional structures; i.e., he must be involved in a personal striving for cognitive coherence or to "accept" the task as a "problem."

One basic question for instructional theory and practice is: What are the processes and conditions that motivate and insure engagement or acceptance of the problem task by the child? The source of "interest" that promotes striving for problem solution is contingent on assimilative-accommodative activity but the specifics remain unclarified in Piaget's theory (cf. Mischel, 1971). Within a structuralist framework—if a structure exists, it must function—multiple cognitive structures provide a dimension of openness that make probable continual sources of disequilibrium from interaction of the internal operational and/or figurative structures activated, as well as by exchanges involving novel experience. And, despite lack of specifications, Piaget is quite clear on his general position: "It is not necessary for us to have recourse to separate factors of motivation in order to explain learning, not because they don't intervene . . . but because they are included from the start in the concept of assimilation . . . to say that the subject is interested in a certain result or object thus *means* that he assimilates it or anticipates an assimilation and to say that he needs it means *that he possesses schema requiring its utilization* [Piaget, 1959, p. 141]." In passing, it might be noted that natural or lifelike contexts seem to provide excellent situations for promoting cognitive change. Unfortunately, too little empirical investigation has been oriented to questions of the natural environmental determinants of curiosity of children at various stages of development and with different experiential backgrounds; i.e., what children recognize as problematic, and what kinds of incongruities are sufficient to motivate change in concepts and/or beliefs.

The notion that disturbances introduced into the child's systems of prior schemas lead to the adoption of a strategy for information processing is the fundamental difference between the equilibration and associationistic theories of learning. For associationistic theories of learning, "what is learned" depends on what is given from the outside (copy theory) and the motive that facilitates learning is an inner state of some sort or other. Equilibration theory proposes that learning is subservient to development; i.e., what is learned depends on what the learner can take from the given by means of the cognitive structures available to him. Further, cognitive disequilibrium (functional need) is what motivates learning; i.e., questions or felt lacunae arising from attempts to apply a scheme to a "given" situation. The child, then, will take interest in what generates cognitive conflict. If the task demands are so novel as to be unassimilable, or so obvious as to require no mental work, the child will not be motivated.

After the period of sensorimotor development, equilibration becomes a process of compensating for "virtual" rather than actual disturbances. At the operational level, intrusions are anticipated by the subject in the form of operations of the system and compensatory activities also consist of anticipations of inverse operations. Further, there need be no external intrusions in order for the equilibration process to be activated. For example, the acquisition of conservation concepts is, in Piaget's view, "not supported by anything from the point of view of possible measurement or perception—it is enforced by logical structuring much more than by experience [Piaget, 1957b, p. 98]." It is the internal factors of coherence—the deductive activity of the subject—that are primary. Equilibration, then, as we noted earlier, is a response to *internal* conflict between conceptual and/or figurative schema rather than a direct response to the character of environmental structure factors.

Operative and Figurative Processes

A considerable amount of confusion concerning Piagetian theory and its implications for both research and instructional practice derives from a failure to consider the figurative and operative aspect of intellectual functioning. In general psychological terms, the distinction is between the selection, storage, and retrieval versus the coordination and transformation of information (Inhelder et al., 1966). More specifically, the development of any sequence of psychological stages, *a la* Piaget, consists of an interactive process of equilibrating functional structures of the organism with sensory event-structures of the perceived environment. Piaget analyzes "experience" into the two components of "physical" and "logical-mathematical" and the distinction is critical to an understanding of his view of the growth of knowledge. Knowledge based on physical experience alone is knowledge of static states of affairs; if a child is wrong, it is easy to demonstrate that to him. Knowledge emerging from logical-mathematical experience is knowledge of transformation of states and quite another matter. If a child is wrong in the first case, it is easy to demonstrate his error, but in the second it is difficult, if not impossible, to convincingly demonstrate, or even to get the child to accept verbal explanation of the "correct" answer. For example, if a child fails to *align* the two endpoints when comparing length of sticks, it is quite easy to correct the mistake. If, however, he fails to display transitive *reasoning* in a task, one or two examples is not likely to "teach" him the concept.

Physical experiences, then, provide for the construction of the invariants (figurative process) relevant to the properties of objects (i.e., states) through exchanges (sensory mechanisms) with objects. For example, one may touch something and it is hard, cold, hot, soft, supple, etc. or one may see something—an object is red, a diamond cutting glass, the shape of a banana, etc. The course of logical-mathematical experience, however, is assumed to be abstractions (operative knowledge) from coordination of actions vis-à-vis representations of "objects," i.e., transformations of the "states" associated with series of discreet physical experiences. The critical difference is that logical-mathematical knowledge demands that a pair (or set) of physical objects not be defined by the temporal-spatial (perceptual) similarities, but rather by invariant relations among or between objects.

Figurative and operational processes represent two types of functional structures necessary to account for knowledge acquisition. Figurations are defined as those action schemes that apprehend, extract and/or reproduce aspects of a prior structured physical and social environment. Such action schemes include components of perception, language, imagery, and memory. Figurations and associated acts are based on physical, as contrasted to logical-mathematical experience and constitute the "empirical" world; i.e., empirical truth is no more than the "representation of past experience in memory."

Operations, on the other hand, do not derive from abstractions from objects and specific events; rather, operational knowledge is derived by abstractions from *coordinated actions* relevant to those events. Thus, operations are those action schemata that construct "logical" transformations of "states." Such "logical" systems of transformations operate either upon representations of events, or on the cognitive system's own logical operations, i.e., reflexive operations.

Figurative and operative structures are two parallel streams with their genetic or developmental origins in the same source (Piaget, 1968, 1970a, 1970b; Piaget & Inhelder, 1971)—the sensorimotor structures. Logical (operational) structures are not generated from the figurative schemata, i.e., not from perception, memory, etc. Reciprocally, figurative structures do not derive from operative schemes but from the representations of past states of events derived from physical experience. And most importantly, figurative structures do not derive from each other, but have unique bases in sensorimotor schema. Imagery, for example, is a derivative of deferred sensorimotor imitation (Piaget & Inhelder, 1971) and not perception.

The postulation of these quite distinct functional structures is one of the cornerstones of Piaget's theory of knowledge acquisition and cognitive development (cf. Furth, 1969). Both the source and function of the structures are theoretically distinct. Operative structures derive from abstractions from coordinated actions, figurative structures derive from sensorimotor and perceptual activity. Operative structures produce "logical" transformations (conservation of invariants) whereas figurative structures reproduce sensory-perceptual consequences of externalized (and, thus "environmental") configurations. The variant operative structures of the intuitive, the concrete, and the formal levels form the discontinuous sequence of stages of cognitive development. On the other hand, figurative structures are static and dependent directly upon the data of experience (sensory-perceptual consequence of stimulation). Piaget makes the fundamental assumption that *all* knowledge acquisition activity is constructive, but the construction of figurative representations is quite a distinct process from the constructive activity at the operative level.

Logically, there are three possible relations between the figurative and operational structures (Langer, 1969). First, they may be unrelated and, if so, as mentally segregated functional structures, do not set limits on the functioning and development of each other. Second, all psychological phenomena might be reduced to one of the types of structures. Langer (1969), for example, suggests that subjective idealists try to reduce psychological phenomena to assimilatory operations while naive realists propose that all knowledge processes are figurative (e.g., perception is knowledge; Michotte, 1963; Garner, 1962). Third, and the one proposed by Piaget, is that of partial communication between figurative and operative structures within the constraints of the assimilation and accomodation processes.

The relations, and the potential forms of interaction, are schematically presented in Fig. 4.2.

Langer, (1969) has examined the organizational and developmental (i.e., transitional) impact of accommodatory figurations (B', Fig. 4.2) on assimilatory operations (A, Fig. 4.2); i.e., how does the child mentally extract and/or represent empirical information about objects and what are the consequences of that activity for the construction of logical concepts. Imitation of an observed event, comparison of one's predictions with the perceived outcome of a physical manipulation, and comparison of an observation (i.e., immediate experience) with the way things have been constructed represent different modes for introducing internal conflict. Generally, Langer's findings were confirmatory, but not definitive, with respect to the Piagetian hypothesis. In any case, if the development of each type of functional structure has implications for, but not direct causal effects upon, the structure and development of the other, current paradigms for the study of concept learning will require considerable modification. The work of the Geneva group concerning memory [B' = f (AB)], Fig. 4.2; analysis of the impact of accommodatory figurations or imitation (Langer, 1969) on assimilatory operations (i.e., A = f B'); and more recent work (e.g., Bruce, 1971; Inhelder & Sinclair, 1969; Kidder, 1976; Leskow & Smock, 1970; Meyer & Elkind, 1975) all represent beginnings in this direction.

The research paradigms involved in such theoretically relevant studies are not the (apparently) straightforward ones common to the behavioristic traditions. But, more and more research reports are indicative that increased knowledge of the complexity of Piaget's theory can stimulate ingenuity and inventiveness of both the psychological and educational researcher. As we argued, many years

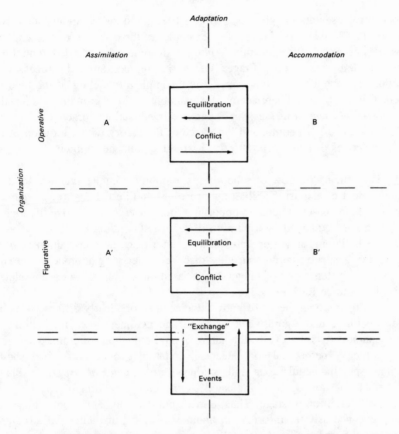

FIG. 4.2   Relations of two invariant processes of adaptation and two types of cognitive structures.

ago, experimental and operational "simplicity" are two quite different things. The fact that we are beginning to face the complexity of psychological developmental processes (even discontinuity) is partially due to the power and viability of Piaget's theoretical constructions.[3]

Psychological Structures and Curriculum Development

The complexity of Piaget's theory is such that a variety of models for educational practice have been proposed. The implication of Piaget's epistemology, his

----

[3]Psychologists and educators alike have been slow to recognize that a constructivist epistemological base (such as Piaget's) leads to the assumption that the environment, essentially, is a black box (von Glasersfeld, 1974) and must be "defined" by the subject. Thus, the stages of psychological development should have their counterparts in terms of "layers" of the environment. Moos (1973) and Gump (1976) provide a starting point for such analyses.

theory of representational processes (Sigel, 1970), and the stage-dependent cognitive skills (Weikart, 1971) are a few examples of the diversity of "essentials" chosen as necessary for education. Although in some cases the differential emphasis is legitimate (e.g., Piaget views the representational processes as functionally separate); in other cases it is incomplete modeling of the theory's practical implications. There seems, for example, to be a growing opinion that the *stage-dependent* processes can be ignored in educational practice (Brainerd, 1978). To do so is to compound ignorance of the theory with confusion of the basic objectives of education. Briefly, I would submit the following:

1. The primary purpose of schooling is to optimize intellectual development in the context of acquiring skills (e.g., reading) and knowledge (e.g., science, history) that increases the child's opportunity for a useful, productive life including becoming "educated"—a purely self-regulated venture.

2. An individual never operates in a vacuum (i.e., no constraints) as often implied by those advocating a strong "discovery" learning approach. The constructivistic epistemology of Piaget is not based on a sophistic (i.e., completely subjective) source for knowledge.

3. The operational theory of knowledge acquisition clearly differentiates between operative and figurative knowledge and assumes *some* interactions of those separate processes. Thus, the nature of environmental structure, whether at the "surface" (perceptual) or "deeper" (relational/conceptual) level should facilitate specific acquisitions and, perhaps, *developmental progress*. Piaget leaves that question open as indicated by the clear rejection of fixed age or "content" definition of stage. Thus, curriculum development, from a Piagetian perspective necessitates information about the logical-mathematical structures characterizing a particular "content" so as to make judgments as to the possibility that a child, in a particular cognitive-developmental stage, will be able to learn at either the figurative or conceptual levels.

4. Finally, the cognitive operational structures are not accessible to direct teaching, but that is not the case for *figurative* knowing, which derives from sensorimotor structures that are as much "stimulated" by the environment as by internal conflicts. The *relevant stimulation,* however, involves providing opportunities for the child to achieve internal coherence from confrontation with correspondences and contradictions inherent in his current interpretations of the environment. To deny the possibility of providing such opportunities is to deny the value of all "schooling" and, ultimately, society which, definition can only exist through a level of "conservation concepts" within the capability of most members.

Implication of Piaget's Theory for Instructional Practices

The model for instructional practices, and for educational system change generally, described below, was developed in the context of the Follow Through

Program (Smock, 1969, 1974), a nationwide research and development effort to improve the educational status of children from low-income families in the public schools. The model (Mathemagenic Activities Program; MAP[4]) principles and specifications concerning the teacher-learning situation were derived from the following assumptions:

1. The structure of a learning environment must be *considered relative to two frames of reference;* i.e., the operational systems controlling the child's interpretation of "environmental" events *and* the "content" to be learned. Operational systems are expressed behaviorally in the coordinated actions of the child confronted with changes in his physical and symbolic world. For example, the mental operations of associativity, reversibility, et cetera are inferred from the manner in which the child attempts to solve problems involving regular environmental contingencies (causality), understanding of spatial-temporal relations, classes, etc. Substantive areas, such as science or mathematics, must be analyzed in terms of their own logical structure since the assimilation-accommodation process and available cognitive structures (figurative and operational) determine what is acquired (i.e., learned). Optimal educational conditions require, then, thorough understanding of the cognitive capacities of the child *as well as* the structures of sequential relations of concepts within a particular curriculum area.

2. *Optimal conditions for structural reorganization,* learning in the broad sense, *require disequilibration* (between different conceptual systems and/ between intrinsic functional structures and the patterning of environmental events). This condition is met when there is an appropriate "mismatch" between the cognitive capacities of the child and the conceptual demand level of the learning task. Too little or too much "pressure" may result in over-assimilation or over-accommodation respectively and not be facilitative of cognitive-developmental change in either the figurative or operational level.

3. Facilitation of learning requires the task analyses be in terms of both the *figurative* and *operative* cognitive functions. The operational theory of intellectual development does not deny the value of "provoked learning," through imitation and/or algorithms, but suggests that such "figurative" learning will be limited (i.e., lack of generalizability) and will have minimal effect on problem solving and reasoning abilities (operational thought). Thus, the "process" by which "content" is learned becomes crucial in setting the limits of schooling effects (See #4).

4. The *nature* and *variety* of the child's "exchanges" with the environment must be considered in planning for children's learning. The *nature* of the interaction refers to the *relative* emphasis on ontogenesis (self-directed) as contrasted to

---

[4]Additional information concerning the operations and outcomes of the Mathemagenic Activities Program may be obtained from the numerous reports of the University of Georgia-Follow Through Program and the U.S.O.E. National Evaluation report (Stebbins, et al., 1977).

exogenesis (environmental or teacher-directed) structure of the learning environment. The *variety* of interaction refers to different types of structured curriculum contents relevant to the child's physical, social, and symbolic experiences. The interlocking nature (i.e., logical-mathematical) of substantive curriculum areas makes it possible to provide a variety of experiences relevant to acquisition of the cognitive "products" that provide representations (memories and/or symbol system) and, at the same time, facilitate the development of cognitive-operational (reasoning) development. For example, analysis of the visual environment (attention or observation skills) as well as cognitive operational structures (e.g., conservation of area) can be emphasized in science, social studies, mathematics and art.

The implementation of these conditions in the classroom requires: (1) Specification of teaching strategy and tactics; and (2) Sequentially structured curricula paralleling, within the limits of our knowledge, both the concept hierarchies of a particular "content" domain and the psychological capabilities of the child. In the case of teacher strategy we provide the teacher with theoretical background and, more importantly we find, specific demonstrations and classroom experiences designed to increase their competencies to implement the following principles in a variety of curriculum contexts:

1. Because the source of motivation for change is provided by a discrepancy (disequilibration between different conceptual systems—ideas) and/or between previously acquired conceptual sytems and environmental task demands, an appropriate *mismatch* (M) is necessary to generate exploratory activities and insure the individual has the prerequisite conceptual basis for learning higher order concepts.

2. Because coordinated actions are the bases for knowledge acquisition, and involve construction of invariants both from properties of objects (physical experience) and from the child's actions on objects (logical-mathematical experiences), the learning environment must be structured so that specific task demands include appropriate *practical, perceptual,* and *mental activity* (A).

3. Because operational thought, and its development, is *relatively* independent of environmental demands and/or structure, the learning environment must include provisions for personal or *self-regulatory* (P) *constructions*. Practically, self-regulation implies a *variety* of options—in terms of level of task difficulty, mode of learning, and choice of activity—are necessary ingredients of developmental change and learning.

Implementing these principles (MAP) is not an easy task for a teacher. A supportive physical and social environment (i.e., instructional aids and learning centers) and helping the teacher acquire a "Piagetian perspective" of children and their development was our beginning point. The second task involved providing the teacher with intensive training and demonstrations in utilization of the MAP principles, especially in mathematics (Davis et al., 1974) and science. Finally, the teachers were given considerable experience (through in-service training) in generating activity-based learning units in a variety of subject matter areas. These experiences were valuable for teacher training directly (e.g., sharpening the teacher' diagnostic skills) as well as providing appropriate curriculum materials which, early on, were not commercially available.

The application of Piaget's theory to education will, in my opinion, not be generally successful until more attention is devoted to development of appropriate curriculum materials and changes in teacher training programs that truly force a restructuring of role functions and classroom resources. Curriculum "contents" based on the *correspondence* between the hierarchical concept structure of a knowledge domain and the psycho-logic (operational and figurative) structures of the child are a necessary condition for educational practices. Until that profound issue is settled (area by area), the more immediate concern is the matter of facilitating the reconstruction of the various knowledge bases in the context of the stage independent process (assimilation-accommodation). The constraint inherent in the stage dependent, cognitive, operational systems should not be ignored, but rather determined in the context of the skills and concepts to be learned. Elkind (1979) provides an excellent example of such efforts for the learning to read process.

In addition, the teacher needs to have procedures for determining "appropriate mismatches" and the extent to which the child's learning is dependent on figurative and/or operative processes.

One approach to providing such information has been suggested by Steffe and Smock (Steffe, 1975) for mathematics instruction. Specifically, it is assumed that the process of concept development involves discontinuities similar to those noted at the macro-developmental (i.e., stages) level. Instruction for concept learning, then, should begin with provision for *exploratory* activities (phase I) followed by problem-solving tasks designed to provide opportunities for *abstraction* and *representation* (phase II), and, finally, *formalization* (phase III) of the conceptual basis of the problem. This teaching strategy guides children toward reconstruction of available knowledge under conditions that recognize both the discontinuity of the learning process and the fundamental nature of all knowledge acquistion, that is, knowledge is always a *personal construction*.

A final note—the variety and richness of the many models for educational programs derived from Piaget's theory are, themselves, a testimony of the constructive nature of knowledge as well as its source within each of our minds. Thus, each of us have made decisions in a garden (Ceccato, 1974) rich in choices—and my flowers may well be your weeds. But, we should keep in mind that Piaget's theory was *constructed* by Piaget and, it is only at that level he would want any disciples.

REFERENCES

Abeles, F. *Structuralism and cognitive development in topology*. New Jersey: Kean College, Bourbaki and Piaget Department of Mathematics, 1976.

Brainerd, C. J. *Piaget's theory of intelligence*. Englewood Cliffs, N.J.: Prentice-Hall, 1978.

Bridgeman, P. W. *The logic of modern physics*. New York: MacMillan, 1961. (Originally published, 1933).

Bruce, A. J. *The effects of age and stimulus structure on serial learning*. Unpublished doctoral dissertation, University of Georgia, 1971.

Ceccato, S. In the garden of choices. In C. D. Smock & E. von Glasersfeld (Eds.), *Epistemology and education*. Athens: University of Georgia, 1974.

Davis, E. J., Mahaffey, M. L., McKillip, W. D., & Steffe, L. P. *MAP teacher training plan*. Athens: University of Georgia, Mathemagenics Activities Program, September 1974.

Einstein, A., & Infeld, L. *The evolutions of physics*. New York: Simon & Schuster, 1952.

Elkind, D. *Stages in the development of reading*. Unpublished manuscript, 1979.

Forman, G. E. *The early growth of logic in children. Influences from the bilateral symmetry of human anatomy*. Paper presented at the Biennial Meeting of the Society for Research in Child Development, Philadelphia, April 1973.

Furth, H. G. *Piaget and knowledge: Theoretical foundations*. Englewood Cliffs, N.J.: Prentice-Hall, 1969.

Garner, W. R. *Uncertainty and structure as psychological concepts*. New York: Wiley, 1962.

Gump, P. V. Ecological psychology and children. *Review of Child Development Research*, 1976, 75-126.

Inhelder, B., Bovet, M., Sinclair, M., & Smock, C. D. Comments on "the course of cognitive growth." *American Psychologist*, 1966, *22*(2), 160-164.

Inhelder, B., & Sinclair, H. Learning cognitive structures. In P. J. Mussen, J. Langer, & M. Covington (Eds.), *Trends and issues in developmental psychology*. New York: Holt, Rinehart, & Winston, 1969.

Kaufman, B. A., & Banet, B. *Will the real Jean Piaget stand up: A critique of three Piaget based curricula, and a rejoinder*. Urbana: University of Illinois, ERIC/ECE, 1976.

Kidder, F. R. Elementary and middle school children's comprehension of Euclidean transformations. *Journal for Research in Mathematics Education*, 1976, *1*, 40-52.

Langer, J. *Theories of development*. New York: Holt, Rinehart, & Winston, 1969.

Leskow, S., & Smock, C. D. Developmental changes in problem-solving strategies: Permutation. *Developmental Psychology*, 1970, *2*, 412-422.

Meyer, J. S., & Elkind, D. From figurative to operative expectancy in the perceptual judgments of children. *Developmental Psychology*, 1975, *6*, 814-823.

Michotte, A. *The perception of causality*. London: Methuen & Co. LTD, 1963.

Mischel, T. (Ed.). *Cognitive development and epistemology*. New York: Academic Press, 1971.

Moos, R. H. Conceptualizations of human environments. *American Psychologist*, 1973, *28*, 652-665.

Piaget, J. *Logic and psychology*. New York: Basic Books, 1957. (a)

Piaget, J. Logique et equilibre dans les comportement du sujet. In L. Apostel, B. Mandelbrot, & J. Piaget (Eds.), *Logique et equilibre. Etudes d'epistemologie genetique* (Vol. 2). Paris: Presses Universitaires de France, 1957. (b)

Piaget, J. Appretissage et connaissance. In M. Goustard, P. Greco, B. Matalon, & J. Piaget (Eds.), *La logique des apprentissages. Etudes d' epistemologie genetique* (Vol. 10). Paris: Presses Universitaires de France, 1959.

Piaget, J. *Le Structuralism*. Paris: Presses Universitaires de France, 1968.

Piaget, J. *Genetic epistemology*. New York: Columbia University Press, 1970. (a)

Piaget, J. *Structuralism*. New York: Basic Books, 1970. (b)

Piaget, J. *Biology and Knowledge.* University of Chicago Press, 1971. (a)

Piaget, J. *Psychology and epistemology.* New York: Grossman Publishers, 1971. (b)

Piaget, J. *Science of education and the psychology of the child.* New York: Viking Press, 1971. (c)

Piaget, J. *To understand is to invent.* New York: Grossman Publishers, 1973.

Piaget, J., & Inhelder, B. *Mental imagery in the child.* New York: Basic Books, 1971.

Sigel, I. The distancing hypothesis: A causal hypothesis for the acquisition of representational thought. In M. R. Jones (Ed.), *Miami Symposium on the Prediction of Behavior, 1968: Effects of Early Experience.* Coral Gables, Fla: University of Miami Press, 1970.

Smock, C. D. *Mathemagenic Activities Program: A model for early childhood education.* Athens: University of Georgia, Research and Development Center, 1969.

Smock, C. D. Constructivism and principles of instruction. In C. D. Smock & E. von Glasersfeld (Eds.), *Epistemology and education.* Athens: University of Georgia Press, 1974.

Stebbins, L. B., St. Pierre, R. G., Proper, E. C., Anderson, R. B., & Cerva, T. R. *Education as experimentation: A planned variation model. An evaluation of Follow Through* (Vol. IV-A). Report to the U.S. Office of Education pursuant to Contract No. 300-75-0134. Cambridge, Ma: Abt Associates, Inc., April 1977.

Steffe, L. P. *Research on mathematical thinking of young children.* Reston, Va.: The National Council of Teachers of Mathematics, Inc. 1975.

Toulmin, S. (Ed.). *Physical reality.* New York: Harper, 1970.

von Glasersfeld, E. Piaget and the radical constructivist epistemology. In C. D. Smock & E. von Glasersfeld (Eds.), *Epistemology and education.* Athens: University of Georgia Press, 1974.

Weikart, D. P., Rogers, L., Adcock, C., & McClelland, D. *The cognitively oriented curriculum.* Urbana: University of Illinois, ERIC-NAEYC, 1971.

5 Continuities and Discontinuities in Structuralism and Constructivism

Rodney R. Cocking
Educational Testing Service
Princeton, New Jersey

INTRODUCTION

The purpose of this chapter is to explore some of the critical aspects in the definitions of Structuralism and Constructivism. The discussion format is a contrastive analysis and the discussion points are presented in ways to evoke comparisons between the two concepts. Hopefully, the effect of such a presentation will differentiate increasingly between Structuralism and Constructivism. Structuralism will always be used as the pivotal framework since it, but not Constructivism, is organized into a theory by way of a set of laws. The test of any theory, according to Campbell (1952) and Kuhn (1962) is in validity and generality of the laws which comprise it, and the contrasts will set up some of those tests.

The attempt to make distinctions between Structuralism and Constructivism does not always result in clear dichotomies. In Assimilation theories of development such as Piaget's, the concept of *Structure* (defined as a system of transformations in Formal Structuralism) becomes continuous with the idea of Construction. It is this particular overlap, in fact, which concerns those of us who subscribe to a Piagetian theory of development. The cause of concern is that Assimilation theories generally present arguments against a basic Structuralism assumption and that assumption is that *meaning* is conveyed by the structure. Assimilations theorists, by contrast, contend that the meaning is "... in the head of the [individual] ... (Brown, 1975, p. 115)." The contrast to the inherent meaning conveyed by the structure is a meaning which is constructed; this is a contrast between *a priori* forms (Structures) and derived forms (Constructions).

A further implication which sparks a contrast between Structuralism and Constructivism is that, based upon the preceding distinction between *a priori* structures and constructed forms, Structure is not coincident with Form, a point acceded by Piaget (1970), but not extensively discussed. Because Structures are the ''givens'' of Structuralism and Forms are the ''products'' of Constructivism, this difference between Structure and Construction will be a primary topic for the discussion.

In order to get a developmental perspective on the issue of Form vs. Structure, it is essential to consider the variations which *Form* and *Structure* can assume. Because Structures have already been described as static, this aspect of the discussion necessarily will shift to Constructivism as the pivotal framework. In that discussion, both aspects of Form (''good'' form and ''bad'' form) will be considered. The purpose will be to highlight the functional aspects of both ''bad form'' as well as ''good form.'' This contrast is an important one for theoretical purposes since some orthodox Structuralists contend that Structures are the ''eternal truths,'' and it is only qualities of enduring value which figure into a formal theory. Developmentalists, however, are obliged to look at the developing organism in terms of ''what works'' and what is functionally relevant to the organism in the growth process. How those ''workable'' solutions change over time is equally important from the developmentalist perspective. For this reason, the relationship between Structure and Construction is a serious issue for developmentalists. This relationship is pronounced in Piagetian theory, where one must reconcile the synergy of assimilation and accommodation, leading to the construction of both ''bad forms'' and ''good forms,'' with the role of both processes in the development of Structures.

ASPECTS OF STRUCTURALISM

The tenets of a formal theory of Structuralism will be the first consideration. In a later section, research in the area of children's language development will be used to challenge some of these tenets and, hence, raise some questions about the theory itself. The three defining characteristics of a structure as described by Piaget (1970) are: (1) wholeness, (2) transformation, and (3) self-regulation. Each of these three points will be elaborated before presenting the specific research data.

Wholeness is a term used to convey the idea that the integrity of a Structure is meaningful in a different sense from the meaning contained in the elements or aggregates which figure into the structure. The nouns and verbs that make up a sentence, for example, convey meaning specific to the elements, but the meaning which is contained in the sentence structure cannot be derived from the elements and is available only when the sentence is structurally intact. A ''Whodunit'' mystery may have the elements of a butler, a rich heiress, and a stabbing, but until the relationships among agent, recipient, and action are mapped, these elements are not useful in decoding the meaning of the situation. Integrated, these elements fall into an overall structure, telling us that the heiress used a dagger to stab the butler. Thus, Wholeness is a principle which indicates that *meaning is mapped within the structure.*

The concept of Wholeness is intended as a contrast with elements or aggregates in how one uses information for constructing the world. The contrast is important for conveying the notion that different interpretations or meanings are constructed when elements are considered, versus the meaning which is constructed on the basis of wholes. The important aspect of "wholeness" is the relationship established among the elements as they constitute a whole. Lenneberg (1971) pointed out that one of the most important properties of language, for example, is the mapping of relationships. He wrote that there is no escape from the necessity of looking toward *relations* as the basis of meaning. Lenneberg illustrates this point by saying that an organism which "has words" does not necessarily have the understanding of the relational constructs that are customarily designated by those words. The process of *knowing,* by Lenneberg's definition, is the process of establishing the relationships within a structure. By this definition, then, the concept of Wholeness is bound to another basic issue— "meaning." Research studies in the area of language comprehension have much to offer for examining the Law of Wholes in the Structuralist theory. More will be said about "meaning" and "the mapping of relationships" in this context, after outlining the other two criterial elements of structures: Transformations and Self-regulation.

The second defining characteristic of Structures is Transformation. Transformations are sets of rules for mapping relationships, such as those discussed in the preceding paragraph. The elements as they comprise a unity have to be considered for their interrelatedness, and the transformational rules for reorganizing these elements must conserve the meanings that have been mapped by these relationships. It is, perhaps, more useful to our understanding of the theory of Structuralism to consider how the child goes about establishing equivalences and setting-up correspondences for mapping relationships than it is to look for the emergence of endless numbers of preformed, static structures, as in the Chomsky tradition. This is one of the major contrasts between Piaget the Constructivist and Chomsky the Structuralist. Piaget has considered all cognitive acquisitions, including language, "... to be the outcome of a gradual process of construction..." whereas Chomsky has tended to look at the universality of linguistic forms (Inhelder, 1978). In order to understand the characteristics that contribute to structural integrity (e.g., Wholeness), however, we need to understand the systems of transformations which are a part of both the Structuralist and Constructivist positions. We will discuss the two issues of correspondences and equivalences which bear upon this distinction when we consider the language data and the Law of Transformation later in this chapter.

The third criterial feature of Structuralism is Self-Regulation. There are, additionally, two important features of self-regulation which need elaboration: (1) self-maintenance and (2) closure. *Closure* means that there is a completeness: the person has to construct a meaningful way of deriving or mapping the relationship without changing the meaning. Closure, therefore, means that the Structure is not open to modification because the meaning would be altered. This is not to say, however, that there are not alternative types of constructions. In fact, involvement at one's own level of competence is the key to *self-maintenance*. Piaget's processes of assimilation and accommodation emphasize that one participates in activities at his or her own particular level of constructive competence.

In order to examine Self-Regulation within the Structuralist theory later in this report, linguistic data which focus upon levels of meaning and different capacities for the extraction of meaning will be presented. The reason for the emphasis upon meaning in this context will be to illustrate that the organic structures which we are discussing, in contrast to physical structures, are unique because of this feature of *meaning*. It will be pointed out, further, that meaning can exist at various levels even within different domains of knowledge, such as the levels of linguistic meaning embodied in syntax, semantics, and dialogue, to name only three. Levels of cognitive competence will also figure into this discussion.

Operations and Constructions

Piaget uses the term *operations* to specify the forms of "... coordination which are general to all actions [Inhelder & Piaget, 1964, p. 291]." Operations are the units of logical thinking and they specify what particular mental activities are involved in deriving a product from mentation (Sigel & Cocking, 1977, pp. 24-25). Piaget's definition of operations becomes relevant in the present discussion of Structure and Form, where errors which enter the system result in "bad form." Piaget defines operations as "perfect regulation," to indicate that errors are excluded from the system. In cybernetic terms, this means that the system of feedback loops results in ongoing adjustments or "corrections." There are certain features internal to the system (e.g., reversibility) that insure the "errors" will be eliminated and never become a part of the structure. What constitutes an "error," then, is an important issue to be confronted. The tack in the present discussion will be to interpret Piaget to mean by this point that "bad form" may be evident to the organism's construction performances, but because of the integrity of the *Whole* and the requirement of *meaningfulness* imposed by the property of closure, errors are not incorporated into the final Structure. But while errors may not be part of a Structure, they do figure into constructions.

Part of the confusion that has crept into discussions of this issue in the past may hinge on a failure to make proper distinctions between operations and constructions. In an early discussion of Construction and its relationship to Structuralism in *Judgment and Reasoning,* Piaget explained the Law of Construction. "The Law of Construction is a combination of relations [p. 195]." "To find the common element in two given classes is to *construct* (emphasis added) the relations between the given individuals and through this construction to reach a classification [p. 196]." It is easy to see that Piaget is describing processes of logical deduction. However, the errors we have been discussing may be evident in the processes of construction of relations when *transduction,* rather than deduction, is the approach to the problem. Transduction is reasoning from particular to particular without the benefit of generalization from the reasoning. Deduction, on the other hand, may be from particular to particular, universal to particular, or particular to universal, with general principles deriving from the relations which are constructed. Because transductive thinking is reasoning without any general principles, we may say that the thinking is syncretic in that there is a fusion of the separate terms that go into the thinking. Piaget says that this is evident in children's thought where separate terms are merely juxtaposed. The juxtaposition does not result in *reversible* thought operations, as in genuine deduction; hence, the syncretic thinking is not reversible thought.

The irreversibility in the thought of the young child explains the absence of any general laws or general principles coming from the constructed relationships. Piaget says that "... a construction *becomes* (emphasis added) rigorous to the extent that it is reversible, and this reversibility of operations is what makes generalization possible [p. 186, fn]." Without the operations (such as reversibility), faulty constructions result. This is how Piaget concludes, as previously pointed out, that operations are "perfect regulation," keeping the system free of error. This does not mean that errors are never present in the system; in fact, we would expect to see errors prevalent prior to the emergence of the operations which regulate the system. To quote from Piaget, "... We simply 'construct' by means of a mental experiment the conclusion that is to be proved ... a mental construction leads to necessary conclusions in so far as it obeys rules, *and these are not the rules of logic* (emphasis added) but previously admitted propositions which are now applied syllogistically [Piaget, 1928, p. 185]." The child's deductions, then, may be based on rules which she/he has extrapolated on the basis of limited experience and the "rules," therefore, themselves may be in error. This, in turn, leads to faulty constructions. Einstein himself provided an anecdote of the value of exploring basic problems with the benefit of formal operations. He said that there were events in his life which he did not explore early on as do most children, discovering them and inventing solutions much later than his peers. He said that he thought his treatment of these problems benefited from being able to reflect on them with the aid of operational thought strategies, while most children had dispensed with those early childhood problems and had gone on to the investigation of more complex problems. Einstein said that the benefit of reflecting on simple problems with formal logic enabled him to approach problems in ways others described as "creative."

Summary

Can we accept all of the tenets of Structuralism? There is some question, particularly with regard to the maxim that every operation is reversible and that erroneous elements are never incorporated into the system. This claim is open to debate, and certainly in need of further study. In language research, at least, where the structures are neither purely logical nor mathematical, we must look for the transformations as they are constructed over time. One might go so far as to say that in language study we ought to consider *classes* of structures as the transformations emerge. Language transformations are regulated by laws which are not operations in the strictest sense. The laws of transformation are not operations because they are not really reversible.[1] Piaget (1970) says that the transformation laws of this modified sort depend upon the interplay of anticipation and corrective feedback, which are, as pointed out in the preceding discussion, the main criteria of *Self-regulation*. It is because of the reliance upon cybernetic feedback-loops and self-regulatory processes that Pragmatism is likely to be more useful to a Constructivist position than to Structuralism. Pragmatism, as a method for solving or evaluating problems of knowledge, always asks the questions "What's the purpose; how does it affect my actions if I follow it or believe it; how does it affect me if I don't follow it or don't believe in it?" The main criterion in pragmatism is the functional utility to the system. This criterion, however, does not mean that behavior is guided only by actions which have forseeable consequences. In pragmatic terms, the reason for asserting whether or not something is true is whether or not it works, and in developmental terms, our constructions result from workable means and ends which we have employed or have observed. Thus, "truth" or "laws" in this psychology of personal constructs are not static. The fact that conceptions change and grow with time is a basic tenet of Constructivism. This point will be continued by discussing both what Constructivism means in language research and at the same time by considering some approaches to evaluating the tenets of Structuralism. This discussion will allow us to look at those instances in which Structuralism and Constructivism are not the same.

Law of Perceptual Wholes

In the introductory remarks on the Wholeness features of Structures it was emphasized that the meaning which may be derived from the elements of a

---

[1]Not all language operations are reversible. In the passive voice transformation, for example, the logical subject becomes the grammatical object and the logical object becomes the grammatical subject. However, not all active voice statements can be subjected to this transformation and still retain a meaning which is synonymous with the active voice statement. *The boy chases the girl* and *the girl is chased by the boy* conform to the reversibility rule, while *Everyone in the room knows at least two languages* is not the same as *At least two languages are known by everyone* in the room (Beilin, 1975, p. 15).

construction is always subordinated to the meaning contained in the integrated, structural whole. In Structuralism, as Piaget presents it (1970), the Law of Perceptual Totalities, or Wholeness, means that the Whole has a qualitative feature of its own, apart from the individual elements. This law also prescribes that there is a quantitative value for the whole which is different from the sum of the parts. This is to say that there is a *law of composition,* which is *nonadditive.* Studies of language comprehension illustrate the nonadditive feature of the law of composition and these studies provide one way of critically examining the Law of Perceptual Wholes in Structuralism.

Language Comprehension.   Ursula Bellugi-Klima (1971) devised a method for assessing syntax comprehension in preschoolers which does not require the child to make any verbalizations. The objective of the technique is to assess the child's understanding of a *complete* sentence. In the task, an array of manipulatable objects is presented for each of a series of different language structures. The child's task is to move the objects according to an experimenter's statements which are framed around particular syntactic forms. For example, the child is presented with two small boy and girl dolls and the experimenter, after demonstrating the verb "chase" in the active voice, asks the child: "Show me: 'The boy chases the girl,' or 'The girl chases the boy.'" The toys are then replaced in the original positions and then the child is asked to perform the same action, but the statement is rephrased to the passive voice. "Show me" 'The girl is chased by the boy,' or 'The boy is chased by the girl.'" That is, the semantic content remains unchanged, but the examiner, in this example, changes the statement so that this item assesses comprehension of the active-passive voice sentence transformation.

A second way of assessing comprehension is to probe the child's understanding of the elements of a sentence (Cocking & Potts, 1976). In contrast to the procedure in which the child is asked to demonstrate, "The boy is pushed by the girl," this second procedure uses an inquiry method and the child is asked, "Who chases?," "Who is chased?" and "Who gets chased?" after the objects are replaced in their original positions and the statement repeated. This second procedure for assessing comprehension looks at the subject-verb-object and the actor-action-acted-upon components of sentences, and the child's understanding of the changes in these elements as a result of sentence transformations.

The issue for discussion is what these different kinds of language comprehension mean in relation to an independent criterion, such as performance involving tasks of new syntactic structures not evident in the child's speech at the time of his/her participation in the study. Cocking and Potts (1976) used both methods, in the order stated above, and the results indicated that performance on new language production tasks was a direct function of the child's knowledge of language as measured by syntax comprehension (the first task) but not related to the child's comprehension of sentence elements as probed through inquiry (the second task).

The Bellugi syntax comprehension score reflected complete sentence comprehension, while the inquiry procedure parceled out the actor, action, and object elements one at a time. Three and four year old children seem to be able to process the unitary elements without too much trouble, but the elements in combination, such as in the Bellugi syntax test, are more difficult. The inquiry-probe procedure would appear to be a refinement of measuring the child's comprehension of both syntactic and semantic *elements,* but the grosser measure reflected in complete sentence comprehension tells us what the child is capable of processing as a string of elements constituting a whole. And what she or he is capable of processing as a string of elements that comprise a whole is what related to performance on a new language learning task.

In addition to the Law of Wholeness, the Law of Composition is relevant to this discussion which posits a *nonadditive* property in the theory of Structuralism. The comprehension studies provide a way of examining the validity of this Law of Structuralism. In the research study cited (Cocking & Potts, 1976), comprehension of the whole sentence unit was more difficult than comprehension of the various sentence elements. The more global comprehension which retained the structural wholeness predicted better to additional generative language learning than comprehension of any of the elements, either alone or in combination. That is, the sum of the elements did not have the same predictive value as the whole. This finding reiterates the Law of Perceptual Wholes as nonadditive.

Law of Associativity

Piaget (1970) describes properties of groups in his discussions of Structuralism because groups are viewed as prototypes of Structures. Groups and groupings are mathematical concepts and as such are not directly applicable to the study of language. Indirectly, however, there are certain features of groups which are useful for understanding how Structuralist principles apply to language development. For example, if we consider the situation of *wanting to express something linguistically,* we are immediately struck by several facts: (1) there are quite a few ways to say essentially the same thing; (2) the actors and recipients of actions in the sentence maintain the same roles regardless of the particular form one chooses for the expression. There are certain identity elements which are preserved regardless of the flexibility in the system for a variety of ways to express a particular meaning; (3) contradictions do not enter into the expression because one alters the mode of expression to edit out contradictory elements; and finally; (4) the route one takes in expressing an idea is irrelevant to arriving at the goal of expressing the intended meaning. These four features are the basic *principles of group structure.* The fourth principle—the route taken being irrelevant to the end goal—is referred to as the Law of Associativity. We will examine this particular law of Structuralism by considering some critical language research.

One Constructivist route for the study of language is to look at the different ways in which children *use* language and how usage changes with development. For example, we see that children use active voice statements primarily in the first stages of sentence construction, and that while the active voice continues as the primary speaking mode even at later ages, passive voice statements are alternatively used. A second example is seen in children's initial failure to use pronoun substitutions for direct and indirect object sentence constructions, although the constructions do appear with a certain degree of regularity at a later point in development. Thus, research has demonstrated that there are predictable and fairly straightforward developmental routes taken in reaching the goal of linguistic expression. The works of Brown (1973), Braine (1963), Menyuk (1963; 1971), Bloom (1970), Cazden (1970), and Potts, Carlson, Cocking, and Copple (1979) have charted the structural development patterns of English grammar, as well as the error or alternate construction patterns. We know, therefore that with experience in a linguistic community, part of the development of linguistic norms is also the development of linguistic alternatives. This is the Constructive process, whereby meaning is abstracted and modes of expression are synthesized. These interactions may be considered as *problems* for a child in that they are encounters which are new to him/her. The child's internal structures determine how the child deals with these problems, and the structures themselves are different at various points in development. Mounoud (1976, p. 170) uses the term *levels of resolution* to describe the internal structures of the child which define the successive stages of development. The levels of resolution tell us a great deal about the construction processes which the child employs in that the child creates new instruments or new organizations for achieving a goal when operations of a given organization fail. Linguistic expression becomes a class of "new problems" as the child's experiences and objects of social interaction expand. The same holds for the need to deal with decoding the expressions of the widening circle of social contacts.

Language Production.   We have followed the issue of *levels of resolution* by studying children's productive language development during the past three years. We have used a prepost research design to study both language comprehension and productive language in a sample of 40 children within the age range of three to five years. Although we have been interested in data which show the child's development-over-time in both language comprehension and production, we have been especially interested in children's alternate routes in linguistic expression. For the production measure, we have used a story completion format in our assessments. Children were individually tested with picture stimuli which depicted the subjects, the actions, and the objects of the stories. The child participated in this activity by completing the stories which the experimenter framed around specific forms of syntax (Potts, 1972). Test development took into account, insofar as possible, the problems of loopholes—that is, responses which were syntactically satisfactory but were other than the designated target form. The interesting aspect of the data was that children continued to exhibit ways of expressing meaning which were different from the prescribed, carefully set up stories as contained in the test. What does this finding mean? For one thing, it's clear that the children understand what it is that you want from them, because their story completions preserve (conserve) the meaning. The children were attending to the aspect we would call "logical necessity": they were not saying someting irrelevant to the task demand or to the task content as contained in the stories or pictures.

The way we have analyzed our data has been to categorize the children's responses to the 39 linguistic structures which were tested across 100 items. The categorizations are: correct target responses, incorrect target responses, and a category of responses in which meaning is preserved but which are clearly alternatives to the target. These categories do not include any responses in which the subject understood the story, attempted the target response, and then made an error: our examples include only children's ways of correctly resolving the story endings.

The following is an example of an item intended to assess the child's knowledge of *Action Nominalization*. The child was given a direct or indirect quotation frame with the nominalization in the subject slot. The child's task was to recognize the nominalization as a subject and give the copula and complement as the response: e.g., "Lee likes to play ball. He says, 'Playing ball _____.' (is fun)." (Potts et al., 1979). Middle class children show a developmental trend of correct usage among three year olds, four year olds, and five year olds of 24%, 41%, and 76%, respectively. However, equally good responses to this target could also be constructed which show variation on the type of adjective used, or the response might even be a definition of the depicted object or activity (e.g., playing ball is a game, . . . is what you do at school, etc.). This happens even with relatively easy items: a targeted response of a *Noun + Plural* construction in which the singular form of the noun ended with an allomorph of the /s/ plural morpheme, thus making it difficult for the child to distinguish between the singular and plural forms, was resolved in various ways. The story and pictures for "This is one glass; here are two _____ ("glasses")" might evoke the error form of "glass," but the correct forms and alternatives to the correct form are the point of this discussion. As an alternative to "glasses," the child might say "cups," which avoids the entire issue of how to pluralize a noun that already sounds plural (Anisfeld, Barlow, & Frail, 1968) by substituting a functional equivalent which doesn't contain the ambiguity.

One might argue that such responses indicate bad test items. From a test-development perspective this may be so, but these types of responses from children also tell us quite a bit about the subjects as active language users. One might ask whether or not these alternate construction responses are common among children. Of the 39 linguistic categories we studied, at least *some* of the subjects constructed alternatives to 19 of them. That is, on half of these structures, there was always someone attempting to approach the problem in slightly different, but correct, way. Is is one or two or just a few children who always do this; just how pervasive is this phenomenon? The specific syntactic structure tested, of course, contributes to the possibilities for variation, but we found that between 15% and 80% of the children showed this type of variation on those 19 structures. That is, on some structures, only 15% chose to approach the targeted syntax differently from what was prescribed; but there were a few structures on which most children tried a variation. The alternatives to the targets were not always produced correctly, but that is not the issue. The point is that the children knew what was required to complete the story and have it make sense, and in their syntax they were expressing different organizational properties from the targeted syntactic form. This is what Mounoud means by *different levels of resolution*.

Law of Transformation

Another way of evaluating the Constructivist position is to explore the meaning of the Law of Transformation as it applies to language behaviors. Children's processes of establishing equivalences and correspondences are ways of looking at the broader concept embodied in the Law of Transformation. In Piaget's Structuralism this means looking at how the child constructs one-to-one correspondence, one-versus-many comparisons, same-versus-different comparisons, and so forth. Roger Brown has considered the roles of equivalence and correspondence in children's very early productive language development (Brown, 1973). Brown was concerned with the ways children construct correspondences in units of *meaning* and units of *sound*. Using the concepts of *morpheme* as a unit of meaning and *phoneme* as a unit of sound, Brown was interested in the equivalences that are established between the sound units and the meaning units (phonemes and morphemes). That is, in English the situation exists whereby phonemic equivalence does not guarantee morphemic equivalence, and this is not exclusive to homophones like ''bored and board.'' Brown studied children's linguistic constructions where the sound units don't always have identical *meaning*. The English suffix ''-er'' in ''runner,'' ''dancer,'' and ''teacher'' does not have the same meaning as the ''-er'' of ''taller,'' ''older,'' or ''stronger.'' The English-speaking child has to learn the so-called ''within'' category equivalences and to ignore the ''between'' category similarities: that is, not to equate comparative and agentive phonemic realizations. Brown argues the case of *language as a system of categories* which have important relations with nonlinguistic categories of thought. The argument is similar to Piaget's Law of Construction, discussed in the preceding section of Operations and Constructions. Brown's thesis is an important and fundamental problem for a general theory of Structure: one has to consider the relation between linguistic and logical structures. The correspondence between the linguistic and logical domains has been studied within two types of research paradigms: the synchrony paradigm which looks for corresponding operations in various performance domains; and the diachronic paradigm, in which differences in development are highlighted. We will consider both approaches.

Synchronic and Diachronic Approaches.   As pointed out in the section dealing with the Law of Associativity, the internal structures of the child determine the stage of intellectual functioning and, consequently, the child's "levels of resolution of various sets of problems" (Mounoud, 1976, p. 170). This means, therefore, that structures are not separable from performance. In the construction of new structures, *assimilation* is the chief function. Assimilation processes are not all of one type, however: Piaget enumerates three specific types— *reproducing, recognitory assimilation,* and *generalizing assimilation.* These various types of assimilation all have the common activity of *relating,* setting up *correspondences,* and of establishing *functional connections.*

There are several ways of studying how children go about establishing these correspondences. Two paradigms which have been utilized within Piagetian research methodologies are the synchronistic approach and the diachronic approach. *Diachronic* aspects concern regulations which appear when the operations of a given organization fail and the subject has to create new instruments of function, or, when possible, to create new organizations. Piaget's own research has dealt, almost exclusively, with studies of the various levels of organization which characterize different stages of development. He saw that it was necessary to specify the various levels of organization prior to specifying the organizing processes themselves. Mounoud (1976) says that *Synchronistic* aspects of behavior concern the regulations made by structures already formed, or the conditions and limitations of the functioning of extant structures. Because this type of study describes status behaviors (i.e., how a structure functions at a given point in time), Mounoud does not believe that synchronistic paradigms are developmental and states, instead, that "Developmental psychology is fundamentally concerned with the diachronic aspects of behavior" (1976, p. 168). Experimental psychology, in contrast, does concern itself with the parameters, conditions, and limitations of the functioning of structures.

It should be pointed out that these two paradigms study different aspects of the same behaviors and, as such, are not quite so exclusive of one another as might be expected. In fact, it will be pointed out that while a research team might adopt the methods of one paradigm, the research data often have considerable bearing on its competing approach. Sinclair-de-Zwart (1973), for example, has concerned herself with issues of *synchrony.* She has looked at development across similar systems, such as the synchrony between linguistic structures and logical structures as they develop in the same children. For example, she studied operational levels in children and related these levels to their use of scalar adjectives.

In that study, Sinclair looked at the relationships between logical operations and adjective marking to determine the synchronous development in cognitive and linguistic systems.

Another way to study this correspondence problem is from a *diachronic* point of view—how systems develop and change. For example, language comprehension and language production are separate language systems and can be studied as different systems of representation (Beilin, 1975, p. 279). Comprehension and production each can be studied also for its relationship to nonlinguistic structures (Beilin, 1975). A diachronic relationship exists when a concept is present in one system prior to its appearance in another modality, unlike synchronous development where the operations appear within similar time frames. The studies, then, look for such differences and for the points where there are correspondences among abilities across functional domains, such as language and thought.

Current work is contributing to our understanding of diachronic functions. Irving Sigel developed a preschool program in which the children are encouraged to employ the assimilative processes of reproducing, recognition, generalizing, setting up correspondences, relating, and establishing functional connections throughout all of the activities of the nursery school day (Sigel, Saunders, & Moore, 1977). That is, the preschool experience promotes what Piaget (1970) and Inhelder (1978) term representational thought which "... transcends the here and now ... and moves the child from the basics of ... sensorimotor intelligence" (Inhelder, 1978, p. 264). The question for this discussion is how nonlinguistic structures appear in the verbal behaviors of the children when there is no direct effort at language training, per se.

The method employed to study this issue was to examine both receptive and productive language in the experimental and control preschool subjects in relation to the psycholinguistic constructs. The design was a 2 × 2 × 6 matrix for studying two levels of treatment (experimental and control nursery school programs), two levels of language knowledge (comprehension and production), and six cognitive-linguistic constructs (future orientation, past-time orientation, negation, conditionals, causal connectives, and questions). Language structures were chosen for their compatability with the constructs of the preschool program which was designed to foster representational thinking. This program utilized a teaching technique termed Distancing strategies, which Sigel describes as teaching efforts which promote the development of psychological distance between the child and the immediate, perceptual world, thereby facilitating representational modes of thought. When the verbal data were analyzed in terms of these distancing categories, and not just as purely linguistic categories (e.g., Time Orientation of past and future for reconstructive and anticipatory cognitive counterparts, negation, question forms, and so forth—see Beilin, 1975), a number of findings emerged which support the diachronic thesis of development. On a combined category for Future orientation, for example, experimental group treatment effects showed significance, indicating that subjects exposed to distancing instructional strategies performed better on this category for both the language they understood (receptive) and the language they used (productive), as compared with a matched control group. In both treatment conditions, however, the children's capacities for dealing with receptive language surpassed their effectiveness for generating the same language structures themselves (productive language). This is a diachronic aspect of those particular cognitive-linguistic constructs. The diachrony transcended the variations in group experience (treatment effects), as well as the type of cognitive-linguistic structure. This latter point deserves some further elaboration, because the conditions and limitations on the functioning of certain structures illustrate that the data are useful toward an understanding of certain synchronistic aspects of early cognitive-linguistic behaviors, too.

A significant distancing treatment effect was also obtained for Past-time orientation, as well as a change-over-time effect for this group. The reconstructive category of Past-time orientation is one of those categories in which it was found that the children who returned for a second year of the experimental treatment program did better than those with just one treatment year and this effect interacted with the specific type of nursery school program to produce an interaction between length of experience and type of program. The latter finding indicates that the experimental, or Distancing program, had more impact on both expressive and receptive linguistic reconstruction and recognition behaviors when the children worked within a program for two years rather than for just one year. Conditionals (clauses), statements involving causal connectives, and Questions showed similar group effects very strongly, as well as the effects of change-over-time. However, these effects were not related to the number of years of nursery school experience as were the reconstruction and recognitory processes of Past-time language.

The results from Sigel's nursery school study are just a sample of the methods currently employed for examining the specific relationships between linguistic and nonlinguistic structures and the changes which occur over time. Beilin (1975) and his colleagues have also examined the diachronic relationship between certain logical and linguistic structures. They found an asymmetry in concepts of conjunction and disjunction as compared with the naturalistic speech samplings of two to three year-olds. The prior emergence of negation relative to other speech expressions of a similar functional category (e.g., connectives) was also found. In somewhat older children, Beilin et al. found the development of logical intersection to be congruent with linguistic comprehension and to *precede* it at each age. These researchers concluded: "In general, comparisons of the development of linguistic and cognitive performance showed that comprehension of many linguistic connectives . . . appeared to develop later than or concurrently with, operational level performance in theoretically related cognitive tasks [Beilin, 1975, p. 299]."

The research paradigms, therefore contrast synchronic and diachronic development but the research data illustrate that there are both correlated (synchronous) and asymmetrical (diachronous) developments occurring in linguistic and logical structures. Thus, although a stage analysis (synchrony) would indicate that Beilin's data show congruent functioning at certain time points, a developmental analysis (diachrony) shows that the logical tasks precede the development of the linguistic comprehension, as in the case of logical intersection. Synchronistic aspects of behavior are useful for structural descriptions of functioning whereas diachronistic aspects illuminate the construction processes.

SUMMARY

As long ago as 1964, Brown and Fraser were pointing out that the systematic errors in children's morphological and syntactic productions were important data sources for the argument that children have construction rules (Brown & Fraser, 1964, p. 337). In the present paper, *Structure was differentiated from Form,* and further, it was asserted that both "good" form and "bad" form are essential to the Constructivist position, especially where developmental data are concerned. The critical question was whether such considerations run counter to Structuralism, which is more closely aligned with synchronic development than with the diachronic aspects of development—the latter are assumed to be more in concert with the constructivist position. Several laws of Structuralism were presented and then reconsidered in the light of some recent language development research. Language comprehension studies were examined as a test of the Law of Perceptual Wholes; next came a consideration of children's own linguistic constructions of alternatives to target responses as a test of the Law of Associativity and self-regulation; finally, structure-function considerations came into the discussion of relationships between linguistic and logical structures, testing the Law of Transformation through function processes of assimilation. These language research studies had the pervasive theme of children's constructive approach to knowledge acquisition, thus bringing into question just how literal one may interpret the Laws of Structuralism which are descriptive of stage functioning. The discussion which pointed to varying degrees of cognitive competencies, as well as the specificity of certain competencies, raised the issue of children's "levels of resolutions" to sets of problems. Throughout this chapter it was intended for the reader to see that there are continuities between Structuralism and Constructivism, but that the two are not necessarily the same.

REFERENCES

Anisfeld, M., Barlow, J., & Frail, C. M. Distinctive features in the pluralization rules of English speakers. *Language and Speech,* 1968, *11,* 31–37.

Beilin, H. *Studies in the cognitive basis of language development.* New York: Academic Press, 1975.

Bellugi-Klima, U. Some language comprehension tests. In C. I. Lavatelli (Ed.), *Language training in early childhood education.* Urbana, Ill.: University of Illinois Press, 1971.

Bloom, L. *Language development: Form and function in emerging grammars.* Cambridge, Mass.: M.I.T. Press, 1970.

Braine, M. The ontogeny of English phrase structure: The first phase. *Language, 1963, 39,* 1-13.

Brown, A. L. The development of memory: Knowing, knowing about knowing, and knowing how to know. In H. W. Reese (Ed.), *Advances in child development and behavior* (Vol. 10). New York: Academic Press, 1975.

Brown, R. *A first language: The early stages.* Cambridge, Mass.: Harvard University Press, 1973.

Brown, R., & Fraser, C. The acquisition of syntax. *Monographs of the Society for Research in Child Development, 1964, 29* (Serial NO. 92).

Campbell, N. *What is science?* New York: Dover Press, 1952.

Cazden, C. Children's questions: Their forms, functions, and roles in education. *Young Children,* March 1970, 202-220.

Cocking, R., & Potts, M. Social facilitation of language acquisition. *Journal of Genetic Psychology Monographs,* 1976, *94*(2).

Inhelder, B. Language and thought: Some remarks on Chomsky and Piaget. *Journal of Psycholinguistic Research,* 1978, *7,* 263-268.

Inhelder, B., & Piaget, J. *The early growth of logic in the child.* New York: Norton & Co., 1964.

Kuhn, T. *The nature of scientific revolutions.* Cambridge, Mass.: M.I.T. Press, 1962.

Lenneberg, E. H. Of language knowledge, apes, and brains. *Journal of Psycholinguistic Research,* 1971, *1,* 1-29.

Menyuk, P. Syntactic structures in the language of children. *Child Development.* 1963, *34,* 407-422.

Menyuk, P. *The acquisition and development of language.* Englewood Cliffs, N.J.: Prentice Hall, 1971.

Mounoud, P. The development of systems of representation and treatment in the child. In B. Inhelder & H. H. Chipman (Eds.), *Piaget and his school: A reader in developmental psychology.* New York: Springer-Verlag, 1976.

Piaget, J. *Science of education and the psychology of the child.* New York: Orion, 1970. (a)

Piaget, J. *Structuralism,* New York: Basic Books, 1970. (b)

Piaget, J. *Judgment and reasoning in the child.* Totowa, New Jersey: Littlefield Adams & Co., 1972 (originally published, 1928).

Potts, M. A technique for measuring language production in three, four, and five year olds. *Proceedings of the 80th Annual convention of the American Psychological Association,* 1972, *9,* 11-13. (Summary)

Potts, M., Carlson, P., Cocking, R. R., & Copple, C. E. *Structure and development in child language: The preschool years.* Ithaca, N.Y.: Cornell University Press, 1979.

Sigel, I. E., & Cocking, R. R. *Cognitive development from childhood to adolescence: A constructivist perspective.* New York: Holt, Rinehard, & Winston, 1977.

Sigel, I. E., Saunders, R. A., & Moore, C. E. *On becoming a thinker: A preschool program.* Paper presented at the Learning Resource Center Workshop, Hightstown, New Jersey, April, 1977.

Sinclair-de-Zwart, H. Language acquisition and cognitive development. In T. E. Moore (Ed.), *Cognitive development and the acquisition of language.* New York, N.Y.: Academic Press, 1973.

6 The Concepts of Adaptation and Viability in a Radical Constructivist Theory of Knowledge[1]

Ernst von Glasersfeld
University of Georgia

Theodore Mischel, to whose memory this chapter on constructivism is dedicated, was interested in epistemology as well as in psychology. In what he did and in what he wrote he never tired of reminding psychologists that their work, if it is to be of real consequence, must be rooted in philosophically firm ground. It is a measure of his success that a panel on "constructivism" can today draw a large and illustrious audience. To add a personal touch, I feel that it is to a large extent due to Mischel's work that someone like myself, whose qualifications as psychologist are rather unconventional, may venture to express ideas on the epistemology of cognition that are certainly alien to, and perhaps even incompatible with, some of the views that have for a long time dominated the branch of science that refers to itself as the study of behavior.

The ideas I shall be expounding owe a great deal to other people. First and foremost among them, Silvio Ceccato, who, 30 years ago, fathered the constructivist approach to cognition in Italy, and Warren McCulloch, the great poet of cybernetics. More recently I have drawn from the works of Humberto Maturana and Heinz von Foerster. Also, as I get into my subject, it will become clear, I am sure, that much of the conceptual basis on which I build was Piaget's long before.[2] However, the following ideas about adaptation and viability are my own concoction and cannot be blamed on anyone else.

[1]A short version of this paper was read in the Theodore Mischel Symposium on Constructivism at the 7th Annual Meeting of the Jean Piaget Society, Philadelphia, May 19-21, 1977.

[2]I shall not cease to thank Charles Smock, who, early on, detected that affinity and then patiently introduced me to Piaget's work.

The purpose of this chapter is to propose a radical reassessment of the meaning of the term ''adaptation.'' I argue that it erroneously implies an adapting activity on the part of the organism and that the particular aspect of evolution to which we want to refer is better expressed by the term ''viability.'' Having stripped away the misleading connotation, I shall try to show that the concept of viability can serve as the mainstay of a consistent constructivist theory of knowledge that eliminates some, if not all, of the age old problems of epistemology.

Since the theory of knowledge I propose is not just constructivist, but *radically* constructivist (von Glasersfeld, 1975), a brief preliminary justification of constructivism will help to clear the ground for the further development. In discussing Piaget and particularly his ideas on the ''construction of reality,'' the question is frequently raised why anyone should want to be a constructivist and hold that the knowing subject *constructs* his or her knowledge rather than obtains it simply by looking at the real world. The question, given our common sense tradition, sounds extremely sensible. Why, indeed, should anyone want to go to all that trouble? Reality appears so obvious, so close, so tangible and even inescapable, that it seems quite absurd to assume that the subject should have to construct it for himself or herself. I have no illusion that a common sense belief so general and so venerable as that one, could be dismantled by one simple argument; but that is all I shall offer here.[3]

Even the most naive of naive realists will at some point come to wonder *how* all the ''information'' one believes one is gleaning from the real world actually gets from that outside world into an individual's system so that the individual can have a cognitive representation of it. In other words, one begins to ask: How do I know? If the individual belongs to our culture and is of a scientific bent, he or she will not be satisfied with introspection but will begin to observe other organisms in order to find out how these organisms come to know *their* environment, which they tacitly but erroneously equate with *the* world (von Glasersfeld, 1976). Because one cannot really get inside the organism that is being observed, one eventually formulates or builds some kind of a model of this process of ''knowing.'' That is what students of perception and the neurosciences in general have been doing and are doing. According to the more or less accepted contemporary models, there are ''receptors,'' ''firings,'' and ''neural networks'' or ''fields'' that compute a ''representation'' out of the firings. In the present context we can say that it is irrelevant whether or not the investigator then claims that the organism's representation is functionally equivalent to, isomorphic with, or, simply, a picture of ''the real world''—whatever an observer says of it, there can be no doubt about the fact that the organism has to *construct* a representation out of such proximal data as it has. In the case of the neuronal model these proximal

---

[3]For a more complete exposition of the bases of constructivism see Ceccato, 1949 and 1964/66; Maturana, 1970; Piaget, 1937; von Foerster, 1972 and 1976; von Glasersfeld, 1975, 1976, 1977a, and 1977b; and Smock and von Glasersfeld, 1974.

data are small elementary events referred to as "firings of neurons." As Hebb (1958) wrote: "At a certain level of physiological analysis there is no reality but the firing of single neurons [p. 461]."

It seems, then, that there is simply no way around the assumption that organisms construct their representations of their world, their environment, or whatever one chooses to call what is outside them. In other words, an activity of construction *has* to be assumed regardless of whether one wants to be a constructivist or not.

Scientific investigators can hardly stop at that point. No matter how diffident or suspicious they might be about questions that smack of philosophy, sooner or later they will be compelled to ask just how adequate, correct, or "true" a representation of an outside world the organisms can construct inside themselves. The moment they ask that question, they are at the very core of traditional epistemology. That is to say, they face the scenario that was set up by the pre-Socratics and then formally and definitively presented by Plato. There is, on one side, an existing, fully structured world and, on the other, a Knower whose eternal task it is to *get to know* that world. This scenario has been welded so firmly to our concept of knowledge that there seems no way of separating the two. In our Western philosophical tradition, the "getting to know" has been viewed either as the activation of innate ideas which automatically match the structure of the real world (because God and, more recently, Evolution have predisposed that match) or it is viewed as the result of the action of our senses. The second, i.e., the empiricist, alternative has dominated science for quite some time now, and it has turned our senses into somewhat mysterious gadgets which, apart from their physiological functioning, have the ability of conveying *information* from outside the organism to its inside. Of course, there have been and still are many hybrid versions that attempt to combine the two alternatives, taking varying percentages of both. The one point in which they all are equivalent is that, owing to their common presupposition of preexisting "objective" structures, they are unable to resolve the question of how we could ever know that the representation inside the organism is really *like* that preexisting world which it is supposed to depict. The question was asked by Socrates and it has remained unanswered to this day.

In the 1930s, as a student of mathematics, like many of my generation, I thought I had found my bible in Wittgenstein's *Tractatus*. I read and reread that book until one fine day, coming to paragraph 2.223, I hesitated—and the beautiful edifice of ideas collapsed. What I read and *understood* for the first time was: "In order to discover whether the picture is true or false we must compare it with reality. (Wittgenstein, 1933/1922, p. 43)." How could one possible carry out that comparison? With that question, although I did not know it at the time, I found myself in the company of Sextus Empiricus, of Montaigne, Berkeley, and Vico—the company of all the courageous sceptics who throughout the history of this civilization have maintained that it is impossible to compare our image of reality with a reality outside. It is impossible, because in order to check whether our representation is a "true" picture of reality we should have to have access not only to our representation but also to that outside reality *before* we get to know it. And because the only way in which we are supposed to get at reality is precisely the way we would like to check and verify, there is no possible escape from the dilemma.

Today, 40 years later, the problems with the traditional scenario of epistemology are clearer to me. In order to make my ideas comprehensible, let me digress for a moment and talk about the concept of adaptation.

In the biological theory of evolution we speak of variability and selection, of environmental constraints and of survival. If an organism survives—individually or as a species—it means that, so far at least, it has been *viable* in the environment in which it happens to live. To survive, however, does *not* mean that the organism must in any sense reflect the character or the qualities of his environment. Gregory Bateson (1967) was the first who noticed that this theory of evolution, Darwin's theory, is really a cybernetic theory because it is based on the concept of constraint rather than on the concept of causation. Somehow we always tend to think that the character of surviving organisms is determined by its environment. We speak of "adaptation", and the idea of causation seems to become associated with that concept so that we end up believing that environmental constraints can *cause* certain biological structures or certain behaviors in organisms. That is a serious conceptual error. In order to remain among the survivors, an organism has to "get by" the constraints which the environment poses. It has to squeeze between the bars of the constraints, to coin a metaphor. The environment does not determine *how* that might be achieved. It does not cause certain organisms to have certain characteristics or capabilities or to be a certain way. The environment merely eliminates those organisms that knock against its constraints. Anyone who *by any means* manages to get by the constraints, survives. We all should know that, from looking around us. If one looks around in Athens, Georgia, one can see cardinals and cockroaches, humming birds, bats, chipmunks, and snakes; daddy longlegs, opossums, frogs, and catfish; and a seemingly infinite variety of mushrooms, moulds, butterflies, and worms. All of them survive in that environment, and they have found entirely different solutions for survival. For all we know, there is an infinite variety of solutions for survival, an infinite number of ways of being viable .Tomorrow, if the environment should change, some of today's organisms may no longer be viable, others may make it in spite of the change. In the ordinary way of speaking we would say that those organisms that survive the change have or are *adapted* to the new environment. This again invites the conceptual error mentioned before, since it suggests that the change in the environment has caused specific *corresponding* changes in the organisms. But that is not the case. Organisms may indeed change, but the changes they manifest are due to their inherent variability, their mutations, genetic drift, or what you will. All the environment contributes is constraints that knock out some of the changed organisms while others are left to survive. Thus we can say that the only indication we may get of the "real" structure of the environment is through the organisms and the species that have been extinguished; the viable ones that survive merely constitute a selection of solutions among an infinity of potential solutions that might be equally viable.

What I suggest now, is that the relationship between what we know, i.e., our *knowledge*, is similar to the relationship between organisms and their environment.[4] In other words, we construct ideas, hypotheses, theories, and models, and as long as they survive, which is to say, as long as our experience can be successfully fitted into them, they are *viable*. (In Piagetian terms we might say that our constructs are viable as long as our experience can be assimilated to them.)

This, of course, immediately raises the question as to what "survival" and "viability" mean in the cognitive domain. Briefly stated, concepts, theories, and cognitive structures in general, are viable and survive as long as they serve the purposes to which they are put, as long as they more or less reliably get us what we want. "Getting us what we want," however, means different things in different realms of experience. In the realm of everyday experience, for instance, Newton's physics serves our purposes well and is perfectly viable. Most of us simply do not enter the realms of experience where the methods and predictions based on Newton's concepts break down. This is not so for the ideal scientist (e.g., as portrayed by Popper, 1934/1965 and 1962/1968) who is perennially searching for concepts and theories that "get by" the constraints encountered in *all* realms of experience and who is, therefore, more concerned with the possible "falsification" of his concepts and hypotheses than with their practical success as means in the pursuit of certain limited ends. This leads to the somewhat peculiar situation that Newton's ideas are quite "true" for the man in the street, the mechanic, and the working engineer, whereas they are "false" for a relatively small group of specialized scientists. What must be stressed, however, is that none of this can change the epistemological status of the ideas, concepts, theories, or models that we consider as constituting our "knowledge."

If we accept this concept of viability, it becomes clear that it would be absurd to maintain that our knowledge is in any sense a replica or picture of reality. It does not have to be, nor indeed could it ever be anything of the sort. On the pragmatic everyday level it has to be useful to us in that it reliably helps us to achieve our purposes. On the scientific level, however, usefulness does not seem particularly relevant. The scientist is looking for consistency, for mutually com-

---

[4]The idea that science or the growth of knowledge resemble or are in some way subject to the "laws of evolution" is certainly not new; but whenever I have seen this idea, it was always contaminated by the conception of adaptation as a progressively *better* match with environment and reality.

patible theories and models, and, ultimately, for a unitary, homogeneous explanation of experience on all levels. Empiricists and statisticians have long been telling us that we can never "prove" a theory—we can only disprove it. In my terms that means that while we can *know* when a theory or model knocks against the constraints of our experiential world, the fact that it does *not* knock against them but "gets by" and is still viable, does in no way justify the belief that the theory or model therefore depicts a "real" world.

In this context it is important to realize that "constraints of our experience" do not necessarily refer to constraints that have to be thought of as inherent in an ontological reality. It was Piaget who has finally made clear that many, if not all, the constraints that govern our actual and potential experience stem from our own construction. Any construction, be it physical or mental, is subject to certain constraints that spring from the material that the constructor employs. It is easy to see that a bricklayer is to some extent constrained in his building by certain basic characteristics that are inherent in the bricks he uses. In much the same way, I believe, the representation we construct of our adult experiential world is constrained by certain basic characteristics of the building blocks we are using, which is to say, the building blocks which we created during the sensorimotor period. We call these building blocks "space," "time," "identity," and "change," and some of their early combinations give us, among others, "objects," "motion," and "causation". All of them are crucial elements in our later picture of the world and determine the kinds of world we can represent to ourselves. As Mischel (1971) formulated it, "What he (the subject) responds to is his construal of the external intrusion, and he is also the one who interprets the outcome of his compensatory activities [p. 324]."

Finally, there is yet another perhaps even more general way in which we can apply the concept of viability. A rather convincing case can be made for the notion that all practical learning may be considered the result of a process of induction. The simplest explication of inductive inference, I believe, is this: If an organism has an experience, and that experience is in some sense successful or satisfactory, the organism will be inclined to repeat it. If there is more experience, the organism will begin to extract or compute regularities from its corpus of experience. As David Hume put it, we repeat what was successful in the past, on the assumption that there is some regularity and that the experience that we have not yet had will not be altogether different from the experience we *have* had. To use this principle in our models of living organisms, it is not at all necessary to presuppose "awareness" or "consciousness" on the part of the organism. Though some behaviorists may be shocked, I would suggest that this basic form of inductive inference is exactly equivalent to Thorndike's "Law of Effect." In any case, both Thorndike's principle and that of induction result in the setting up of more or less reliable regularities. These regularities, regardless of whether we consider them predictions, explanations, instruments for achieving goals, or merely learned patterns of behavior, are regularities that have been established in past experience, and as long as they are replicated in the organism's further experience, they "survive." Repetition thus creates and perpetuates the "viability" of posited regularities. We speak of "confirmation" or "corroboration" (Popper, 1962/1968), but again we must beware not to interpret perpetuated viability as correspondence to a "real" world or as "truth" in the traditional sense.

If we can accept this view of inductive inference as the establishing of regularities that survive and remain viable as long as our experience does not falsify them, and if we conclude that, by and large, we have no better way of explaining, predicting, and governing our experience, then we can take one further step that is relevant to the problem involved in what Piaget (1975) has called *équilibration majorante,* i.e., the incremental equilibration that proceeds in spirals, incorporating more and more items and events in the developing organism's experience. This constitutes a problem because of the tacit assumption that such an effort of incrementation could be explained only by some specific form of motivation. I would now suggest that one reason for this tendency to increment the range of experience within which equilibration is attempted by the organism, may be quite simply that the organism comes to make an inductive inference about the principle of induction itself. In other words, given that inferring regularities has been successful in the organism's past experience, to infer regularities will be likely to become a goal in its own right and the organism will begin to enlarge its range of experience, and will foster or create new experience simply for the sake of establishing regularities. Once such a tendency is established—and if living organisms can be described as "inductive systems" (Maturana, 1970), it could not help being established—it would lead the adult organism to engage in some of the activities that seem to defy utilitarian or other simple explanations. Activities such as solving puzzles for the sake of solving them, or, to use a more romantic traditional expression, to pursue truth for the sake of truth alone, fall under this rubric. This, clearly, is no more than a conjecture, and all that can be said to make it more plausible is that it *would* seem to be a logical consequence of the idea of viability presented here.

To sum up, then, according to the radical constructivist view, we must never say that our knowledge is "true" in the sense that it reflects an ontologically real world. Knowledge neither should nor could have such a function. The fact that some construct has for some time survived experience—or experiments, for that matter—means that up to that point it was viable in that it bypassed constraints that were inherent in the range of experience within which we were operating. But viability does not imply uniqueness, because there may be innumerable other constructs that would have been as viable as the one we created.

This principle applies as much to the epistemological model suggested here as to any other model constructed. Thus, it should be emphasized that I am not claiming ontological status for the proposed model. The model being developed here is one that might allow us to think of knowledge and the activity of knowing *without* the basic contradiction that is inherent in traditional epistemology.

As a parting comment, let me borrow yet another idea from Piaget: the concept of decentration. Piaget has observed that not only the child in his or her ontogenetic development moves from egocentricity to states of increasing decentration, but so does our species. Looking at our intellectual history and the progression of cognitive constructs and explanatory models, Piaget singled out Copernicus who successfully abolished the egocentric notion that the little planet on which we live must be the center of the universe. We know that it was a difficult step to take and that resistance against it lasted longer than a century. It seems that now there is yet another, even more difficult step in that direction we shall have to make, namely, to give up the notion that the representations we construct from our experience should in any sense reflect a world as it might be without us.

REFERENCES

Bateson, G. Cybernetic explanation. *American Behavioral Scientist,* 1967, *10*(8), 29–32.

Ceccato, S. Il Toceono. *Methodos,* 1949, *1*(1), 34–55.

Ceccato, S. *Un tecnico fra i filosofi* (Vol. I). Padua, Italy: Marsilio, 1964.

Ceccato, S. *Un tecnico fra i filosofi* (Vol. 11). Padua, Italy: Marsilio, 1966.

Hebb, D. O. Alice in Wonderland or psychology among the biological sciences. In H. F. Harlow & C. N. Woolsey (Eds.), *Biological and biochemical bases of behavior.* Madison, Wisc.: University of Wisconsin Press, 1958.

Maturana, H. *Biology of cognition.* BCL Report Nr. 9.0. Urbana, Ill.: University of Illinois, 1970.

Michel, T. Piaget: Cognitive conflict and the motivation of thought. In T. Mischel (Ed.), *Cognitive development and epistemology.* New York: Academic Press, 1971.

Piaget, J. *La construction du réel chez l'enfant.* Neuchâtel: Delachaus et Niestlé, 1937.

Piaget, J. *L'équilibration des structures cognitives.* Paris: Presses Universitaires de France, 1975.

Popper, K. R. *The logic of scientific discovery.* New York: Harper Torchbooks, 1965. (Originally published, 1934).

Popper, K. R. *Conjectures and refutations.* New York: Harper Torchbooks, 1968. (Originally published, 1962).

Smock, C. D., & von Glasersfeld, E. (Eds.) *Epistemology and education.* MAP Report Nr. 14. Athens, Georgia: Follow Through Publications, 1974.

von Foerster, H. Notes pour une épistémologie des objets vivants. In E. Morin & M. Piattelli-Palmarini (Eds.), *L'unité de l'homme.* Paris: Editions du Seuil, 1972.

von Foerster, H. Objects: Tokens for (eigen) behaviors. Paper presented at the Meeting for the Celebration of Jean Piaget's 80th Birthday. *Cybernetics Forum,* 1976, *8,* 91–96.

von Glasersfeld, E. Piaget and the radical constructivist epistemology. In C. D. Smock & E. von Glasersfeld (Eds.), *Epistemology and Education,* 1974.

von Glasersfeld, E. Radical constructivism and Piaget's concept of knowledge. In F. B. Murray (Ed.), *Impact of Piagetian theory,* Baltimore: University Park Press, 1978.

von Glasersfeld, E. Cybernetics and cognitive development. In P. B. Vrtunski (Chair) Relevance and perspectives of cybernetics in psychology. Annual Meeting of the American Psychological Association, 1976. *Cybernetics Forum,* 1976, *8,* 115–120.

von Glasersfeld, E. *Notes on the epistemological revolution*. In von Foerster (Chair) The general systems paradigm: Model for a changing science. SGSR/AAAS Symposium, Denver, Colo.: 1977. (a)

von Glasersfeld, E. *A radical constructivist view of knowledge*. In B. A. Kaufman (Chair) Implications of constructivism for human development. Paper presented at Annual Meeting of AERA, New York, 1977. (b)

Wittgenstein, L. *Tractatus logico-philosophicus*. London: Kegan Paul, Trench, Trubner, 1953. (Originally published, 1922).

THEORY

7 Cognitive Development: Construction of New Structures or Construction of Internal Organizations

Pierre Mounoud
Université de Genève

The purpose of this chapter is to present the hypothesis that cognitive development can be considered as the construction of *internal* organizations of contents (construction of internal models) and *not* as the construction of new structures as Piaget states since the formal structures of our actions and our reasoning (Piaget's general coordinations of action) are preformed. It is on the basis of these preformed structures, that internal organizations of contents (representations) occur if new coding capacities appear. As we know, Piaget considers that structures or coordinations of our actions and thinking are constructed. He defines them as what is general or common to all our actions, all our reasoning, and all subjects . . . epistemic subjects! He specifies that he refers to the *form or structure* of our behavior, independent of different contents to which they apply.

This position gives the environment a secondary and nonspecific role: it may accelerate or decelerate the construction of structures.

To begin with, we shall examine how Piaget studies the problem of cognitive development in terms of constructions of new structures. It is possible to distinguish two principal origins of his way of studying cognitive development: his epistemological project and his structural approach.

PIAGET'S EPISTEMOLOGICAL THEORY

Piaget cannot be considered a psychologist. In fact, he refuses to be considered as such. His theory is not a psychological theory but is essentially an epistemological one, his main interest being in biology. From his biological-epistemological point of view, I consider myself in Piaget's camp even though I have developed a strong critique of the psychological aspect of his work.

Historically, the essential problem for Piaget was to explain the *appearance of new forms or structures* in the living world. This was the main concern of many biologists at the end of last century. When he was observing limnetic watersnail, mollusks in Swiss lakes, he was investigating the influence of different environments on the form of the snails. The particular emerging form was considered a result of the interaction between genotype and phenotype, i.e., between the genetic structure and its appearance. The emergent form or structure of the snails was considered a new and original one. In his actual research on sedum (a plant), that he tirelessly transplanted, Piaget always tried to solve the same problem: how new forms appear, how the hereditary aspects of the plant can be affected by the present conditions of the new environment that have produced the actual phenotype. To solve that kind of problem, he had to study many generations of the same plant. In the biological area, Piaget does take the environment into consideration, attending to its specificity and particularities. The environment affects evolution of the species and is related to the appearance of new forms, whereas in any view in psychology the environment does not have this specific action influence.

Let me show how Piaget transposes the problem of the advent of new forms using a biological model for the field of psychology. He starts by considering cognitive development as successive advents of new structures. For him, these structures are determined by the interaction between the subject's previous structures and properties of the environment. But from the biological to the psychological level an important change takes place. For Piaget, the initial structures of the child's behavior at birth are considered as equivalent in all individuals. Piagetian structures can be defined as *formal* because they can be to some degree independent of the content and of the context to which they are applied. As for the environment, Piaget only takes into consideration the physical aspects of reality which he considers equivalent around the world. Piaget therefore concludes that interactions between equivalent structures and constant environmental features produce new equivalent structures for all subjects. At a biological level, interactions between the individual and the environment account for the emergence of new *specific* forms because environments are particularized. At a psychological level, however, the emergence of nonspecific new forms or structures are attributed to interaction with common environmental features. Paradoxically, the effect of the environment is nonspecific in the case of cognitive development of the child whereas the environmental effects are specified in the development of various plants and animal forms. The only variations in development that can occur are those of speed of development but never of form. Yet, in development, individual differences are observable in regard to ways of acting and reasoning to physical and social reality. We also accept the notion that certain aspects of our way of reasoning are determined both by hereditary factors and by characteristics of the environment (specific as well as general, social as well as physical aspects). In order to understand these individual differences, we must reject the hypothesis that the children build common formal structures.

Let us see how Piaget explains the advent of new structures through this method.

PIAGET'S STRUCTURAL APPROACH

For understanding the sensorimotor period, Piaget uses his observations of the behavior of children as the basis for his inferences regarding development of structures. Behavior was analyzed in terms of epistemological categories such as objects, space, causality, time, etc.

In his study of the period of concrete operations (2 to 10 years), Piaget emphasized his structural approach. Specific *situations* were designed in order to gather evidence of the formal structures of the reasoning of the child for each separate category of time, speed, space, and so on.

These specific situations consist of a simplification of a situation focusing on a particular dimension selected by the researcher. In this context, the object is considered *one-dimensional,* as if no longer possessing other significant attributes. The purpose of the method is to determine if the child understands the object and the particular dimensions selected by the experimenter. Objects, for example, become "lengths" and the experimenter observes if the child can make a series of "lengths" defined by a particular attribute; or if the child can conserve "length" after modifications of the state of the object are made such as moving the object, e.g., translation or rotation.

The aim of such a method is to discover at what age the child handles a particular transformation. Further, it is assumed that it is possible to infer the subject's cognitive structures or operations from his/her behavior in these particular situations. Piaget infers the achievement of a structure by the way the child handles a given situation and at what age he/she does it. If the child cannot handle such a situation it means that he has not yet achieved that given structure.

COGNITIVE DEVELOPMENT AS A CONSTRUCTION OF NEW FORMAL STRUCTURES

If we consider psychological development as the construction of new structures, difficulties appear when behavior of different levels are described by the same formal structures. Piaget was confronted with this difficulty when he discovered that matter, weight, and volume conservations were not achieved by the child at the same age, even though there was an equivalent formal structure. It is because of this problem that Piaget defined the horizontal decalages, as a characteristic of children's reasoning during the concrete operations period.

This problem is also relevant during the formal operation period. A subject can reason in a formal way in a given situation and not in another. It becomes difficult therefore to say whether a given structure is present or not on the basis of a given behavior or reaction to a particular situation.

This problem was also encountered in the study of the sensorimotor period. Piaget, using the idea of the structural equivalence between different stages, demonstrated that the sensorimotor coordination in sucking behavior at birth and locomotion at 18 months could be described by the same mathematical structure (the displacement group) at all the stages of this period. To distinguish these organizations Piaget characterized them as "practical," "subjective," and "objective" organizations, thereby introducing distinctions between the child's point of view and the observer's point of view as well as between child and external world. Further, when Piaget studied later stages of development the objective displacement group (or the sixth stage) has been renamed "practical group." From this point of view it becomes difficult to talk about construction of *new* structures and above all to consider that these formal structures result from the interaction between the subject and the environment.

From careful observation of babies' behavior, we concluded that the formal structures of actions, in the sense of general coordination of action, are *preformed*. Our rationale for such a conclusion is as follows: the coordinations for activities such as walking, handling, imitating, and visual exploration, etc. are observed among young children. The baby does not build these coordinations, he does not construct the complex structures which determine the sequences of contraction and decontraction of various muscular groups (antagonistic and synergist) and of several organs simultaneously. These structures exist already. They are the ones that will define the form or pattern of subsequent actions. They define the pattern of reflex and voluntary walking, of first prehension and of voluntary prehension, or pseudoimitation or of real imitation.

To summarize, we have discussed the way in which Piaget has tried to grasp the structures, the formal instruments of knowledge, without taking into consideration the content of the activity. From our point of view he has studied the elaboration of certain contents that are common to a great number of objects that are the least specific. He has studied how certain properties of objects isolated by the experimenter are mastered by the child, but he did not take into account the process by which the child extracts or identifies these attributes. Therefore, it is not possible to talk about the genesis of structure but rather of structuring or of organizing contents more or less generally, more or less specifically, by means of structure that we consider preformed.

COGNITIVE DEVELOPMENT AS A CONSTRUCTION OF INTERNAL ORGANIZATIONS (MODELS)

The interaction between the subject and his environment is organized in a complex way at every level of development and particularly at the time of birth. It is evident that birth cannot be considered as an absolute beginning. At birth the exchange between the child and the environment is defined by a reflex organization that we will call *sensorimotor internal organization* (or sensorirepresentation). This sensorimotor organization is responsible for all the baby's movements (sucking movements, arm, hand, eye movements, etc.). In other words, this sensorimotor organization specifies the movements in relation to the information given by the sensori receptors. It is not an abstract formal structure, detached or indetermined from contents. Rather, it is a specific organization where the way the object will be handled, i.e., gathering information, is already specifically defined. This organization contains a formal structure involving central processing and coordination. It is in the sense of a programmed processing and coordination that we consider the formal structure of the sensorimotor period preformed. Nevertheless, even though there is development or construction (which we do not doubt), that behavior is only partially determined, that is to say, the subject tries to attain goals that he can only partially achieve.

Behavior is only *partially determined* because *new internal* coding capacities appear by maturation. Consequently, information defined by the initial sensorimotor organization will have to be redefined by means of these new capacities. This leads to the construction of a *new internal organization* that will be called *perceptivomotor*. This *perceptivomotor* organization partly corresponds to what some psychologists call mnemonic traces, configurations of perceptual indices, gestalts or meanings. From this perspective, behavior of the newborn can be considered simultaneously as *entirely determined* by the internal sensorimotor organization and as *partially determined* by the newly constructed *perceptivomotor* organization. This new organization is built upon the previous internal organization and the characteristics of the environment by means of new coding capacities.

This reorganization will be more or less satisfactory or complete depending on the particularities of the situations, the people encountered and the integrity of the initial organization. It is evident that the environment plays a specific and determinant role in this conception.

Let us briefly mention that development is characterized by a succession of internal reorganizations. For example, around 18 months of age new coding capacities appear. These new capacities entail a new reorganization of contents. This new internal organization will be called *conceptuomotor* and it is constructed in a similar way as the previous perceptivomotor organization.

These internal organizations or reorganizations (sensorimotor, perceptivomotor, conceptuomotor, etc.) can be more or less structured according to the nature of the situations encountered. But *these internal organizations will never become formal structures detached from content,* nor will they differ from the structures hereditarily given.

What we have described as internal organizations of contents does not correspond to figurative thought which Piaget defines as knowledge of states and properties of objects, rather than knowledge of transformations of objects. As for the study of formal structures (or operative thinking), Piaget has tried to grasp the development of figurative mentations as a general means to translate or represent states of objects (coding capacities). In fact, what Piaget has studied is the development of representation of the more general aspects of objects and not the development of coding capacities. This is the reason why most of the experiments designed to study the development of mental image and language are the same as those designed to study the structures of operative thought (Piaget & Inhelder, 1966; Sinclair, 1967). In this field Piaget and collaborators have again adopted the structuralist method. For Piaget, the figurative aspects of thought are symbols, signs, and perceptual indices but not organized by transformation rules. How is it possible to study signs, symbols, perceptual indices without these transformation rules? As Piaget has stated, these two figurative and operative aspects of knowledge are indissociable. Moreover, we think that they cannot be studied as general aspects of thought. Once again what Piaget has studied is the development of representation (figuration) *of the more general contents* and not the development of general figurative thought and consequently certain aspects of internal organization of contents.

We will now make some comments on the different methods used in the study of development.

METHODS OF STUDY OF COGNITIVE DEVELOPMENT

We have seen how Piaget developed a method that we have called structuralist for the study of formal structure of behavior. The child is faced with a simplified situation where a property or a transformation of an object is isolated as far as possible. The generality of organizations put in evidence depends on the universality of preformed structure and on the general aspects of the chosen reality (the common aspects to a great number of objects).

For studying more directly the construction of internal organization (representations) it is necessary to face the child with objects that have *multiple properties* (Osiek, 1977), in opposition to unidimensional objects. Presenting the child with such objects, we can identify aspects of the problem the child must solve in organizing his or her reality. First the child must dissociate, isolate, and identify the different properties of the object prior to organizing them. To understand how the child accomplishes these dissociations and compositions, it is necessary to present the child with *purposeful situations* in which the object becomes the means to obtain or realize a goal. With this type of realistic situation we can understand how the child discovers a property or a dimension of an object and how they vary. While acting on an object to obtain a goal, the child will discover or rediscover the properties which will first be isolated and then composed. While modeling plasticine to make a sausage the child will discover the different properties of this object, their variations and their covariations.

EXPERIMENTAL APPROACH

A. Construction and Use of Tools

Ten years ago I studied the construction and use of tools with children from 4 to 8 years of age. One of the experimental situations consisted of pulling out a piece of wood with a ring from a bottle with a narrow neck using different tools. In such a situation, it is possible to understand how the child discovers simultaneously the characteristics of his action and those of the situation. It is very instructive to study how the child uses the adequate tool for a given task. Most children solve the problem in a certain number of their attempts. Their behavior shows that they are capable of taking into account and organizing the different aspects of the situation. That is, by means of what we have called perceptivomotor organization. On the other hand, the way the children justify their failure or their success reveals *another type of organization*. The justification of the 4-year-olds referred generally to their actions or to their own capacities. But very quickly it was the length of the tool that was declared responsible for the result even though the tool used was long enough to touch the bottom of the bottle. All tools estimated as being longer than the others were considered to be the best. These justifications reveal the construction of the conceptuaomotor organization. By means of this organization the 4-year-old children take into consideration only this particular aspect of the situation, the "length." This aspect gives the situation its conceptual meaning. We distinguish the simultaneous presence of two internal organizations that determine the behavior of the child:

—On one hand, the conceptuomotor organization (or conceptual representation) revealed by the children's verbalizations. At 4 years of age their organization takes into consideration only some aspects of the situation which determines the modifications, the corrections and choices made.

—On the other hand, the perceptivo motor organization (or perceptual representation) directs and controls their actions in the use of tools, and takes into consideration the relevant aspects of the situation.

The way the child handles the situation makes it possible to understand how he discovers a particular property of the object—the length—as a distance to overcome. The tool is considered as long enough or not long enough according to the success or failure of the child's action, independently from the fact of touching or not the bottom of the bottle. The whole situation is assimilated to this aspect (partial organization). We can ask what meaning the experiment of length conservation has for a 4-year-old child. This dimension—length—can only be studied in the context of a goal-seeking action. The aspects "longer" or "shorter" are directly related to the success or failure of the action and not to the relationship between the tool and the bottle. What we consider important to understand is precisely the way in which the child can *dissociate and isolate the characteristics of his action and the properties of the objects.*

At around 5 years of age the child focuses his interest in the prehensive aspects of the tool and of his action. If he fails in the use of a tool he will ask for another one that "pinches" or "grasps" the object. The conceptuomotor organization is improved by another aspect of the situation and of his action. These different aspects are discovered and isolated by the child but they are still not coordinated.

It is only around 6 years of age that the different properties of objects and the different categories of actions (reaching, grasping, etc.) involved in the situation are regrouped or coordinated. The child can anticipate a tool that fulfills the function of reaching, grasping, etc. and usually he refuses every object that does not correspond to his internal organization (representation). Usually the tool anticipated (or chosen) by the child is not adequate because the child does not yet master the necessary relationships between the different parts of the tool and the situation. At this stage around 6 years, the tool is more a substitute for action than for association.

Between 6 and 9 years of age the child progressively masters the relationships that the different parts of the tool should have to solve the problem. The conceptuomotor organization loses progressively its rigidity and becomes more flexible or general.

We have understood the construction of an internal organization because we have confronted the child with purposeful situations with multiple properties objects. The conceptuomotor organization is constructed on the basis of the perceptivomotor organization that directs initially the activity of the child. Justifications, corrections of mistakes, choice, are progressively determined by the conceptuomotor organization.

Parallel with this research on concrete problem solving, Piaget and I have done several studies on causality (Piaget & Mounoud, 1969a, 1969b; Piaget et al., 1972a, 1972b, 1973a, 1973b). From these studies, it was possible to understand through discourse with the children the conceptual organization they built. But we could not generate evidence to indicate how the organizations were constructed. I believe this is due to the artificiality or simplicity of the tasks. Piaget also seems aware of this difficulty. More recently Piaget has also used purposeful situations in his research (Piaget, 1974a, 1974b).

Studying cognitive development only on the basis of the child's verbalizations has led to great misunderstanding. Most of the studies done on children during the concrete operation period ignore completely the perceptivomotor organizations of the situations observed. It is in the perceptive elaboration, more precisely in his *activities* that the child discovers the new properties (of his actions and of objects) that he elaborates conceptually. From our point of view, the dynamics of the development are based on the divergences between the perceptivomotor and the conceptuomotor organization (Mounoud, 1968, 1970). It is then possible to reject the hypothesis of equilibrium (Piaget, 1947, 1957, 1975) as well as the hypothesis of conflicts between operations of the same level (Inhelder, Sinclair, & Bovet, 1974). The famous improvement Piaget and Inhelder (1968) reported in memory performance can be better understood if a perceptivomotor organization (of the situation) is recognized and if regulations between the different organizations (perceptivomotor and conceptuomotor) of the same reality are taken into account (Mounoud, 1978).

After the research on the use of tools we wanted to study the perceptivomotor organization of content that determines the activity of the child under 3 years of age, and particularly the way the baby acts progressively on objects.

B. Prehension of Objects

Our main problem is to find out how certain physical and spatial properties of an object are taken into consideration by the child in the preparation for and performance of relevant actions. Variations in physical and spatial properties of objects perceived by visual means (texture, height . . .) may or may not be correlated with variations in their respective weights. Thus, from the subject's point of view, the weight of an object *may or may not be predictable* depending on the visual information available to him and on his internal organization or models (Mounoud, 1973; Mounoud & Bower, 1974).

The subject will become aware of the object's weight through the characteristics of his action. When he is holding or lifting objects, his movements will vary in amplitude, rapidity and regularity. Variations in these different parameters result simultaneously from the properties of the object and from the motor command initiated by the child. The child has to discover and control the *variations in the characteristics of his own actions* (force, amplitude, velocity, etc.) on the one hand, and the *variations in properties of objects* (weight, height, etc.) on the other hand. It is only by taking hold of objects, lifting them and so forth that the child can explore weight perceptually and process proprioceptive and tactile information as they relate to visual information. It is important to note that these proprioceptive indications of weight perception are necessarily bound to a motor action.

Our aim is to characterize the degrees of preparation for movement in terms of *perceptual-motor programming*. Let us clarify what we mean by program. The behavior of lifting objects is the result of a series of contractions by antagonist and synergist muscular groups. We suggest using the world "program" for these *sequences of contractions and their coordination*. The varying dimensions of these programs are the intensity and the length of contractions or relaxations. These dimensions can only be defined by a certain number of *parameters* relative to the situation (position, height, weight, destination of the object, etc.) and to the body itself (position of the arm, amplitude, direction, speed of displacements, etc.).

We will take into consideration two types of programs:

1. *Preprogramming* of the action (totally determined before its performance) which engenders rapid, precise, smooth movements.
2. *Programming* of the action (requires *picking up information during the course of action*), which engenders slow, irregular, awkward movements in opposition to the preceding type (Evarts, Bizzi, Burke, Delong, & Thach, 1974; Teuber, 1974; White, Castle & Held, 1964).

However, we do not envisage development as the mere passage from an initial level of partial programming to a later level of preprogramming. We believe that the entire development consists in a *succession* of transitions leading the child: (1) from an initial level of preprogramming to a level of programming, and then (2) from this level of programming to a new level of preprogramming. Each of these levels is bound to the degree of elaboration of internal organization (Mounoud, 1976).

In order for preprogramming or programming to be possible in holding and lifting movements, the physical properties of the objects (such as weight and volume) must be predictable mainly from visual information. Such predictions result from the degree of elaboration of internal organization. These are accomplished at various levels of processing an object's properties during development.

We have studied the following movement: lifting objects of constant or variable weight and height. The subject sits facing the experimenter and lifts objects vertically placed on a support in front of him. The behavior is recorded on videotape (subject in profile). Videotape analyses (recording on the TV screen the position of the object every 100 ms. from the beginning of movement) makes it possible to study more exactly the characteristics of the carrying phase in the movement (displacement, velocity, time).

I will discuss the results of one specific item called the substitution item. In the *substitution item* we present the subject with an object (150 gr. or 330 gr.) several times and we then substitute a visually identical but lighter object (10 gr. or 30 gr.). Let us examine the performances of subjects between 6 months and 5 years of age in this substitution item.

In this figure, we have represented six examples of velocity curves for the substitution item (lifting phase). The dotted lines represent the first three liftings of the heavy object. The black lines represent the first lifting of the light object. The effect of substitution manifests itself in two ways: (1) a more or less large *increase* in the velocity of the liftings of the light object (Fig. 7.1a); (2) *no significant increase* in the velocity of liftings of the light object (Fig. 7.1b).

Three examples at different ages are given, for each of these categories of effect, in the Fig. 7.1.

Seventy-five children were subjects in the experiment under conditions that were not entirely systematic. Most of the subjects have been tested twice giving a

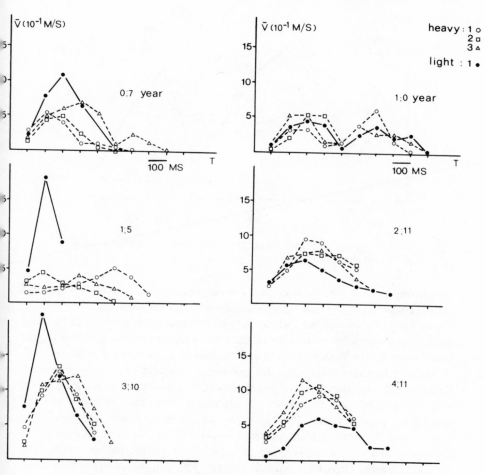

FIG. 7.1. 6 examples of the substitution item. Dotted lines: three liftings of the heavy object; black lines: one lifting of the light object. 1a: 3 subjects with whom we observe an increase in velocity when the heavy object is substituted by the light one; 1b: 3 subjects with whom we observe no increase in velocity when the heavy object is substituted by the light one.

sum of 137 substitutions. These data are summarized in Fig. 7.2, giving us indications relative to development.

It appears that the development of subject's performance in the substitution item is not linear. At 6 to 10 months, 15 months to 2:5 years and 3:6 to 4:5 years, we obtain an increase in the velocity for the light object. At 11 to 14 months, 3:0 to 3:5 years and 4:6 to 4:11 years, there is no such effect. The fact that a performance is globally the same at different moments during development means that the same reality is organized several times. It should not be consid-

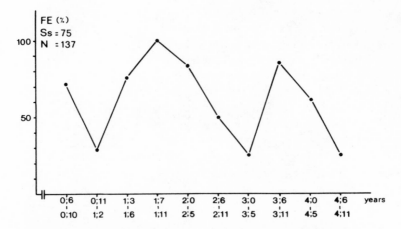

FIG. 7.2.   Percentage of items per age group (FE) showing an increase in velocity for the light object after substitution.

ered as regressions. On the contrary, the reappearance of partially comparable performances reflects a new internal organization of the same content.

We have tried to look not only at the global aspect of the reaction of the child in the substitution item but also at the intrinsic characteristics of action, the morphology of the velocity curves and we have tried to classify them.

Methodologically it appeared that the videotape analysis had to be improved. Subsequently, we started using a potentiometer, allowing us to record a signal corresponding to the lifted object's displacement. The object is bound to a rod moving the potentiometer. The parameters of acceleration and velocity are obtained from the signal which is treated numerically. From these recordings we have been able to define six types of velocity curves that we have regrouped following Brooks (Brooks, Cooke & Thomas, 1973) in two categories: continuous and discontinuous movements.

The lifting movements will be called ''continuous'' when they have only one maximum velocity, and ''discontinuous'' when they present more than one maximum velocity.

Sixty-two children from 2:0 to 4:11 years were studied with the new device (Hauert, 1980). This population is divided into six groups (of six monthly intervals).

Figure 7.3 shows the evolution with age of the continuous movements when lifting the heavy object (330 gr.) in the substitution item. The black line refers to all the lifting movements of this object and the dotted line refers to the last lifting movement (before the substitution). We should point out that the highest percentage of continuous movements is found at the end of the third year (3:6—3:11). At this age we have also found the highest percentage of acceleration effect to substitution.

The difference between discontinuous and continuous movements is the kind of control the subject uses. Discontinuous curves depend upon a series of feedback loops relative to the intermediate states of the course of action. They are *locally programmed* and require picking up information on intermediate states of action so that performance can continue.

Continuous movements are preprogrammed before performance. The regularity of velocity curves means that the movements are preprogrammed.

The different morphologies in velocity curves explain various degrees of *action preparation and programming* as well as different *degrees of knowledge of the object's physical properties*. This morphological diversity is typical of children of 6 months to 5 years of age (the population on which we worked until now), in contrast with adults, in whom we found continuous movements. With adults discontinuous movements appear occasionally in the first trials of a new item.

We have described briefly the way in which we now study the cognitive development of the child by a detailed analysis of the characteristics of

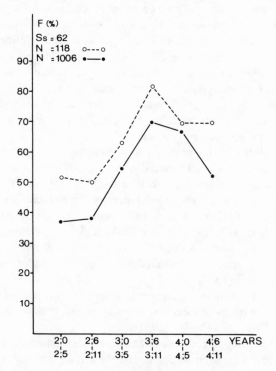

FIG. 7.3.   Percentage of continuous movements in the lifting of the heavy object (substitution item) per age group. Black line: all the lifting movements; dotted line: the last lifting movement.

movements. This method allowed us to describe a series of stages relative to diverse possibilities of action programming. These possibilities of action programming can be related to different levels of internal organization of properties of objects and characteristics of actions.

A program can be already built or in the process of elaboration. The stages of partial programming are of great importance to understand the process of development. During these stages of partial programming, the child actively controls his behavior. He experiences the effects of his actions on objects as well as the effects of objects on his actions. His activities are locally programmed and need picking up information during the course of action. These intermediate stages are the stages of reconstruction of new internal organizations.

CONCLUSION

Following Piaget, we have previously interpreted our research work in terms of structure development. Presently we consider structures as *preformed*. By means of new capacities of representation the child constructs *internal organizations* (representations) resulting from the application of these preformed structures to reality. *Thus, our conception of development is an elaboration of successive internal organization of content, instead of a construction of successive structures*. Structures characterize only the formal aspects of behavior without specifying objects or situations. On the contrary, internal organization of contents (representations) characterize the organization of specific objects and situations including the goals to be attained.

Logical structures of our actions and our thinking are preformed. The new coding capacities to construct internal organizations appear successively by a process of maturation which depends to a small degree upon the environment. We have tried to reinterpret the development in this perspective.

What we call internal organization of contents (representation) is partly similar to traces, schemas. It is important to make a clear distinction between structures or general cognitive functions that we actually consider as preformed and the results of their application to reality that we call internal organization (representation) (Mounoud, 1977).

This distinction is almost nonexistent in Piaget's theory except in a few places where he writes of traces or figurative remembrances, but they are mainly static (Piaget, 1961; Piaget & Inhelder, 1968).

We suggest defining internal organization (representation) as analyzing (sampling) and organizing aspects of reality and their variations, or as analyzing and organizing object's properties and their relations, or moreover as analyzing and organizing a person's characteristics and their interrelations. These analyses and organizations are progressively built by means of preformed structures, previous organizations and new coding capacities.

Internal organizations or representations are theoretical constructs, they can only be inferred from the different types of activity (gestural, facial, verbal expressions). Some activities can be materialized in the form of drawings, writings, object construction like tools, etc. Since expressive activities are a sequence or a succession of actions, we analyze them by means of programs (algorithms, strategies). A program is an indicator of the degree of elaboration of internal organizations (Mounoud, in press).

With this new perspective, we have seen how the characteristics of the internal organization are determined by the *specific* and *nonspecific aspects* of environments. At the end we have given experimental data to illustrate our approach.

REFERENCES

Brooks, V. B., Cooke, J. D., & Thomas, J. S. The continuity of movements. In R. B. Stein, K. G. Pearson, R. S. Smith, & J. B. Redford (Eds.), *Control of posture and locomotion: Advances in Behavioral Biology*, Vol. 7. New York/London: Plenum Press, 1973.

Evarts, E. V., Bizzi, E., Burke, R. E., Delong, M., & Thach, W. T. Central control of movement. *Neurosciences Research Symposium Summaries*, Vol. 6, Cambridge, Mass./London, Eng.: M.I.T. Press, 1974.

Hauert, C.-A. Propriétés des objets et propriétés des actions. *Archives de Psychologie*, 1980, *XLVIII, 48*, 95-168.

Inhelder, B., Sinclair, H., & Bovet, M. *Apprentissage et structures de la connaissance*, Paris: Presses Universitaires de France, 1974.

Mounoud, P. Construction et utilisation d'instruments chez l'enfant de 4 à 8 ans. *Revue Suisse de Psychologie*, 1968, *27*, 1, 200-208.

Mounoud, P. *Structuration de l'instrument chez l'enfant*. Neuchâtel et Paris: Delachaux et Niestlé, 1970.

Mounoud, P. Developpement des systemes de representation et de traitement chez l'enfant. *Bulletin de Psychologie* (Université de Paris) 1971, XXV, 5-7, 261-272. (Translated by B. Inhelder & H. Chipman [Eds.], Piaget Reader, New York: Springer Verlag, 1976.)

Mounoud, P. Les conservations physiques chez le bebe. *Bulletin de Psychologie* (Université de Paris), 1973, *312*, XXVII, 13-14, 722-728.

Mounoud, P. Les révolutions psychologiques de l'enfant. *Archives de Psychologie*, 1976, XLIV, *171*, 103-114. (Translation available)

Mounoud, P. L'utilisation du milieu et du corps propre par le bébé. In J. Piaget, P. Mounoud, J.-P. Bronckart (Eds.), *La Psychologie*, Paris: Encyclopédie de la Pléiade, Gallimard, in press.

Mounoud, P. Relations entre les régulations biologiques et les processus cognitifs. Vers l'Education Nouvelle. *Cahiers du CEMEA*, 1977, 173-180.

Mounoud, P. Gadachtnis und intelligenz. In *Die Psycholgie des 20. Jahrhunderts* (Band 7, 3. Teil), Kindler Verlag, Zurich, 1978, 859-872.

Mounoud, P., Bower, T. G. R. Conservation of weight in infants. *Cognition*, 1974, *3*, 1, 29-40.

Osiek, C. Interferences entre differentes proprietes de l'objet chez l'enfant. *Archives de Psychologie*, 1977, XLV, *44*, 279-326.

Piaget, J. *La Psychologie de l'Intelligence*, Paris: Armand Colin, 1947.

Piaget, J. Logique et équilibre dans les comportements du sujet, *Etudes d'Epistémologie Génétique*, 1957, *II*, 27-117.

Piaget, J. *Les Mécanismes perceptifs*, Paris: Presses Universitaire de France, 1961.

Piaget, J. *La prise de conscience*, Paris: Presses Universitaires de France, 1974. (a)

Piaget, J. *Réussir et comprendre,* Paris: Presses Universitaires de France, 1974. (b)

Piaget, J. *L'équilibration des structures cognitives: Problème central du développement,* Paris: Presses Universitaires de France, 1975.

Piaget, J., & Inhelder, B. *L'image mentale chez l'enfant,* Paris: Presses Universitaires de France, 1966.

Piaget, J., & Inhelder, B. *Mémoire et Intelligence,* Paris: Presses Universitaires de France, 1968.

Piaget, J., & Mounoud, P. L'explication d'un mécanisme de rotation et d'enroulement, *Archives de Psychologie,* 1969, XL, 157, 30-39. (a)

Piaget, J., & Mounoud, P. L'explication d'une coordination des mouvements d'un jouet, *Archives de Psychologie,* 1969, XL, 157, 57-71. (b)

Piaget, J. Bliss, J., Bovet, M., Ferreiro, E., Labarthe, M., Szeminska, A., Vergnaud, G., & Vergopoulo, T. *La transmission des mouvements.* Paris: Presses Universitaires de France, EEG XXVII, 1972. (a)

Piaget, J., Bliss, J., Dami, C., Fluckiger-Geneux, I., Graven, M.-F., Maier, R., Mounoud, P., & Robert, M. *La direction des mobiles lors de chocs et de poussees.* Paris: Presses Universitaires de France, EEG XXVIII, 1972. (b)

Piaget, J., Chollet, M., Fluckiger-Geneux, I., Henriques-Christophides, A., de Lannoy, J., Maier, R., Mosimann, O., & Szeminska, A. *La formation de la notion de force.* Paris: Presses Universitaires de France, EEG XXIX, 1973. (a)

Piaget, J., Bliss, J., Chollet-Levret, M., Dami, C., Mounoud, P., Robert, M., Rossel-Simonet, C., & Vinh-Bang. La composition des forces et le probleme des vecteurs. Paris: Presses Universitaires de France, EEG XXX, 1973. (b)

Sinclair, H. *Acquisition du langage et développement de la pensée,* Paris: Dunod, 1967.

Teuber, H. L. Concluding session: Panel discussion. *Brain Research,* 1974, *71,* 535-568.

White, B. L., Castle, P., & Held, R. Observations on the development of visually-directed reaching. *Child Development,* 1964, 349-364.

8

Language and Thought: Thistles Among the Sedums[1]

Harry Beilin
City University of New York
Graduate School and University Center

Piaget's approach to language acquisition is not easily characterized. One reason is that recent statements provide no guide as to whether earlier views have been retained or superceded. Some examples of this will become evident in this chapter, the principal purpose of which is to detail some limitations in Genevan notions of language, with indications as to how extensions in Piaget's theory may address these limitations.

LANGUAGE AND EGOCENTRICITY

In his early observation on language (Piaget, 1955) Piaget emphasized the developmental progression in which speech advanced from an egocentric function to one in later childhood indicative of "communicated intelligence." These observations were part of an effort to demonstrate the egocentric nature of the child's logic (i.e., more intuitive than deductive, little emphasis on proof or the checking of propositions, use of personal schemes of analogy, visual schemes to support deductions, etc.). His thesis was that the egocentricity of thought was reflected in the way the child communicates with other children and by how other children are understood. It is often forgotten, particularly by his critics, that the actual question posed by Piaget was, "to what *extent* do children of the same age think by themselves and to what *extent* do they communicate with others . . . (and

---

[1]This title is something of an inside joke. Piaget is a long time collector and student of sedums, "a large group of mainly perennial herbs with fleshy stalks. . . ." (Webster's); thistles to a farmer are weeds.

with) older and younger children . . . (and with) parents [p. 67]." (Emphasis added.) The same questions were addressed to the *extent* of understanding between children. In other words, the emphasis on *extent* reflected an effort to explore a developmental thesis and not to deny that a child could think in any way other than egocentrically.

The early research on language, despite its emphasis on the egocentricity of thought, manifested what has become Piaget's principal thesis concerning the relation between language and thought: that language is one means by which thought can be understood, but is not in itself the origin of thought. Recent research on communication competence, even when this research is in sympathy with Piaget's theory, shows however only a very general relation between language forms (egocentric or social) and the ostensibly parallel cognitive system, whether conceived by the early Piaget as moving from an intuitive egocentric logic to a later logic of justification, or as conceived later by Piaget, as a system of thought following a law of decentration, defining the increasing ability to shift from a given cognitive perspective (Piaget, 1962a).

Although Piaget now interprets his findings as showing that the decline in centration and egocentrism tells more about the development of mental operations than about language, some of his critics maintain nevertheless that the decline in centration and egocentrism appears much earlier than Piaget proposes. As indicated, inasmuch as it is a question of relative proportions, even a Piagetian would expect that a certain amount of early language and communication would show the effects of decentration. A more significant question is whether decentering is associated with a changed operational system such that significant changes in thought processes have really occurred, or derive instead from some other source. Although there is evidence that some forms of social and linguistic perspective taking appear at young ages (as early as 2:9), it is not evident as to what types of operational structure and their extent are minimally necessary to permit or facilitate decentration in the capacities that enter into communicative aspects of language use. In essence, then, recent research in communication competence, while challenging the purported intimate relation between cognitive and linguistic structure, suffers in turn from an inadequate account of the source of the intellectual power basic to early linguistic perspective-taking.

IMITATION AND LANGUAGE

A later addition to Piaget's account of language development is associated in part with the nature of imitation and the accommodative adaptation of schemes (Piaget, 1962b). The development of linguistic imitation in the sensorimotor period (from about 0 to 18 months) was said to parallel the stage-like development of sensorimotor schemes, progressing from response to auditory "signals" and "indexes" eventually, at the end of the sensorimotor period, to the social signs that constitute exterior language. At the end of the sensorimotor period, when representative imitation occurs, exterior language is "interiorized" and language becomes representative of thought, paralleling other interiorization processes by imitation, such as image formation.

It is not at present clear, however, how willing Piaget is to tie language acquisition to imitation. In a brief 1966 account of language development (Piaget & Inhelder, 1969) Piaget took note of Chomsky's claims, particularly in regard to his view of language as a creative instrument and Chomsky's argument that syntactic development cannot be accounted for by passive imitation, with apparent endorsement. At that point Piaget appeared less inclined it would seem to accept imitation as the basis of language acquisition, except possibly as it applies to phoneme differentiation in the 11th or 12th month (Piaget & Inhelder, 1969, p. 85). If this is a fair characterization of his position it differs from earlier views, or at least modifies those views, which characterized language as one of the forms of the emerging symbolic or semiotic function, differing from thought in that language has its origins in the "imitations of patterns provided by adults" (Piaget, 1967, p. xvi), whereas thought itself derives ultimately from action. In attempting to define the mechanism by which the semiotic function is formed, Piaget makes clear that in his view, four of the five principal forms of symbolic behavior he describes, deferred imitation, symbolic play, drawing and mental imagery, are based on imitation. Language differs from other symbolic forms in that the others are invented by the child, while language is a social invention. Nonetheless, language is "necessarily acquired in the context of imitation." "The acquisition of language, rendered accessible in those contexts of imitation, finally overlays the whole process (by which representation is disassociated from external action and by internal outlines of action is ready to become thought), providing a contact with other people which is far more effective than imitation alone, and thus permitting the nacent representation to increase its powers with the aid of communication [Piaget, 1967, p. 56]."

In this quotation Piaget is very careful not to say that language acquisition is due to imitation, only that it occurs in the context of imitation's role in the acquisition of the other examples of the symbolic function. What seems to be implied is that language is tied to the internal schemes of thought that are disassociated from actions and objects and is another system, different in kind, because its origin is external to the subject, whereas the other symbolic instruments are internally created for the purpose of representation.

In another statement, Piaget asserts again that language plays an important role in the formative process of the semiotic functions, which "detaches thought from action and is the source of representation" (Piaget, 1967, p. 86), but unlike images which are created by the individual, language is socially created and "the individual learns this system and then proceeds to enrich it [p. 87]." How this learning occurs is not spelled out, except that Piaget later emphasizes that the acquisition of language presupposes the prior formation of sensorimotor intelligence, and as Sinclair argues, where the processes of repetition , ordering and associative connecting that define the coordinations of sensorimotor schemes provide the source for linguistic operations (Piaget, 1970).

Piaget appears to be saying the following about imitation: (1) language is a socially constructed system of verbal signs; (2) this system is learned in the "context of imitation" by which other forms of the symbolic or semiotic function are acquired at the end of the sensorimotor period; (3) in essence, language is acquired by other than (passive) imitation; (4) the acquisition of language presupposes the prior development of the structures and functional relations of sensorimotor intelligence.

A clear formulation of language acquisition in relation to imitation does not emerge then from the foregoing statements. Piaget believes language like thought to be creative, but not, as Chomsky asserts, innately given. As a socially created system and external to the subject, it is evidently learned, but the role of imitation is no longer clear. If there is an acquisition process other than imitation to account for language Piaget does not allude to what it might be. To assert that language acquisition presupposes the prior development of sensorimotor structures and functions does not define how language is acquired. Instead it reasserts Piaget's thesis that learning is under the control of development. This issue should be considered further.

STRUCTURAL RELATIONS BETWEEN LANGUAGE AND COGNITION

If imitation is not the critical mechanism of language acquisition, what is the Genevan alternative? In one respect the Genevans, like most everyone else, accepted the Chomskyan thesis that language acquisition could not result from exposure to specific models. Most everyone, including Piagetians, were impressed by the proposal that children approach learning their mother tongue "with some idea of what the structure of human language is like [Sinclair, 1976, p. 212]." Sinclair suggests there are two senses in which children may be thought to approach acquisition with a basic schema for learning their language. One, is the sense in which Chomsky appears to use it, that of a positing an innately given schema. This position is consistently rejected by the Genevans (Sinclair, 1976). The weaker sense of having a genetically-given *predisposition* to develop language is accepted by Sinclair and presumably by Piaget. This predisposition is either enhanced or realized through the development of the structures of practical intelligence of the sensorimotor period, which establishes the pattern of all later cognitive structures. This group of sensorimotor action patterns "also serves as the heuristic model for language learning (Sinclair, 1976, p. 212)." Language learning thus results from a genetic predisposition augmented by a set of "basic assumptions permitting an oriented approach to the input [p. 212]." From actual utterances heard, the child acquires knowledge of the unobservable and underlying system of syntactic rules and structure. The simple heuristic model provided by sensorimotor structures provides that start and achieves through a constructive and creative process the full capacity that results in adult language (p. 217).

In place of imitation what is proposed then is a set of cognitive capacities and processes that enable language learning to occur. First, is the species-specific genetic predisposition to create and acquire language. Second, is the development of cognitive structures in the preverbal sensorimotor period that provides a heuristic for the processing of degraded or partial linguistic inputs. Third, is the construction of linguistic rules by processes common to both language and cognition.

Let us consider each of these proposals or assumptions briefly:

There should be little argument concerning the weak nativist position represented by the genetic predisposition thesis, except by radical empiricsts and radical nativists. One would have to be more radical an empiricst than Locke, however, to hold that human language is somehow not related to the nature of the species that created and uses it. At the other extreme, it is important to be clear as to what a nativist like Chomsky claims. "We may suppose," says Chomsky, (1976) "that there is a fixed, genetically determined initial state of mind, common to the species . . ." "The mind passes through a sequence of states under the boundary conditions set by experience, achieving finally a " 'steady state' at a relatively fixed age . . ." "The initial state of mind might be regarded as a function characteristic of the species, which maps experiences into the steady state. Universal grammar is a partial characterization of this function, thus a partial characterization of the initial state. The grammar of a language that has grown in mind is a partial characterization of the steady state attained [p. 3]." In other words, according to Chomsky, "universal grammar" is hereditary, not the "linguistic competence" gained in knowing a specific language (e.g., English or French). (Chomsky feels that the Genevans have misunderstood him on this score.)

I do not see that the notion of "properties or conditions that constrain" language acquisition [p. 17fn] is very different from the idea favored by Sinclair of innate predispositions. In both Chomsky's case and the Genevans', the mechanism by which the initial state function transforms experience into the steady state, or the predispositions plus cognitive structure and experience that become adult language, is only programmatically stated. For Chomsky, it is merely a function characteristic of the species; for Piaget and presumably Sinclair it is abstraction and reflexive abstraction in the service of constructing the lexicon and syntactic structure. Although the latter have the advantage of explaining and differentiating between the ways in which physical and logicomathematical knowledge are acquired, they are little more than metaphors in explaining the acquisition of language. Thus the mechanism (a "discovery procedure" in

Chomsky's terms) by which initially given hereditary elements become transformed into language is not really specified in either theory (nor in any other, for that matter).[2]

For Chomsky, language is only one of a number of cognitive systems "that interact in the most intimate way in the actual use of language [p. 3]." He nonetheless argues against the Piagetian idea that preverbal cognitive structures are necessary for language acquisition. What he implies instead is that structures inherent in language should be sufficient to account for language acquisition. In fact, linguistic theory (i.e., universal grammar) to be adequate must provide specification of a "discovery procedure" by which a grammar is abstracted from the linguistic corpus made available to a child. The Genevan alternative proposes that the starting point is not some generally characterized initial hereditary structure and a similarly vague "discovery procedure," but some specifiable set of cognitive structures plus a mechanism of abstraction.

Needless to say, the Piagetian preverbal cognition thesis has generated a great deal of interest, and has been used not only by Sinclair but a number of others (including Beilin, 1975; L. Bloom, 1970; R. Brown, 1973; Nelson, 1973; and Slobin, 1971). Despite a considerable literature on the issue, Chomsky dismisses the Piagetian claim as not factually supported or theoretically justified. Chomsky cites instead specific linguistic structures that would have to "arise on the basis of the same kinds of principles that account for the child's early sensorimotor constructions and the like [p. 8]." This he asserts is not shown either by Genevan argument or evidence. The research evidence (from Geneva and elsewhere) in fact does show a moderate though not a substantial relation between the development of cognitive structures and the development of some specific linguistic structures. What is reasonable to conclude is not that Chomsky is correct and that a relation between cognitive and linguistic structures is denied but that a *one-to-one* cognitive-linguistic structural relationship has not been demonstrated. (See Beilin, 1975 for review and discussion.) The research evidence instead denies both the Chomskyan and original Genevan theses. What it suggests is that the theoretical relation between cognition and language is one of partial autonomy for each system. That is, nonlinguistic cognition, reflected in each aspect of the symbolic-semiotic function (viz. symbolic play, deferred imitation, imagery, etc.) has system characteristics unique unto itself. So does language. Neither system, however, is wholly unique; each appears to have system properties in common with the other. If it were not so, language could not be considered as cognitive, which even Chomsky recognizes it to be. Thus, the most simple and plausible way to conceive of the relation between cognition and language is as each deriving from some common, more abstract, structure. Again, in light of

---

[2]For Chomsky, the "universal grammar" specifies the "abstract conditions that unknown (i.e., actual) mechanisms must meet" (Chomsky, 1976, p. 9). The actual mechanisms he feels do not bear specification with present knowledge of the brain and the manner in which it functions.

the nature of linguistic and nonlinguistic cognition, the most abstract commonalities are formal. They are reflected in the logical structures of cognition and in the logical or formal relations of language. Although some logical relations can be posited at present to be held in common, it is premature, considering the state of knowledge of the formal properties of both language and cognition, to propose which logical system would most aptly model such a relation. Propositional and modal logics, for example, do not appear fully equal to the task, but that does not preclude the possibility that more elegant logics will become available to fulfill that mission.

The partial autonomy of linguistic and nonlinguistic cognitive systems appears to be accepted in a recent commentary of Piaget's (Piaget, 1971), as well as the recognition of the possibility that common structures are realized in both linguistic and nonlinguistic cognition.

A difficulty with the notion, appealing as it is, that preoperational sensorimotor schemes represent later linguistic structures and that a logic of coordinated actions exists prior to language, is that when language appears it embodies logical structures and relations that far outdistance in complexity and power the logical structures evident in nonlinguistic cognition of that period. Additionally, the linguistic structures parallel logical structures of the later concrete operational period. A simple example of this is the comprehension of the passive, which, at least in non-Genevan research, appears at an early age, about 3-4 years (Beilin, 1975), whereas the reversibility logic inherent in its structural relations is not acquired in nonlinguistic contexts until about 6 or 7. It appears then that language follows cognitive structure and also anticipates it, which suggests that no simple relation of priority exists between the two domains. Thus, if language anticipates later developing general structures, it may very well be that language is in fact necessary to the attainment of operations in a constructive sense and not only as "an instrument of formulation and reflection (Piaget, 1963)."

LANGUAGE AND REPRESENTATION

Another feature of the relation between language and thought plays a central role in Piaget's theory. It concerns the representational function of language, that is, language considered as a semiotic vehicle for communicating fact and meaning to others and oneself. In this instance, as already indicated, Piaget views language as a socially constructed, conventional sign system designed to convey meanings, usually from sources other than language itself. There are two ways of looking at the representational relation of language to thought. In one, the view that has prevailed in Geneva, language comprehension cannot exceed the level of operational (nonlinguistic) knowledge. In this interpretation, as Sinclair (1976) describes it, language is: "no more than a formal translation of physical experience, which does not in itself create new structures [p. 217]." This, to Sinclair, appears to be the proper role for natural language, even if it does not aptly describe the formal role of logic to physical experience. She says, "It is difficult to imagine that language creates new structures that announce or make possible new scientific discoveries—language would then be richer and more powerful than what it describes.[3] A language is indeed essentially a system of representation (and a rather inadequate one at that, it lacks the capacity of creating new knowledge and as such it would take a subordinate place in epistemology [p. 217]."

Sinclair however recognizes that this is too narrow a characterization of language. The Chomskyan insight that surface structure provides only a partial indication of deeper structure is said to bring linguistic theory closer to the biological and physical sciences, and particularly to mathematics, which in its structure goes far beyond the naturalistically observable reality. Linguistics with its own formal models and theories goes equally beyond the merely observable in human speech. Even though language itself does not appear to create knowledge, for Sinclair, the fact that the child constructs the underlying rule system of language, which is both a constructive and creative cognitive activity, qualifies language for an important function in epistemology. In this way, language is reinstated as a significant object of epistemological concern with more than a representational significance for Piagetian theory.

As important as this development is for Piagetian theory, it does not go far enough in my view. First, one can take as a model the implicit distinction made between mathematics and the physical sciences, and the languages in which they are expressed. The power of mathematics, in creating new knowledge, for example, comes not only from its theories or ideas as Sinclair implies, but also from its created languages and formalisms. Ideas concerning number, for example, could make no progress until there was a notational system for representing numbers,[4] first in the natural language and later in more abstract notations. In fact, the full import of the number system is still not fully understood. Nonetheless, the creation of the number system and its formalism provided power that enabled mathematical reasoning to go well beyond the prevailing level of knowledge. In a sense it has taken operational knowledge a long time to catch up with the knowledge inherent in the formal system. Inasmuch as languages (natural and artificial) are constructed by the same processes of mind as nonlinguistic constructions, it is purely arbitrary to hold that these constructions are incapable of yielding new knowledge when other constructions are able to. If language is viewed as a system in part independent of other systems of cognition, instead of

---

[3]One presumes that there is more than redundancy in this statement. That is, it says more than that language as a product of mind cannot go beyond mind.

[4]The zero is a good example of a singularly important notational device, in addition to having conceptual and theoretical significance.

as a product of mind alone, then it can be the source of knowledge just as readily as any other processing system.

A second issue relates to the role of language vis-à-vis operations. Piaget specifically asks whether the development of thought is connected to the acquisition of language as such, or to a more general semiotic or symbolic function (Piaget, 1963). The difficulty with rejecting the identification of thought with the development of language, which Piaget recognizes, is that thought, when viewed as conceptual representation, is evident at the same time as the appearance of language (about 1 to 1½ years). This correlation of appearance is not judged by Piaget to be indicative of a causal relation between language and thought. It is indicative instead of their common interconnection with the appearance of the more general semiotic function. The evidence that Piaget invokes in favor of this interpretation is the appearance of other symbolic forms, such as symbolic play and deferred imitation. Unfortunately one cannot dismiss the possibility that language is the significant symbolic mediator in these instances, inasmuch as it appears concurrently with the manifestation of these other symbolic forms in behavior. Another limitation of this thesis is that Piaget ties the development of representative symbolic behavior so closely to imitation, saying, at the least, that deferred imitation and interiorization ensure differentiation between expression and meaning, between the signifier and the signified. In light of the questionable status now accorded to imitation in the origin of language, it is equally questionable as a source for any symbolic activity. Thus, while the notion is theoretically appealing that thought as a conceptual representative function is more generally identified with the semiotic/symbolic function than with language alone, the possibility is far from excluded that thought in the sense defined by Piaget is possible only with language.

Furthermore, according to the Piagetian position, operative experience may lead to the construction of language but linguistic experience does not lead to the construction of operations. The reason for this is that the origin of knowledge is action and neither perception, imitation, nor language can lead to operational knowledge. This is a theoretical assertion and is ostensibly supported by data from various training studies including those of Sinclair (Inhelder, Sinclair & Bovet, 1974). As an extensive body of research makes evident, however, there is little empirical basis for this claim. A sufficient number of studies, utilizing the strongest criteria proposed by Piaget as a test of operational knowledge, have demonstrated that operational knowledge can be achieved by linguistic training based on verbal rule-instructional methods (Beilin, 1976).

If, as I noted earlier, linguistic structures and cognitive structures are derived from common logical or structural schemes, there is no reason in principle why operational structures cannot be constructed by linguistic means any less than linguistic structures require the acquisition or prior operational structures or are induced by operational means, the view held by Piaget and Sinclair.

LANGUAGE AND ACTION

Another problem is created by the strong Piagetian claim that operations result only from actions carried out by the subject either overtly or covertly. The difficulty resides in the definition of action. From what Piaget has written it appears that action is to be interpreted in the very broadest sense. It ranges from large muscle movement to movement of the eyes, to the "action" of the mind in thought. In this way, it is only a question of relative activity that is at question, inasmuch as life itself is defined by some form of activity. Operations are thus clearly inducible as long as there is "activity" in thought. Linguistic activity has as much claim then to activity as nonlinguistic activity. I suggest then that linguistic forms and linguistic activity are fully capable of inducing operational structures either by algorithmic or heuristic means (Beilin, 1976) and language plays a significant role not only in the child's developing operational knowledge but in knowledge considered educationally, historically, and epistemologically.

LANGUAGE AND CREATIVE EDUCATION

Piaget has made much of the educational implications of activity, at the same time portraying emphasis on learning through language as the villain in educational backwardness. If one wants to produce encyclopedic compilers of facts, says Piaget, teach by way of linguistically focused methods; if one wants creative thinkers teach through activity-based methods. Thus Piaget identifies intellectual rigidity and stereotyped thought with language and linguistic methods of instruction. This is an error.

Consider the fact that practically all advanced thought is associated in one sense or another with language. Consider too that almost all advanced education is based on the use of language whether it involves the creative use of mind or more pedestrian uses. The same is true, even if somewhat less so, at less advanced educational levels. It is counter-intuitive to suppose that culture so deeply infused as it is with linguistic forms plays only a minor role and possibly no role at all in the creation of cognitive schemes. Piaget is willing to concede such a role for formal operational thought. The evidence is compelling that language plays a greater role in creating cognitive structures than Piaget is willing to concede.

If products derived from contemporary educational practice are poor, as Piaget has long argued, the fault is not to be put at the feet of language but to the way in which language is used in education. Language need not be identified solely with rote learning but is involved in fact in most forms of so-called creative instruction that foster decision making and inference forming and discovery.

Language, both natural and formal, is as necessary to present day education as it has always been. If activity is also necessary to the development of the creative use of mind and intelligence, as Piaget asserts, then linguistic activity should play a major role in that development. As I have indicated, there is every justification for this within the bounds of Piagetian theory and Piagetian practice. Even casual observation of a protocol involving the use of the clinical (or critical) method favored by Genevans shows that the experimenter (or examiner, or teacher) is involved in an analysis not only of the child's understanding but of his language. Thus, if the construction of operations is to be understood in the context of Piagetian methods of exchange and exploration, it requires understanding too of the ways in which language is known and used in the context of learning, understanding, and communicating.

In consideration of the foregoing, it is time for Piagetians to rethink their position on language and instead of relegating it to a position secondary to activity, to see linguistic activity as a dynamic and necessary force in intellectual and social development.

REFERENCES

Beilin, H. *Studies in the cognitive basis of language development*. New York: Academic Press, 1975.

Beilin, H. Constructing cognitive operations linguistically. In H. W. Reese (Ed.), *Advances in child development and behavior*, Vol. 11. New York: Academic Press, 1976.

Bloom, L. *Language development: Form and function in emerging grammars*. Cambridge, Mass.: MIT Press, 1970.

Brown, R. *A first language: The early stages*. Cambridge, Mass.: Harvard University Press, 1973.

Chomsky, N. On the biological basis of language capacities. In R. W. Rieber (Ed.), *The neuropsychology of language: Essays in honor of Eric Lenneberg*. New York: Plenum, 1976.

Inhelder, B., Sinclair, H., & Bovet, M. *Learning and the development of cognition*. Cambridge, Mass.: Harvard University Press, 1974.

Nelson, K. Structure and strategy in learning to talk. *Monographs of the Society for Research in Child Development*, 1973. (Serial no. 149).

Piaget, J. The language and thought of the child. New York: Meridian Books, 1955. (French Edition, 1923.)

Piaget, J. *Comments on Vygotsky's critical remarks*. Cambridge, Mass.: MIT Press, 1962. (a)

Piaget, J. *Play, dreams and imitation in childhood*. New York: Norton, 1962. (b) (French Edition, 1945.)

Piaget, J. Le langage et les operations intellectuelles. In J. de Ajuriaguerra et al., *Problèmes de psycho-linguistique*. Paris: Presses Universitaires de France, 1963.

Piaget, J. Language and thought from the genetic point of view. In J. Piaget, *Six psychological studies*. New York: Random House, 1967. (Swiss Edition, 1964.)

Piaget, J. *Structuralism*. New York: Basic Books, 1970.

Piaget, J. Preface. In E. Ferreiro, *Les relations temporelles dans le langage de l'enfant*. Geneva: Droz, 1971.

Sinclair, H. Developmental psycholinguistics. In D. Elkind & J. H. Flavell (Eds.), *Studies in cognitive development: Essays in honor of Jean Piaget*. New York: Oxford University Press, 1969.

Sinclair, H. Epistemology and the study of language. In B. Inhelder and H. H. Chipman (Eds.), *Piaget and his school*. New York: Springer-Verlag, 1976. (Original article appeared in 1971.)

Slobin, D. Developmental psycholinguistics. In W. D. Dingwall (Ed.), *A survey of linguistic science*. College Park, Md.: Linguistics Program, University of Maryland, 1971.

9 The Influence of Piagetian Theory on the Study of the Development of Communication

Roberta Michnick Golinkoff
University of Delaware

The purpose of this chapter is to discuss the utility of Piaget's theory for the study of the development of communication during the first year of life. It should be noted, however, that Piaget did not specifically emphasize the early development of communication in his writings. Nonetheless, as will be illustrated below, Piaget's theory is most relevant to understanding the relationship between communication development and cognitive development.

Piaget's theory provides information about three aspects of language development and communication: first, the development of representation, second, the relationship of the development of various cognitive structures to linguistic structures, and third, the phenomenon of egocentric speech in communication. The first topic, the development of representation, was examined by Piaget in *Play, Dreams and Imitation* (1962), and to a lesser extent in *The Origins of Intelligence* (1952), and *The Construction of Reality* (1954). Some language researchers have speculated about the link between the development of object permanence, one manifestation of representation, and its relationship to early word use, although there has been little systematic research (Corrigan, 1978; Kavanaugh, 1979; Zachry, 1978). A number of writers have used Piaget's theory and particularly his treatment of the development of the symbolic or semiotic function in their explanations of language development (e.g., Ingram, 1978; Moerk, 1975; Morehead & Morehead, 1974). The second topic, the relationship between cognitive and linguistic structures, has received considerably more attention, beginning with Sinclair's (1969) work on children's use of dimensional adjectives and their ability to conserve, and more recently by Beilin's (1975) work.

The third topic, egocentric speech, was discussed primarily by Piaget in *The Language and Thought of the Child* (1955) and brought back to the attention of psychologists by Flavell and his colleagues (Flavell, Botkin, Fry, Wright, & Jarvis, 1968). The conditions associated with the occurrence of egocentric speech (e.g., Goldstein, 1977) and the sophisticated nature of children's social speech, e.g., Garvey and Hogan (1973), are still issues addressed in the burgeoning literature on the development of communication.

Whereas the areas mentioned above continue to be of considerable interest to researchers, other aspects of Piaget's theory are relevant to the very origins of the child's language development—namely, the child's initial attempts to communicate through the use of prelinguistic means. Interest in communication within the field of language development is motivated by a number of concerns: first, language development can no longer be viewed as just the acquisition of semantic, syntactic, and phonological structures. The development of "communicative competence," or the use of these language structures in social situations must be considered (Halliday, 1975; Hymes, 1971). As Bruner (1974) has written:

> Neither the syntactic nor the semantic approach to language acquisition take sufficiently into account what the child is trying to do by communicating. As linguistic philosophers remind us, utterances are used for different ends and use is a powerful determinant of rule structures . . . one cannot understand the transition from prelinguistic to linguistic communication without taking into account the uses of communication as speech acts [p. 283].

In other words, to paraphrase a statement by Ervin-Tripp and Mitchell-Kernan (1977) the development of formal language structures is in part caused by changes in communicative intent. To ignore the *functions* which language serves is to fail to account for the motivation behind language change.

The second reason there is renewed interest in communication is that the impact of nativistic theories of language development has diminished. Following Chomsky, researchers in the 1960s studied the child's word combinations since their focus was on the acquisition of syntax. Following the generative semanticists (Chafe, 1970; Fillmore, 1968), researchers in the 1970s emphasized the acquisition of semantics. In order to understand many of the concepts purportedly expressed in early utterances, the sensorimotor constructions of the prelinguistic period increased in importance. Now at the end of the 1970s researchers, influenced by the study of pragmatics in linguistics (Austin, 1962; Searle, 1965), are turning their attention to the origins of language in the child's prelanguage communication. Investigations of these origins have focused on communication conducted mainly through nonverbal gestures and prelinguistic vocalizations although manipulations of facial expressions and body posture for communicative ends needs more attention. The remainder of this chapter will examine the usefulness of Piaget's theory to this line of research. Just as some cognitive counterparts of semantic categories may be constructed during the prelinguistic period (e.g., Golinkoff, 1975; Golinkoff & Kerr, 1978; Sinclair, 1973), some communicative functions of language probably have primitive prelinguistic counterparts (Halliday, 1975). The thesis of this chapter is that Piaget's theory of infant development, represented in his trilogy of books on infancy, has been and will continue to be useful to researchers who study the early communicative aspects of language development.

"Communication" is defined as the exchange of information between a sender and a receiver, either through vocal (and not necessarily verbal) or gestural channels (the latter includes hand gestures, facial expression and body postures). Specification of the channels of communication rules out a broad definition of communication that includes information exchange with the inanimate environment. Authors, e.g., Moerk (1977), who use such a broad definition only trivialize the concept of communication. Communication occurs prior to the time when infants are capable of intentionally communicating since much of their behavior is interpreted as communicative by those attending the infant (Bates, Camaioni & Volterra, 1975; Bruner, 1975; and Snow, 1977) and therefore is apparently successful in relaying information. Indeed the response infants engender from adults may be one way infants learn to endow their signals with communicative meaning (Ryan, 1974). In other words, there is a time in the infant's development when communication occurs through the adult's reading of child behaviors which were not necessarily used in service of communicative ends at all. At some point in development, however, the infant begins to try in a purposeful way to contact others. As Schaffer (1977) put it, "the contrast is between the baby who cries because he has a pain and the baby who cries in order to summons his mother to deal with the pain: the one responding reactively, the other with an eye to the future [p. 10]." Regardless of the intent behind the cry, mothers (and other caregivers) will make attributions about the infant's state thus endowing the child's behaviors with a signal value which the behaviors do not necessarily possess. What is interesting from a developmental standpoint and what has been the focus of a number of investigations (e.g., Harding & Golinkoff, 1979) is the point at which the infant does begin to communicate intentionally.

As a further example of intentional communication, consider the following observation of Jacqueline by Piaget (1954):

> ... Jacqueline at 1;3(30) makes the adult intervene in the particulars of her games, whenever an object is too remote, etc.: she calls, cries, points to objects with her finger, etc. In short, she well knows that she depends on the adult for satisfaction; the person of someone else becomes the best procedure for realization [p. 312].

Jacqueline appears to be communicating intentionally in this sequence using call vocalizations, conventional gestures such as the point, and probably alternating glances at the object and the eyes of the adult. She seems to understand that her signals need to precede the desired results (i.e., adult intervention) and that people (as opposed to objects) are her best bet for obtaining assistance. In the literature intentional communication is often operationally defined by the alternation of gaze between a desired object and the adult's eyes or by the use of a gesture (e.g., pointing) with alternating eye contact and/or by behaviors which can be interpreted as sending messages, e.g., the infant handing an object to the mother presumably requesting her to operate it (Bruner, 1975; Bates, Camaioni, & Volterra, 1975; Harding & Golinkoff, 1979; Lock, 1976; Sugarman-Bell, 1978). These intentional behaviors may occur with or without an accompanying preverbal vocalization.

Interpreting the transition from unintentional to intentional communication within a developmental constructivist theory such as Piaget's, it is necessary to investigate what infants need to know about the world in order to direct intentional communications to another human being. It is proposed that infants must possess the following four prerequisites:

1. Although perhaps a simplistic point, it is necessary that the infant has the ability to distinguish self from nonself (Schaffer, 1977; Werner & Kaplan, 1963). If infants are not aware of the existence of others, to whom (other than themselves) would they send messages? Infants must know that there is someone else "out there."

2. Infants must also have something to communicate about; that is, infants must have some ideas they want to convey. These could be as general as "pay attention to me" in which case communicating or contacting another is the end in itself or as specific as "get me X" in which case the communication is about something outside the self.

3. Infants must have the ability to see events as ordered causal sequences with one event (their gestures or vocalizations) occurring prior to and capable of causing later events. In other words, infants must know something on the order of "... my signal must precede the effect I wish to achieve." Only if infants have this idea of a causal sequence, will they be able to formulate a plan of sorts designed to reach the end result.

4. Infants must be able to see other animate beings as potential agents, capable of serving as a means to an end.

Thus, the ability to distinguish self from nonself is not sufficient; infants must distinguish *between* the categories of nonself objects in the world. People and objects can help in the pursuit of goals in different ways. People are autonomous self-motivated beings who cannot be triggered into action like machines since they may have their own goals different from the goals the signal sender has in mind.

Piaget's theory of infant development treats each of the four factors necessary for communication although Piaget did not discuss the development of communication itself at any length. For example, on point one—distinguishing self from nonself—Piaget described in the *Construction of Reality* how infants' consciousness develops from a state of relative undifferentiation between subject and object with no distinction made between the self and nonself to a state where infants conceive of themselves as just cogs in the universe. As Piaget (1954) put it:

> During the first months of life the child does not dissociate the external world from his own activity. Perceptual images, not yet consolidated into objects or coordinated in a coherent space, seem to him to be governed by his desires and efforts, though these are not attributed to a self which is separate from the universe. Then gradually as progress is made in the intelligence which elaborates objects and space by spinning a tight web of relations among these images, the child attributes an autonomous causality to things and persons and conceives of the existence of causal relations independent of himself, his own body becoming a source among other sources of effects integrated in this total system [p. 424].

If the child did not recognize the existence of other objects, there would be little reason to attempt to send messages. But more than just recognizing that there are objects to be distinguished from the self in the world, the child comes to know that some of these are capable of action. Most of the research on early communicative development has focused on the latter part of the first year when the primitive distinction between self and nonself is present. However, as the ontogeny of intentional communication is studied, it is necessary to go further back in developmental time to when the infant's concept of self is less differentiated. For example, when the infant uses what Piaget calls "procedures" such as waving the arms and kicking the feet during sensorimotor stage 3, he/she expresses a desire for objects or the re-creation of interesting events. Piaget (1954) has claimed (pp. 267–272) that these procedures are not used to contact the adult present since the child cannot yet conceive of the adult as an objective center of action capable of causing events. In terms of the development of communication, infants could not be said to be intentionally contacting another when they use procedures. If Piaget's analysis is correct and the child still feels omnipotent and does not distinguish between the self and the external world, then the child should continue these procedures even when the adult who has caused the event leaves the scene. If the child does not continue his procedures, this might indicate that the child was intending to signal to the adult, or minimally, that the child had an association between the adult's presence and the attainment of goals. Even the latter instrumental knowledge—"something to do with that person gets me what I want"—may be an important step in the insight necessary for separation of the self from others and therefore for intentional communication. Although Piaget's writings (e.g., see observation 132, II, 1954, p. 270) contain examples of children performing procedures even in the absence of an adult, this is one of the issues research on early communication development should address. When does the infant make the distinction between the self and the nonself and stop employing procedures when potential help in the form of a person leaves the scene?

With regard to the topics or content of communication, Piaget's infancy trilogy is replete with examples of infants' knowledge. The schemes the preverbal child uses to act on the world are an index of how the child thinks of it, i.e., there are objects to bang with, to suck on, etc. Halliday (1975), among the language researchers, has written most extensively about the contents or meanings conveyed by children's preverbal vocalizations. Halliday's emphasis is on language as rooted in the child's social construction of reality, a construction which by nine months (in Halliday's single subject) consists of a self and a nonself, the latter being the environment composed of inanimate objects and persons. Through the use of prelanguage vocalizations Halliday's 9 month old son was capable of signaling four communicative functions with four distinct vocalization patterns: the instrumental (as in "I want"), the regulatory (as in "do as I tell you"), the interactional (as in "me and you"), and the personal (as in "here I come") (p. 36). If Halliday did not require a constant "content-expression" relation (that is, if the same content could be signaled by more than one prelinguistic vocalization), he might have found these functions to appear earlier or in a different order. What has not been done by Halliday or others is an analysis of what specific cognitive capabilities are required for these different communicative functions to emerge. Further, such a specification and test using Piaget's notions would be one way of seeing if these putative communicative functions have psychological reality.[1] On what basis, for example, does Halliday (1975) distinguish "I want" from "do as I tell you"? His descriptions of their uses are not detailed enough to tell. Drawing upon Piaget's description of the development of causality, "I want" or the instrumental function may be unintentionally communicated through the infant's procedures. The infant may still have global undifferentiated schemes which link his/her action to the desired end. However, to signal "do as I tell you" it seems that the infant would need to know that others are autonomous centers of causality. "Do as I tell you" implies that the infant is purposely contacting the other, perhaps through the alternation of gaze between the adult and the desired object. Other researchers have proposed slightly different communicative functions. Bates, Camaioni and Volterra (1975) have focused on what seem to be Halliday's regulatory function (they call it the "protoimperative") and his interactional function, (their "protodeclarative"). Independent cognitive evidence is needed to validate the existence of any functions proposed. An analysis (like the one above on "I want" vs. "do as I tell you") drawing on Piaget's theory of what knowledge is required for what function could be most heuristic.

The last two factors necessary for communication—understanding means-end relations and distinguishing between the action capabilities of animate and inanimate objects—was also discussed in depth by Piaget (1954) and has been the focus of a number of studies on prelinguistic communication (Bates, Camaioni,

---

[1]Francis (1979) has just made several of these points in an article critical of the work of Halliday and others who claim to detect pragmatic functions in prelanguage vocalization.

& Volterra, 1975; Harding & Golinkoff, 1979; Lock, 1976; Olswang, 1978; Snyder, 1978; Sugarman-Bell, 1978). Piaget's work on the development of causality has been most often used by these researchers probably because as Bates, Benigni, Bretherton, Camaioni, and Volterra (1979) have written "there is something about causal development from 9–13 months that is a particularly sensitive indicator of social and communicative developments in the first year of life [p. 378]." Bates et al. go on to cite Piaget's (1954) statement ". . . causality must definitely be conceived as intelligence itself to the extent that the latter is applied to temporal relations and organizes a lasting universe [p. 357]." As the following studies indicate, the development of intentional communication seems to be closely tied to the child's understanding of the causal workings of the universe.

Lock's (1976) position on how the child makes the transition from unintentional to intentional communication is based on Piaget's description of secondary circular reactions and the way in which the latter reflect the child's incomplete causal knowledge. Lock noted how without understanding the causal mechanisms involved, his single subject learned to use procedures (e.g., arm waving) to get an event repeated. The fact that this is interpreted by the parent as wanting the event repeated, indicates the child's "natural powers" of unintentional communication. Lock wrote "through the mediation of social transaction and the child's 'reflective intelligence' this situation can be transformed into one in which communication is intentional; this transformation is instrumental in changing R's latent 'natural powers' into potential 'personal power' [p. 151]." In other words, infants learn first, what things they can do to reach goals, i.e., carry out a procedure, second, through observing which objects in the world seem to aide in carrying out their goals, i.e., people and not objects, infants learn to contact the adult intentionally in order to use the adult as an agent. Lock seemed to be discussing causal achievements which characterize stage 5 in Piaget's system.

Bates, Camaioni and Volterra (1975) explicitly identified stage 5 causal developments as prerequisite to the appearance of the "illocutionary" or intentional stage of preverbal communication. Since stage 5 heralds the child's recognition that causality can reside in external agents and that new means can be used to achieve familiar ends, the child now would have the ability to use his signals (the "new means") in an intentional way to get an adult to act (adult as "external agent"). Bates et al. provided some confirmation for their hypothesis when they administered informal stage assessments to their two subjects. Both subjects were able to use tools to obtain objects and to pull a cloth to obtain a desired object resting on it—stage 5 behaviors—around the same time that they were observed to use intentional communicative signals. Consider the following example of Carlotta who is about 13 months old:

C is seated in a corridor in front of the kitchen door. She looks toward her mother and calls with an acute sound "ha." M comes over to her, and C looks toward the kitchen, twisting her body and upper shoulder to do so. M carries her into the kitchen and C points toward the sink. M gives her a glass of water and C drinks it eagerly [p. 217].

This example contains more than one communicative device, namely, gaze direction (at the mother first, then the kitchen), pointing, and a nonlinguistic vocalization. As such, it reflects much sophistication and perhaps even stage 6 causal development since the child is apparently envisioning a means (the use of her mother as agent) to obtain an unseen end (water in the kitchen). Further research by Harding and Golinkoff (1979) suggests that the use of a vocalization in that sequence may be developmentally advanced relative to communicative episodes in which vocalizations are not employed, although both types could still be in stage 5.

Harding and Golinkoff (1979) developed a case for stage 5 causal developments as prerequisite for the use of intentional *vocalizations*. They defined intentional vocalizations as vocalizing that occurred simultaneously with eye contact with the mother (seated to one side). This breakthrough in the use of the vocal medium may be one of the first things the infant learns about language. To test their hypothesis about the importance of stage 5, they observed 46 infants ranging in age from 8-14 months in two frustration situations devised to elicit intentional vocalizations. In addition, two independent measures of the child's level of causal development were used (Mehrabian & Williams, 1971; Piaget, 1954, pp. 267-271) which permitted them to assign children to either stage 4 or 5. Their results supported the hypothesis in that stage 5 causal abilities were found to be necessary, but not sufficient, for a child to use illocutions. Of the infants classified as either "transitional" (these passed one of two causality tests at stage 5) or in stage 5, 68% were using intentional vocalizations. No infant classified as in stage 4 on the causality tasks used intentional vocalizations. Also, infants who were using illocutions performed many more nonvocal communicative behaviors such as pointing to the object or giving their mother the toy to operate on than did the infants not using illocutions who were in stage 5. However, the fact that infants not using intentional vocalizations did employ some gestural communicative behaviors suggests that "intentionality in communication may develop gradually, with intentional vocalizations being added to already existing sequences of intentional attention-directing behaviors . . . the addition of vocalizations to the communicative repertoire seems to require abilities beyond those necessary for nonverbal attention getting, for example, the stage 5 abilities to sequence events and to invent new means for achieving goals" (Harding & Golinkoff, 1979, p. 38).

Thus, the Harding and Golinkoff study used performance on Piaget's sequence in the development of causality to predict the ability to produce intentional vocalizations. A type of discriminant validity to support the importance of causal development was provided by the finding that object concept development was not found to be predictive of whether infants were using perlocutions (nonintentional vocalizations) or illocutions (intentional vocalizations).

The ability to use novel means-end relations (stage 5) in order to be able to intentionally communicate is recognized in the work of Sugarman-Bell (1978). Children using stage 5 means-ends relations and operational causality as assessed on the 1966 version of the Uzgiris and Hunt (1975) scales, were able to engage in what Sugarman-Bell called "coordinated person-object" exchanges (p. 54). These consisted of genuinely social overtures to adults apparently designed to achieve the infant's object-oriented goals. An example from Sugarman-Bell is "child vocalizes to adult—reaches toward chair—adult places child in chair [p. 54]." The features of these coordinated person-object exchanges were that the child approached the adult *socially*—as opposed to manipulating the adult's involved body part (stage 4)—and attempted to use the adult as an agent. In much the same way that the stage 5 child was able to subordinate the use of one physical object to obtain another, the child coordinated one means (signaling an adult) to the end of obtaining an object. In other words, the child began to "show an intent to communicate, apart from an intent simply to accomplish something [p. 62]." Before that time infants' schemes for objects and persons were kept separate even though they became increasingly complex. That is, the child moved from being able to perform only one repetitive action with either a person or an object (secondary circular reactions) to being able to perform differentiated actions on either a person or an object.

Sugarman-Bell (1978) briefly mentioned that she studied the development from unitary repetitive schemes to coordinated person-object schemes in a group of institutionalized infants. Whereas these children seemed to develop person-object integration at about the same age and developmental stage (stage 5) as the home reared subjects, they acquired language about 6 months later than the home reared group. Unfortunately, no description of the institutionalized group's linguistic level or communicative facility was given nor were any cognitive assessments done. That information would have been useful for hypothesizing the source of the language delay and for examining the characteristics of the language once it emerged. Sugarman-Bell (1978) believed the difference in language onset might be explained by representational lags in the institutionalized infants. Research by Snyder (1978) with children who were inefficient communicators may point to a different cause, however, for delay in communication and language. Both segments of Snyder's sample (normals and inefficient communicators) had attained stage 6 of object permanence. Although all Snyder's subjects had reached stage 5 on Uzgiris and Hunt's means-ends scales, only the normals had attained stage 6. Thus, while stage 5 means-end relations and person-object integration is associated with prelinguistic intentional communication and was apparently achieved by Snyder's subjects and Sugarman-Bell's groups, Sugarman-Bell's institutionalized subjects may have been delayed in their entry into stage 6 of means-ends behavior. Stage 6 means-end behavior, or the ability to represent means-ends solutions internally, appears to be necessary to use language effectively, as a tool, in social interaction.

Olswang (1978), in a study similar to Sugarman-Bell's (1978) and Harding and Golinkoff's (1979), and also drawing extensively on Piaget's ideas about the development of causality, sought to relate the child's expression of agency in one- and two-word speech to cognitive understandings of agency. To do that she traced children's communication skills before and after language emerged. Unlike other researchers she reported that intentional communication (what she called "directive multiple recipient acts" [p. 74]) appeared at about 14 months of age. This later onset may be because her criterion for when the child was using intentional communication of a gestural nature (as opposed to procedures for making interesting things last) was a stringent one: the child must attempt to use a *new* adult as his tool in obtaining goals. Olswang (1978) considered this to be stage 5 in Piaget's scheme. However, this is more than Piaget would require for stage 5 since in many of his examples the child uses the parent who has just been seen engaging in the event, e.g., "Laurent replaces in or on my hand a toy I have just thrown, to make me do it again (Piaget, 1954, p. 312)." When Olswang considered that infants had only achieved an *"apparent* recognition of others-as-agent" (emphasis added) she in fact used stage 5 behaviors for her criterion. This level had been attained by her three subjects by the start of her study when the children were all close to 11 months old. This earlier onset accords with the mean ages for the onset of intentional communication reported by Harding and Golinkoff (1979), Sugarman-Bell (1978), Bates et al. (1975), and Bruner (1975).

Bruner's work (e.g., 1974, 1975) on early communication supports and complements the research cited above. His work has focused on two issues: first, how mother-infant interaction serves to lay the groundwork in *action* for the case concepts of agent, recipient, etc. (Fillmore, 1968) that will later be expressed in language; and second, how mothers require that their infants "clarify" their intentions even on the preverbal level. Bruner's observers' coded aspects of mother-infant interaction designed to detect the molecular communicative components of their "joint formats." He described the child's responses without recourse to Piaget's theory because "The Piagetian formulation of internalization and symbolization of action schemes is suggestive but rather too vague to be satisfactory . . . [p. 9]." Nevertheless, the following is an attempt to show how readily Bruner's observations on the development of communication can be related to developments in the domain of causality: first, Bruner noted, the mother is always the agent in action games and the child, recipient. The child indicates his/her desire for a repeat of the action by a "typical level of excitement." Very likely, this excitement reflects procedures to make interesting sights last—Piaget's stage 3 of causal development. The child next begins to become the agent of the action, e.g., of handing over an object to the mother's *hand,* but never making eye contact with the mother. This is parallel to stage 4 in the development of causality when the child still considers that his activity on the mother's previously acting body part is necessary to set her in motion. At the next phase, it seems that infants have begun to communicate intentionally; they make eye contact with the mother and vocative sounds while looking at their mother's eyes. From the research cited above, e.g., Harding and Golinkoff (1979) it is likely that children are now in stage 5 of causal development because they seem to recognize that the adult is an autonomous center of activity. Although the present interpretation of Bruner's results fits well with the findings of the related research reported above, it is only speculative since no independent assessments of cognitive development were done. Where Bruner's research complements the related research is in its focus on how communicative interactions evolve through mutually constructed games between mother and child.

FINAL COMMENTS

The purpose of this chapter has been to show how Piaget's theory has much utility for researchers interested in studying the origins of communication. The progress that has been made up to now can be attributed in part to Piaget's (1952; 1954; 1962) description of the sensorimotor period, and particularly the development of causality. Researchers have drawn upon the work on causality most extensively to try and understand the way the child's mode of communication evolves from an apparently unintentional to intentional means at the child's disposal. Upon reflection, the intersection between the development of intentional communication and the development of causality is really not unexpected; Piaget's discussion of the development of causality is, to a great extent, a discussion of how the child comes to affect events in the world. Communication is a uniquely social route for making things happen. In order to be able to operate on the external world with any effectiveness the child must first, distinguish himself from the world; second, understand cause-effect relations and how to employ means to achieve ends; and third, be able to anticipate what sorts of things in the world can be directly influenced by the self's actions, e.g., inanimate objects, and which can be only indirectly influenced, e.g., animate objects. These three aspects of causal knowledge were three of the four factors considered necessary for intentional communication in the introduction to this chapter. They are indicative of stage 5 of causal development. The fourth factor posited in the introduction—infants must have some content to communicate about—fits with Piaget's ideas too. As it is discussed in the literature, e.g., Halliday (1975), Bates et al. (1975), the content the infant expresses are various communicative functions similar to the adult's imperative, declarative, etc. However, unlike the other three factors, the argument was made in this chapter that Piaget's theory needs to be plumbed more deeply to provide support for the existence of the posited functions.

It might be noted that the development of object permanence was not found to be particularly useful for understanding aspects of intentional communication

(Harding & Golinkoff, 1979; Snyder, 1978), despite the fact that it was the relationship between object permanence and the beginnings of language that many researchers speculated about, e.g., Bloom (1973). When language development is seen as beginning with the appearance of communicative phenomena, object permanence declines in its theoretical and empirical importance relative to other sensorimotor constructions. Advanced representational capacities are not seen as necessary for the achievement of intentional communication. By the time the first words appear and representational abilities are present, the infant has learned much about how to express content and intentions through nonverbal means. Certainly, as Piaget and others have pointed out, language involves the ability to represent absent objects and events and the transition to the use of conventional signs is an important issue. However, the current emphasis on other cognitive abilities, particularly causality, reflects a necessary broadening of perspective. The field of language development in the past probably concentrated too exclusively on the ability to deal with symbols (although not much research resulted) to the exclusion of the critical communicative aspects of language development.

Although Piaget's theory has been and probably will continue to be most heuristic for studying the development of communication there are of course many questions which remain. The following is just a sample of questions that will need more exploration in future research.

First, what is the relationship between the development of intention in general and the intention to communicate? Whereas Piaget (1972; 1954) dates the development of intentional behavior to stage 3 of the sensorimotor period, there is some disagreement as to what constitutes intentional behavior (Bruner, 1974). Harding (1979) in an examination of these issues has written:

> This difference in identifying the initial appearance of intention may, however, be more apparent than real; Bruner and Piaget appear to be focusing on different aspects of the concept. Various components included within intention (cf. Ryan, 1970) may have distinct developmental courses and "intention" as a unified pattern may not appear in an all-or-nothing fashion. . . . It is hypothesized that changes in the use of communicative behaviors may occur in part because of the infant's increasing ability to intentionally organize his/her own behaviors in relation with the intentions of others in pursuit of a goal [p. 21].

Second, how do all the communicative devices mentioned in this paper, e.g., pointing, gaze direction, vocalizing, etc. enter into the child's repertoire? What accounts for their entry when they do appear? For example, why do intentional vocalizations come after looking at the mother's eyes? How does the child learn to use communicative devices in combination, e.g., pointing and alternating gaze between the adult and the desired object? What cognitive and social factors can help account for the course of communication development?

Third, what is the role of the environment and particularly parental style in the child's breakthrough into intentional communication? Piaget's general theoretical position (as interpreted by Sinclair, 1970) seems to be compatible with this concern, "language acquisition can be understood only by taking into account what is already known of cognitive development in particular and also of affective and social development [p. 4]" since "producing and understanding speech proceeds basically... through complex interaction between the individual's inner structures... and, the objects and people around him... [p. 1]." However, Piaget's theory is not designed to study individual differences and that is what this question is addressing. Others have at least considered (Bruner, 1975; Ryan, 1974; see Schaffer, 1977) how a mother's interaction with her infant could influence the infant's communicative skills but little systematic research has appeared. Parents in general, as pointed out above, cannot resist interpreting their infant's behaviors as though they were intentional communications. Does an overly attentive and perceptive mother cause the infant to fail to refine his communicative skills as readily as a less attentive mother? On the other hand, does a mother who fails to anticipate the infant's wants delay the child's understanding of his role as an agent in the world and hence his potential communicative effects? As a first pass at these issues, Harding and Golinkoff (1978) correlated various maternal demographic variables and maternal perceptions of her child to the number of the child's intentional vocalizations as assessed by Harding and Golinkoff (1979). The number of intentional vocalizations was significantly correlated with the mother's educational level ($r = .29$, $p < .05$) and with the extent to which the mother believed she could figure out what her baby wanted from its sounds ($r = .36$, $p < .05$). Clearly, many more fine grained analyses of maternal behavior and mother-infant interaction need to be done.

The fourth question is when does the infant know that it makes sense to direct one's messages to only potential agents, e.g., animate beings, and not to objects? At some point in the development of communication the infant may be attempting to direct signals to inanimate objects. Piaget (1954) is not entirely clear on when the child's concept of an agent includes only animate objects. In stages 1–3 when the infant is still differentiating the self from the universe, objects—like everything else—are under the infant's control and require the infant to set them in motion through his/her own efficacious gestures. In stage 4 the infant seems to endow inanimate objects with the potential for self-motivated action as when Lucienne (Piaget, 1954, p. 302) directs her procedures to her doll (she does not know Piaget is present) to get it to resume shaking. In stage 5 the infant has objectified causality to reside in others in the world. Although infants have made a large advance over the previous stages, they still seem to endow inanimate objects with the potential to act. For example, Jacqueline (p. 309) puts her toy down rapidly, expecting it to move unaided. In stage 6, apparently the child can still think objects can act (p. 346). Thus, while at stage 5 the infant seems to know that people can be used as agents there is still some confusion about what inanimate objects can do. Unfortunately there is little research on the general question of what and when children know about inanimate and animate objects. The research available is mostly of children's responses to two-dimensional vs. real faces (e.g., Field, 1979), although two studies (Golinkoff, 1975; Golinkoff & Kerr, 1978) used films of real objects. Generally, the issue and its ramifications for communication development remains to be resolved.

The final issue has to do with the relationship between the development of intentional communication and the acquisition of language. For one thing, are the continuities in prelanguage and language functions suggested by the language researchers really there? The hypothesis of developmental continuity is a difficult one to prove in any case (Schaffer, 1977). Given that language may involve a different set of cognitive abilities (e.g., the development of representation) than the onset of intentional communication, why would one predict continuity? Piaget's theory (1962) suggests that words are first used as part of action schemes and may have only minimal communicative effect. What sorts of cognitive achievements are required for the child to use language in a communicative fashion? Snyder (1978) suggested that stage 6 means-end behavior is important in this regard but more work is needed.

To conclude: although the precise relationship between cognitive, social, and communicative functioning has not yet been definitively established—and perhaps never will be (Bates, Benigini, Bretherton, Camaioni, & Volterra, 1977)—Piaget's insights have helped and will continue to help us to pose interesting questions relevant to communication. Interest in this area will probably continue to grow since as Garvey (1978) wrote, "communication is of central importance to the development of the individual and to the structure of the interactions, relationships, groups, and communities which comprise the environment of human growth [p. 1]." Where Piaget's theory is most useful, "the development of the individual," is in understanding the very origins of the communication skill.

ACKNOWLEDGMENT

A much abbreviated and different version of this paper was coauthored by Carol G. Harding and presented at the annual meeting of the Jean Piaget Society, June, 1979. I wish to thank Carol Harding, Frank Murray, and Irving Sigel for their most helpful comments on earlier drafts of this chapter. Patsy Howaniec's secretarial skills merit thanks as well.

REFERENCES

Austin, J. L. How to do things with words. New York: Oxford University Press, 1962.
Bates, E., Benigni, L., Bretherton, I., Camaioni, L., & Volterra, V. From gesture to the first word: On cognitive and social prerequisites. In M. Lewis, & L. A. Rosenblum (Eds.), Interaction, conversation and the development of language. New York: Wiley, 1977.

Bates, E., Benigni, L., Bretherton, I., Camaioni, L., & Volterra, V. *The emergence of symbols: Cognition and communication in infancy.* New York: Academic Press, 1979.

Bates, E., Camaioni, L., & Volterra, V. The acquisition of performatives prior to speech. *Merrill-Palmer Quarterly,* 1975, *21,* 205–226.

Beilin, H. *Studies in the cognitive basis of language development.* New York: Academic Press, 1975.

Bloom, L. *One word at a time.* The Hague: Mouton, 1973.

Bruner, J. S. From communication to language: a psychological perspective. *Cognition,* 1974, *3,* 255–287.

Bruner, J. S. The ontogenesis of speech acts. *Journal of Child Language,* 1975, *2,* 1–19.

Corrigan, R. Language development as related to stage 6 object permanence development. *Journal of Child Language,* 1978, *5*(2), 173–189.

Chafe, W. L. *Meaning and the structure of language.* Chicago: University of Chicago Press, 1970.

Ervin-Tripp, S., & Mitchell-Kernan, C. Introduction. In S. Ervin-Tripp, & C. Mitchell-Kernan (Eds.), *Child discourse.* New York: Academic Press, 1977.

Field, T. M. Visual and cardiac responses to animate and inanimate faces by young term and preterm infants. *Child Development,* 1979, *50,* 188–194.

Fillmore, C. The case for case. In E. Bach, & R. T. Harms (Eds.), *Universals in linguistic theory.* New York: Holt, Rinehart, & Winston, 1968.

Flavell, J. H., Botkin, P. T., Fry, C. L., Wright, J. C., & Jarvis, P. E. *The development of role-taking and communication skills in children.* New York: Wiley, 1968.

Francis, H. What does the child mean? A critique of the 'functional' approach to language acquisition. *Journal of Child Language,* 1979, *6,* 201–210.

Garvey, C. *The origins and growth of communication.* Proposal for a summer institute sponsored by the Society for Research in Child Development. Submitted to the Carnegie Foundation, June 1978.

Garvey, C., & Hogan, R. Social speech and social interaction: Egocentrism revisited. *Child Development,* 1973, *44,* 562–568.

Goldstein, D. The situation in egocentrism research. *The Genetic Epistemologist: Quarterly Newsletter of the Jean Piaget Society,* 1977, *VI,* 1–3.

Golinkoff, R. M. Semantic development in infants: The concepts of agent and recipient. *Merrill-Palmer Quarterly,* 1975, *21,* 181–193.

Golinkoff, R. M., & Kerr, J. L. Infants' perceptions of semantically-defined action role changes in filmed events. *Merrill-Palmer Quarterly,* 1978, *24,* 53–61.

Halliday, M. A. K. *Learning how to mean.* London: Arnold, 1975.

Harding, C. G. *The development of the intention to communicate. Human Development,* 1981, in press.

Harding, C. G., & Golinkoff, R. M. *The relationship between cognitive development, maternal behavior, and the occurrence of intentional vocalizations in prelinguistic infants.* Presented at Jean Piaget Society Meetings, May 1978.

Harding, C. G., & Golinkoff, R. M. The origins of intentional vocalizations in prelinguistic infants. *Child Development,* 1979, *50,* 33–40.

Hymes, D. Competence and performance in linguistic theory. In R. Huxley, & E. Ingram (Eds.), *Language acquisition: Models and methods.* London: Academic Press, 1971.

Ingram, D. Sensorimotor intelligence and language development. In A. Lock (Ed.), *Action, gesture and symbol: The emergence of language.* London: Academic Press, 1978.

Kavanaugh, R. D. Relationship between cognition and language in infancy. Presented at Jean Piaget Society Meetings, June 1979.

Lock, A. Acts not sentences. In W. von Raffler-Engel, & Y. Lebrun (Eds.), *Baby talk and infant speech.* Holland: Sivets and Aeitlinger V. B. V., 1976.

Mehrabian, A., & Williams, M. Piagetian measures of cognitive development up to age two. *Journal of Psycholinguistic Research,* 1971, *1,* 113–126.

Moerk, E. L. Piaget's research as applied to the explanation of language development. *Merrill-Palmer Quarterly*, 1975, *21*, 151–170.

Moerk, E. L. *Pragmatic and semantic aspects of early language development*. Baltimore: University Park Press, 1977.

Morehead, D. M., & Morehead, A. From signal to sign: A Piagetian view of thought and language during the first two years. In R. L. Schiefelbusch, & L. L. Lloyd (Eds.), *Language perspectives—Acquisition, retardation, and intervention*. Baltimore: University Park Press, 1974.

Olswang, L. B. *The ontogenesis of agent: From cognition notion to semantic expression*. Unpublished doctoral dissertation, University of Washington, 1978.

Piaget, J. *The origins of intelligence in children*. New York: International Universities Press, 1952.

Piaget, J. *The construction of reality in the child*. New York: Ballantine, 1954.

Piaget, J. *The language and thought of the child*. Ohio: The World Publishing Co., 1955.

Piaget, J. *Play, dreams, and imitation in childhood*. New York: Norton, 1962.

Ryan, J. Early language development. In M. P. M. Richards (Ed.), *The integration of the child into a social world*. Cambridge, England: Cambridge University Press, 1974.

Ryan, T. A. *Intentional behavior*. New York: Ronald Press, 1970.

Schaffer, H. R. (Ed.). *Studies in mother-infant interaction*. London: Academic Press, 1977.

Searle, J. What is a speech act? In M. Black (Ed.), *Philosophy in America*. Ithaca, N.Y.: Cornell University Press, 1965.

Sinclair-de Zwart, H. Developmental psycholinguistics. In D. Elkind & J. H. Flavell (Eds.), *Studies in cognitive development*. New York: Oxford University Press, 1969.

Sinclair-de Zwart, H. The transition from sensorimotor behavior to symbolic activity. *Interchange*, 1970, *1*, 119–126.

Sinclair-de Zwart, H. Language acquisition and cognitive development. In T. E. Moore (Ed.), *Cognitive development and the acquisition of language*. New York: Academic Press, 1973.

Snow, C. E. The development of conversation between mothers and babies. *Journal of Child Language*, 1977, *1*, 1–22.

Snyder, L. Communicative and cognitive abilities and disabilities in the sensorimotor period. *Merrill-Palmer Quarterly*, 1978, *24*(3), 161–188.

Sugarman-Bell, S. Some organizational aspects of preverbal communication. In I. Markova (Ed.), *The social context of language*. New York: Wiley, 1978.

Uzgiris, I., & Hunt, J. *Assessment in infancy*. Chicago: University of Illinois Press, 1975.

Werner, H., & Kaplan, B. *Symbol formation*. New York: Wiley, 1963.

Zachry, W. Ordinality and interdependence of representation and language development in infancy. *Child Development*, 1978, *49*, 681–687.

10

The Conservation Paradigm: The Conservation of Conservation Research

Frank B. Murray
University of Delaware

> *Our contention is merely that conservation is a necessary condition for all rational activity . . . conservation appears then to be a kind of functional* a priori *of thought.*
>
> J. Piaget and A. Szeminska
> *The Child's Conception of Number.*

The psychological construct, *conservation,* like the constructs *seriation, class inclusion, horizontality, egocentrism, decentration,* is in its clearest sense simply a label for an experimental paradigm or a set of research procedures. It is merely a procedure to assess children's realization that the equivalence of some aspect of two objects is preserved (or conserved) when one of the objects is transformed in some other respect. The labels, *conservation* and *nonconservation,* also serve as the description of children's characteristic ''success'' and ''failure'' responses to the tasks the procedures place before them. Because the constructs are completely redundant with the child's behavior they can provide no explanation of why or how children above and below seven years or so respond in the consistently different ways they do to the tasks. At this level the constructs provide only circular explanations of the behavior. Reifications of the construct conservation occur in the literature when, for example, researchers speak about ''conservation ability'' etc., but these have the limited explanatory value of any other reified construct.

The explanation of children's conservation behavior and the break in the lower level circularity of the conservation construct reside in the development of higher order constructs which carry sufficient general nonoperationalized surplus meaning to explain not only conservation, but other related behaviors. The

143

Genevans have proposed the construct, *concrete operation*, to explain conservation behavior and virtually all other cognitive developments between about seven and eleven years. Such non-Genevan higher order constructs as *discriminative conditioning, working memory, imitation, maturation, concept learning*, etc., compete with the concrete operations as potential explanations of conservation behavior and related cognitive behavioral changes.

LIMITATIONS OF THE GENEVAN MODEL

Although a complete presentation and critique of the Genevan account of operativity is beyond the scope of this chapter, some limitations in the explanation can be outlined. The concrete operations are by definition a system of operations (structure d'ensemble) which can be modeled by various *groupings*—a logical invention of Piaget's. Osherson (1974) and Sheppard (1978) review the formal weaknesses in the Genevan grouping model which have been given by such logicians as Quine, Beth, McKinsey, Kneale, Hempel, Parsons, Grize, Granger and present some attempts by them to reformulate the model. For example, Sheppard proposes a new entity, the groupoid, to handle the problems of concrete operational behaviors.

It is not clear what kind of empirical evidence could provide unequivocal support for the grouping model (see Pinard & Laurendeau, 1969 and Flavell, 1977, for review of the issues). In part the central theoretical issue is the degree of asynchrony a structural stage theory can tolerate before the nonstructural components vitiate completely any clarity and explanatory power the stage construct confers on the phenomena. A theoretical F test is needed to comprehend the point at which the within stage variation so exceeds the between stage variation that the stage construct can no longer be defended. This issue is *not* an empirical question. Were the criterion merely that the diverse behaviors defined by the concrete operational stage intercorrelate or load on a single factor as they could be expected to, the model would have some empirical support in the findings of Hamel and van der Veer (1972), Toussaint (1974), Stephens et al. (1972) and Dihoff (1975) for example. On the other hand the grouping model could be expected to predict asynchronous clusters of positive intercorrelations or factors rather than a general factor intercorrelation because the Genevans have postulated eight separate groupings each linked theoretically to some existing or yet to be discovered behaviors (Flavell, 1963). Ideally, the factor analyses of the concrete operational tasks should yield oblique factors representing the known groupings. Although factor analyses of the tasks (e.g., Berzonsky, 1971, De-Vries, 1973, Hathaway, 1972, Jamison, 1977) usually yield separate factors for the concrete tasks, they are not always interpretable in terms of one or another of the groupings. A biunivocal multiplication of relations grouping factor on which conservation task performance should theoretically load is rarely found, although the various conservation tasks do intercorrelate positively and significantly (e.g., Goldschmid and Bentler, 1968). However, factor analyses of sets of conservation tasks have sometimes yielded as many as four separate factors (e.g. Winkelmann, 1973). It may be that the dynamic relationships among the groupings may be revealed in their structural equation analysis and that causal models may provide clearer explication of the behaviors than a logical group model (see Cornelius et al., 1978). Asynchrony appears to be the common finding (e.g., Weinreb & Brainerd, 1975) and the fact that these time lags are often unpredictable has led Piaget to conclude that it is not possible to have a general theory of these lags and that explanations of them, while possible, are inevitably *post hoc* (Piaget, 1971, p. 11). The construct, *horizontal decalage,* incidentally, is also merely a label for the asynchrony and is not an explanation or mechanism for it as some have suggested (e.g., Jamison, 1977). The creation of higher order constructs for the horizontal decalage within the conservation is a prime problem for developmental theorists. It would seem in any case that the Genevan explanation for conservation is somewhat flawed and as Piaget has admitted, no doubt faceitiously, his explanation, like so many others, may very well have missed the heart of the conservation problem (Piaget, 1967).

A close examination of the lowest level of the conservation construct, namely the paradigm, is undertaken in the remainder of this chapter to make clear the gaps in our explanation of this significant aspect of children's cognitive development despite nearly a 20 year saturation of research journals with articles on the topic.

THE CONSERVATION PARADIGM

Step 1. Two objects, A and B, of the same material which are identical with respect to at least two attributes, x and y, are presented to the child. The attributes x and y are independent of each other or at least not perfectly correlated and often x is quantitative and more abstract than y. Commonly researched x attributes are the object's length, number weight, area, volume, duration. The object's shape, location or position are commonly used y attributes.

The equivalence of the objects with respect to x and y may be established by the experimenter's fiat or preferably by some measurement procedure or testing action (ta), however primitive (e.g., eyeballing, hefting, or counting, etc.). In any event the child must acknowledge the equivalence of A and B at least with respect to x.

Thus $A_{xy} = B_{xy}$.

Step 2. One of the objects (say B) is transformed with respect to y by an action, t, which changes y but not x.

Thus $B_{xy} \rightarrow B'_{xy'}$.

Optional addition to Step 2.   Some guarantee is often provided that the child was aware of the transformation, *t,* and its result, $B'_{xy'}$, by asking the child to describe the events *t* and $B'_{xy'}$ or by asking the child if $B'_{xy'}$ *looks* different from A or B with respect to x or y.

Step 3.   The child is presented with A_{xy} and $B'_{xy'}$ and asked (Q1), whether or not A_{xy} equals $B'_{xy'}$ with respect to x. A_{xy} and $B'_{xy'}$ must be presented in such a way that the question cannot be correctly answered by comparing or measuring them in any way by *ta.* If the child's response to Q1 is made on the basis of how A and $B'_{xy'}$ look or feel, the child's judgment, even though it is correct, could not indicate conservation and the presence of operational competence. It is only conservation if the response to Q1 is a deduction (Inhelder, Sinclair, & Bovet, 1974).

Thus, the response, $A_{xy} = B'_{xy'}$, is called a conservation response; and the response, $A_{xy} \neq B'_{xy'}$, is called a nonconservation response. Responses to Q1 and Q1 itself may be nonverbal. Retention measures for the information in Step 1, and sometimes Step 2, may be made.

Step 4.   The child may be asked (Q2) why he said what he did in response to Q1 in Step 3. The criteria for an acceptable reason are given in the various theories of conservation.

Step 5.   Since the judgment, $A_{xy} = B'_{xy'}$, can be a deduction from the evidence in Step 1 and what the presence of concrete operations allows him to construct out of the evidence in Step 2, a determination of the child's feeling of the necessity of his response should be made. For example, the child may be asked whether the outcome of applying the transformation could ever have been different, or whether the outcome would always or just sometimes be what his response to Q1 indicated it was.

Step 6.   Some additional criteria may be applied. The common ones are:

1. Durability. Steps 1–4 are repeated at later time intervals up to one or two months.
2. Resistance to countersuggestion. This is an assessment similar to that in Step 5, but in this case counter-evidence, pressure, argument is offered by the experimenter in an attempt to change the child's response to Q1 on the assumption that necessary conclusions are not modifiable. Easily changed responses to Q1 indicate pseudo-conservation.
3. Specific transfer. Steps 1–4 are repeated with different *A*'s and *B*'s with respect to the same *x* but perhaps with different *y* and/or *t* (different objects and transformations may be used).
4. Nonspecific transfer. Steps 1–4 are repeated about different *x* attributes and the same or different *y* attributes and transformations. Occasionally the

appropriate paradigm steps may be applied to other concrete operational tasks (e.g., seriation, transitivity, class inclusion).

5. Trainability. This criterion is in some sense the converse of the counter suggestion criterion since, unlike this criterion, it is applied to the nonconservation response to Q1 (and Q2) on the assumption that a quick and abrupt change in response to Q1 and Q2 after feedback, hints, cues, etc., indicates that the original nonconservation was not valid (or was pseudo-nonconservation).

These paradigm criteria, especially Steps 4-6, are requirements of the Genevan school and support their interpretation of the significance of conservation behavior. Less demanding criteria for the behavior (viz. Steps 1-3 or only Step 2) have permitted experimental paradigms that favor alternate explanations of the behavior (e.g., Bever, Mehler, Epstein, 1968; Braine & Shanks, 1965; Bryant, 1974; Gruen, 1966; Gelman, 1969; Mehler & Bever, 1967). No empirical evidence can clarify or resolve the differences between these competing explanations as they are arguments over different criteria and paradigms and not arguments about the data each has generated (see Reese & Overton, 1970 for an elaboration of this point).

Still, the criteria embedded in Steps 1-3 (and perhaps 4) are straightforward and unbiased toward one model of another except insofar as they require some linguistic competence. However, nonverbal assessment alternatives exist for each paradigm step (e.g., Murray, 1970) to correct much of this deficiency. Nevertheless the behavior emanating from the paradigm requires explanation, even if only Steps 1-3 or Steps 2 and 3 (the so-called identity conservation paradigm, Elkind, 1967) are adhered to.

THE LOGIC OF CONSERVATION AND NONCONSERVATION COMPETENCE

A further analysis of the conservation paradigm reveals that the conservation conclusion cannot be deduced from the information presented in the experimental procedure. The child must supply two additional premises. To the initial premise in Step 1 that, $A_{xy} = B_{xy}$, the child must add a premise, $B_{xy} = B'_{xy'}$, and a transitivity premise (viz., "if $A = B$ and $B = C$, then A must equal C") to complete the argument that $A_{xy} = B'_{xy'}$, the conservation deduction. These two additions which guarantee the logical necessity of the conservation conclusion also demonstrate that the conservation problem is not solely a logical reasoning task even though success on it is taken by Piaget (1960) as the best indicator of the presence of the logical groupings of operational thought. The conservation problem tells us as much about the child's understanding of certain natural regularities as it does of his understanding of logical necessity. The problem, as Piaget (1971, p. 32) and others (e.g., Osherson, 1974) have noted, is contaminated by a mixture of logical and physical principles. The information that $B_{xy} =$

$B'_{xy'}$ and the information that the particular relationship which x entails is transitive both have non-logical sources. From the premises that A has a relationship to B (ArB) which B also has to C (BrC) one cannot conclude that A and C have the same relationship (ArC) as may be quickly seen if the relationship were "A loves B," etc. or "A is the father of B." Thus, before the initial information $A_{xy} = B_{xy}$ can lead him to the conservation deduction, the child must come to know somehow which relationships are transitive and which are not, as well as the fact that t left x unchanged so that $B_{xy} = B'_{xy'}$.

Had the child supplied different premises, as well he might have, a nonconservation judgment also could be deduced from the paradigm with a force of necessity equal to the usual conservation deduction. If the child believed that $B_{xy} \neq B'_{xy'}$ and knew a different transitive relationship, viz. "if A = B and B ≠ C, then A ≠ C', he would and should conclude that $A_{xy} \neq B'_{xy'}$," which is a nonconservation deduction. If the child followed this reasoning pattern, his nonconservation judgment would be a proper deduction and should indicate the same operational competence that is implicated in the conservation deduction. In sum, the nonconservation judgment, $A_{xy} \neq B'_{xy'}$, follows necessarily from the premises $A_{xy} = B_{xy}$ and $B_{xy} \neq B'_{xy'}$ when the relationships between A_{xy}, B_{xy}, and $B'_{xy'}$ are seen as transitive.

Indeed there is evidence (Murray & Armstrong, 1976) that some nonconservers feel their judgments necessarily follow from the premises of the task. In a subsequent study it was found that 16 out of 38 nonconservers, as well as all the conservers, acknowledged all the appropriate premises and felt their different conclusions were equally necessary. Specifically these nonconservers believed $B_{xy} \neq B'_{xy'}$, knew the transitivity relationships and felt their nonconservation conclusion had to be true, would always follow, and could not be different, no matter how many times the task was presented.

These nonconservers respond very much like adults who occasionally fail to conserve. When we find problems on which adults fail to conserve, we do not think it is because they have failed to develop operational competence, but rather that, for some reason, they are employing a set of premises that leads ineluctably to a nonconservation conclusion. For example, Murray and Armstrong (1978) and Hufnagel and Murray (1978) have researched a number conservation problem which only 20% of adult samples conserve. Ironically, significantly more third graders seemed to solve the problem correctly than college students. However, it now seems clear that the third grader's superiority is more parsimoniously attributed to their misunderstanding of the problem. The problem is a numerical equivalence conservation problem in which the initial equality is between the number of red beads in jar 1 and blue beads in jar 2. In the transformation, ten red beads are taken from jar 1 and mixed with the blue beads in jar 2 after which any ten beads are returned from jar 2 to jar 1. The question is whether the number of red beads (or blue beads) in jar 1 equals the number of blue beads (or red) in jar 2. The surprising answer, at least to 80% of the adults sampled, is that the number of red beads in jar 1 always equals the number of blue beads in jar 2 regardless of the proportion of red and blue beads that happened to be returned from jar 2 to jar 1. The adults' performance on more traditional operativity measures unquestionably indicates they have operational competence. Moreover they are confident that their nonconservation judgment is necessary because the problem is taken as indeterminate. If it is the case, as is claimed here, that young nonconservers in some circumstances exhibit operational competence in their reasoning, we should expect to see the other common aspects of operativity in their reasoning. Indeed, as we shall see below, nonconservers understand the traditionally accepted conservation reasons. A benefit operational competence is thought to confer upon the child is the ability not only to treat more than one aspect of an event but to integrate these into a system of compensating actions. There is evidence that a large number of nonconservers can do this and appear thereby to appreciate an INRC set of relations among the attributes in a conservation problem. For example, Murray and Johnson (1975) showed that nonconservers who thought making a clay ball colder made it heavier also thought making it warmer made it lighter. Coupled with their knowledge of the effects adding and subtracting clay had on a clay ball's weight, they acted as though they possessed the INRC group depicted in Fig. 10.1. Both adding clay and making colder were correlates (C) that made the ball heavier. The effects of adding clay to the ball could be reversed by its negation (N), subtracting clay, or by its reciprocal (R), making it warmer. Even though the nonconserver's thinking is in error with respect to the effects of temperature on weight, his reasoning has these INRC features of operativity.

These conclusions are based on the effects of single discrete transformations in which, say, clay is added to the ball, and after it is restored to its original condition, the ball is made warmer. A better test of the INRC characteristics might come from an examination of double transformations which could be sequentially or simultaneously carried out. These are represented by the horizon-

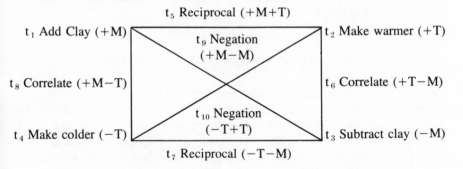

FIG. 10.1.   INRC Group of nonconservation of weight transformations of mass ($\pm M$) or temperature ($\pm T$). Single transformations (t_1, t_2, t_3, t_4) are represented at the juncture of three lines. Double transformations (t_5, t_6, t_7, t_8, t_9) are represented by the vertical, horizontal and diagonal lines and indicate the simultaneous or successive performance of single transformations on the same object.

tal, vertical and diagonal lines in Fig. 10.1 which portray, for example, a clay ball which is made colder and added to (C transformation), or made warmer and subtracted from (R transformation). Hrybyk and Murray (1978) have investigated these double transformations to substantiate the INRC character of some nonconservation judgments. However, their nonconservers on the single transformations were unable to accept the double transformation task and when pressed seemed to base their judgments only on one of the two transformations. Conservers' performance on the double transformation task need to be determined but it seems likely that a more advanced form of operativity is required to respond to the double transformation in the same consistent and coherent way that is found with the usual single transformation task.

In conclusion, we find again the force of the Genevan maxim that the more significant clues in the diagnosis of a child's intellectual status are not in the correct response but in the examination of the errors. For some nonconservers the error doesn't seem to be incompetent or immature reasoning but misinformation about the transformation's effects. At the very least, this indicates that nonconservation is no more a certain criterion for preoperational thought than conservation is for operational thought. Success on the conservation task, according to this analysis of the competence requirements for it, is dependent on the child's ability to supply the missing premises of the logical argument. The source of these premises is the heart of the conservation problem. With them the valid logical argument they produce is sufficient for the problem's solution. Not only may the source of these premises reside in sets of nonlogical factors, the logical competence which has just been demonstrated to be sufficient for the problem's solutions may not be necessary for the solution if the child employs a nonlogical strategy. The logical competence required for the conservation deduction may be sufficient, but not necessary for the problem's solutions (especially if only paradigm Steps 1–4 are used). The complete account of the conservation requires an examination of these nonlogical or nonstructural factors that influence the child's response to Q1.

NONSTRUCTURAL PARADIGM FACTORS

Each step of the conservation paradigm carries with it a set of nonlogical or nonstructural factors which influence the child's solution to the problem. The voluminous conservation literature contains demonstrations of correlational links between conservation and a large number of subject characteristics. It is beyond the scope of this chapter to document these but soon conservation, like IQ, will have been correlated with every conceivable psychological variable. Sohan and Celia Modgil have catalogued nearly every "Piagetian" study in an eight volume series, *Piagetian Research: Compilation and Summary,* published by NFER Publishing in 1976. Those volumes and the research bibliographies published in the *Genetic Epistemologist* (Vol. VII, No. 4; Vol. VI, No. 5; Vol. VI, No. 1), the newsletter of the Jean Piaget Society, provide a reasonably complete compilation of the research findings on subject characteristics. Briefly, conservation performance has been related to the child's IQ, MA, CA, SES, M-space, anticipatory imagery, eye movement patterns, cultural and national background, constructive memory, language development, category clustering, concept formation strategy, various cognitive styles, school achievements, prior knowledge and special experiences, lateral dominance, genotype, hearing and vision, school attendance, mental health and sex. Some of these relationships are theoretically trivial, some are equivocal, others are manifestations of third factor causes, and some serve to tie the conservation construct to universally recognized constructs in cognitive psychology. The best predictor of conservation appears to be the child's mental age, although the relationship between CA, MA, and IQ is not simple (Brown, 1973). The MA prediction holds only after a certain CA is reached (6 years in Brown, 1973) which suggests that a minimum level of necessary experiences, marked by CA, provides a threshold above which differential conservation performance becomes more closely related to MA than CA. Below the CA threshold MA is not predictive of conservation.

Although some aspects of the paradigm factors have been as widely investigated as the subject characteristics, there remain some significant gaps which inhibit an adequate explanation of conservation. The exposition of these can be organized around the content of the Steps in the conservation paradigm presented above.

A and B Factors

A and *B* refer to the stimuli or materials presented to the child in Step 1. Although the influence of many aspects of the materials is negligible (e.g., color) and is confounded with other features of the experimental procedures, many apparently trivial differences between materials seem to influence conservation. As one example Uzgiris (1964) found conservation of mass, weight, or volume was affected by whether the material was clay, metal, or plastic. On the other hand, material differences which appear equally or more salient, desirable, or familiar than those Uzgiris used are not found to influence conservation performance (see Miller, 1978 for a review of some of these studies). Although the results from contrasts of various types of conservation stimuli are equivocal, there are two common notions of material differences that require further elaboration because they have been invested with some theoretical significance—namely whether material is discontinuous or continuous and whether its mode of presentation is concrete or abstract.

Discontinuity-Continuity. The discontinuity-continuity dimension was introduced by Piaget and Szeminska (1952) and refers to whether the material is composed of discrete particles (sand, beads) or not (liquid). Although they reported no difference between quantity conservation of liquids and beads, subsequent researchers (e.g., Elkind, 1961; Smedslund, 1961) found that discontinuous materials were conserved before continuous ones. The finding fitted with a Genevan notion of atomism and the related notion that conservation of quantity develops from the idea that whole substances are decomposable into and composed of small discrete, enumerable parts which simply change their locations in relation to each other when the substances are transformed in the conservation experiment. Recently the discontinuity-continuity discrepancy has figured prominently in the Genevan conservation training studies (Inhelder, Sinclair, & Bovet, 1974) as basis for inducing cognitive conflict between discontinuous and continuous task judgments. Smedslund (1961) noted the pedagogical significance of initiating instruction with discontinuous materials.

Still, the dimension has not been systematically researched and the reported differences are found as marginal findings in experiments designed to explore other factors. When Murray and Holm (1975) analyzed the dimension with 90 primary school children (K–2) for conservation of length, substance, and weight on a series of materials of graduated discontinuity (water, flour, bird sand, BB shot, and glass marbles), they found absolutely no effects that could be attributed to differences in the materials although the usual age and time lag effects were found in the proportions of conservers and nonconservers at each grade. This finding held for an identity conservation task in which glass marbles were depicted as repeatedly dividing until they finally melted and fused in response to five temperature increases. It would appear that the discontinuity-continuity dimension is not a significant factor in conservation. Also in the standardization sample of the Conservation Assessment Kit (Goldschmid & Bentler, 1968) continuous materials were easier than discontinuous ones on Forms A and B, although the differences were insignificant. Fleck (1972) in replication of the Conservation Assessment Kit confirmed the no difference finding between continuous and discontinuous materials as well as finding that only half the tasks of each Form discriminated subjects in grades K, 1 and 2. Finally, Peisach and Hardeman (1975) found no differences in quantity conservation performance between crude salt and water in their exploration continuity-discontinuity dimension.

Concrete-Abstract. The limited data on the concrete-abstract dimension of the mode of presentation follow a similar course to the continuity dimension, although the variable has not been directly explored by the Genevans. Still, the expectation from the general Genevan claim that mental operations develop from the gradual transformations of overt actions, suggests that children might be differentially sensitive to abstract stimuli modes. Transitive relationships expressed verbally have been found more difficult than those presented with concrete objects. Hans Aebli, Piaget's colleague, has suggested (Flavell, 1963), that instruction:

> might begin by having the child operate directly on physical entities, then on pictorial representations of these entities, then have him proceed to cognitive anticipation and retrospections of operations not actually performed at the moment, and so on, until the originally external actions can take place internally and in complete autonomy from the environment [pp. 368-369].

In two experiments (Murray 1970) the power of the concrete-abstract dimension was analyzed in between and within subject formats in which children were presented the conservation stimuli as concrete objects (clay balls and poker chips), photographs of the objects, line drawings of the objects, and verbal descriptions of the objects. No differences in the proportions of conservers and nonconservers were found between stimulus modes, although the usual age and SES differences were found. These findings were replicated by Burnett and Kroger (1974) and hold for each problem and for the youngest children who might be expected to show maximal sensitivity to the dimension.

An argument could be made that the expected facilitation from the concrete mode was balanced by facilitation from the other conditions in which the transformation was simply described and therefore not as seductive as if it had been performed. Although their results are not supported by the present data, Shantz and Smock (1966) claim, for example, more distance conservation with drawings than with objects ($p < .12$). The expected difficulty of the verbal condition, moreover, may have been mitigated by the lack of a perceptual confrontation that was most strongly present in the concrete condition.

The importance of the perceptual confrontation in conservation has been emphasized by Frank (1966), but its importance has been challenged by Silverman and Marsh (1969). The matter of whether the transformation need actually be performed or only imagined by the subject is not clear in the literature. For example, Elkind (1961) found that as much conservation and nonconservation occurred when children predicted the outcome of a transformation before it was performed as when they judged the situation after it was performed. However, Smedslund (1963) and Pratoomraj and Johnson (1966) found more conservation when the outcome was anticipated or predicted than when the situation was judged after the transformation was actually performed. The abstractness dimension data, nevertheless, indicate that a transformation is as seductive when it is simply described and imagined by the subject as when it is actually performed.

In view of the concept formation, verbal learning literature, and logical reasoning literature on the facilitative effects of concrete stimuli, it is surprising that conservation appears so strongly insensitive to the abstractness dimension in these studies and yet at the same time sensitive to the traditional conservation variables. No doubt some resolution to the puzzle will come from experimental designs which separate the abstractness dimension from the perceptual saliency of the transformation.

Animate-Inanimate materials.   It is not clear from contemporary developmental theories, including Piaget's, how conservation performance might be expected to change if the materials were animate instead of inanimate as they usually have been. For example, should the child's greater familiarity with his own body facilitate conservation of his own length, mass, weight, volume, and age, or should his feelings of uniqueness, etc., cause him to resist a renewed identification with these physical concepts, or are the traditional conservation concepts tied so closely to inanimate objects that generalization to animate objects is difficult. Or like Asch and Nerlove's (1960) analysis of double function words (brittle, hard, bright) which may be applied to people and objects, do the animate and inanimate conceptual systems develop relatively independently, with inanimate preceding animate which develops independently of it and is later integrated with it. The literature indicates conservation performance is sensitive to the animate material variable, but the direction of the difference is unclear. Curcio, Robbins and Ela (1971) and Montada (1972) found that conservation of the number of fingers after a "spreading" transformation is easier than number conservation for equivalent numbers of physical objects under analogous transformations. Murray (1969) found, on the other hand, that the child's conservation of his own weight was more difficult than his conservation of a clay ball's weight under analogous transformations (e.g., crouching). Macready and Macready (1974) report the opposite result and further that no differences exist between conservation of the self and other's weight. Piaget claims (Gruber & Voneche, 1977, p. 568–569) synchrony between the child's concept of age and physical time in that the development of age and time concepts are "precisely parallel." The distinction between animate and inanimate, between people and things, is a profound construction and it is not surprising that it might influence conservation judgments. How it does is another matter in need of clarification.

X Factors

The particular invariant attribute of the conservation paradigm is the X factor. With respect to the various attributes much has been made of the time lags in the onset of the conservations of them. There is no theory of these lags, although many, like the mass, weight, volume lag in conservation, are stable enough to have diagnostic value (Inhelder, 1968). A complete explanation of conservation has been delayed by the need to discover the dimension or dimensions upon which these tasks scale. The various post hoc explanations do not provide it, and it is difficult to imagine the dimension which yields the following fairly universal scale of difficulty: number, quantity and mass, length, area, weight, time, volume, density, momentum, etc. The scale does not seem to be one of dependence even for the familiar mass, weight, volume sequence since all the attributes are independent (e.g., the concept of weight can be understood and defined quite apart from considerations of volume and vice versa, as they do not share a common metric or unit). The number of relevant transformations does appear predictive of the lag, as there is just one way to change mass (viz. ± matter) three ways to change weight (± matter, ± matter of largest proximal object, ± distance between them), four ways to change volume (± matter, compression, stretching. enclosure). However, as the conserving child is not aware of all of these factors (Murray & Johnson, 1975), it is unlikely that the scale dimension is the number of possible relevant transformations which define the concept, or even the ratio of relevant to irrelevant. Moreover, young conservers are distinguished from nonconservers by and large by their belief that there is an addition or subtraction of matter way to change mass, weight and volume, but it is the *only* way to change them (Nummedal, 1970). It is possible that the magnitudes of the environmental correlations between x and y would be predictive of the lag sequences, but these have not been empirically determined. Or it is possible that some x attributes are more concrete and conserved earlier for that reason. However, weight that has clear sensory consequences occurs later in the squence than the more abstract attributes of number or mass. Finally, it is possible that, despite the identity of the paradigm, the demands various attributes make upon working memory and attention are not equivalent, e.g., volume must be evaluated in three dimensions whereas length and area involve only 1 and 2 dimensions. Even if the entire time lag range of concepts were not a single scale, certain groups, like the mass, weight, volume sequence, do form an exceptional scale. Even a label for it would be helpful; what is it a scale of besides difficulty, which is the very thing in need of explanation? Under some conditions the mass, weight, volume sequence may disappear. For example, Murray (1969) and Nummedal (1970) found no evidence of the sequence when the concepts were operationally defined by various hypothetical "machines" that measured mass, weight and volume. Children answered the conservation question by predicting the scale readings on the dials of the machines.

Whereas conservation researchers have limited themselves generally to the object attributes Piaget originally researched (e.g., number, amount, length, area, weight, time, volume, etc.), this limitation has been self-imposed, because the conservation paradigm can be applied without exception to any concept. When it is, it provides a diagnostic technique for measuring a person's understanding of a concept that is as old as Platonic dialectic, wherein various concepts like justice, virtue, goodness, etc., were each subjected to a series of relevant and irrelevant transformations to determine whether they had changed or even had ceased to be. By this process the essence of the concept was constructed and understood. For example, whereas it is just to repay a debt, is it just to repay it if the repayment will injure the creditor as might be the case if a borrowed weapon were to be returned to its now deranged owner? The point is that there is nothing in principle to distinguish the traditionally researched conservation concept from any other that might be of interest to the curriculum developer.

It has been claimed by Piaget (1968) that conservation is reserved for quantitative and not qualitative attributes, but this claim must give way to the child's, not the researcher's, notion of a quantitative concept. The concept of substance or mass may be quantitative for the physicist, but it is probably not for children (and many adults), and yet it is conserved by children about 7 years of age. Moreover, Saltz and Hamilton (1968) have shown that conservation of qualitative concepts follows the same patterns that Piaget and others have claimed for quantitative concepts.

Step 1 and correspondence factors.   How does the child convince himself of the initial equality between the objects A_{xy} and B_{xy}, especially when x is somewhat abstract and not immediately given perceptually? Upon what is the child's acknowledgment or determination of the initial equality based? Both conserver and nonconserver acknowledge the equality, although the conserver tends to accept it more easily as a given or a condition of the problem than the nonconserver who often requires that certain minor, often imperceptible, adjustments be made in the amounts of x before the equality between A and B is acknowledged. In some sense the child's correct understanding of the initial question begs the whole conservation question since it could be thought that the knowledge which is sufficient to establish the equality of A and B, particularly if they appeared unequal to the child initially, would be sufficient to preserve, or recreate, the equality after the transformation?

In his treatment of correspondences, some 40 years ago in the *Child's Conception of Number* and now more recently at a symposium of the Jean Piaget Society, Piaget (1978) actually suggests as much since the correspondences which set the initial equality come to have an operational base or link. Currently three stages are portrayed in the link between operations and correspondences. In the first the initial correspondences are simply empirical comparisons which precede the transformations, followed by an interactive stage between correspondences and transformation in which correspondences between changes of state engender transformations which in turn permit new correspondences between states. At the third stage correspondences result from the construction of the operational system itself and are, for that reason, necessary correspondences which can be deduced from the operational structure. Although there are reciprocal correspondences, there are no inverse correspondences, and in that fact lies the irreconcilable difference between them and operations. "Therefore," argues Piaget (1978) "we are dealing with two sorts of systems that are distinct, but both indispensible, both necessary . . . there is a solidarity between operations and correspondences and even if their forms of equilibration are different, the forms are complementary forms that have nothing contrary or contradictory in relation to each other [p. 27]."

In all operational or preoperational activities, of whatever sort, there are correspondences (Piaget, 1978, p. 19) and presumably the nonconservers and conservers employ different ones in Step 1 even though their conclusions about the relationship between A_{xy} and B_{xy} are identical. With exception of the research on one to one correspondences (Piaget & Szeminska, 1952) and Gelman and Gallistel's (1978) research on the development of "counting principles," we have very little idea about how the child handles the demands of Step 1 or the conservation paradigm in other than the number conservation task.

With respect to the other conservations, considerable research of the Gelman and Gallistel mode is needed before we understand how children determine length, area, weight, time, volume, substance, etc., equalities. Wallach (1969) in an analysis of the experiential basis of conservation proposed the existence of certain perceptible indicator properties, the "sameness of which indicates equality and difference inequality [p. 207]." These properties coupled with the knowledge of certain actions, procedures, transformations which we have called testing actions (*ta*), provide the basis for the determination of the equality in Step 1. If the result of the performance of the *same* operation upon each of the quantities of two objects is their having the same value of an indicator property, the quantities must have been equal in the first place. Thus, the test of whether two quantities, whose equality is in doubt, are equal is that when the same thing is done to both of them the resulting identicator properties are identical. If they are not, the quantities were initially unequal. Experiences with a wide variety of indicator properties and testing actions, Wallach argued, would provide the basis of conservation since "the recognition of transformations as quantity-conserving seems to be based on observing that they have no effect on the values of properties that indicate equality by sameness and inequality by difference brought about by any actions [p. 216]."

Although the presence of such indicator properties would violate the deductive criterion of paradigm Step 3, their presence certainly figures in Step 1 and provides the basis of the Step 1 judgments, *a fortiori*. An important research task is to discover the indicator properties and testing actions the children use.

Murray (1972) reported evidence from two studies which indicated that knowledge of these testing actions or "procedures for making things the same and different" was a critical feature which distinguished conservers from nonconservers. In one experiment 200 children's understanding of substance, weight, and volume was established from their responses to ten pairs of stimuli that varied in weight and volume. In each of nine conservation problems that followed (three transformations for each of three concepts—mass, weight, and volume) subjects were asked to select from six stimuli two that were equal with respect to the conservation concept under consideration and to explain how they had made the selection. They were then asked to think of ways to change the amount of substance (weight or the amount of space taken up) of the objects they had selected. The experimenter prompted the subject for additional ways until no more, if any, were given before he assessed conservation in the traditional manner.

In the second experiment after conservation of number, length, and weight were measured in the traditional manner, 57 subjects were asked if they could think of anything that could be done to both stimuli that would make them the same again. After the child had answered, various objects were presented and it was suggested by the experimenter that they might be of help in making the two objects equal once again. After the child had responded, the experimenter used the objects to perform actions that demonstrated or proved the equivalency of the conservation stimuli and asked the child if the action had produced equivalency with respect to the concept under consideration. In short, subjects were asked to produce, to recognize and acknowledge actions that demonstrated and proved the equality of two stimuli whose equality was in doubt.

In both studies conservation as usual was found to be positively and significantly associated with age, and as well the traditional horizontal decalages were found for the concepts investigated.

In the first experiment, those subjects in all grades who argued that the objects could be changed only by the addition and/or subtraction of material were invariably conservers and those who argued that other transformations would be effective were always nonconservers. Nonconservers for each concept at each grade level sometimes suggested only irrelevant transformations but generally suggested relevant and irrelevant transformations.

In the second experiment, the conservers could cite significantly more equivalency producing actions than the nonconservers could even with hints or by recognition of those the experimenter produced.

The data provided evidence for the hypothesis that the child's knowledge of the effects of various testing actions on the properties of objects is a necessary condition, but probably not a sufficient condition, for the conservation of the properties. Conservation under, for example, a shape transformation occurred only when subjects recognized that shape was an irrelevant variable, and believed that only the addition and/or subtraction of material could change substance, weight, or volume of the transformed object. The results of the second experiment further suggest that conservers differ from nonconservers in that they, the conservers, possess a repertoire of testing actions that can be performed on both objects. This allows the child to establish the equivalency of any two objects whose equivalency is in doubt. Still the relationship between this testing action repertoire and the conservation deduction is far from clear since the paradigm prohibits their use in Step 3 when the conservation judgment is called for.

Step 2 and the y and t factors.   The irrelevant attribute, y, and the transformation, t, are not easily dissociable since t is defined as an action which changes y but not x. As the critical relationships between x, y and t have not received much experimental investigation, we have little information about why the young child is seduced by some changes in attributes of A and B and not others. For example, Murray and Johnson (1975) have shown the nonconservers of weight from changes in a clay ball's shape, temperature, or texture, etc., conserve the weight of the clay ball when it is changed in other ways (e.g., its position).

Although it is the case that the x and y attributes are functionally independent, they are not uncorrelated. The exact relative frequencies of large heavy objects, small light objects, large light objects, and small heavy objects in the child's environment have not been determined, but if they were, the large–heavy and small–light frequencies would no doubt dominate the scatter plot and support the nonconservation inference. Zimmerman (1976) has observed in this connection that in randomly tossing sets of poker chips 80% of the time the more numerous sets fall in patterns that occupy more space than the less numerous sets. The clarification of the naturally occurring x and y frequencies could be served with Egon Brunswick's notion of ecological validity and the intraecological correlation (Hammond, 1966). The environmental correlations between size and weight, height and age, length, density and number, and so forth could be determined as Brunswick determined the correlations between proximal and distal cues or the correlations for the Gestalt organizational principles.

Whereas the magnitude of the correlations could be instructive and might clarify some of the time lag phenomena, the basis of the child's response to these various frequencies and imperfect regularities would still require explication. Some attractive hypotheses are that (1) the x-y link is essentially psychophysical, i.e., y is linked to x by a perceptual illusion (e.g., Braine & Shanks, 1965; Smedslund, 1963; Murray, 1968) or (2) the changing salience of various y attributes precludes or enhances the consideration of x at various times (Odom, 1978); and (3) that x-y link is semantic. The last hypothesis has considerable promise because it provides a basis for a theory of the conservation transformations.

Of all the transformations that can be performed on an object, why is it that some lead to nonconservation and some to conservation of some property of an object? Why do young children think, for example, that changing a ball's shape changes its weight, while changes in some other equally irrelevant characteristic of the ball do not affect their judgment of the ball's weight? There is at present no theory of conservation transformations or explanation for what might be called the "transformation decalage" or the fact that the conservation of an object's properties is easier under some transformations than others. The thesis is that transformations based upon words that are connotations of the label for the x concept to be conserved will lead to nonconservation. Moreover, the stronger the connotative relationship between the label for the concept and the label for the transformation the more difficult it will be for the child to conserve that transformation. If the word or concept, *heavy*, connotes hard, rough, or strong, for example, then transformations that change an object's hardness, roughness, strength, etc., will be expected to be effective conservation of weight transformations. This was the case in the study by Nummedal and Murray (1969). The thesis was extended in Murray and Tyler (1978) over a wider variety of transformations that were based upon words that were connotatively and not connotatively related in varying degrees to the words, *heavy* and *light*. The measure of the strength of a connotation was simply the absolute magnitude of the factor loading of a word (or pair of words) on a semantic differential factor on which the adjective pair, heavy-light, was loaded. The notion was that adjective pairs that loaded significantly on the same factor on which "heavy-light" was loaded were connotatively related to weight and would serve, therefore, as the basis of effective conservation of weight transformations. Word pairs that were not significantly loaded on the factor or loaded on other factors should be unrelated to conservation and transformations upon them should not be seductive. These expectations were born out in significant positive correlations between the degree of nonconservation as measured by the number of nonconservers on each of 25 problems, and the degree of connotation to weight, as measured by the factor loadings of each of the 25 adjective pairs on the factor on which heavy-light loaded significantly. Correlations were insignificant between nonconversation and the factor loadings of the adjective pairs on factors on which heavy-light did not load significantly. These correlational results provide reasonable support for the thesis that effective transformations are connotatively related to the concept to be conserved. Also supported is the claim (Ervin-Tripp, & Foster, 1960) that young children accept the connotation as a denotation.

These findings have been replicated and extended in Murray and Markessini (unpublished manuscript). In this study a children's measure of connotation and denotation was developed based upon the notion that the attributes a concept or word denotes are always connected to it while the connotative attributes of the concept are only sometimes connected to it. Thus children were asked whether "heavy" (light) things are always (sometimes) strong (weak, big, small, tall, short, rough, smooth, etc.) and their responses compared to whether they conserved the weight of objects which were transformed and made stronger (weaker, bigger, smaller, etc.). Moreover, following the reasoning of Saltz and Hamilton (1968), it was expected that the child would fail to conserve the weight of an object if a transformation changed an attribute of the object the child had accepted as denotation of "heavy" or "light" even though the attribute might be only a connotation of weight for an adult.

By and large this expectation was confirmed. It was also found that the direction of nonconservation (i.e., whether the transformation made the object heavier or lighter) was related to whether the adjective which labeled the transformation was marked or unmarked. Transformations labeled by unmarked adjectives were judged to make the object heavier while marked adjective transformations made the object lighter. As "heavy" is an unmarked adjective and "light" is a marked adjective, these results have a certain coherence and permit predictions of the directionality of nonconservation from semantic marking.

The semantic roots of the transformations were also portrayed in Murray (1970) which employed a purely semantic transformation. When a clay ball was labeled smaller (as it was when it was next to a large ball), it was judged to have become lighter in weight, and when it was labeled larger (as it was when it was next to a small ball) it was judged to have become heavier.

Finally, in addition to the matter of double transformations which has been treated, some attention might profitably be given to determining the strength of the transformation. Although the outcome of manipulations of the strength of the transformation on conservation is equivocal (see Miller, 1978), most studies find in balance that the nontransitional conservation judgment is an "all or none" judgment quite independent of the strength of contrary perception generated by the change in y (e.g., Murray, 1967). Setting aside its influences on conservation, the effects of the strength of the transformation upon nonconservation is a relatively unexamined question and can be treated by adding an ordinal question to the paradigm. Instead of simply determining that the child thinks the transformed object is simply heavier, the question of "how much heavier" could be raised with the child. The child's responses to such ordinal questions may shift our understanding of the transformations and their links to the x and y attributes from a nominal to an ordinal scale.

Step 3 Paradigm Factors. The nonstructural features in Step 3 of the paradigm center on the manner in which Q1, the conservation question, is asked. The literature on the various question formats, synonyms, word orders, etc. have been reviewed recently by Siegel (1978) and need not be treated further here except to comment that some nonverbal measures of Q1 result in assessments that are identical with the verbal forms of Q1 (Murray, 1970) while others are more demanding than the verbal measures. Although conservation assessment is sensitive in yet unexplained ways to variations in Q1, it cannot be claimed that nonconservation is merely a linguistic artifact which reflects only the child's misunderstanding of the question.

Step 4 Paradigm Factors. The principal issue in Step 4 is the criterion for acceptability of the supporting reasons for the conservation judgment. It is worthwhile to examine the adequacy of the traditional conservation reasons in some detail.

Like the items on an IQ test, the conservation task is simply one of many tasks that could be used to assess the status of the child's reasoning competence. Its significance in Piaget's theory is little more than any diagnostic device's significance, although educators may view the child's success on the task itself as an important curricular accomplishment. Because the child's "yes or no" judgment of whether two objects have remained the same in some respect after one of them was transformed in another respect is likely to be unduly influenced by guessing, etc., and because such a simple "yes-no" response tells us little of the child's basis for the judgment, researchers have tried to probe the child's reasoning competence more directly by having the child explain and justify his conservation or nonconservation judgment. The attendant false positive and negative risks in this probe are that the child's response may be uninterpretable or the child may be unaware of or be unable to articulate the basis of his correct or wrong opinion. The criteria for what constitutes a good, or even correct, reason from children are often misunderstood by researchers in the field. For example, the traditionally accepted good reasons, e.g., identity and reversibility by cancellation and reciprocity, are inadequate and in some cases totally irrelevant to the conservation deduction and an understanding of the concept in question.

Some researchers, like Brainerd (1973), have argued that the child's reasons for his conservation judgment should not be sought at all on the theoretical grounds that language cannot provide an adequate access to operativity anyway since we always know more than we can tell. Others, like Tuddenham (1970), have argued more practically that scoring conservation reasons "entails a degree of subjectivity in classifying responses and almost forces resumption of the *method clinique* to classify obscure or incomplete explanations by the subject [p. 53]." Most researchers have followed Piaget's (1960a) initial practice and sought reasons for the judgment and found not surprisingly that a significant number of children who were correct in their judgment cannot support that judgment with a reason the researcher finds acceptable (Gruen, 1966). Some attempts to standardize operativity assessment procedures have required reasons (Goldschmid & Bentler, 1968) while others have not (Tuddenham, 1970).

An evaluation of what might constitute an adequate reason entails an analysis of the conservation paradigm itself to determine what kinds of information and competence the child must employ to solve the conservation task correctly. Such an analysis will reveal what reasons or pieces of information in fact support a correct judgment.

As Piaget (1971, p. 32) has noted, the conservation problem is contaminated by a mixture of logical and physical principles in the sense that the physical manipulations which furnish the content of the task are insufficient to impose necessity. A critical premise in the conservation deduction depends upon having the appropriate information about the properties of the conservation material. To conserve, that is to conclude that the clay pancake equals the clay ball in weight, for example, the child must know these two premise relationships between the objects:

1. $A_{xy} = B_{xy}$ (object A equals object B with respect to x and y where x is weight and y is shape).
2. $B_{xy} = B'_{xy'}$ (object B equals the transformed object B' with respect to x but not y).

From these, as we have already noted, he can conclude the conservation judgment, $A_{xy} = B'_{xy'}$, by the general principle of the transitivity of quantitative relationships. What should constitute an adequate reason or justification for this conservation conclusion? An acknowledgment of the necessity of the conclusion would be appropriate along with a statement of the source of the child's knowledge that $B_{xy} = B'_{xy'}$.

The knowledge that $B'_{xy'}$ can be directly (by reversibility) or indirectly (by reciprocity) converted to B_{xy} does not imply or require that B_{xy} equal $B'_{xy'}$. That A_{xy} can be transformed to $A'_{xy'}$ such that $A'_{xy'} = B'_{xy'}$ (by identical action) could not provide the information that $B_{xy} = B'_{xy'}$ either or lead to the conservation conclusion in its place. The knowledge (identity) that nothing was added to or subtracted from B also does not provide the information. In fact all these reasons—reversibility, reciprocity, identical action, and identity—together or separately do not logically entail the second premise, $B_{xy} = B'_{xy'}$, of the conservation argument. Yet *all* of these reasons are routinely given by conservers in support of conservation judgments and *all* are readily acknowledged by nonconservers as well. For more than 30 years the Genevans have known that nonconservers may be aware of one or another of the traditional reasons and have insisted that "the only legitimate answer" (Inhelder, Sinclair & Bovet, 1974, p. 21; Piaget, 1960a, p. 141; Piaget & Inhelder, 1969, p. 99) to the conservation problem is a child's justification that cites *all* the reasons—identity, reversibility, and reciprocity—as they are interdependent, each entailing the other.

Nummedal (1969) found that nonconservers of substance, weight, and volume were indeed aware not just of one of the reasons, but all of them. What distinguished the conservers and nonconservers was not knowledge of all these operativity reasons but the fact that the conservers thought that the only way to change substance, weight, or volume was to add or subtract matter, whereas nonconservers, who also knew this, did not think it was the only way to change the quantities in question. Moreover, Murray and Hufnagel (unpublished manuscript) have found that college students do not give, even when prompted, *all* the classical reasons in support of their conservation judgments. Reversibility and reciprocity reasons rarely were cited while identity or a statement of the irrelevancy of the transformation was cited unanimously.

Consider a clay ball conservation of weight task in which the transformation is x-raying instead of flattening. In the evaluation of whether the x-rayed ball equals the un-x-rayed ball, of what use is the information that (1) no clay was added to or subtracted from the x-rayed ball; or (2) the x-rayed ball could be de-x-rayed somehow (reversibility); or (3) the x-ray effects could be neutralized by a y-ray (reciprocity) or that the x-ray was composed of two rays in which an increase in one always resulted in a decrease in the other (reciprocity)? None of this information generates the critical information that x-rays do not alter the weight of clay balls. Strictly speaking it is irrelevant to the conservation problem.

That the traditional conservation reasons form, severally or as a whole, an inadequate, even irrelevant, basis for the conservation judgment may not be the problem for genetic epistemology it appears to be, even though it leaves some aspects of the origins of conservation in doubt. Operational thought, it has been claimed, drives and governs the experimental and other search procedures by which the child discovers the information required in the conservation conclusion and invents the transitivity rule which makes the conclusion necessary. These arguments for the inadequacy of the traditional conservation judgments, sound as they may be, shed no light on the fact that young conservers cite them and use them to instruct nonconservers in conservation (Murray, 1972). Moreover, the same college students who themselves do not cite reversibility reasons as support for their conservation response, do cite it as an instructional principle and demonstration they would use with a nonconserving pupil (Murray & Hufnagel, unpublished manuscript). In this sense this empirical "reversibility" action could fulfill the criterion of a testing action which can be performed on A_{xy} and B'_{xy}, and yield identical indicator properties in A_{xy} and B_{xy}. This would only be the case if the particular inverse of the transformation was one of the set of testing actions.

Step 5 and Necessity.   Rarely is a direct assessment of necessity made although the critical distinction between genuine and pseudo conservation is that the former has the force of a logical necessity while the latter does not. However, the direct assessment of necessity is complicated by the fact that while logical deductions always follow from the prior events, could not be otherwise given the prior events, etc., nonlogical physical laws have many of these same properties. The recognition of physical uniformity and universality is not to be confused with necessity. None of the physical laws are necessary since the universe could be otherwise than it is, whereas when A = C the relationship between A and B and B and C could not be other than what it is.

No doubt the Genevans have avoided direct probes of necessity in the conservation task because the assessment of operativity in its place guarantees the criterial necessity. Nevertheless, an assessment of the child's feelings of necessity can only strengthen the claim that conservation is a manifestation of an operational system of necessary relations even though the problem itself has nonlogical components.

Step 6 Criteria.   The criteria of durability, transfer, counter training (or extinction), and trainability, like all experimental criteria, fulfill certain implicit and explicit theoretical requirements. Like all criteria they also are somewhat arbitrary (e.g., how long does something need to be remembered before we say it was learned?). The durability, counter suggestion-extinction and training criteria are all indirect criteria for necessity because the feeling of necessity, like Calvinistic grace, is permanent and unmodifiable. Thus, the genuine conservation judgment should, once acquired, last indefinitely and should be fairly resistant to contrary empirical evidence. The data from extinction attempts are equivocal with some showing 100% regression to nonconservation after an initial conservation judgment (e.g., Smedslund, 1961; Kingsley & Hall, 1967), others considerably less (e.g., Brison 1966; Murray, Ames, & Botvin, 1975). The authenticity of these regressions is questionable, because the child's interpretation of the extinction task is not clear (Smedslund, 1969) and the procedure has some methodological shortcomings (Miller, 1976). Robert and Charbonneau (1978) conclude that in some circumstances (viz. modeled nonconservation) the yielding children alter only their public response in reaction to social pressure while they maintain conservation privately. Murray, Ames, and Botvin (1978) found absolutely no extinction effects in "natural" and newly trained conservers with a most demanding extinction procedure. The procedure capitalized on the cognitive conflict generated when a child pretends to believe the opposite of what he truly believes. Whereas the procedure was extremely effective in inducing conservation in nonconservers, it utterly failed to influence the conservation judgments of any conservers, either those trained or those who conserved from the start.

The trainability criterion refers to the possibility that as with conservation, there may be circumstances in which nonconservation is not genuine and that true operational competence may be masked by certain performance factors. Thus if genuine conservation should not be easily modifiable by extinction training, pseudo-nonconservation should be. Very quick effortless training of conservation would indicate that the nonconservation was not genuine and that the apparently nonconserving child, adult, or old person was in fact competent to conserve, even though they failed to in the original assessment of their conservation status.

The transfer criteria are more difficult to justify since they have no clear relationship to necessity. Although it is expected that firmly held ideas, like genuine conservation, would transfer positively and widely, the existence of the time lags attributable to x, y, and material factors cloud our expectations of specific and nonspecific transfer. The defining point of the concrete operational stage is that the logical operations are not applied uniformly across all possible x, y, and A-B factors. Thus the failure to find generalization cannot invalidate the claim of genuine conservation in the specifically assessed domain. The degree of transfer to other tasks that should be expected to establish a particular conservation judgment as genuine is much more an empirical rather than a theoretical question.

The $P_a \times P_b{}^{(1-k)}$ Summary Model.   Flavell and Wohlwill (1969) have presented a model which can be used to summarize and integrate the factors presented so far. They argue that the probability of a person conserving (P) is a function of three factors: (1) the probability (P_a) that the requisite competence has been developed and is functional; (2) the probability (P_b) that the competence will function in the specific task; and (3) an individual difference constant (k), an exponent of P_b, which weights it to reflect the degree to which the relevant features of the task will be processed. They suggest the relationship between the variables is multiplicative, viz. $P = P_a \times P_b^{(1-k)}$, and that each varies between 0 and 1. The mathematics of the relationships requires that as k approaches 1 the subject will attend to, remember, etc. all the relevant task variables since $P_b^{(1-k)}$ is 1. Performance then will be controlled by the competence factors. When $P_b^{(1-k)}$ is less than one, performance is always less than the competence probability. Although this model doesn't explain performance, it suggests that the interaction between the competence and nonstructural factors controls the child's performance.

In this chapter the P_a factors were the child's capacity to acknowledge the premises presented in the experimental procedure, supply two other premises, and deduce the conservation or nonconservation conclusion. The k factors were catalogued as subject characteristics, and the P_b factors were discussed as the nonstructural aspects of the conservation task.

The link between x and y and the source of premise $B_{xy} = B'_{xy}$. Although the basis of the x, y, t relationship has been cast as an environmental correlation, as a psychophysical illusion, or as a semantic connotation, the critical aspects of the relationship can be clarified quite apart from these sources. The effects of t on y are not uniform since y must be thought of as a set of at least two components $y_1, y_2, \ldots y_n$, which t invariably affects in different ways, usually increasing some while decreasing others. Shape, a typical y attribute, is composed minimally of height (y_1), width (y_2), depth (y_3) and the t which changes shape must influence each y differently. The relationships between y_1, y_2 and y_3 are constrained by the material (A and B) and the x attributes. Similarly, changes in the x attribute are constrained by the values of y within A and B. Table 10.1 presents a summary of the constraints on the relationships for a given A or B of x and the y's. Thus in line 1, increases in y_1 and y_2 require increases in x where y_1 and y_2 are the height and width of a jar and x the amount of liquid in the full jar. When y_1 and y_2 increase x *must* increase. Or in a number conservation task where y_1 is the length of a row of objects, y_2 is the density of the row and x the number of objects, an increase in y_1 and y_2 mandates an increase in x. Similarly in a length conservation task in which y_1 is the stick's left alignment and y_2 is the right alignment, an increase in both, i.e. shifts to the left and right, can only happen if x, the length of the stick, increases. The entries in Table 10.1 for any task reveal that the following changes in y_1 and y_2, viz. both increase, both decrease, only one increases or decreases, require that x must increase or decrease. There are necessary relationships between these changes in x, y_1, y_2, etc., such that changes in y_1 and y_2 signify that x was changed also. However, when y_1 increases and y_2 decreases or y_1 decreases and y_2 increases (lines 3 and

TABLE 10.1
Necessary Relationships Between Values of y_1, y_2 and x

Transformations of y Attribute		Changes in x from changes in y_1 and y_2[1]
1.	$+ (y_1)$ $+ (y_2)$	x must be increased $(+)$
2.	$- (y_1)$ $- (y_2)$	x must be decreased $(-)$
3.	$+ (y_1)$ $- (y_2)$	x may be increased, decreased, or remain unchanged $(+, -, 0)$
4.	$- (y_1)$ $+ (y_2)$	x may be increased, decreased, or remain unchanged $(+, -, 0)$
5.	$0 (y_1)$ $0 (y_2)$	x must remain unchanged (0)
6.	$+ (y_1)$ $0 (y_2)$	x must be increased $(+)$
7.	$- (y_1)$ $0 (y_2)$	x must be decreased $(-)$
8.	$0 (y_1)$ $+ (y_2)$	x must be increased $(+)$
9.	$0 (y_1)$ $- (y_2)$	x must be decreased $(-)$

[1]If y_1 and y_2 were increased, this could not be done without increasing x in line 1; or in line 6 if only y_1 were increased, x would need to be increased, etc. For conservation of liquid amount changes y_1 and y_2 might be changes in heighth and width; in conservation of number changes in y_1 and y_2 could be changes in row length and density; in conservation of length changes in y_1 and y_2 could be changes in right and left alignment with the standard, with $+ (y_1)$, for example, being a shift of the left end to the left, $- (y_1)$ a shift in it to the right, and with y_2 being a shift in the right end of the stick to the right $(+)$ or left $(-)$.

4), no changes in x are required although they could occur. These are the conservation task conditions, and it is apparent that no one need conclude x was unchanged since x could also be more or less under these changes in y. The application of some testing action could determine whether the increases and decreases in y_1 and y_2 exactly compensated each other and in the event they did, x would have to remain unchanged. However, as the testing action or measurement is prohibited by the conservation paradigm, the judgment that x had to remain unchanged must be based upon some knowledge about x since observations about y_1 and y_2 do not guarantee that x was unchanged but permit only the possibility that it was unchanged. How that possibility becomes a necessity is the heart of the conservation problem. How can the child eliminate the other possibilities that x increased or decreased and guarantee the necessity of the third alternative?

If the child knew that the transformation (t) was not among the ways to change x, then x could be fixed as unchanged. However, this determination obviously could be made quite apart from the child's observations about y_1 and y_2. Conservation in that case would be unrelated to any information the child

TABLE 10.2
The Group Structure of the Necessary
Relationships Between the Increase
(+), Decrease (−), Constancy (0)
Values of the y_1, y_2, and x Attributes
of the Conservation Materials

y_2	y_2 Attribute		
Attribute	+ (y_1)	− (y_1)	0 (y_1)
+ (y_2)	+ (x)	0 (x)	+ (x)
− (y_2)	0 (x)	− (x)	− (x)
0 (y_2)	+ (x)	− (x)	0 (x)

might have about y_1 or y_2. The child could conserve simply by ignoring y, or learning to ignore y, and conclude quite sensibly that x must be unchanged and equal to itself if nothing was done to change it. The conserver may deduce this conclusion from what he knows about x and t or upon the integration of that with the implications of the changes in y_1 and y_2, but he need not. The Genevans claim, nevertheless, that he does and that operational thought is manifested in conservation only when it is based upon the coordination of the y_1, y_2, and x. The Genevan evidence from the correspondences (Piaget and Szeminska, 1952; Piaget, 1978), particularly the third stage operational correspondences, suggests that the child can generate the conservation equivalence solely from the considerations of y_1 and y_2. Be that as it may, when +(y) and −(y) are connected with no change in x (0 x), the variables y_1, y_2 and x form a mathematical group (Table 10.2) of the nine relationships shown in Table 10.2, viz. + − 0. The increases (+), decreases (−), constancies (0) of the values x, y_1, y_2 fulfill the group properties viz. closure, inversion, identity, associativity. Whether the possibility of such a group structure when 0(x) is uniquely determined for changes in y_1 and y_2, produces that determination, or whether that determination creates the possibility of the group structure is not at all clear. Nor is it clear whether the operations which compare −(y) and +(y) with respect to x create the possibility of 0(x) and the elimination of +(x) and −(x) or vice versa.

Educational implications. The nature of the educational implications of any theory, or part of a theory as is the case with conservation, is quite complex. At the highest criterion level, theoretical implications are those that can be deduced formally from the theory which means that their failure as educational practices would invalidate the theory. Few psychological theories are stated with the precision needed to construct formal deductions in any case, and perhaps for this reason there are no statements of educational recommendations derivable from any conservation theory (Piaget's in particular) which would invalidate that theory if they were proved false by empirical failure (see Murray, 1980, for an elaboration of this claim).

Because it does not seem possible at the present time to ground the statements of educational implications in formal deductive links to theory, a lower level criterion for an implication might be that it at least be compatible with the theory in the sense that it not be specifically proscribed by it. Of course the same educational practice may be equally compatible with different theories as is the case, for example, with Montessori practices which are compatible with Piagetian theory, operant theory, and naturally Montessori theory.

By this weaker compatibility criterion the broader implications of Piagetian theory of intellectual development are, not surprisingly, that schooling should simulate natural human development by linking the instructional practices to the natural mechanisms of intellectual development. More precisely, good schools are those which place a high premium upon self-initiated and self-regulated "discovery" activities in situations which require social interactions which expose the pupil to slightly higher stages of functioning than his present stage and provide cognitive conflict provoking activities which focus upon the anomalies and inconsistencies in the pupil's thinking. The good curriculum places a higher premium on thinking and the knowledge of necessary relationships than on learning information and skills. Although these foregoing statements are compatible with the theory, they provide precious little guidance to the educator.

Regrettably, the implications from the conservation theories provide only slightly more guidance and more only because of their specificity rather than the theoretical links. They occur in three categories—assessment, curriculum design, and instruction.

Assessment. The conservation paradigm, as has been noted, provides a procedure for the assessment of the pupil's understanding of *any* concept that might be part of the curriculum. Moreover, the information on the relationships between the structural and nonstructural components of conservation tasks suggests that the pupil's understanding of concepts is likely to be stubbornly tied to idiosyncratic features of the exemplars of the concept.

Curriculum. There are no theoretical recommendations about curricular content, although the paradigm has generated substantial empirical information about specific curricular concepts and the "natural" difficulties children of various ages have in mastering them. There is also considerable evidence about the "natural" sequences and hierarchies in the child's grasp of these concepts which are not implications of any theory inasmuch as only post hoc explanations have been offered for these sequences. The paradigm can be applied to the construction of curriculum models for curricular concepts (see Johnson & Murray, 1970 and Murray & Johnson, 1975 for an example of a descriptive model for the concept of weight).

Instruction. The paradigm has been richest in its generation of instructional procedures. Between 1961 and 1978 over 150 research studies were published that were designed specifically to teach young children to conserve some x attribute. Quite apart from the theoretical reasons that motivated and legitimized the attention archival journals gave to the training of conservation, a number of precise teaching techniques were created and more importantly evaluated even if toward the end they added ever diminishing amounts of information of theoretical significance (e.g., Jeffrey, 1975).

A number of reviews of this training literature exist (viz. Beilin, 1971, 1977; Brainerd, 1973; Brainerd & Allen, 1971; Glaser & Resnick, 1972; Goldschmid, 1971; Peill, 1975; Strauss, 1972, 1974, 1975; Murray, 1978). There is no longer doubt that nonconservers can be taught to conserve, although there is the somewhat pessimistic result that training, even highly individualized training, is either successful with about half the nonconservers in the sample or only half the gains in conservation that could be made are made by the nonconservers, when the gains fulfill the more demanding durability, extinction, and specific transfer criteria of the paradigm. This result seems quite independent of teaching time, although it is often, but not always, constrained by the child's substage of development (see Murray, 1978).

By and large these procedures focus upon one or another of the factors in the paradigm, often violating some paradigm constraints to elicit the conservation judgment. They divide into procedures which assume nonconservation is due to a competence deficiency and those which assume it is due to a performance limitation. Competence theorists often use a fixed trials procedure while performance theorists who assume the competence is masked by a performance factor employ trials to criterion procedures. Some procedures are designed to strengthen the child's tendency to base his judgment solely on the changes or absence of changes in the attribute x by: (1) classical feedback (tangible or intangible) of the x based response; (2) lowering the saliency of the changes on the y attribute through fading, cue reduction, shaping, or screening; (3) providing a verbal algorithm to ignore y and attend to x. Other procedures have had the pupil separate the x and y factor combinations by: (1) classical discrimination and oddity training paradigms; or (2) the making of a previously acquired discrimination, an analogy or metaphor for the current task situation. Some merely attempt to reduce the processing load of the paradigm by providing external props and cues, retention insurances, familiar materials, a reduction in number of task elements, etc. Still others attempt to build competence through a simulation of the equilibration mechanisms the Genevans propose, by providing conflicts between the effects on x from changes in y_1, y_2 and x.

Others base the procedure upon imitation, cognitive dissonance, and social conflict paradigms and theories while some adhere to direct training upon one or another of the defining Piagetian features of an operation (viz. inversion and reciprocity) or a related operational member of the "structured whole" (e.g., seriation, classification).

All of the procedures can be shown sufficient within the limits cited for cognitive growth while none seem necessary for it. The success of any one relative to another, however, provides no guarantee that it more closely models the "natural" acquisition of a conservation than its inferior.

The generation of these various training strategies constitutes the chief instructional legacy of the conservation paradigm and the various theories of the source of the child's nonconservation and conservation. The source of the critical premise $B_{xy} = B'_{xy'}$ supplied by the child remains unclear, and training procedures that focus solely upon the judgment $A_{xy} = B'_{xy'}$ are not likely to clarify the source, although they will provide the pupil with a correct response.

What remains is the development of a theory from which necessary and sufficient instructional strategies could be deduced. These presumably would provide the child not only with the correct response, but with the feeling and awareness of the necessity of it. The issues raised in the chapter mark how far our field is from such a theory and the need to conserve research on topic.

REFERENCES

Asch, S., & Nerlove, H. The development of double function terms. In B. Kaplan and S. Wapner (Eds.), *Perspectives in Psychological Theory: Essays in Honor of Heiz Werner*. N.Y.: International University Press, 1960, 47-60.

Beilin, H. The training and acquisition of logical operations. In Rosskopf et al. (Eds.), *Piagetian Cognitive-Development Research and Mathematical Education*, Washington, D.C.: National Council of Teachers of Mathematics, Inc., 1971.

Beilin, H. Inducing conservation through training. In G. Steiner (Ed.), *Psychology of 20th Century, Piaget and Beyond*, Vol. 7. Bern: Kinder, 1977.

Berzonsky, M. D. Interdependence of Inhelder and Piaget's model of logical thinking. *Developmental Psychology*, 1971, *4*(3), 469-476.

Bever, T., Mehler, J. & Epstein, J. What children do in spite of what they know. *Science*, 1968, *162*, 921-924.

Braine, M. D. S., & Shanks B. The development of the conservation of size. *Journal of Verbal Learning and Verbal Behavior*, 1965, *4*, 227-242.

Brainerd, C. J. Neo-Piagetian training experiments revisited: Is there any support for the cognitive-developmental stage hypothesis? *Cognition*, 1973, *2*, 349-370.

Brainerd, C. J., & Allen, T. Experimental inducements of the conservation of first order quantitative invariants. *Psychological Bulletin*, 1971, *75*, 128-44.

Brison, D. W. Acceleration of conservation of substance. *Journal of Genetic Psychology*, 1966, *109*, 311-322.

Brown, A. Conservation of number and continuous quantity in normal, bright, and retarded children. *Child Development*, 1973, *44*, 376-379.

Bryant, P. *Perception and understanding in young children*. N.Y.: Basic Books, 1974.

Burnett, J., & Kroger, J. Conservation and stimulus mode. *New Zealand Journal of Educational Studies*, 1974, *9*, 134-138.

Cornelius, S. W. et al. *Structural equation analysis of a neo-Piagetian causal model: relationships among performance variables, concrete operations, and social inferential reasoning.* Paper presented at the Fifth Biennial Southeastern Conference on Human Development, Atlanta, Georgia, April 1978.

Curcio, F., Robbins, O., & Ela, S. S. The role of body parts and readiness in acquisition of number conservation. *Child Development*, 1971, *42* 1641-1646.

DeVries, R. *Relationships among Piagetian, achievement, and intelligence assessments.* Paper presented at the annual meeting of the American Educational Research Association, New Orleans, March 1973.

Dihoff, R. E. *Multidimensional scaling of Piagetian task performance* (Technical Report No. 316). Madison, Wisconsin: The University of Wisconsin, Wisconsin Research and Development Center for Cognitive Learning, February 1975.

Elkind, D. Children's discovery of the conservation of mass, weight, and volume: Piaget replication study II. *Journal of Genetic Psychology*, 1961, *87*, 219-227.

Elkind, D. Piaget's conservation problem. *Child Development*, 1967, *38*, 15-27.

Ervin-Tripp, S. H., & Foster, G. The development of meaning in children's descriptive terms. *Journal of Abnormal and Social Psychology*, 1960, *61*, 271-275.

Flavell, J. *The developmental psychology of Jean Piaget*. New York: Von Nostrand, 1963.

Flavell, J. *Cognitive Development*. Englewood Cliffs, N.J.: Prentice Hall, 1977.

Flavell, J., & Wohlwill, J. Formal and functional aspects of cognitive development. In D. Elkind & J. Flavell (Eds.), *Studies in Cognitive Growth: Essays in Honor of Jean Piaget*. N.Y.: Oxford University Press, 1969.

Fleck, J. Note on the concept assessment kit—conservation. *Psychological Reports*, 1972, *31*, 118.

Frank, F., Oliver, R., & Greenfield, P. In J. S. Bruner (Eds.), *Studies in Cognitive Growth*. New York: Wiley, 1966.

Gelman, R. S. Conservation acquisition: A problem of learning to attend to relevant attributes. *Journal of Experimental Child Psychology*, 1969, *7*, 167-187.

Gelman, R. S., & Gallistel, C. *The child's understanding of number*. Cambridge, Mass.: Harvard University Press, 1978.

Glaser, R., & Resnick, L. B. Instructional psychology. In P. H. Mussen & M. Rosenweig (Eds.), *Annual review of psychology*. Palo Alto, Calif.: Annual Reviews, 1972.

Goldschmid, M. The role of experience in the rate and sequence of cognitive development. In D. R. Green, M. Ford, & G. Flammer (Eds.), *Measurement and Piaget*. New York: McGraw-Hill, 1971.

Goldschmid, M., & Bentler, P. *Conservation assessment kit manual*. San Diego: Educational and Industrial Testing Service, 1968.

Gruber, H. E., & Voneche, J. (Eds.). *The Essential Piaget*. New York: Basic Books, 1977.

Gruen, G. E. Note on conservation: Methodological and definitional considerations. *Child Development*, 1966, *37*, 977-984.

Hamel, B., Remmo, B. R., & van der Veer, M. A. A. Structure d'ensemble, multiple classification, multiple seriation and amount of irrelevant information. *The British Journal of Educational Psychology*, 1972, *42*, 319-325.

Hammond, K. Probabilistic functionalism: Egon Brunswick's integration of the history, theory and method of psychology. In K. Hammond (Ed.), *The psychology of Egon Brunswick*. New York: Holt, Rinehart & Winston, Inc., 1966.

Hathaway, W. E., Jr. *The degree and nature of the relations between traditional psychometric and Piagetian developmental measures of mental development*. Unpublished manuscript, 1972.

Hrybyk, M., & Murray, F. B. *Logic in nonconservation: an application of the INRC Group*. Paper presented before the Jean Piaget Society, Philadelphia, PA, May 1978.

Hufnagel, P., & Murray, F. B. *Children's "conservation" without understanding on an adult nonconservation problem*. Paper presented before the Jean Piaget Society, Philadelphia, PA, May 1978.

Inhelder, B. *The diagnosis of reasoning in the mentally retarded*. New York: Intext, 1968.

Inhelder, B., Sinclair, H., & Bovet, M. *Learning and the development of cognition*. Cambridge, Mass.: Harvard University Press, 1974.

Jamison, W. Developmental inter-relationships among concrete operational tasks: An investigation of Piaget's stage concept. *Journal of Experimental Child Psychology*, 1977, *24*, 235-253.

Jeffrey, W. Editorial. *Child Development*, 1975, *46*, 1-2.

Johnson, P. E., & Murray, F. B. A note on using curriculum models in analyzing the child's concept of weight. *Journal of Research in Science Teaching*, 1970, *7*, 377-381.

Kingsley, R. C., & Hall, V. C. Training conservation through the use of learning sets. *Child Development*, 1967, *38*, 1111-1126.

Macready, C., & Macready, G. Conservation of self, others, and objects. *Journal of Experimental Psychology*, 1974, *103*, 372-374.

Mehler, J., & Bever, T. Cognitive capacity of very young children. *Science*, 1967, *158*, 141-142.

Miller, P. Stimulus variables in conservation: An alternate approach to assessment. *Merrill-Palmer Quarterly*, 1978, *24*, 141-160.

Miller, S. A. Extinction of Piagetian concepts: An updating. *Merrill-Palmer Quarterly*, 1976, *22*, 257-281.

Montada, L. Personal communication, August 1972.

Murray, F. B. Conservation of illusion-distorted length and illusion strength. *Psychonomic Science*, 1967, *7*(2), 65-66.

Murray, F. B. Phenomenal-real discrimination and the conservation of illusion distorted length. *Canadian Journal of Psychology*, 1968, *22*(2), 114-121.

Murray, F. B. Conservation of mass, weight, and volume in self and object. *Psychological Reports*, 1969, *25*, 941-942.

Murray, F. B. Verbal and nonverbal measures of conservation of illusion-distorted length. *Journal for Research in Mathematics Education*, 1970, *1*, 9-15.

Murray, F. B. The acquisition of conservation through social interaction. *Developmental Psychology*, 1972, *6*, 1-6. (a)

Murray, F. B. *Conservation and knowledge of relevant transformations*. Paper presented before the Eastern Psychological Association, New York, April 1972. (b)

Murray, F. B. Teaching strategies and conservation training. In A. M. Lesgold, J. W. Pellegrino, S. Fokkema, & R. Glaser, (Eds.), *Cognitive Psychology and Instruction*. New York: Plenum, 1978, 419-428.

Murray, F. B. The generation of educational practice from developmental theory. In S. Modgil (Ed.), *Toward a Theory of Psychological Development Within the Piagetian Framework. NFER*, 1980.

Murray, F. B., & Armstrong, S. Necessity in conservation and nonconservation. *Developmental Psychology*, 1976, *12*, 483-484.

Murray, F. B., & Armstrong, S. Adult nonconservation of numerical equivalence. *Merrill-Palmer Quarterly*, 1978, *24*(4), 255-263.

Murray, F. B., Ames, G., & Botvin, G. The acquisition of conservation through cognitive dissonance. *Journal of Educational Psychology*, 1977, *69*(5), 519-527.

Murray, F. B., & Holm, J. *The absence of lag in the child's conservation of discontinuous and continuous materials.* Paper presented before the American Educational Research Association, Washington, D.C., April 1975.

Murray, F. B., & Hufnagel, P. *Adults' conservation reason.* Unpublished manuscript.

Murray, F. B., & Johnson, P. E. Relevant and some irrelevant factors in the child's concept of weight. *Journal of Educational Psychology*, 1975, *67*, 705-711.

Murray, F. B., & Markessini, J. *A Semantic interpretation of the child's failure to conserve concepts.* Unpublished manuscript.

Murray, F. B., & Tyler, S. J. Semantic characteristics of the conservation transformation. *Psychological Reports*, 1978, *42*, 1051-1054.

Nummedal, S. *The existence of the substance-weight-volume decalage.* Unpublished doctoral dissertation. University of Minnesota, Minneapolis, 1970.

Nummedal, S., & Murray, F. Conservation and connotative-denotative meaning. *Psychonomic Science*, 1969, *16*(6), 323-324.

Odom, R. A perceptual-salience account of decalage relations and developmental change. In L. Siegel & C. Brainerd (Eds.), *Alternatives to Piaget*, N.Y.: Wiley, 1978.

Osherson, D. *Logical Abilities in Children*, Vol. 1 & 2. Hillsdale, N.J.: Lawrence Erlbaum Associates, 1974.

Peill, E. J. *Invention and discovery of reality: The acquisition of conservation of amount.* New York: Wiley, 1975.

Peisach, E., & Hardeman, M. The role of atomism in the development of conservation. *Journal of Genetic Psychology,* 1975, *126,* 217-225.

Piaget, J., & Szeminska, A. *The child's conception of number.* London: Routledge & Kegan Paul, 1952.

Piaget, J. *Psychology of intelligence.* Patterson, N.J.: Littlefield, Adam, & Co., 1960. (a) (First published in 1947.)

Piaget, J. *Logic and psychology.* New York: Basic Books, 1960. (b)

Piaget, J. Cognitions and conservations: Two views. *Contemporary Psychology,* 1967, *12,* 532-533.

Piaget, J. *On the concept of memory and identity.* Barre, Mass.: Clark University Press, 1968.

Piaget, J. The theory of stages in cognitive development. In D. Green, M. Ford, & G. Flammer (Eds.), *Measurement and Piaget.* New York: McGraw-Hill, 1971.

Piaget, J. Correspondences and transformations. In F. B. Murray (Ed.), *The Impact of Piagetian Theory.* Baltimore: University Park Press, 1978.

Piaget, J., & Inhelder, B. *The psychology of the child.* New York: Basic Books, 1969.

Pinard, A., & Laurandeau, M. "Stage" in Piaget's cognitive-developmental theory: Exegesis of a concept. In D. Elkind & J. Flavell (Eds.), *Studies in cognitive growth: Essays in honor of Jean Piaget.* New York: Oxford University Press, 1969.

Pratoomraj, S., & Johnson, R. Kinds of questions and types of conservation tasks as related to children's conservation responses. *Child Development,* 1966, *37,* 343-353.

Reese, H., & Overton, W. Models and theories of development. In L. R. Goulet, & P. Baltes (Eds.), *Life-span developmental psychology.* New York: Academic Press, 1970.

Robert, M., & Charbonneau, C. Extinction of liquid conservation by modeling: Three indicators of its artificiality. *Child Development,* 1978, *49,* 194-200.

Saltz, E., & Hamilton, H. Concept conservation under positively and negatively evaluated transformations. *Journal of Experimental Child Psychology,* 1968, *6,* 44-51.

Shantz, C., & Smock, C. Development of distance conservation and the spatial coordinate system. *Child Development,* 1966, *37,* 943-948.

Sheppard, J. L. A structural analysis of concrete operations. In Keats, J. A., Collis, K. F. and Halford, G. S. (Eds.), *Cognitive Development: Research Based on a Neo-Piagetian Approach.* N.Y.: John Wiley & Sons, 1978.

Siegel, L. The relationship of language and thought in the preoperational child: A reconsideration of non-verbal alternatives to Piagetian tasks. In L. Siegel and C. Brainerd (Eds.), *Alternatives to Piaget.* N.Y.: John Wiley, 1978.

Silverman, I., & Marsh, K. On the production of images within the conservation experiment. Paper presented at the meeting of the Society for Research in Child Development, Santa Monica, March 1969.

Smedslund, J. The acquisition of conservation of substance and weight in children: III. Extinction of conservation of weight acquired "normally" and by means of empirical controls on a balance. *Scandinavian Journal of Psychology,* 1961, *2,* 85-87.

Smedslund, J. Patterns of experience and the acquisition of conservation of length. *Scandinavian Journal of Psychology,* 1963, *4,* 257-264.

Smedslund, J. Psychological diagnostics. *Psychological Bulletin,* 1969, *71,* 237-248.

Stephens, B., McLaughlin, J. A., & Miller, C. K. Factorial structure of selected psychoeducational measures and Piagetian reasoning assessments. *Development Psychology,* 1972, *6,* 343-348.

Strauss, S. Inducing cognitive development and learning: A review of short-term training experiments. I. The organismic-developmental approach. *Cognition,* 1972, *1,* 329-357.

Strauss, S. A reply to Brainerd. *Cognition,* 1974/75, *3,* 155-185.

Toussaint, N. A. An analysis of synchrony between concrete-operational tasks in terms of structural and performance demands. *Child Development,* 1974, *45,* 992-1001.

Tuddenham, R. A. "Piagetian" test of cognitive development. In W. B. Dockrell (Ed.), *On Intelligence*. London: Methuen & Co., Ltd., 1970.

Uzgiris, I. C. Situational generality of conservation. *Child Development*, 1964, *35*, 831–841.

Wallach, L. On the bases of conservation. In D. Elkind & J. Flavell (Eds.), *Studies in Cognitive Growth: Essays in Honor of Jean Piaget*. New York: Oxford University Press, 1969.

Weinreb. N., & Brainerd, C. J. A developmental study of Piaget's Groupment Model of the Emergence of Speed and Time Concepts. *Child Development*, 1975, *46*, 176–185.

Winkelmann, W. *Factorial analysis of children's conservation task performance*. Paper presented at the meeting of the International Society for the Study of Behavioral Development, Ann Arbor, Michigan, August 1973.

Zimmerman, B. Personal communication, May 1976.

11 Confounding with Cognitive Style Factors: An Artifact Explanation for the Apparent Nonuniversal Incidence of Formal Operations[1]

Edith D. Neimark
Douglass College, Rutgers University

In the summer of 1973 when I reviewed all the evidence then available on formal operations thought and its development there were some disturbing signs that the theory was not supported by the evidence (Neimark, 1975a). In the intervening years additional evidence has accumulated, all pointing to the same conclusion. By far, the most damaging, and depressingly consistent, evidence concerns the nonuniversal attainment of the final-stage of adult thought (Blasi & Hoeffel, 1974). Even among college students, who, presumably, are selected for their ability at abstract thinking and who are expected to engage consistently in that activity, incidence of attainment of formal operations seems to be below 100% (e.g., Dulit, 1972; Neimark, 1975a, p. 577). Entire segments of the adult population of the world seem to perform at a much lower level than the modal college sophomore or to fail to evidence formal operations at all. Among groups in this category are the aged (Papalia, 1972), the less educated (Goodnow, 1962; Graves, 1972; Peluffo, 1962, 1967), members of other cultures—especially non-Western ones (Dasen, 1972)—, and, for some measures, women (e.g., Elkind, 1961, 1962; Leskow & Smock, 1970). Moreover, when task batteries are administered, obtained intercorrelations among formal operations tasks, while

---

[1]This is a modified version of a talk presented at the 7th annual meeting of the Piaget Society in Philadelphia, May 20, 1977. Since its delivery more relevant—and generally supporting—evidence has appeared. Although it is tempting to rewrite the paper in light of the later evidence, it would be improper to do so, especially in light of the fact that some of that evidence cites this manuscript. On the other hand, total omission of later evidence would be a disservice to the reader. My compromise has been to include references to later work without substantive revision in light of them. The literature on formal operations has been reviewed by Neimark (1975a, 1979); the relation of operational level and the cognitive style of field dependence has been reviewed by Huteau (1980).

generally positive and statistically significant, are not impressively high (e.g., Martorano, 1977). Thus, the bulk of the evidence strongly suggests that formal operational thought, as described by Piaget and assessed by the Inhelder tasks (Inhelder & Piaget, 1958), seems to constitute an optimal level of performance attained unevenly, if at all, by most adults and subject to loss with advancing age. Although that is a very disheartening empirical picture of the nature of adult thought, which on a priori grounds one should be loathe to accept as a basis for theory construction, there has been widespread acceptance of the data at face value.

One natural reaction to this evidence is to conclude that Piaget's theory is wrong and must be abandoned. Most critics who urge this course (e.g., Strauss & Kroy, 1977; Smedslund, 1977; Blasi & Hoeffel, 1974 for a recent sample) do not, however, offer a comparable alternative theory by way of replacement. The available alternatives are for the most part either cast at a level of ad hoc empiricism promising very little power or generality, or at so speculative a level as to be almost impervious to empirical test. In light of those alternatives one should be loathe to jettison in toto a theory which has been so productive of research and insights concerning the earlier stages of cognitive development. Another approach has been to take the data, and the procedures which produce them, at face value and to modify the theory to fit the evidence. This seems to be the course of action adopted by Piaget himself (Piaget, 1972) although it has some very disturbing implications for the ultimate status of any resulting theory of adult thought. How does one select among bits of rapidly accumulating evidence those which necessitate further revision as contrasted with those which may be attributed to chance or other lawfully determined sources of variability? i.e., where does the process of empirical adjustment end? It seems to me that there is a logical middle ground between the two extremes of summary rejection of or endless tinkering with the theory of formal operations; and I find it to be the most sensible and useful course of action for guiding future research. It is to retain the theory of formal operations as it now stands but to subject our methodology for testing and interpreting it to more searching critical scrutiny. Let us ask, in other words, whether the existing evidence does provide direct, appropriate, and unequivocal evidence concerning the nature of adult thought or whether it may be subject to some artifacts leading to bias or error.

AN ARTIFACT EXPLANATION

To better identify potential sources of bias let us first consider what it means to say that an individual "has formal operations." There is widespread agreement that formal operations is not a simple directly identifiable property like freckles, or even left-handedness. Rather, it is a presumed condition, or capacity, inferred from a variety of observations of performance. In the language which some of us used as graduate students in a bygone era, it has the status of an *intervening variable* (MacCorquodale & Meehl, 1948). Moreover, as is also well known, the class of independent variables which affect performance is not isomorphic with the class of independent variables determining competence. Or, to put it another way, although capacity or competence is assumed to be a major determinant of performance quality, it is by no means the sole determinant. There are a host of factors, differing in relative pervasiveness and importance, which may be operating to enhance or obscure underlying ability: some are situational, some are specific to the task or the conditions of its administration, others are specific to the individual or his momentary state, etc. One may do poorly on a test not only because of inherent stupidity, but also because one has not studied, or is distracted by unfavorable environmental conditions, or is temporarily indisposed, or because the questions are poorly worded, etc. (through the whole litany with which every instructor is well acquainted). Clearly, one may have the requisite ability but fail to manifest it for a great variety of reasons.

Before attempting to identify one or more specific sources of performance bias, let's indulge in a simple *gedanken* experiment to explore the general utility of an artifact, or performance bias, explanation. Let us assume that people differ in their readiness to apply maximum intellectual potential in a given situation. That seems like a very reasonable assumption. All of us know some individuals who ponder and analyze even when confronted with simple problems while still others of our acquaintance seize the first available option even in matters of great importance. To provide a useful handle on this aspect of individual differences, let's—by way of illustration—equate it with cognitive style as characterized on the familiar continuum of field dependence/independence. Specifically, let's assume that field independent individuals, because of their tendency to analyze a situation and disembed relevant aspects, are more likely to manifest formal operational thought than field dependent individuals whose approach is more global (for a systematic theoretical derivation of this prediction, see Pascual-Leone & Goodman, 1979). Bear in mind, we assume that the individuals are equivalent with respect to native ability (i.e., are fully formal operational) but differ only in readiness to manifest that ability: for tasks at an appropriate level of difficulty, the field independent individual is likely to perform at a formal operational level whereas the field dependent individual is not. Now, assume that we give such an appropriate task to a random sample of individuals drawn from a general population of normal (i.e., formal operational) adults. Roughly half of them should perform at a formal operational level (since field dependence/independence is defined in terms of a median split). For subjects sampled from special subgroups the observed proportion displaying formal operations should vary predictably depending upon the composition of the group: For groups known to have a high proportion of field-dependents, e.g., women, older persons, the less formally educated, and members of many non-Western cultures, the observed proportion performing at a formal operational level should fall between 0% and 50%. For known field independents, on the other hand, e.g., mathematicians, scientists, academically gifted adolescents, etc., the observed proportion of formal operators might well approach 100%. The predictions are also consonant with results of studies (e.g., Case, 1974; Scardamalia, 1977) in which high performance levels are obtained from subjects preselected for field independence. The predictions from our simple *gedanken* experiment are in sufficiently close correspondence with all the available evidence to encourage pursuit of an artifact explanation framed in terms of individual differences.

To make the *gedanken* experiment more credible it is necessary to establish two links in the chain of inference: first to show that performance on formal operations tasks is, indeed, related to cognitive style measures, and, second, to demonstrate that there is a feature common to all widely used tests of formal operations which evokes the operation of cognitive style differences. Once these two links are established, we can seriously entertain an artifact explanation and proceed to explore its implications for future research practice.

Cognitive style effects upon formal operations performance.   In view of the mountains of published material reporting correlation of some individual difference measure such as cognitive style to some other measure such as intellectual performance, one might reasonably expect that relevant evidence showing a clear link between, e.g., field dependence/independence and formal operations should be abundantly available. Surprisingly, it is not. Although Witkin and his associates (Witkin et al., 1973, 1974, 1976) maintain excellent comprehensive bibliographies of research on field dependence/independence, my search through this material yielded only three directly relevant studies which are readily available in the public domain (Lawson, 1976; Neimark, 1975b; Saarni, 1973) and three which are not (Pascual-Leone, 1969; Case, 1973; Pulos & Adi, 1977). These studies differ sufficiently with respect to index of cognitive style, measure of formal operations, index of relation, and subject populations to make direct comparison difficult. Nevertheless, all of them do report a statistically significant relation. Moreover, group comparison of frequency distributions of performance on a test of formal operations for field dependents, vs. field independents (Neimark, 1975b; Pulos & Adi, 1977) in two studies both reveal clear separation of the two distributions. Thus, although the relevant evidence is neither as abundant nor as consistent as one might wish, it is all in support of the assumed relation: field independent individuals are more likely to perform at a formal operational level than field dependent individuals of comparable intellectual ability. I am reasonably confident that more supporting evidence will be forthcoming. Until it is, the assumed relation does seem to be tentatively established.

Perhaps an anecdote will give the reader a better intuitive understanding for the approach of field dependent individuals to formal operations tasks. I had just prepared a group-administered water level test for my undergraduate class and decided to try it out on an unsuspecting colleague who wandered into my office. She started out confidently enough but became increasingly hesitant and uncertain until a glance at my amazed expression stopped her completely. "I'm doing something stupid, aren't I?" she asked. "I'm sure there is some simple general principle that applies here, but I don't know what it is. I've never thought about this before." As you might guess, the water levels she had drawn on the tilted bottles were not horizontal. Although other explanations have been offered for the performance of adult women on the water level task (Thomas, Jamison & Hummel, 1973) there is consistent and compelling evidence that drawing of water levels which deviate from horizontal is correlated with field dependence (Pascual-Leone, 1969; St. Jean, 1976). This colleague, despite her field-dependent style, is a distinguished classicist, a full professor, and a department chairperson; prolonged past acquaintance leaves me with no doubt whatsoever as to her status as a first-class formal operational thinker.

The role of ambiguous instructions in formal operations tasks. We come now to the problem of demonstrating that there is a factor common to most formal operations tasks which serves to maximize the presence of cognitive style variation. The most direct solution is provided not by a consideration of formal operations tasks but, rather, by a consideration of tests of cognitive style to find the necessary enstating condition common to all of them, regardless of the style in question. That defining property is a stimulus situation lacking in structure but rich in ambiguity. If one provides a situation rich in potential for a variety of alternative responses but without an obvious criterion for selection among them, individual variability will appear in abundance. By way of contrast, in a well-structured task situation where the behavior to be studied is almost dictated by the stimulus context, variation attributable to individual style differences is virtually eliminated: The subject either does or does not emit the behavior. Such a well-structured context constitutes the most appropriate test for assessment of competence.

Let us now consider the usual procedure for assessing formal operations in relation to optimal conditions for evoking cognitive style variation. To the extent that the most frequent criticism of Piaget's *methode clinique* is the absence of standardized procedures for scoring and administration of tasks, one is, of course, hard pressed to point to "a typical formal operations task." Instead, one can only characterize some vague modal norm for administration of the set of Inhelder experiments. Nevertheless, the major common property of that modal norm seems to be the use of unstructured tasks and ambiguous instructions. The subject is confronted with an array of stimulus materials and told to discover "how a balance works" (Inhelder & Piaget, 1958), "what makes a difference in bending," "what makes a difference in how fast the weights go back and forth," etc. There is not even consistency across experimenters within a given task (e.g., the pendulum task). The subject is provided with no explicit objective, no means of evaluating alternate routes to it, nor, even, a basis for knowing when or if it has been attained. If this reasoning is correct then one would expect to find that (1) formal operations tasks, as traditionally administered, assess individual differences in coping with ambiguity as much as intellectual competence per se; and (2) removal of ambiguity leads to a marked reduction in performance variability. An experiment directly supporting the second prediction is now available.

Danner and Day (1977) administered two tasks under traditional instructions: either the Inhelder bending of rods or the pendulum task, followed by the spinning wheel task (Case, 1974). After each of these tasks, they gave a graded series of prompts[2] (based on observed performance inadequacies) designed to provide progressively more structure and to assess the child's response to additional assistance. A third and final task (either pendulum or bending of rods, whichever had not been given first) was given only with the traditional unstructured instructions. Although all age groups showed improvement as a result of the prompting, very few fifth graders performed at a formal level on the final task whereas virtually all of the twelfth graders did so; a third group, of eighth graders, were inferior to the twelfth graders. On the other hand, a control group of twelfth graders who had not received the prompts showed no improvement on the third task relative to the first two. These findings, as well as scattered results from earlier training studies such as Fischbein, Pampu & Manzat, 1970, clearly show improved performance resulting from explicit structuring of the task—i.e., demonstration of competence—only at those ages where it would normally be expected.

Summary.   The purpose of this first section has been to demonstrate that the apparent nonuniversal incidence of formal operations might be explained by the operation of an artifact, such as an individual-difference factor, common to most available research which serves to confound and obscure evidence concerning intellectual competence per se. For the sake of argument that factor was initially coordinated with cognitive style as indexed by the field dependence/independence continuum. Obviously, other style factors, or some combination of them, might also serve this purpose. Some post hoc predictions concerning performance of specific subgroup samples were then derived and compared with existing data. Two necessary assumptions entailed by the hypothesized artifact explanation (correlation of measures of field dependence/independence with

---

[2]The prompts consisted of: a) asking S to identify any untested variable and to test it; b) providing a general rule of testing—the all else constant rule; c) stating the rule along with a demonstration; d) direct prompting to test each variable in turn according to the rule; e) showing S how to test each of the four variables according to the rule provided. Later research by Stone and Day (1978) showed specific details of the prompting procedures to be noncausal in differentiating those Ss who spontaneously perform at a formal operational level from those who do so only after prompting (the latent formal Ss). A subsequent study by Stone and Day (1980) showed that spontaneous formal operational subjects were more field independent (as assessed by WAIS blocks) than the latent formal subjects.

measures of formal operations, and the role of ambiguous instructions in evoking cognitive style factors) where then explored to further strengthen the credibility of the explanation.

Although data in support of the two assumptions are in the predicted direction, they constitute only piecemeal support. A direct test of the artifact explanation requires an experimental design in which formal operations tasks are administered in a factorial design varying cognitive style and degree of procedural ambiguity (possibly with mental age as an additional variable). Recent evidence (Linn, 1978; Huteau & Rajenbach, 1978; Pascual-Leone & Goodman, 1974) provides clear evidence of the predicted interaction of style and task variables. Pascual-Leone and Goodman (1974) demonstrate a task in which field dependent individuals excell field independents—a state of affairs comparable to that reported by Zelniker and Jeffrey (1976) for younger children and a different style index.

Having demonstrated that the proposed artifact explanation is tenable and worth experimental test, the remainder of this paper will be devoted to a preliminary exploration of its implications for (1) future research methodology in assessing formal operations competence; and (2) a theory of adult thought and its development.

IMPLICATIONS FOR FUTURE RESEARCH

Implications for research methodology. If, as suggested, existing measures of formal operations provide a biased measure of true competence because they are confounded with individual difference effects resulting from ambiguous instructions, then the solution is obvious: the sources of bias must be removed. Although the logic of the solution is obvious, the specific details of its implementation are not; there is no "how to" manual on creating appropriate tasks or procedures. In this instance, the general form of the solution has already been suggested: remove conditions which evoke individual variation and create a task designed to evoke competence. The form of the general solution I am suggesting derives from a psychometric strategy quite similar to that originally proposed by Binet for the assessment of intelligence: first establish a basal level and proceed from there. A basal level, in principle, is provided by the *least* demanding test of competence: does the skill exist at all? To determine if there are any conditions under which the skill occurs one generally starts with optimal conditions (i.e., those most likely to evoke the behavior). If the skill is manifest in this easy test one can then proceed to test the generality of its occurrence (i.e., is it widely used or situation specific?) and facility of its application.

A general prescription for optimal conditions for assessment of basal competence requires that one provide the subject with all requisite information concerning task requirements as well as the means of solution. With respect to information about the task, necessary components include (1) its goal or purpose; (2) available alternative means for attaining the goal (from which, generally, one best method is selected); and (3) the criterion (or criteria) to be used by E in evaluating performance. Because, for some (probably historical-cultural) reason, experimenters rarely provide explicit information concerning any of these task components, it is useful to consider them in more detail. Where a statement of purpose is explicitly provided it is often inaccurate and may serve to evoke behavior incompatible with the true purpose (e.g., ''we are going to play some games,'' which is commonly used in presenting assessment tasks to children possibly evokes a playful attitude incompatible with ''we want to see how smart you are''—which is automatically assumed to evoke anxiety). In the absence of an accurate statement of purpose the subject (who must assume some purpose if he is to be motivated to respond at all) generally provides his own; and his purpose may well differ from the experimenter's. Glick (see chapter 14 in this volume) and many other writers (e.g., Scribner & Cole, 1973) have elaborated at length on cultural and subgroup differences in task interpretation; that they exist is established beyond doubt. Only when the task S is performing coincides with the one intended by E can it be legitimately interpreted within the directing theoretical framework. Thus, removal of ambiguity in the subject's interpretation of a task is a necessary (and, one hopes, also a sufficient) condition in removing ambiguity from E's interpretation of resulting performance.

A full description of alternative means for goal attainment ensures that the subject's selection from among them is not the result of inadequate knowledge (e.g., he may be capable of the correct solution but have overlooked it because it was not salient). The potential effect of cognitive style differences is especially obvious here: an analytic subject will first consider possible alternatives before acting whereas a more impulsive one may chose the most immediately obvious. Similarly, field dependence or independence will be expected to be a factor depending upon how much intellectual and/or perceptual processing (i.e., dis-embedding) is required for identification of alternatives. Only when all alternatives are explicitly presented can the experimenter ensure that they are potentially available to the subject and that the resulting selection from among them reflects an informed judgment. The effect of information concerning evaluative criteria is quite similar to the effect of goal information: where it is lacking the subject may be expected to supply his own best guess. Thus, if the subject assumes that speed is desired, he or she may sacrifice accuracy; whereas if encouraged to ''take your time and do the best you can'' he or she may perform quite differently. More-over, some subjects may assume that any solution is acceptable whereas others will spontaneously search for the best, or most elegant, solution—often making the task harder than E had intended.

Finally, even where full information concerning all component ingredients of the task is provided, the task may be sufficiently novel or unfamiliar that S cannot readily produce the requisite solution behaviors (e.g., he may not have the appropriate algorithm or lack skill in its execution). To remove all possible ambiguity here it is desirable to indicate what is required, if need be with appropriate demonstration. It may seem, at first blush, that the procedures I have recommended for removal of ambiguity will also result in the removal of all task difficulty and, therefore, all possible value as a basis for inference about competence. Performance under the prescribed conditions may show nothing more than whether or not the subject is capable of imitation. Is that a test of competence? Is it at all compatible with the Piagetian clinical method? The answer to both questions is "yes." As every student of Piaget knows, imitation is the source of all symbolic representation; the child imitates only what he or she can understand and assimilate to existing schemes. What cannot be imitated is presumably beyond the bounds of comprehension. Thus, imitation constitutes a perfectly appropriate test of basal level of competence as is well demonstrated by the Danner and Day experiment. Simple nonoccurrence of behavior in a complex or difficult context, on the other hand, does not constitute adequate justification for inferring incapacity as I have attempted to demonstrate in the preceding discussion. In order to conclude that some behavior is lacking in an individual's repertoire one must show that it cannot be caused to occur under conditions in which it should reasonably be expected. Once existence of the behavior in an individual's repertoire has been established clinical questioning, or a series of standardized transfer tasks, or some combination of the two, are then appropriate for finer assessment of the strength and generality of competence beyond the basal level. An additional advantage of the proposed procedure of starting from a basal level of competence is likely to be the resulting enhancement of the subject's motivation and/or sense of accomplishment.

In the foregoing discussion, I have expanded at length on the need for removing all possible sources of ambiguity and a very general means of doing so without offering any specific detail concerning task content or response measures. These details, it seems to me, must be determined in relation to the specifics of the experimental question being raised. The Inhelder tasks are by far the most widely used in assessment of formal operations and will probably continue to be the preferred method despite their requirement for special materials and time-consuming individual testing (which also places considerable demand upon experimenter skill). As our knowledge of the nature of component skills of formal operational thought increases it is likely that simpler and more direct methods for assessing them will be devised. At this point it is easier to prescribe the "how" of assessing formal operations than the "what."

In this regard, it may be noted that most reported attempts at the development of "better" formal operations tasks have retained the structure of the Inhelder tasks but modified the content—generally in the direction of introducing more familiar material. In the case of some logical inference tasks—mostly notably, the four card problem (Wason & Johnson-Laird, 1972)—content changes have led to dramatically improved performance: In general, subjects do much better on a realistic problem with familiar materials (such as postage stamps) than with arbitrary combinations of conventional symbols (such as letters and digits). Although there is also some scattered evidence suggesting performance variation in a number of Inhelder tasks as a result of change to more familiar content (e.g., Sinnott, 1975; Peel, 1971; Kuhn & Brannock, 1977) the effect is neither large nor consistent. Although predictions of improved performance on tasks with familiar content might seem to follow logically on intuitive or common sense grounds, it should be noted that there is no theoretical basis whatsoever for predicting either the existence or direction of effects of content modification. The existing equivocal evidence on effects of content variation, therefore, is quite understandable. On the other hand, as noted earlier, there is theoretical rationale for change in task structure through removal of ambiguity.

Theoretical implications. My motivation for demonstrating that current methodology for assessing formal operations is a better candidate for rejection than the theory which underlies it derives from a firm conviction in the reality of adult thought as qualitatively distinct from child thought. Certainly every human society makes the distinction and enforces institutional rules to insure that decisions of major importance for the society are made only by adults—and responsible adults, at that. Although science (as a formalized body of knowledge and associated technologies) is a relatively recent cultural development not yet characteristic of all cultures, every human society has areas of endeavor such as jurisprudence, legislation, and long-range planning of group activities, which are the exclusive province of select adults. Although psychologists may ultimately conclude that Piaget has characterized adult thought in terms of too narrowly restricted a set of properties—or of properties too closely associated with the trappings of Western science—they will, undoubtedly agree that he was correct in characterizing it as a qualitatively distinct level of competence. I have tried to show that the use of standardized tasks, objective response measures, and unambiguous procedures will reveal that competence to be more universal in incidence and more orderly in attainment than it is currently believed to be.

The methodological artifact which I proposed to account for the apparent nonuniversality of formal operations is, in principle, not necessarily confined to the stage of formal operations; it might be more generally applicable to evidence at the lower developmental stages as well. Whereas the generality, in principle, cannot be gainsaid, its relevance, in practice, is probably diminished at younger ages. To the extent that earlier stages of cognitive development are more fully determined by relatively universal conditions of maturation and rearing, there should be less opportunity for variations attributable to individual differences to arise. Furthermore, the experimental procedures employed in work with younger children generally tend to be more tightly structured and less reliant upon verbal instructions (i.e., already less prey to ambiguity). On the other hand, certainly no harm could result from increased concern with the need for unambiguous assessment procedures in the study of childrens' intellectual competence.

In focusing upon inferred competence as a central topic of theoretical concern, individual difference factors, and all the stimulus components of ambiguous experimental procedures which give rise to them, may be dismissed as sources of noisy variability or bias to be eliminated at all cost. However, when interest shifts to description of performance as a legitimate topic of theoretical interest, then all these banished "undesirables" come flooding back demanding attention. A complete psychological theory, and its application to everyday problems, require a full account of how competence is translated into performance and how it is masked or amplified by a plethora of varying conditions. Why do some individuals spontaneously manifest available competence whereas others do not? How invariant is this apparent difference in approach across context variation? What factors determine which aspects of competence are evoked in relation to a variety of environmental conditions? These, and a host of related questions, are logically inescapable but currently unanswerable. Recent discussions of developmental theory have, however, increasingly differentiated performance from competence theories. Concomittant with this trend has come a shift toward interest in performance variables.

Among contemporary theorists of cognitive development only Pascual-Leone (1969, 1980) has attempted a comprehensive systematic account of conditions determining performance. In his theory the factor corresponding most directly to competence or operative level is M, the maximum number of schemes that can be activated in a single mental operation. Performance results from modulation of and interaction with M by three classes of factors: learning factors (L and C, where L roughly corresponds to logic and C to content), field factors (F operator) and affective, motivational, personality factors (A and B structures), each of which affects the likelihood of activation of particular schemes. A detailed study of the effects of learning and field factors upon performance by 12 and 15 year-olds on five formal operations tasks recently reported by Pascual-Leone and de Ribaupierre (1979) provides the first direct test of his theory on formal operations performance. The results support the validity of formal operations as a unique stage of competence and show that the relative weighting of moderating factors changes with age. The results also suggest that the artifact explanation proposed here, while partially correct, is also undoubtedly incomplete. Although field dependent adolescents do show less propensity for utilizing available competence, (the central property invoked in the *gedanken* experiment proposed earlier) Pascual-Leone accounts for the propensity in terms of available repertoire of planning skills, a learning factor, rather than simply in terms of field factors such as stimulus ambiguity.

REFERENCES

Blasi, A., & Hoeffel, E. C. Adolescence and formal operations. *Human Development*, 1974, *17*, 344–363.

Case, R. *The relationship between Field dependence and performance on Piaget's test of formal operations.* Unpublished pilot study, University of California, Berkeley, 1973.

Case, R. Structures and strictures: Some functional limitations on the course of cognitive growth. *Cognitive Psychology,* 1974, *6,* 544–573.

Danner, F. W., & Day, M. C. Eliciting formal operations. *Child Development,* 1977, *48,* 1600–1606.

Dasen, P. R. Crosscultural Piagetian research: A summary. *Journal of Crosscultural Psychology,* 1972, *3,* 23–39.

Dulit, E. Adolescent thinking à la Piaget. *Journal of Youth and Adolescence,* 1972, *1,* 281–391.

Elkind, D. Quantity conceptions in junior and senior high school students. *Child Development,* 1961, *32,* 551–560.

Elkind, D. Quantity conceptions in college students. *Journal of Social Psychology,* 1962, *57,* 459–465.

Fischbein, R., Pampu, I., & Manzat, I. Effect of age and instruction on combinatory ability in children. *British Journal of Educational Psychology,* 1970, *40,* 261–270.

Goodnow, J. J. A test of milieu differences with some of Piaget's tasks. *Psychological Monographs,* 1962, *76,* No. 36, Whole No. 555.

Graves, A. J. Attainment of conservation of mass, weight, and volume in minimally educated adults. *Developmental Psychology* 1972, *7,* 223.

Huteau, M. Dependance-independance a l'egard du champ et developpement de la pensee operatoire. *Archives de Psychologie,* 1980, *48,* 1–40.

Huteau, M., & Rajenbach, F. Heterogeneité du niveau de developpement operatoire et dependance-independance a l'egard du champ. *Enfance,* 1978, 181–195.

Inhelder, B., & Piaget, J. *The growth of logical thinking from childhood to adolescence.* New York: Basic Books, 1958.

Kuhn, D., & Brannock, J. Development of the isolation of variables scheme in experimental and "natural experience" contexts. *Developmental Psychology,* 1977, *13,* 9–14.

Lawson, A. E. Formal operations and field independence in a heterogeneous sample. *Perceptual and Motor Skills,* 1976, *42,* 881–882.

Leskow, S., & Smock, C. D. Developmental changes in problem-solving strategies: Permutation. *Developmental Psychology,* 1970, *2,* 412–422.

Linn, M. C. Influence of cognitive style and training on tasks requiring the separation of variables schema. *Child Development,* 1978, *48,* 874–877.

MacCorquodale, K., & Meehl, P. E. On a distinction between hypothetical constructs and intervening variables. *Psychological Review,* 1948, *55,* 95–107.

Martorano, S. A developmental analysis of performance on Piaget's formal operations tasks. *Developmental Psychology,* 1977, *13,* 666–672.

Neimark, E. D. Intellectual development during adolescence. In F. D. Horowitz (Ed.), *Review of Child Development Research,* Vol. 4, Chicago: University of Chicago Press, 1975, 541–594. (a)

Neimark, E. D. Longitudinal development of formal operations thought. *Genetic Psychology Monographs,* 1975, *91,* 171–225. (b)

Neimark, E. D. Current status of formal operations research. *Human Development,* 1979, *22,* 60–67.

Papalia, D. E. The status of several conservation abilities across the life-span. *Human Development,* 1972, *15,* 229–243.

Pascual-Leone, J. *Cognitive development and cognitive style: A general psychological integration.* Unpublished Ph.D. dissertation, University of Geneva, 1969.

Pascual-Leone, J. Constructive problems for constructive theories: the current relevance of Piaget's work and a critique of information-processing simulation psychology. In R. Kluwe & H. Spada (Eds.), *Developmental Models of Thinking.* New York: Academic Press, 1980.

Pascual-Leone, J., & de Ribaupierre, A. Formal operations and *M* power: A Neo-Piagetian investigation. *New Direction for Child Development,* 1979, *5* 1–43.

Pascual-Leone, J., & Goodman, D. *Cognitive style factors in linguistic performance.* Paper given at Canadian Psychological Association, Windsor, 1974.

Pascual-Leone, J.,& Goodman, D. Intelligence and experience: A Neo-Pagetian approach. *Instructional Science,* 1979, *8,* 301-367.

Peel, E. A. *The nature of adolescent judgment.* London: Staples, 1971.

Peluffo, N. The notions of conservation and causality in children of different physical and sociocultural environments. *Archives de Psychologie,* 1962, *38,* whole no. 151, 275-291.

Peluffo, N. Culture and cognitive problems. *International Journal of Psychology,* 1967, *2,* 187-198.

Piaget, J. Intellectual evolution from adolescence to adulthood. *Human Development,* 1972, *15,* 1-12.

Pulos, S., & Adi, H. Individual differences in formal thought among college students. AESOP report #ID-45, May, 1977.

Saarni, C. I. Piagetian operations and field independence as factors in children's problem solving performance. *Child Development,* 1973, *44,* 338-345.

Scardamalia, M. Information processing capacity and the problem of horizontal decalage: A demonstration using combinatorial reasoning tasks. *Child Development,* 1977, *48,* 28-37.

Scribner, S., & Cole, M. Cognitive consequences of formal and informal education. *Science,* 1973, *182,* 553-559.

Sinnot, J. D. Everyday thinking and Piagetian operativity in adults. *Human Development,* 1975, *18,* 430-443.

Smedslund, J. Piaget's psychology in practice. *British Journal of Educational Psychology,* 1977, *47,* 1-6.

St. Jean, D. *The water-level task as a measure of field dependence-independence.* Unpublished M.A. thesis, Rutgers University, 1976.

Stone, C. A., & Day, M. C. Levels of availability of a formal operational strategy. *Child Development,* 1978, *49,* 1054-1065.

Stone, C. A., & Day, M. C. Competence and Performance Models and the characterization of formal operational skills. *Human Development,* 1980, *23,* 323-353.

Strauss, S., & Kroy, M. The child is logician or methodologist? A critique of formal operations. *Human Development,* 1977, *20,* 102-117.

Thomas, A., Jamison, W., & Hummel, D. D. Observation is insufficient for discovery that the surface of still water is invariantly horizontal. *Science,* 1973, *181,* 173-174.

Wason, P. C., & Johnson-Laird, P. N. *Psychology of reasoning. Structure and content.* Cambridge, Mass.: Harvard University Press, 1972.

Witkin, H. A., Cox, P. W., Friedman, F., Hrishikesan, A. G., & Siegel, K. M. *Field dependence-independence and psychological differentiation.* Supplement I. Princeton, N.J.: ETS Research Bulletin RB 74-42, 1974.

Witkin, H. A., Cox, P. W., & Friedman, F. Field dependence-independence and psychological differentiation, Supplement II. Princeton, N.J.: ETS Research Bulletin RB 76-28, 1976.

Witkin, H. A., Oltman, P. K., Cox, P. W., Ehrlichman, E., Hamm, R. M., & Ringler, R. W. Field-dependence-independence and psychological differentiation. Princeton, N.J.: ETS Research Bulletin RB 73-62, 1973.

Zelniker, T., & Jeffrey, W. Reflective and impulsive children: Strategies of information processing underlying differences in problem solving. *Monographs of the Society for Research in Child Development,* 1976, *41*(5), Serial No. 168.

12 A Revised Interpretation of Piaget (1932)

James Youniss
Boys Town Center
Catholic University of America

This is a review of Piaget's (1932) book: *The moral judgment of the child.* Although 45 years late, the review offers an interpretation which revises the standard meanings attributed to the book. This interpretation allows the book to be seen as a statement within the framework of *relational* theory (cf., Macmurray, 1961; Sullivan, 1953). Relational theory posits a self whose existence is known through and dependent on other persons. Development is of relations per se so that the self is always a confined term. The self finds its individuality in relations but never becomes the person apart, the so-called autonomous personality which other theories emphasize.

The relational interpretation of Piaget has been discussed in a series of papers (Youniss, 1975, 1977, 1978a, 1978b, 1978c) and presented with empirical data in a recent book (Youniss, 1980). The goal of the present essay is to pull together major ideas around two points: Why has Piaget's work, which is well-known to researchers of social and moral cognition, not been seen as a relational statement? And, what are the significant implications which follow from viewing his work within a relation framework?

SUMMARY OF RELATIONAL THEORY

Before addressing the two questions, I will summarize relational theory as it is found in Piaget's (1932) study. The reader is cautioned that familiar terms like self, interaction, relation, and so on, do not have conventional meaning. If they are taken in their common connotation, the relational core of the proposal will have been missed.

The Child.   Piaget describes the child as an agent who acts on the world and seeks order through these actions. Order is constructed from actions. But since actions engage other agents, like parents, siblings, or other caretakers, the child's focus must be dualistic. The child is one source of action and other persons are a second source. If order is to be constructed, the construction must take account of both sides. It must pertain to *interpersonal interactions*.

The logic in this argument is consistent with Piaget's analysis of the child in the physical world. The child acts and physical objects act in return. Balls move away when the child throws them. Walls block the child when he approaches them. Water runs over the body when the child touches it. Actions of objects reveal their agency. If the child is to understand objects, order must be constructed from the meeting of self-object interactions. Knowledge is not of objects *qua* objects but of relations in which they actively participate with the child (Piaget, 1970).

Interactions.   Piaget proposes that order can be constructed if the child assesses the *forms* of interaction rather than the content. Piaget identifies form as recurring, generalized *methods* or *procedures*. For example, one procedure would be that when the child hesitates, an adult steps in to remove doubt. Another example, would be that when a child gives an assertion, another child presents an alternative assertion. Procedure refers to ways actions are exchanged. Content refers to details of actions, for instance, how an adult might remove doubt or how another peer states an assertion.

Procedures are not facts to be perceived but forms which the child constructs. Technically, the child cannot construct them alone. Two persons are required since the referent is interaction. Whereas one can say that the child constructs reality, the very process of construction involves two agents. The child operates on reality simultaneously with other operators. Thus, construction of social reality is by necessity a process of cooperation and coconstruction.

Relations.   Forms of interactions constitute social existence. The child exists through participation in these forms with other persons. Knowledge of oneself is knowing oneself in relations with others. Knowing the other is dependent on relations with oneself.

Piaget distinguishes practical knowing, which pertains to pragmatic interacting, from knowing oneself and the other in a stabilized, conceptual way (pp. 96–98). The latter derives from the former. Once established, the child knows self as one term in a relation and knows the other person as another term. Neither person is known in an absolute or objective sense. One is the referent for the other and vice versa (cf. Macmurray, 1961).

Insofar as there are distinguishable forms of interaction, the child can know self and other as existing in different relations. Piaget emphasizes two relations as important in social development. One is the relation of unilateral authority or unilateral constraint. It arises from procedures in which persons are not equals. One person possesses more knowledge and the right to demand conformity to this knowledge. The other person possesses less knowledge and does not have the right to impose it on the first person (Hinde, 1976).

Piaget suggests that this procedure is found typically in adult-child interactions. He refers here to form and not content. Much has been made in developmental psychology of content differences among styles of child-rearing. For example, one parent may discipline through stringent punishment and another through a technique in which reasons for acting are expressed in verbal explanations. These techniques differ in detail as to how the child and the adult act. But both techniques partake of a common form. The adult is controlling and directing the child. The child is expected to adopt the adult's position when that position is not negotiable (cf. Gadlin, 1976).

The second relation is called cooperative. It comes from procedures in which persons interact as equals. Each possesses knowledge and neither possesses power to demand the other's adherence to a position. Through experiencing what could be a continuing stalemate, the persons learn to construct positions together. They present ideas and listen to ideas. They argue, debate, discuss, and compromise. The result is adoption of a general procedure of reciprocal influence.

Piaget proposes that interactions between peers best exemplify this procedure. The product of peer experiences is establishment of a relation of cooperation. The goal of this cooperation is to construct an order for reality. Because of the method, the construction process involves cooperation and the persons within it are known as reciprocating equals. Again, content is not the issue. Peers might fight, disagree, and compete as frequently as they work to gain compromise. The common form which subsumes this variety of content is that neither peer has the unilateral right to step outside interactions and demand adherence to a position.

The Self. It should now be evident that the child is not a person apart, an isolated thinker. The self is constituted through relations with other persons. The self's development is therefore contemporaneous with development of interpersonal relations. The self neither begins as an individual entity nor attains maturity by reaching a state of self-assured individuality.

Piaget proposes two lines of development of self, at least up to adolescence. One line pertains to the self in relations of unilateral authority. This self sees an order to reality which adults know and toward which the child strives. This self feels most confident when actions are built to complement actions of knowing adults. This self senses trust in exchange of conformity for approval and obedience for granting of privilege.

The second line pertains to the self in relations of cooperation. Here the self sees order as attainable by means of reciprocal exchange. There is confidence in democratic procedures, with assurance that order can be constructed with others. Trust in self is trust in the process of reciprocal influence between equals.

Social Knowledge.   For Piaget social knowledge consists of two facts. First, the child's knowledge of social reality is not solely the child's own but is *socialized* through processes of joint construction. Second, social knowledge is of interpersonal relations and interactions occurring within them. Socialization is inherent to the definition of child as agent through the process of construction. Knowledge is not simply social because it is about social objects or persons. It is social in its formation. It is also social in its objective which is to gain order in the meeting of self with other.

Piaget's emphasis is on the types of social knowledge which are possible in interpersonal relations. The focal point is *mutuality* or shared understanding. Relations of unilateral authority allow only minimal mutuality. Shared understanding is restricted because the form of this relation has not involved direct, step-by-step, cooperative construction. Authority figures already posses knowledge. They present it to children who then have the burden to reach the authority's position. Adults might simplify and tailor communication toward children but they ordinarily do not hope to gain knowledge of the order of reality through discussion or debate with children. Consequently, children must construct or try to reconstruct the position adults already have.

A high degree of mutuality should be possible when two persons construct ideas together. Each presents a position and listens to the other's side. There is going back-and-forth which allows full disclosure of ideas as they are being formed. The two parties need not agree and, in fact, disagreement is an important vehicle for seeing one's own idea recast in another light. Agreement aside, the process of joint construction through direct reciprocity, logically leads to mutuality between persons.

DIFFERENCES FROM STANDARD THEORIES

The Piaget which appears in contemporary writings on social and moral cognition is not the same that has been just recounted. It is more a Piaget seen through constructs like egocentrism, role-taking, intentionality, autonomy, and so on. Let us first inspect some of these in light of the relational Piaget.

Egocentrism.   This construct typically refers to the young child's incapacity to know anything but the self's version of reality. Egocentrism, so defined, is incompatible with mature social functioning. Unless the self knows of the other and modulates the self accordingly, social experience remains essentially a self-contained endeavor. Thus, egocentrism is said to be an early state of mind which wanes with increasing age.

Piaget (1932) speaks of this type of egocentrism but his main argument pertains to another type. It is the egocentrism which *results* when the child recognizes that the other has a point of view and tries to match it but must do it on his or her own. Unilateral authority relations are the context for this egocentrism. Specifically, the child thinks the other's position has been matched but in the absence of cooperative construction, there is little mutuality (p. 36). The point is clarified further in Piaget (1970) who proposes the term *sociocentrism* (p. 729) in its stead. This emphasizes that the result, subjective thought, does not come from ignorance of the other but arises from the social condition and socializing process of unilateral authority.

The point bears repeating since Piaget has clarified these meanings and still contemporary theorists single-mindedly use egocentrism in the nonsocial sense of a capacity limitation. Piaget assumes that from early in infancy, children recognize that other persons think and act differently from them. The question is how clearly the child can grasp another's view and vice versa. The answer depends on the achievement of mutuality, which, in turn, varies with the degree of coconstruction. Therefore, those who argue that children remain in egocentric ignorance of others until they acquire skills to infer and penetrate others, are arguing plausibly but outside of Piaget's epistemology.

Role-taking. This construct has become ubiquitous in contemporary theories, representing the vehicle by which the child's "natural state" of isolation is broken and the child's thought reaches accord with the thoughts of other persons. There are several specific accounts of role-taking as a construct and a process. What these accounts have in common is a single description of its function. That is, role-taking allows the child to enter into social life with others at levels of thought, feeling, motivation, and the like. The child moves into the place of the other and begins to experience reality as the other does.

Piaget (1932) speaks of a similar line of development but approaches it differently than most theorists do today. The following distinctions seem most pertinent. First, social existence is not problematic in Piaget (1932). The fact of agency and the implication of relation, insures that the self is in contact with the thoughts of others. Second, forms of interactions put the topic of thought into social terms so that the child continually has to deal with the other's views on reality. Third, the self does not grasp the other, penetrate the other's mind, but forms a way of knowing *with* the other.

Fourth, Piaget's emphasis is on mutuality, which will vary according to the forms of interaction in which self and other participate. Mutuality is not the same as knowing the other's role but pertains to understanding it relative to one's own. Fifth, mutuality is not an all-or-none phenomenon. Persons can progress in it, depending on the relation they share. Sixth, there are several ways by which to know a person. Each depends on the relation one is in with that person.

Autonomy. For some theorists, the outcome of development is an individual motivated from within, able to stand outside the mass and act freely with confidence. One sees this autonomous individual especially in theories of morality which picture higher stages as a step beyond conventional views and not needing support from conventional others. Stress is on independence in one's individuality.

For Piaget (1932) autonomy requires interpersonal dependence if thought is not to deteriorate into subjective embeddedness. One's criteria for what is good or correct are not solely self-generated but come from coconstructions with other persons. Standards are established jointly and it is precisely in social agreement that standards become more than personal preferences. Outside of intersubject validation, the risk is utter subjectivity.

The notion of freedom makes the point sharply. Piaget (1932) proposes that subjugation of self to jointly constructed standards is the basis of free choice. This is not a matter of internalizing values when following them but of forming values with others so that what one holds has been checked by others. Resistance from others is essential. Without it, any person risks entrapment in self-embedding subjectivity.

An associated example is altruism. As usually treated, altruism is action for another in which there is no payoff for self, even to the extent of entailing risk. In Piaget (1932) altruism does not involve heroic individuality but applies to normal interpersonal relations. When the self acts to maintain relation no distinction can be made between the self's or the other's benefit. To parse the act and distribute its returns unequally, is to deny the supraordinate goal of relation which is enhancement of the self through the other and vice versa.

Ideologies

The foregoing illustrations exemplify differences between Piaget (1932) and now familiar extensions of this book found in current theories. The obvious question is why are there differences? Why has Piaget's relational framework been overlooked? The following discussion presents speculative answers.

One reason seems to be ideological. As Sampson (1977) has demonstrated, much of social psychologists' thinking builds from the premise that persons are individuals by right. This thinking spawns a Hobbes-like view on society. Society is populated by individuals, each with a self-interest. Social life is possible only because individuals consent to function by a contract in which persons keep themselves in check.

An immediate match can be seen between this ideology and that possibly applicable to developmental psychologists' thinking. The child is naturally idiosyncratic. Left alone, the child would wander freely but insofar as external agents give the child direction, self-interest can be checked by social considerations. This essential check takes place either through classical social learning or through the child's own construction via role-taking.

A second part of this ideology refers to development after the thoughts of others are internalized. There still remains a strong push to be an individual. Hence, the interest in the adolescent's search for identity and movement beyond convention. The infant's self-interest is egocentric, even hedonistic. The mature adult's self-interest is enlightened since it has been informed by the self-interest of others, has passed through conformity with others, and then moved beyond others knowingly.

If this assessment of ideologies is plausible, our original question can be partially answered. In the 1960s there was a renewed interest in Piaget's writings. There was, however, an already established way of viewing social functioning and social development. The prospect of seeing Piaget's work as a relational statement was unlikely. The more likely prospect was to see those parts as important which fit existing ideologies. Egocentrism matched idiosyncracy. Role-taking served to explain the check on self-interest. Autonomy seemed to fit the definition of the free acting, individual adult.

Epistemology.   One can hardly ignore the fact that Piaget's relational outlook differs from familiar theories, especially those prevalent in the 1960s. Still today, there seems to be a general belief that self as actor constructs reality or that reality (other agents) instruct the self. The choice is offered as an exclusive disjunction. Given this context, it is difficult to see that Piaget suggests that both views are correct and compatible.

A similar problem pertains to the construct, person. For instance, one reads regularly that social development is an extended process of perception of the other. The other, in this case, is much like an object whose properties are attributes like motives, thoughts, or feelings. Persons are, of course, contained entities. But they are also agents who reveal themselves dynamically through interactions. If the other is an agent, so is the self. Consequently, the very term perception pales. A dynamic agent is difficult to grasp and hold for parsing. Nevertheless, this agent can be known if the focus is on interactions, forms they express, and relations which subsume them. To know another thus means to place one agent in a relation with another agent when the relation remains open to development by the practice of interactions and the discovery of new forms.

Piaget's (1970) definition of knowledge as a relation (cf. Furth, 1969; Macmurray, 1961) defies a ready translation into models where one self knows and another is known. In those models, relation is a loose term standing for any of several specific processes. In Piaget's theory, relation refers to the nature of knowing possible for an agent who must deal with other agents on dynamic grounds. Relation is ultimately a convention constructed by the agents, an agreement to take positions with regard to one another. Each change of position requires modification of the other agent's position. All that could be stable in such a reality would be this agreement to cooperate in agency and therefore to achieve mutual understanding.

IMPLICATIONS

A general problem in many theories of cognition concerns the connection between knowledge or judgment, on the one hand, and action or performance, on
the other hand. The problem is sometimes put in terms of morality as follows. A
person may know what is correct, but does this knowledge predict behavior? The
answer is that knowledge is not a specific predictor. For example, in the moral
domain a person might know right from wrong, see a difference between two
courses of action, but decide to follow either path.

The question can be seen to come from a perspective in which knowledge is a
distinct process from action. Knowledge refers to mental processes like reflection, classification, or judgment. Action refers to doing which is a separate
process depending on other factors like motivation, circumstances, and so on.
This division is by theoretical choice and once made, requires other processes
which serve to bridge the separation. If not done, the theory accounts only for
knowledge as an ideal state of mind but gives up hope for explaining what
persons actually do.

Relational theory opens us to other sides of this problem. Without trying to
predict how persons will act, relational theorists attempt to explain how persons
understand implications of their actions. To rephrase the problem, relational
theory is concerned with the question: Do persons understand the consequences
of their actions? Can they see the implications of following one rather than
another line action? For instance, one course may lead to a momentary rift in a
relation while another may more severely upset a relation. The issue is not which
course will be chosen but the person's knowing that there are two options and
being able to follow each through to its logical extension.

Piaget (1932) gives several examples of how relational theory helps to approach the problem. For example, consider a young boy functioning in a unilateral relation of authority with his mother. Unilateral authority describes the terms
which lead to obedience as a norm or expectation. Additionally, the terms say
that the mother will give approval, praise, or reward when the boy obeys. From a
relational view, obedience and approval make for a reciprocity by complement
which serve to keep the child and parent in a known bond. When expressed at the
level of interaction, the terms affirm the relation.

The child's knowledge of the norms does not necessitate that he always
choose to obey. Piaget recognizes that children do not and cannot consistently act
in accord with norms. What the theory requires is that the child see the different
implications of obedience and disobedience. That is; does the child understand
that disobedience represents a deviation from the norm? Does the child realize
that disobedience must be reacted to for a reestablishment of the norm? Does the
child know what to do to initiate repair of the relation?

Piaget (1932) reports several observations illustrating children's articulation
in answering these questions. Children admit that disobedience represents de-

viance from the terms of the parent-child relation. They also say that adults expect to take note of disobedience, for example, by punishing or explaining. They further realize that acceptance of punishment is a step toward reestablishing the norm and repairing the relational breach. In other words, children, whether or not they choose to obey, comprehend the interactions that are likely to follow from adherence to and deviation from terms of interpersonal relations (e.g., p. 213; p. 225; p. 261).

Much work remains to be done before a full account of the knowledge-action connection can be made theoretically definite. For the present, however, one can see the possibilities in Piaget's position. It considers knowledge not as a judgmental conclusion but as an account of the dynamics of social exchange. Knowledge of relations is supra-ordinate to interactions, interactions being composed in order to affirm, repair, or change the terms of a relation. This approach frees us from having to look on knowledge as a judgment from which particular actions should emanate. Actions vary from moment to moment by circumstance or what have you. Social knowledge is the source from which these variations can be given meaning, each interaction having identifiable consequences for existing relations.

KNOWLEDGE AND AFFECT

The second implication pertains to the connection between social knowledge and affect. One general complaint about theories of social cognition is that they treat the person too much as a logician and too little with regard to personal feelings, biases, and preferences. This criticism would seem to apply especially to Piaget who has generally emphasized the logic in structures of knowing.

Piaget (1932) makes three definite points which bear on the problem. First, instead of treating affect as a state within an individual, Piaget sees feelings and emotions as parts of relations. Second, affective states are treated as coming from relations so that one expects different feelings to derive from unilateral authority than cooperative relations. And third, feelings and the like are understood to be products which are instigated and changed by interpersonal activities.

Points one and two belong together. Piaget (1932) presents observations showing that children describe themselves and others in different relations as having different feelings or emotions. For example, children see adults as offering trust, security, credibility, anger. They see themselves with respect to adults as being trusted, confident, believable, guilty, and the like. For peers, a different set of emotions apply. They include fairness, likeability, trustworthiness, caring, and so on. The issue is not whether one can experience the same emotion in two relations but how each relation tends to generate feelings appropriate to its terms.

As to the dynamic side of affect, Piaget (1932) is equally clear. Children understand that their interactions are likely to have consequences for their own and other persons' affective states. For example, not playing fair is a deviation from the norm of friendship which may make the offended peer upset. Calling attention to this feeling, the offended peer can make the offender feel apologetic and even relationally isolated. When repair is successfully undertaken both friends may feel relieved at the reduction of tension and feel happy that they are together again (e.g., pp. 231–232; pp. 282–283).

As with the above issue, Piaget's ideas are incomplete but show the possibilities contained in the relational viewpoint. Affect is different from knowledge but when knowledge is seen as guiding interactions, feelings and motives become its products. Social life without affect is a contradiction. One of Piaget's contributions may be the offer of a position in which social knowledge of interpersonal interactions leads persons to appreciate each other not as objects but as persons, with all that would imply for affect.

These points are clearly made with the data reported in Youniss (1980). Children supplied accounts of interactions between friends or child and parent when outcomes were designated. Not only did children frequently posit feelings surrounding the outcomes, but they clearly showed knowledge of means by which friends operated on feelings to modify them. For example, children knew how to diminish feelings of loneliness as well as how to heighten a sense of isolation. Moreover, they regularly described friendship as a vehicle for discussing feelings and clarifying them through self-exposure and commentary.

Here one can again see how far some theorists have departed from the relational model offered by Piaget. They point to a need to reintegrate cognition with affect, as if they assumed cognition was identical with rationality and affect were the synonymn for irrationality. To think of interpersonal relation apart from affect is a tour de force not permitted in Piaget's relational proposal. Worse, to say that role-takers have to guess about feelings of others is to deny the core of relational theory in which friends construct affective meanings together and freely expose their affective selves to one another for validation or clarification on a continuing bases.

CONCLUSION

The relational position which Piaget articulated 45 years ago has been neglected by most theorists. The position is based on an epistemology and a way of viewing the child which do not readily fit traditional models in the field. The position requires changes in assumptions and necessitates a new look on the self and on the forms of adult-child and peer relations. It addresses the dynamics of social functioning with regard to knowledge and performance and knowledge and affectivity. Although some may still prefer to deal with the more familiar interpretations of constructs of egocentrism, perspective-taking, and the like, others may find value in studying the child as agent whose existence is constituted through relations with others. The prospect for a new approach to social development is clear and interesting (see, Youniss, 1980).

REFERENCES

Furth, H. G. *Piaget and knowledge.* Englewood Cliffs, N.J.: Prentice Hall, 1969.

Gadlin, H. *Spare the rod: Disguising control in American childrearing.* Paper of the American Association for the Advancement of Science, Boston, February, 1976.

Hinde, R. A. On describing relations. *Journal of Child Psychology and Psychiatry*, 1976, *17*, 1-19.

Macmurray, J. *Persons in relations*, London: Faber and Faber, 1961.

Piaget, J. (1932) *The moral judgment of the child*, New York: The Free Press, 1965.

Piaget, J. Piaget's theory. In P. H. Mussen (Ed.), *Carmichael's manual of child psychology*, Vol. I. New York: Wiley, 1970.

Sampson, E. E. Psychology and the American ideal. *Journal of Personality of Social Psychology*, 1977, *35*, 767-782.

Sullivan, H. S. *The interpersonal theory of psychiatry*, New York: Norton, 1953.

Youniss, J. Another perspective on social cognition. In A. Pick (Ed.), *Minnesota Symposium on Child Development*, Vol. 9. Minneapolis: University of Minnesota Press, 1975.

Youniss, J. Socialization and social knowledge. In R. K. Sibereisen (Ed.), *Newsletter Soziale Kognition*, Berlin: Technical University of Berlin, 1977.

Youniss, J. The nature of social development. In H. McGurk (Ed.), *Issues in Childhood Social Development*, London: Methuen, 1978. (a)

Youniss, J. Dialectical theory and Piaget on social knowledge. *Human Development*, 1978, in press. (b)

Youniss, J. *Parents and Peers in Social Development.* Chicago: The University of Chicago Press, 1980.

Youniss, J., & Volpe, J. A relational analysis of friendship. In W. Damon (Ed.), *New Directions Sourcebook*, San Francisco: Jossey-Bass, 1978. (c)

13 Social Experience in the Development of Representational Thought: Distancing Theory

Irving E. Sigel
Educational Testing Service
Princeton, New Jersey

This paper, while in the structuralist orientation of Piaget, is an extension and elaboration of Piagetian theory, particularly with respect to the role of social factors in cognitive development.

The epistemological perspective espoused is that the scientific system one holds is derived from an underlying belief system. A Piagetian perspective, for example, is accepted because of some positive sense of affiliation with an authority whose perspective seems to resonate with one's construction of reality. There is a sense of trust that the system will help answer the unanswerable, that methods for study will be employed which fit a value system about human development, and further, that the topic of interest is consonant with what one thinks and feels is important. To argue that acceptance or rejection of a theory is rational and independent of one's basic belief systems is to ignore the phenomena that individuals, including scientists, come to every situation with some sense of that situation and where it may or may not fit into their construction of reality. To pose the issue metaphorically is to say it is the metaphor of the constructor, the active builder, with the critical capacity to evaluate experience on the basis of previous constructions. Evaluation of new experiences is in part a function of those previous constructions.

Social reality is constructed through experiences in the social and physical world. As time binding organisms capable of integrating past and future, held together by strands of the ongoing present, we are continuously experiencing.

The question of how to conceptualize "experience" is not new, of course, to psychologists or philosophers. According to Heath (1967):

> As to the content of immediate experience there are characteristic differences of
> opinion. At one extreme lie the theories of direct realism, whose claim is that

material objects are immediately given so that no real difference arises between the naked and clothed experience, sensation and perception or for that matter appearance and reality; apart from perceptual error there is this no "problem of knowledge". At the opposite pole are theories . . . for whom immediate experience presents only an undifferential mass of feelings or sensation in which even the contrast between subject and object has not begun to appear [p. 157].

These differences of opinion arise from a failure to agree on what is the "given." The sense datum theories argue that appearances and actions of objects are external to the individual, impinging on the senses implying veridicality. These "experiences" provide foundations of knowledge. Yet, we know that sense data are not veridical sources of knowledge. The most obvious example is the shape of the earth. From visual data it is flat. Experiencing the earth sensorially alone provides knowledge from one perspective. The knowledge so derived may be incomplete and inconsistent with knowledge acquired through other sources.

The argument shifts from sensory experience as the determinant of knowledge to an argument that construction of experience (sensory included) leads to knowledge acquisition. Constructions are products of abstractions from experience. What characteristic attributes of experience are abstracted depends on the developmental level of the individual as well as sociocultural features which guide or influence the experience.

I subscribe in part to Piaget's (1977) conceptualization which holds that there are two types of experiences:

First there is experience in the empiricist sense; groupings controlled by the properties of the external objects, followed by selection as a function of success or failure.

But there is another form of experience which we have called logicomathematical. There information derives not from the objects as such, but from the actions that are performed on the objects and from the general coordination (order, classes, correspondences, etc. between the actions). This is no longer an Aristotelian abstraction, but a reflecting abstraction that extracts certain operations from the active coordinations themselves [p. 9].

By eschewing a priori assertions regarding the specific conceptualization of experience, Piaget set out to investigate the origins and development of concepts. The major concepts studied by Piaget are regarded as constructions from our actions. Transactions between the individual and the physical world (including social and nonsocial objects) become internalized; the shift is from nonorder to a definite pattern of order. In the course of this development the child comes to know physical, social and logicomathematical concepts.

If we argue that "coming to know" physical and abstract concepts is a result of experience, then we ask if experience with objects is sufficient.

My contention is that, whereas experience as actions and internalization of actions with objects is a necessary condition for cognitive development, it is not sufficient. What is an additional necessity is a particular set of social experiences—interactions with others.

For Piaget, experience acquired through contact with the external physical environment is a factor in cognitive development (Piaget, 1970). Piaget considers experience heterogeneous, including physical experiences ranging from extracting information from the objects themselves to directly acting on objects. There is no implication that knowledge is extracted; logicomathematical knowledge "seems to be derived from the objects because it consists of discovering by manipulating objects, properties introduced by action which did not belong to the objects before these actions [p. 721]." These types of events are in fact discoveries of relations among events.

Piaget does not detail *social* experience as part of the experiential world of the child. Rather, he refers to the social environment in general terms as a third factor influencing the development of intelligence. He asserts that social or educational influences and physical experience can be effective only if the child "is capable of assimilating them, and he can do this only if he already possesses the adequate instruments or structures (or their primitive forms) [p. 721]."

Yet for Piaget, (1973) the relationship between social environmental features and the development of cognitive structures is interdependent:

> ... in the case of structures in the process of constitution or continual reconstitution (as with biological structures), exchange is no longer limited to internal reciprocities, as is the case between the substructures of a completed structure, but involves a considerable proportion of exchange with the outside, to enable these structures to obtain the supplies necessary for their functioning. This is so with structures in the formative stage, as regards the development of the intelligence, when the subject must constantly have recourse to trial and error (even in the case of specifically logico-mathematical experiments, when the information is drawn not from the objects as such, but from the actions exerted upon them) [p. 16].

In spite of this assertion, Piaget does not conceptualize this exchange process either in terms of the personal conditions or the ecological contexts.

My position is that the social exchange needs specification of form and function like Piaget's conceptualization of physical experience. By so doing we move from gross labelling of social experience to greater precision. In this way the theory is enriched, in a sense, a contribution to filling existent lacunae. Essentially, the exigesis presented, although written in a Piagetian framework, is revisionist in nature.

CONCEPTUAL FRAMEWORK

Basic assumption. To provide a context for the conceptualization, some of the basic underlying assumptions will be presented. These assumptions were influenced by Piaget (1966), Kelly (1955), Polanyi (1958) and Werner (1948).

1. The individual is an active, outreaching organism, constructing and reconstructing its physical, social, and personal reality from conception to death.

2. The construction process involves the employment of representational thinking. The concept of representational thinking has been defined by Piaget as the ability to transcend the immediate, evoke the past, as well as anticipate the future. Representational thought involves the development of the semiotic function (Piaget & Inhelder, 1969). The child comes to transform actions into mental events, and to employ symbols and signs to communicate either to himself or to others. Translating these ideas into specific thinking skills involves transcending the physical environment, relating past and present events, anticipating the future, and understanding the rules that experience can be *re* = *presented* and/or represented in a medium other than its original one: the dog can be represented in words, drawings, photogrpahs, or other arbitrary signs. This latter capability enables the individual to both send and receive messages as they are expressed in particular symbol systems. Representational thinking, while fundamentally a biologically ordained human capability, is actualized when appropriate environmental opportunities are experienced by the individual.

3. The process of reality construction and reconstruction and concomitant representations is continuous, and results in an organized network of constructs (representations) which serves as the cognitive map guiding the interactive process continuously. This network is modifiable if at least two conditions are met: (a) *appropriate social* experiences ''confront'' the given system and (b) the boundaries of the cognitive map are *permeable*. The social experiences appropriate for change are those that contribute to the creation of *discrepancies*. It is the dynamic movement toward discrepancy resolution that creates the potential for cognitive construct reorganization (Sigel, 1979).

4. The specifications of social experience relevant to the development of representational thinking are *distancing behaviors,* a class of events and interactions which ''demand'' the child to separate himself/herself mentally (via representation) in space or time from the ongoing observable field.

The theme of this chapter is to demonstrate that distancing behaviors have a particular significance in fostering representational thinking since they can serve to create, maintain and resolve discrepancies. Representational thought is the cognitive mode involved in coping with the discrepancies. Although the origins of representational thought are considered to be intrinsic to the biological nature of the human, it is the quality that takes its form from social experience. *The hypothesis is that the level of representational thinking an individual will attain is a function of the quantity and quality of distancing experiences.*

Conceptualization and Definition of Distancing Behavior

Distancing strategies create psychological distance between the individual and the ongoing environment. Distancing behaviors are operationalized to include those types of behavior which demand the child to reconstruct past events, to employ imagination in dealing with objects, events, and people, to plan and to anticipate future action (with particular attention being paid to articulate such intention), and finally to comprehend the transformation of such experience into various symbol systems. Distancing behaviors, whether emanating from others (parents, teachers, peers) or from the physical environment, make demands on the person (individual of any age) to infer from the observable present. In the course of making such inferences, the child has to represent to himself and to transform these experiences into representational systems to communicate the outcomes of reconstructions or the predictions of events. Representational thinking may be on the *figurative level,* i.e., creating images of events, or on the operational level, employing mental operations, i.e., thinking in terms of classifications, propositions, etc. (Sigel, 1970).

Characterization, form and function of distancing strategies. The *form* of the distancing strategy can be telling—i.e., presenting a message; or posing a question. The content can focus on *interpersonal, intrapersonal,* and *nonpersonal* phenomena. Thus, a distancing strategy can involve *telling* the child something about a relationship (e.g., "When you hit Mary, she will go away and not play with you"), or *asking* (e.g., "What will Mary do if you hit her?").

Although each of these does place some demand on the child to represent the experience, the *hypothesis* is that the *asking,* the *inquiring,* maximizes the development of representational thought in the young preschool child. *Inquiry,* when employed *systematically,* serves to create continuous cognitive dialogue for the participant to engage in social interchange. Such continuous dialogue has the potential to create opportunities for generating and resolving discrepancies. Inquiring of a child how events A and B might be related generates a discrepancy, while asking the child to come to some conclusion on the basis of the previous discussion is asking for a closure response. Thus, the inquiry in this context may serve two functions: (1) generating discrepancies and/or (2) resolving discrepancies.

Distancing behaviors vary in the degree to which they activate the separation of the person from the ongoing present. Where simple declarative statements require passive listening and associative responses, open ended inquiry demands active engagement (Sigel & Cocking, 1977). Thus, such cognitive activity *demands* "function as *instigators, activators* and *organizers* of mental operations [p. 213]."

According to Sigel & Cocking (1977), discrepancies created by inquiry "propel the organism to change because of the inherent nature of the organism's inability to tolerate discrepancies [p. 216]."

In sum, by creating discrepancies, distancing behaviors contribute in a major way to cognitive development. The contention is that the inquiry generates tension while creating a discrepancy, thereby increasing the stress level, and this stress causes disequilibrium, which the child strives to resolve via some mental action (Sigel & Cocking, 1977). The resolution is perhaps short lived. Another question can reinstitute the cycle and it is this cyclical aspect that is central to the thesis that distancing strategies are critical determinants of cognitive growth.

Concept of Discrepancy

We take our lead from the Piagetian perspective that holds that representational though evolves through changes from a dynamic equilibrated state to a dynamic nonequilibrated one (Piaget, 1977). We refer to the change in state or disequilibrium as *discrepancy* (Sigel & Cocking, 1977). A discrepancy is a dynamic state of disequilibrated tension, whose resolution yields a reorganization to a new state. Where no discrepancy exists, the status quo or the dynamic balance reigns and there is no external or internal need to change. The child believes what he sees; his construction of reality is such that the world appears ordered.

Discrepancies refer to the differences between the given and the desired, the belief and the counterbelief, the expected and the unexpected. Salient discrepancies create the potential for change in the child's construct system of physical and social reality. The readiness to change, however, depends on the permeability of the boundaries within the construct network, the potency of the activating actions of the "*other,*" and the developmental level of the child. Discrepancy resolution is a life-long process, changing in form and content. With increasing maturity and capability to comprehend the symbol systems, e.g., learning to read, learning to comprehend pictures, signs, etc., discrepancies can occur on a symbolic level as well as on an action level, with internal dialogues functioning similarly to the interpersonal inquiry generated through reading, etc. Fundamentally, change occurs when the equilibrium of the individual is disturbed by whatever source, activating the person to resolve this state. The resolution may result in a new orientation.

Discrepancies may take any of the following forms:

1. Discrepancies can occur between an internal perspective and an external demand. For example, in a conservation experiment with two balls of clay where one of the balls is deformed, the child argues that the deformed ball has more clay than the other ball. The discrepancy is identified by the child. If when told that nothing was added or taken away, the child does come to realize the two balls although different in appearance have the same amount of clay, the discrepancy between the observed and the inferred state (amount) is resolved. If, however, the child continues to reject the idea of similarity and continues to accept the difference in appearance and amount as true differences, then the discrepancy remains.

2. Discrepancies can occur between two internal events. For example, the child is asked, "Will you tell me the best ways to drive to your house?" when

there are two routes to the house. The child may be in conflict as to which route to present.

3. Discrepancies can occur where both events are external, e.g., the child is shown clear water and a set of colored powders. He is asked to predict what would happen if two of the colors were mixed (red and blue) and put into the water. After the colors are mixed another question is posed, "Why do you think the water is colored purple and not red or blue." The discrepancy in this case arises in the context of the action and is external to the child.

It will be recalled that resolution of discrepancies, whatever their type, was proposed as a necessary step in cognitive development. My argument does further, contending that Socratic and/or dialectic inquiry is the inquiry procedure of choice to foster resolution of the discrepancy. Let us turn now to an explication of this point of view.

THE PROCESS OF INQUIRY

Socratic dialogue is not just a simple posing of questions, but rather has a set of rules. Stevens and Collins (1977) present 24 such Socratic rules. Further, for Stevens and Collins as well as for us: "The different rules are triggered by specific situations, but there is no explicit control structure that specifies when tutors [in our case, teachers] use particular strategies, select particular cases, or discuss particular parts of the causal structure [p. 5]."

Socratic rules are, in fact, one type of distancing strategy. Types of Socratic rules can be used in solving causal problems. Imagine a case with an extreme wrong value [e.g., if the student has not yet mentioned temperature with respect to rice growing, the teacher posing this fact, forces the student to pay attention to a factor he is ignoring (Collins, 1977)]. In fact, the Socratic rules serve the cause of cognitive development because they *activate* representational thought and give it form and direction.

This point is crucial for the argument regarding distancing theory. For example, when an individual asserts something, e.g., rainfall is a necessary factor for plant growth, a counter example can be stated: How come plants grow in sheltered places such as homes or greenhouses? The argument follows that rainfall is not a *direct* cause but is an *indirect* cause, since it provides water which in turn becomes available for watering plants indoors. Take another example: Prediction statements are requested. In a conservation of mass task, after having attested to the equivalence of the amount of water in two jars, the child is asked how high the water will go if it is poured into a tall, thin cylinder.

In each of these cases the teacher poses the problem by asking an explicit question which focuses the child's attention on a particular set of events in particular situations. In either case, to answer the question the child has to reconstruct from the past (retrieve) and integrate that knowledge with the presenting problem. Further, she/he has to assimilate the ongoing event. Through inquiry and close attention to the child's response, the teacher can determine at what level the child is thinking as well as what his knowledge base is. The child is reasoning within the confines of the problem posed by the teacher.

You may ask whether this set of inquiry strategies precludes the autoregulatory functions of the child in striving to solve problems. The argument is quite the contrary. The child is doing the mental work along with the teacher (they are mutually engaged in trying to solve a problem). To be sure, the teacher has the control since she/he is structuring, and even defining the problem. However, this need not be the case. The teacher can observe the child as she/he is engaged in a task and enter into a dialogue. In this case, the child has chosen the problem and the teacher is taking advantage of this opportunity to help elaborate and articulate the child's involvement. In either case the child and teacher are *actively* engaged.

Within an inquiry context, the dialogue the teacher engages in must be *dialectic*. This is the process where the teacher employs rules of inquiry which do involve counterexamples, contradictions, etc. The teacher can compare and contrast instances to create a unity. All of these processes are involved in coming to acceptable resolutions.

In either physical or social problem solving, the child and the teacher begin with incomplete knowledge; that is, the teacher does not know what the child knows and the child probably does not have the information necessary to solve the problem, and if he does, he may not be aware that he has it or how to apply it. The inquiry may serve five functions: (1) to elicit what knowledge the child has and thereby the teacher becomes informed; (2) to provide an opportunity to relate bits of knowledge that the child does not see as related or even relevant; (3) to provide a basis for the child knowing what he does not know; (4) to tell the teacher what the child does not know or what he needs to know; and (5) to foster decentration. The degree(s) to which the dialogue enhances the child's movement toward problem solving and, in fact, thinking will be dependent on the subsequent steps the teacher and the child take to complete the knowledge base (Sigel & Saunders, 1979).

From the perspective of either teacher or child, the interaction described serves to demonstrate that inquiry is in fact an experience and an exercise in discrepancy creation and movement toward resolution. Most important, it provides an experience that can contribute to the child's awareness of his knowledge and of the gaps in his knowledge. It is also an opportunity for the child to objectify by articulating what he does and does not know. This movement toward objectification and articulation is a step in the direction of providing opportunities for checking one's knowledge about events with others.

Knowledge is organized at different levels of "knowing." In the case of the young child, knowledge to be used from an inquiry encounter will be limited to the child's capability to assimilate and concomitantly to accommodate to this new information. Children come to "know" an event and to understand the operations as well as the implications involved relative to their developmental level. Knowledge acquisition can be described in terms of levels, e.g., figurative-operative, where levels of knowledge are constructed and integrated and subsequently reintegrated, proceeding in a spiral-like progression as the child's competence to abstract and to integrate experience increases. This is analogous to Piaget's notion of equilibration (Piaget, 1977).

Telling may become effective as the child matures, since she may have evolved *internal* dialoguing—a consequence of experience with inquiry. Internal dialoguing refers to internalized inquiry—asking oneself questions as a reaction to "telling" statements, e.g., asking oneself what does the speaker mean or why should that reflect causal relations? With the acquisition of internalized dialoguing, older children and/or adults may not need to engage in complex levels of inquiry. This is not to say that inquiry cannot play an important role in the developing representational competence with older children or adults, it is to say that the function of "telling" may converge with inquiry to the degree that the individual engages in *internal dialoguing*. Whereas direct empirical support for this assertion is still lacking, the logic seems reasonable. Observations of adult-adult interactions, e.g., individuals altering their ideas as a function of listening to a lecturer, suggest that with increasing maturity, individuals can react to a didactic presentation as if they were reacting to an inquiry. Internal dialoguing may function as a mediator between a didactic presentation and reorganization of a listener's response.

Secondary effects of inquiry. Although discrepancy resolution and consequent competence to deal with representations may be the primary consequence sequence of inquiry, there are secondary effects which emerge from the interaction. They are referred to as secondary because they are not the intentional goals of the inquirer, but rather "fall out" from the inquiry method.

Secondary effects of inquiry can be positive—encouraging the child to become engaged—or negative—discouraging the child from becoming a constructive participant. This is because questions, irrespective of the benign appearance of the content, convey latent as well as explicit messages. The speaker may not be aware of the affective features of the message. The affective overtones of the interaction can be independent of the actual verbalizations. Questions can be characterized as hostile, arrogant, "put downs," etc. Reactions by the receiver will be influenced by his/her interpretation of the emotional features of the message, e.g., emotional tone, inflection, etc. Personal-social considerations require sensitivity not only to emotional tone and manner of the inquiry, but also to the readiness of the receiver to engage in a social interaction dialogue. The question form is common as an introductory or warm-up technique used by adults and children. Questions such as, "How are you?" "Why does an airplane fly?" may serve to engage, to establish contact. What is unique about the question is that it demands a response—an engagement. Of course, the recipient of the question may not participate and may leave the scene. That is always possible, but less likely with an inquiry perceived as benign. A dialogue is inherent in the inquiry context. This is in contrast to telling, which usually implies that the speaker knows more and/or knows something that the receiver does not know or should know. Chances for engagement, as well as the quality of the engagement, and interaction would be less than when a question is used. Telling does not generate a necessary response. These are complex issues beyond the scope of this chapter (Sigel & Saunders, 1979). In any event, whichever mode is used, inquiry or telling, there are surplus meanings conveyed—meanings which may not even be intended. Surplus meanings, then, can be critical features which influence the quality of a social interaction.

The values of the speaker may be involved. The content, whether in telling or asking, does in itself express the speaker's values. The speaker selects aspects of the situation that he considers important. In the context of inquiry, the value issue can be pervasive, subtle, and potentially insidious. First, there is the value the speaker shows by asking a question with particular intent. Second, evaluation of the person is expressed by his tone of voice and general demeanor. Third, there is the value placed on the nature of the subsequent responses. There are many risks a responder takes in responding to questions: anywhere from making an error, indicating ignorance, indicating tactlessness by answering in a way that may be offensive to the speaker, etc. Thus, the value and attitude domains of the speaker in hearer and vice versa are intrinsic dimensions embedded in inquiry-social interaction.

SUMMARY

In sum, the use of inquiry should be considered in the context of its distancing function and concomitant role in creating, maintaining or resolving discrepancies. It is in this role, that inquiry does activate representational thinking and in so doing does provide the child with opportunities for developing constructions, since children evolve constructs through such social and nonsocial experience. Use of inquiry—in terms of the child's maturity level—challenges the established constructions, and thereby sets the stage for change. The change, however, comes about through a discovery process which, while supported by the teacher or some other relevant inquirer, is carried out by the child. The way it is carried out and the consequences of such encounters are always embedded in a social-emotional context. The change process is the basis for the quality of cognitive growth.

EMPIRICAL EVIDENCE FOR THE DISTANCING HYPOTHESIS

Working within the conceptual model described, two preschool programs were established: one from 1969 to 1973 with disadvantaged children aged 2½, and a second from 1974 to the present with children from middle income families. In the latter situation, 4 year old children were enrolled.

In the first program, the underprivileged children were enrolled in a preschool program with teachers trained to use distancing strategies and where the entire program emphasized understanding rules regarding transformation of objects and providing experience with symbol systems. These children performed at significantly higher levels on tasks involving representational competence—anticipation, reconstruction, understanding of causal relations (Sigel, Secrist, Forman, 1973). Two years after leaving the program, the children were performing at a higher level in reading and math, each involving transformations of experience into symbol systems relative to a control group. Yet, more of the children in the experimental program were considered disruptive by their public school teachers because they asked too many questions, and were not always interested in the classroom routines (Cataldo, 1977).

Two major themes dominated the programs with the middle class group: (1) distancing strategies as the basic teaching strategy, and (2) emphasis on transformation of experience into various representational modes, e.g., motor action into a picture, or a picture into a story. The latter involves dealing with signs or symbols—namely, external representations. Thus, the educational program dealt with both internal representations and their externalization.

Working with groups of children enrolled in the distancing program and control and comparison groups, it was found that the teachers in the "distancing programs" did, in fact, use inquiry significantly more often than teachers in control or comparison programs and did follow through more consistently (Rosner, 1978), indicating the program was what it was said to be. Pre-post assessments were done with a number of tests assessing representational competence. The results from these two programs reveal significant differences between experimental and nonexperimental classrooms.

Language assessment. Language comprehension and language production were examined because it was hypothesized that children in a distancing program would manifest greater competence in complex expressive and receptive language. The rationale for this is that the distancing program created more demands for expressive language as a response medium to questions. Because different distancing strategies demand the use of different conceptual categories, children in the distancing program should have differential competence to express themselves conceptually. For example, present time descriptions are posited as being less difficult than future orientations which involve anticipations or past event time which involves *recognition, reconstruction,* and *reproduction.* Thus, one can posit that present tense expressions may require less distancing than demands placed in future tense or past tense. To assess language a task devised by Dr. Rodney R. Cocking was used (Cocking, 1974). This task allows for determination of the child's language comprehension and production in the frame of distancing categories.

Children's language knowledge was analyzed in terms of the cognitive categories represented by the distancing behaviors, rather than along strictly linguistic lines. What this means is that select language categories that corresponded to cognitive operations were of more interest in these analyses than grammatical ones. For example, time orientation expressions are the linguistic counterparts of anticipatory (future) and reconstructive or recognitory (past) cognitive operations. The classes of anticipatory, reconstructive and recognitory memory are among the key elements in teachers' strategies used in the Distancing Program. Therefore, in the language performance analyses, the differential program effects were examined analyzing the ways children used past time and future time expressions, how they utilized linguistic means for conveying notions of negation, etc., as opposed to treatment differences in particular ways of expressing negation grammatically (e.g., "not" versus "un-"). Although there was no direct effort in the classroom toward language training exercises, it was found that the children from the Distancing Program performed significantly better on items requiring comprehension *and* production of future time orientations (linguistic expression of anticipatory events). Similar results were found with comprehension and production of past time, use of causal connectives, and conditionals. Use of such categories indicated linguistic knowledge for expressing reconstructive memory, causality, and conditionality (Cocking, 1977).

Conservation of continuous quantity.   As will be recalled, one of the components of representational thinking as considered in this chapter is that representational thought involves the ability to anticipate or to predict. Such an ability requires an understanding of the relationship between actions or events at one time period and outcomes at a subsequent time. To assess such anticipatory thinking, Piaget's conservation of liquid task was used. Although interest was in whether children could conserve and justify their decisions, this task can also be interpreted as assessing the ability to predict—specifically, in this case, imagining outcomes of physical transformations. Essentially the task involves presenting the child with the problem of predicting the level the water will reach when poured from one short and wide cylinder to a tall and thin one. To make the correct prediction, the child has to employ the principle of compensation. The task among others was administered to all the children enrolled in each of the two types of preschool programs—a distancing program and a so-called traditional child development program. No significant differences were found between the two groups at the outset. However, on the second testing at the end of the school year, more children in the distancing program were able to provide appropriate predictive statements than in the comparison program. Further, no significant changes were found for the comparison group between the two time periods. Sigel and Cocking (1977) concluded that these results indicated that "the discrepancy between Time 1 and Time 2 performance begins to close for children who experience the systematic use of distancing strategies by instructing adults [p. 224]."

Children's verbalizations as they draw.   Cocking and Copple (1979) studied verbal behavior of children as they drew pictures in small groups. They hypothesized that children who made planning statements in drawing would also be likely to make evaluative or critical statements about their own drawings and those of peers. Such behavior which would seem to reveal a more reflective tendency in representational efforts, was hypothesized as emerging later than less self-conscious types of evaluation children might make about their drawings such as labeling or describing. Results indicate that children from the distancing program did exhibit significantly more self-naming and planning than children in a nondistancing program.

Although we found evidence that distancing strategies do influence the children's thinking in a school setting, this is not enough to generalize the influence of "distancing" beyond the classroom. Since the general hypothesis is that "distancing" behaviors are a critical social experience impacting representational competence, the effect should be found in family settings where parents do play the role of teachers.

Effects of parental use of distancing strategies.   A dissertation by A Donovan (1974) on middle-class children found that mothers of boys who manifested greater representational competence used more distancing strategies and fewer coercive control strategies.

Preliminary analysis of data for a large scale family study of birth order and child spacing in which four year old children and their parents were studied and which involved observation of parents teaching their children a structure task (paper folding), revealed that those children whose parents were rated high on distancing strategies did significantly better on representational tasks than children whose parents were rated low (McGillicuddy-DeLisi, Sigel & Johnson, 1979). These results were consistent with results from the preschool studies.

CONCLUSIONS

The aim of this presentation was to elaborate on the role of social experience in developing representational thinking. Distancing behaviors, a class of social interactions, were proposed as causally linked to the development of representational thought. The Representational thinking was conceptualized in Piagetian terms as intimately involving representation of the past, transcendence of the present and anticipation of the future. The temporal and spatial emphasis in distancing interactions, especially when in the form of inquiry in the context of discrepancy generation or resolution, did influence the level of the child's representational thinking.

The interactional model focuses on a Socratic-type inquiry process which is essentially instructional in nature. Although the employment of distancing strategies in the classroom or the home may not be a new topic, the approach proposed here, particularly the theoretical base for it, does make it a viable and relevant general instructional strategy. To be sure, it is not being advocated as a total approach. There are certain types of knowledge which can only be mastered by rote. What is being advocated is a heavy emphasis on inquiry as a critical element in the instructional complex.

The model presented, while compatible with Piagetian structuralism, does make explicit a type of individual environment exchange that seems in fact to influence representational thought. At this stage of our research, the role of inquiry as the interactional (and instructional) method is the strategy of choice if enhancement of representational competence as defined in this paper is an objective.

Further, the empirical results reported in this chapter suggest that the distancing strategies have general applicability. The results from school and family studies indicate that the quality of representational thought may well be influenced by the form of social exchange—to use one of Piaget's terms. The argument in this presentation is simply this: To understand the source and course of cognitive growth, the detailed analysis of social experience is necessary—it is the interaction that is crucial—*decontextualizing* the child's cognitive development is just as much in error as denying the role of internal processing by the individual. Spelling out the critical features of the environmental and individual components and their intersection will enable us to move ahead in our understanding of "how" representational thought evolves. I have presented *one* form of social experience. Others may be identified, yielding a broader understanding of the *what*, the *how,* and perhaps the *why* of cognitive growth.

REFERENCES

Cataldo, C. Z. A follow-up study of early intervention (Doctoral dissertation, State University of New York at Buffalo, 1977). *Dissertation Abstracts International,* 1978, *39,* 657-A. (University Microfilms No. 78-13990).

Cocking, R. R. *A language production instrument.* Princeton, N.J.: Educational Testing Service, 1974.

Cocking, R. R. *Evaluation of a program employing teacher distancing strategies.* Paper presented at the meeting of the New Jersey Psychological Association, Morristown, April 1977.

Cocking, R. R., & Copple, C. E. Change through exposure to others: A study of children's verbalizations as they draw. In J. Magary (Ed.), *Proceedings of the Eighth Annual UAP-USC Conference on Piagetian Theory and the Helping Professions*. Los Angeles, Calif.: University of Southern California, 1979.

Cocking, R. R., & Sigel, I. E. The concept of décalàge as it applies to representational thinking. In N. R. Smith & M. R. Franklin (Eds.), *Symbolic functioning in young children*. Hillsdale, N.J.: Lawrence Erlbaum Associates, 1979.

Collins, A. M. Processes in acquiring knowledge, In R. C. Anderson, R. J. Spiro, & W. E. Montague (Eds.), *Schooling and the acquisition of knowledge*. Hillsdale, N.J.: Lawrence Erlbaum Associates, 1977.

Donovan, A. L. Mother–child interaction and the development of representational skills in young children (Doctoral dissertation, State University of New York at Buffalo, 1975). *Dissertation Abstracts International*, 1975, *36*, 1403B. (University Microfilms No. 75-18,793).

Heath, P. L. Experience. In P. Edwards (Ed.), *The Encyclopedia of Philosophy*. New York: Macmillan Publishing Co/The Free Press, 1967.

Kelly, G. A. *The psychology of personal constructs* (2 vols.). New York: Norton, 1955.

McGillicuddy-DeLisi, A. V., Sigel, I. E., & Johnson, J. E. The family as a system of mutual influences: Parental beliefs, distancing behaviors and children's representational thinking. In M. Lewis & L. A. Rosenblum (Eds.), *The child and its family: The genesis of behavior* (Vol. 2). Plenum, 1979.

Piaget, J. *Psychology of intelligence*. Totowa, N.J.: Littlefield, Adams & Co., 1966.

Piaget, J. *Science of education and the psychology of the child*. New York: Norton, 1967.

Piaget, J. Piaget's theory. In P. H. Mussen (Ed.), *Carmichael's manual of child psychology* (3rd ed., Vol. 1). New York: Wiley, 1970.

Piaget, J. *Main trends in interdisciplinary research*. New York: Harper, 1973.

Piaget, J. *The development of thought: Equilibration of cognitive structures*. New York: Viking Press, 1977.

Piaget, J., & Inhelder, B. *The psychology of the child*. New York: Baisc Books, 1969.

Polanyi, M. *Personal knowledge*. Chicago: University of Chicago Press, 1958.

Rosner, F. C. An ecological study of teacher distancing behaviors as a function of program, context and time (Doctoral dissertation, Temple University, 1978). *Dissertation Abstracts International*, 1978, *39*, 760A. (University Microfilms No. 78-12235).

Sigel, I. E. The Piagetian system and the world of education. In D. Elkind & J. H. Flavell (Eds.), *Studies in cognitive development: Essays in honor of Jean Piaget*. New York: Oxford University Press, 1969.

Sigel, I. E. The distancing hypothesis: A causal hypothesis for the acquisition of representational thought. In M. R. Jones (Ed.), *Miami Symposium on the Prediction of Behavior, 1968: Effect of early experiences*. Coral Gables, Fla.: University of Miami Press, 1970.

Sigel, I. E. Consciousness raising of individual competence in problem solving. In G. W. Albee & J. M. Joffe (Eds.), *Primary prevention of psychopathology* (Vol. 3): *Social competence in children*. Hanover, N.H.: University Press of New England, 1979.

Sigel, I. E., & Cocking, R. R. *Cognitive development from childhood to adolscence: A constructivist perspective*. New York: Holt, Rinehart & Winston, 1977.

Sigel, I. E., & Saunders, R. An inquiry into inquiry: Question asking as an instructional model. In L. G. Katz (Ed.), *Current topics in early childhood education* (Vol. 2). Norwood, N.J.: Ablex Publishing Corp., 1979.

Sigel, I. E., Secrist, A., & Forman, G. Psycho-educational intervention beginning at age two: Reflections and outcomes. In Julian C. Stanley (Ed.), *Compensatory education for children, ages two to eight: Recent studies of educational intervention*. Baltimore, Md.: Johns Hopkins University Press, 1973.

Stevens, A. L., & Collins, A. *The goal structure of a Socratic tutor* (BBN Report No. 3518). Cambridge, Mass.: Bolt, Beranek and Newman, March 1977.

Werner, H. *Comparative psychology of mental development*. New York: International Universities Press, 1948.

14 Functional and Structural Aspects of Rationality

Joseph Glick
CUNY Graduate Center

Most developmental psychologists are, at once, intrigued and bothered by the Genetic Epistemological approach. The approach is intriguing in that it provides a nicely integrated set of concepts and structural descriptions which serve to give some sense of order to diverse phenomena displayed by children and to culturally ideal notions of rationality. Yet there is something disturbing in all of this as well. Many of the phenomena placed in order under the theoretical descriptions are revealed only under conditions designed to elicit them. Many of these elicited behaviors run counter to our naive expectations about what children are likely to know. Accordingly, there has emerged within developmental psychology in the United States of America and Britain a concerted effort to probe the Piagetian elicitation paradigm in order to find experimental artifacts and paradigm-specific features which serve to produce the phenomena which seem so disturbing (Larsen, 1977; Bryant, 1974). In general, these attempts have gone beyond cleaning up the methodology to a position which redefines the meaning of the phenomena measured. Thus, in many instances the operational distinctions made within Piagetian theory have been redefined into a variety of information processing subprocesses, with an accompanying redefinition of the child's performance into specific processing disfunctions (e.g., Klahr, 1973).

Another approach which has been taken has been to provisionally accept the operational distinctions made within Genetic Epistemological theory, and to probe for the performance constraints which may, or may not allow for a given operational structure to be manifested on any occasion. This approach has tended to examine the issues from a cross-situational, and cross-cultural perspective. Although accepting the centrality of operational distinctions researchers working in this tradition seek to examine the influence of performance rules and conditions for the application of operational structures to a given task domain (Flavell & Wohlwill, 1969). Likewise, cross-cultural studies have sought to examine issues of operational structure by searching for universal and nonuniversal aspects of functioning (e.g., Dasen, 1977).

From this latter perspective the important issues are not the redefining of operations into other things (subprocesses) but rather the examination of the relationship between structure and occasion. From this view the issue is how "typical" is the operation of the performance. Questions of typicality may require additional theoretical constructs which may allow us to put structure and behaviour together. One may procede with certainty along these lines so long as it is remembered that the problem is to unite psychologist's and genetic epistemologist's concerns, and not to redefine one in terms of the other.

The problem of the gap between psychological and epistemological interests emerges with increasing force at higher developmental levels. Piagetian descriptions of operational progress within the sensori-motor period appear to be robust, with a good deal of intracultural replication and converging findings from widely different cultures seeming to show a universality in the order and timing of stages (see Glick, 1975 for a review of this literature).

If, in fact, progress during the sensorimotor period involves a progressive mapping of an initially small set of activities onto a physical world which serves as a stable substrate for these activities, one might not expect the physical world to vary much from place to place and hence we would not expect much cultural variation. Additionally, it should be remembered that studies of sensorimotor development tend to be observational in nature so that the studies largely classify spontaneously occuring behaviors. Accordingly we would not expect that problems of experimental paradigm, of elicitation of performance, etc., would be particularly manifest in this developmental period.

With the transition from preoperations to concrete operations there has been simultaneously more evidence of intra and inter cultural variability. Piagetians themselves have generated evidence which suggests alteration in timing (though not in form) of various concrete operational achievements (Bovet, 1974; Dasen, 1972, 1977; Glick, 1975; Piaget, 1974, 1970). The explanation for whatever variations exist is not clearcut: ranging from the possibility that there are differences in the opportunities for structuration experiences that various environments and cultures provide to the possibility that various cultural rules and understandings may determine the expression of concrete operational abilities (Bovet, 1974; Cole, Gay, Glick & Sharp, 1971; Greenfield, 1966).

In the remainder of this chapter this latter view will be extended and developed with respect to the relationship between psychological and epistemological accounts of intellectual functioning.

The basic position is that cognitive processes, rather than captivating, or controlling as it were, the mind, are processes that are deployed, and selected from a set of alternatives, both by a subject of psychological studies and by the formulation of the studies themselves. The basic idea is that rather than constituting rationality, certain operational cognitive processes are deployed as instruments of rationality—on—and this is most important—occasions seen as conductive to their application.

Three examples from earlier cross-cultural work may serve to give an idea of some of the phenomena that have led to this sort of position.

In the project from which these examples are selected (Cole, Gay, Glick & Sharp, 1971) theoretical interest was in the relation of cultural factors to certain basic operational features such as classification, logical inference making, etc. The strategy was to use stable semantic features of the native language (the Kpelle language spoken by the Kpelle tribe of Liberia and Guinea) as a guide to probable areas of classification ability and disability. It was expected that wherever the language made stable distinctions this would be related to efficient classification abilities (from either the linguistic determinist point of view or from a cognitive developmental view that the occurrence of stable semantic features at least reflects if it does not create stable class structures).

The first experiment in the field was rather perplexing. Starting with clear cases we decided to check out our basic generative notion by testing classification abilities in areas where the language made stable classifications. This was almost in the nature of an equipment check.

Using stable classes, derived from extensive semantic elicitation procedures (see Cole et al., 1971 for a description) we arrived at a heap of objects instantiating five instances each of foods, clothes, tools and eating utensils. These objects were heaped on a table and subjects were asked to classify them ("put the ones together that go together"). The results of this instruction were that the subjects made many categories, relating two objects functionally, e.g., the knife and the orange go together, because the knife cuts the orange; or the hoe and potato go together, because the hoe digs the potato. We attempted to push and to rephrase, but always got functional classifications of this sort. When asked for reasons, the answers were often in terms of how "smart people" would choose to relate just such and such objects. When asked if there were other ways to do things, we were flatly rejected with the caveat that a "wise person" would do it in such and such a way. When exasperated, we finally asked "how would a stupid man do it?" The answer was both beatific and categorical. A "stupid man" would organize things into classes like tools, foods, etc.

What was at issue in this experiment was an issue in the deployment of cognitive abilities. It is still not clear what the stupid man/smart man distinction glosses in terms of the tactics of cognitive deployment—but we do know that such deployment occurred.

The next example is another in the class of factors of deployment determiners. Using a similar logic to generate experiments that had to do with the use and deployment of elementary logical operators such as conjunction, disjunction, etc. we explored the relationship between conjunctive and disjunctive concept attainment in a language group that makes clearer distinctions between the various sorts of disjunction than does English. The expectation was that the oft noted advantage of conjunctive over disjunctive concept learning might be mitigated in a case where the logical connectives were encoded in an equally clear manner. A procedure was devised which was to be a model for more serious studies of the matter. The procedure was as follows:

S was told to look at some nearby natural object with the following instruction:
You see that_____I will either be thinking of it or not, at first you will have to guess whether I am thinking of it, but after a while you will be able to know every time. To show you I will be putting my hands out like this (two hands out) like this (left hand out) like this (right hand out) or like this (neither hand out). Each time I will ask you 'am I thinking of the _____?' and I will put out my hands. You are to tell me whether I am not thinking of it. I will tell you if you are right or wrong.

Our initial results with this procedure were quite disappointing. Whereas American children will solve the problem in one run through the instances, our African subjects, both children and adults, showed no learning at all. They would make guesses every time but those guesses were unrelated to the protoconcept involved (e.g., two hands = conjunction, either hand = exclusive disjunction, etc.) When probed for the source of their answers, the African subjects would indicate that they had, in fact, been monitoring various sorts of cues; but these were precisely not the cues that had been intended as critical. Subjects looked for inadvertant glances as a cue, tightness of closing of hands as a cue, etc. It seemed as if the logic of their responding was to look for information that was given off ''in spite of oneself'' and to disregard the information that we had intended, and told them was central.

A chance comment by one of our subjects allowed us to understand what was going on. Our subjects were puzzled by a situation where we asked a question to which we obviously had the answer. The resultant implication was that, in fact, there was some sort of trickery going on; that our intent was never ''straight'' and that, therefore, in order to solve the ''real'' rather than the ''ostensive'' problem it was their job to read through the trickery. The solution to that problem was to pay close attention to those things over which we had little control (like inadvertent tip-off cues that are used in games where hiding is to be confuted). A simple reformulation of the procedure, making the subject ask the question ''are you thinking of it?'' and framing our hand gestures as an answer to that question, served to produce learning, this time oriented to the focal information, and which was fully equivalent to that produced in the United States of America. This device, which in no way altered the reality that we knew the answer, served nonetheless to allow the situation to be interpreted as being a ''normal'' and not a tricky one. If only politicians could learn from cross-cultural field work.

A third example is once again in the domain of classification. We wanted to examine classification abilities with abstract dimensions when semantic categories were not in question. Yet we wanted to use "normal" "everyday" objects. Fortunately, we thought, the town that we were working in abounds with several sorts of beer brands. There were Guiness Stout bottles (which are short and brown), Club beer bottles (which are tall and brown), and various other brands which come in either tall or short green bottles. A bunch of empties were collected and subjects were asked to classify them into the ones that go together. This time there was absolute refusal to classify at all. "Smart people don't classify garbage." Doing the same task with filled bottles (and the labels off) led to classification.

Two points may be made at this juncture: First, one of the major issues in these examples is the question of the deployment of the skills that subjects were capable of exercising. We simply had no idea that these skills were "deployed." The fumbling efforts made by us to reformulate the experiments so that they would work served in fact to reveal deployment rules which aligned the subject's and the experimenter's conception of what was going on. Second, it seems as if the issue of deployment arose because the tasks were not taken simply as hypothetical games, but were rather taken as tokens in social intercourse. It was somehow important for the subjects to locate their doings in terms of a personalized world having as some of its inhabitants, "tricksters," "smart doers," "fools," etc..

Neither of two easy conclusions is warranted at this point. The first conclusion is that Africans, as an index of their primitivity, live in a social world inhabited by tricksters, fools and others. We all do. The second conclusion to be ruled out is that translating "pure" cognitive tasks into social ones necessarily obscures cognitive activities. This is not so for three reasons; first there is a yet to be discovered rationality of social doings; second, certain social constructions can lead to the display of operational knowledge more readily than certain nonsocial contexts; and, third, the task results are not limited to the social realm.

Before elaborating further, an odd distortion that has been introduced should be noted. We generally tend to think that the formal operational period is marked by, first and foremost, the introduction of a certain hypothetical attitude toward reasoning from the possible to the necessary. The operations that distinguish between concrete and formal levels are based on this hypothetical attitude. Yet the examples that have been provided are largely concrete operational examples, and allow for the utilization of this hypothetical attitude. I mean to suggest that even such concrete level operations as classification occur in contexts where the pragmatic is divorced from the theoretic in a principled way.

We often tend to think of classification as an obligatory feature of cognition. Functionalist arguments have been raised to suggest that were it not for information reduction capabilities we would soon be swamped by an informational surplus that would overtax our minds (e.g., Bruner, Goodnow & Austin, 1956). Classification is seen by these theorists not simply as a way of eliminating small differences, but as an essential ingredient for psychological economy whereby members of conceptual categories might be considered equivalent and hence knowledge about one of the members applies to other members as well. Yet it is equally clear that some of the classes that we, and others, used in our research are taxonomic in nature, without any functional equivalence implied. Thus, whereas a computer, a language and a screwdriver are all "tools," we learn precious little from knowledge about one of them that can be applied to the others. In some sense, to indulge in this classificatory action one must suspend notions of practicality and play with notions of a definitional sort—and this is hypothetical in some important sense.

In large measure the African experiments dealt with classification not from the point of view of the deployment of operational structures with respect to classes (no matter how composed), but were rather looking at conditions for the composition of classes. The latter reflects a psychological rather than an epistemological concern. Where Piaget's theory is relevant to what has been done is in the attempt to circumscribe operational structures within a functional sphere. What is different from Piaget's theory in the position taken here is that the structural descriptions of operational intelligence (whether concrete or formal) are valid descriptions of only an area of human capability. Structures of operational intelligence are, however, circumscribed in their execution. The fundamental requirement for the application of these forms of thought is some form of hypothetical posture which implies a "contemplative" attitude (Werner & Kaplan, 1963).

What are requirements for contemplation? To operate contemplatively one requires either explicit indication to do so or a freedom from the consequences of action. Taking the latter first, under conditions where moves have consequences and the pressure to act is strong, one is likely to find that processes of rational construction are truncated, and more local scenarios or prescriptions for recognizably competent behaviour are utilized. When the pressure is on—to operate in real time at a rapid pace—people tend to use formalized roles and ritualized performances. The invocation of "smart men"—also often glossed as Kpelle man—is an invocation of precisely that level of concept. In lay society, even in this society, the intellectual approach is subject to social valuations—many of them negative—and we do distinguish between intellectual and "smart." Recent research on social understandings, an area which is most subject to the sort of pressure to be visibly and immediately competent, (perhaps at the cost of rational reflection) has demonstrated that there are a number of short-cut devices, which serve to reduce informational loads and uncertainties. These have been called "social scripts." (Schank & Abelson, 1973.) Similar effects may be obtained by increasing time pressure in the doing of operational tasks.

Within the cognitive domain, Bruner, Goodnow and Austin (1967) have demonstrated that information is processed quite differently depending on whether it is framed in terms that are conducive to contemplation or terms which place the information in the domain of the socially judgeable. In a study which looked for strategies of treating information, they constructed a set of 81 cards which were defined in terms of the intersect of four three-valued dimensions. Thus, cards could be made up from any of three colors, applied to any of three shapes in any of three numbers, with any of three numbered borders. Careful records of the manner in which a next card was chosen after a subject was given a positive intance, served to identify three basic sorts of strategies. In one strategy, subjects seemed to operate according to formal operational principles, performing combinational contrasts which efficiently served to eliminate dimensions for consideration. At the other extreme were subjects who jumped to a guess and simply tested its validity through a number of instances. For geometrically defined problems, such as that described above, the former, combinatorial strategy was dominant. However, when the material for concept identification was transformed into representative material, depicting e.g., humans of different sexes, sizes, etc. instead of geometrical dimensions, the mode of solving the problem changed. Given a stimulus set of equal information complexity, subjects now opted for a strategy of seizing upon hypotheses and testing their implications out. It is as if, the human, social, form of the problem served to turn everyone into clinicians, where before they were combinatorial logicians.

Similar results could be obtained by preserving the geometrical problems and instead increasing pressure to identify the concept (e.g., by timing or other devices). Again, a truncation of the combinatorial into the intuitive occurred. What can be seen so plainly in these experiments is that rational contemplative action is fragile and requires essentially protected spaces in which to occur. Its form has been elegantly described by Piaget (1970), but the conditions of the application of this form have not.

The approach taken here is concerned with the conditions of application and this probably requires a theory of a different sort than has heretofore been offered. Operational functioning is not an automatic consequence of development, it is rather a product of developmental acquisition and a directed intelligence oriented to act in particular real world ways. Some recent studies have been exploring the implications of this approach using classically operational areas, such as conservation. In our experiment (White & Glick, 1978) we were concerned with the problems that have been stated above, but in inverse form. We asked whether strategically encouraging children to deploy social categories could be used as a device to enhance, rather than inhibit, operational functioning. We reasoned that a "trickster" figure, from whom one would expect various sorts of illusory fabrications, might lead children to pay careful attention to the usual transformations, which do not cause quantitative changes in the conservation task. We expected that the experimenter who was a "trickster" might indeed lead children to exhibit earlier signs of conservation reasoning than a "straight" experimenter. The experiment used video-taped scenarios which had the following general form—two children had equal amounts of differently flavored kool-aid. One of the children desires an exchange because he prefers the flavor that the other child has. The possessor of the preferred flavor resists a trade saying that he would trade only if he got more in exchange. At this point the desiring child consults the trickster "Jimmy Cool" and receives advice. After receiving advice (which is whispered and unavailable to the audience) he returns to the trading post and does a classic conservation manipulation, first aligning level of liquid establishing correspondence, and then pouring the nonpreferred into a narrower glass; thereby effecting a trade. The audience children were then asked what was tricky about what he did, and why? Control conditions, where just the transformation and its consequence were shown, and control conditions where the same script was followed but no trickster character, etc. were run. Results indicate that the trickster manipulation was effective in advancing the display of conservation judgments and explanations, particularly among transitional children.

The upshot of these considerations is that it is particularly important to pay attention to the conditions of elicitation and the functional spheres within which rationality is displayed. This is not simply a problem of décalage. Décalage refers basically to different acquisitions within a functional sphere. With décalage it is assumed that individuals are trying to operate with similar principles and we ask if they are able to do so across various contents. I have in mind something more profound. It is possible that there are multiple rationalities—or as Werner might have put it—multilinearities in development. Piaget has offered us an elegant and precise description of only one type of rational development—culminating with the possibilities of scientific reasoning. There is at least the entertainable hypothesis that there are other sorts of rationalities, for example, rationalities of smartness rather than of science. We as yet have little idea of what a formal theory of that sort of rationality might look like. It appears rather, at this point, as if it is noise in our attempts to measure rationalities of the first sort. Yet it may be that these other rationalities are not a degraded form, nor merely noise, but forms of rationality not yet identified.

We may in fact be dealing in our developmental cognitive analyses with an uncertain interweaving between at least two formally integral systems. These may be called out in different degrees and in completely uncontrolled manners in our attempts at psychological measurement—which is, after all, what experiments are all about. In order to approach fundamental problems examining the development of cognitive structures, we shall have to work assiduously to determine what the "normal" course of reasoning is. In this way we may find a place for the kind of structures that the Genevan school has so elegantly and excitingly brought to light.

Perhaps, in this manner, some greater light can be shed upon problems of décalage, on the influences of sociocultural variables on cognitive functioning, and the like. Perhaps we may gain some purchase on the relationship between logically rational and the socioculturally rational that seems so often out of joint.

As a final note I should like to point to an implication of this approach which was pointed to, though not explicitly developed, by Mounoud (Chapter 7) and raised again by Murray (Chapter 10) and Sigel (Chapter 13). Mounoud pointed out that the interest in various logically derived aspects of thinking led to experimental approaches which tended to isolate concepts such as time, or number, or causality. This segregation, for purposes of study, may have obscured fundamental organizational and reorganizational features of intelligence. Murray and Sigel pointed out various sources of methods variance which in one way or another obscure "true" measurement. Neimark (Chapter 11) has pointed to stable personal-variation in the same vein.

The approach taken here is that even if we were to pursue the error-free measurement of various cognitive abilities, we would be missing a fundamental point. This is the point that Mounoud made and which I have just developed. Our experiments themselves create—as the focus of our interest—just some possibilities of knowing, and obscure others. By doing a good experiment, we "protect" as it were a special sphere of functioning—we arrange things so that, *that*—and just *that*—can happen. What we miss in all of this, in our search for cleaner ideas of structure, is the natural flow of thought as it is deployed in nature. Thus, we tend to create a domain of possible results—and to close down on asking some very important questions about the tactical deployment of thought.

REFERENCES

Bovet, M. Cross-cultural study of conservation concepts: Continuous quantities and length. In B. Inhelder, H. Sinclair, and M. Bovet, *Learning and the Development of Cognition*. Cambridge, Mass.: Harvard University Press, 1974.

Bruner, I. S., Goodnow, J. J., & Austin, G. A. *A study of thinking*, New York: Wiley, 1956.

Bryant, P. *Perception and understanding in young children*. New York: Basic Books, 1974.

Cole, M., Gay, J., Glick, J., & Sharp, D. *The cultural context of learning and thinking*. New York: Basic Books, 1971.

Dasen, P. Cross-cultural Piagetian research: A summary. *Journal of Cross-cultural Psychology*, 1972, *3*, 23-29.

Dasen, P. *Piagetian psychology: Cross-cultural contributions*. New York: Gardner Press, 1977.

Flavell, J. H., & Wohlwill, J. F. Formal and functional aspects of cognitive development. In D. Elkind & J. H. Flavell (Eds.), *Studies in development: Essays in honor of Jean Piaget*. New York: Oxford University Press, 1969.

Glick, J. Cognitive development in cross-cultural perspective. In F. D. Horowitz (Ed.), *Review of child development research. Vol. 4*. Chicago: University of Chicago Press, 1975.

Greenfield, P. M. On culture and conservation. In J. S. Bruner et al. *Studies in cognitive growth*. New York: Wiley, 1966.

Klahr, D. An information processing approach to the study of cognitive development. In A. D. Pick (Ed.), *Minnesota Symposium on Child Psychology*. Vol. 7. Minneapolis: University of Minnesota Press. 1979.

Larsen, G. Y. Methodology in developmental psychology: An examination of research on Piagetian theory. *Child Development*, 1977, *48*, 1160-1166.

Piaget, J. Necessité et signification des recherches comparatives en psychologie genetique. *International Journal of Psychology 1*, 3-13. (English Translation in J. W. Berry & P. R. Dasen (Eds.), *Culture and cognition: Readings in cross-cultural psychology*. London: Methuen, 1974.)

Piaget, J. Piaget's theory. In P. Mussen (Ed.), *Carmichael's manual of child psychology, Vol. 1.* New York: Wiley, 1970.

Schank, R. C., & Abelson, R. P. *Scripts, plans, goals and understanding: An inquiry into human knowledge structures.* Hillsdale, N.J.: Lawrence Erlbaum Associates, 1977.

Werner, H., & Kaplan, B. *Symbol Formation.* New York: Wiley, 1963.

White, D., & Glick, S. *Interpretive frameworks and conservation.* Paper delivered at the Jean Piaget Society Meetings, Philadelphia, PA., May 1978.

IV

APPLICATION

15 Application of Piaget's Theory to Education: The Preoperational Level

Constance Kamii
University of Illinois at
Chicago Circle and
University of Geneva

Early childhood education has been in existence for a long time in the form of nursery school, kindergarten, and early elementary education in the United States. A chapter on the application of Piaget's theory to education at the pre-operational level might, therefore, begin by asking what Piaget's theory has to contribute beyond what is already known and practiced in this field.

I think Piaget's theory has a great deal to contribute to progress in early education, and I would like to make the following two points in this chapter: (1) Piaget's theory makes it possible to evaluate the theories on which all programs are based, and (2) the theory makes it possible to identify the best practices developed to date and to go beyond them.

THE USE OF PIAGET'S THEORY TO EVALUATE THE THEORIES ON WHICH ALL PROGRAMS ARE BASED

Before discussing this point directly, it is necessary to clarify the relationship between Piaget's theory and other theories on which programs are either explicitly or implicitly based. I would like to begin by comparing Piaget's theory with classical behaviorism because classical behaviorism is a particularly clear and scientific example of the empiricist-associationist current on which education has traditionally been based.[1]

---

[1] It was necessary to oversimplify many points in the original version of this chapter. After the Symposium, the paper had to be reduced to almost half of its original length. The following discussion is, therefore, a simplification of an oversimplification that does not deal with the relationship between empiricism as an epistemological theory and behaviorism as a psychological theory. The reader is referred to Piaget and Inhelder (1969) for a clarification of the epistemological context within which behaviorism came into being.

Behaviorism and Piaget's Theory

There is a tendency today to view behaviorism and Piaget's theory as two alternative theories. This presumed relationship can be expressed with two circles as shown in Fig. 15.1(a) which represent a mutually exclusive relationship. This conceptualization is incorrect. As can be seen in Fig. 15.1(b), behaviorism is much more limited than Piaget's theory and can, in fact, be encompassed by it.

Piaget's theory is broader and more powerful than behaviorism because it can explain every intellectual and moral phenomenon explained by behaviorism, whereas behaviorism cannot explain most of Piaget's findings. Let us take the example of Pavlov's dog which is interpreted by behaviorists as demonstrating conditioning and extinction. Piaget's interpretation of the same phenomena is different in that, for him, after the repeated presentation of the bell and meat, the bell comes to be a signal for the appearance of food (Piaget, 1947, 1967; Piaget & Inhelder, 1966). If the meat subsequently stops appearing, the organism simply stops anticipating it. Piaget thus explains conditioning and extinction in terms of the organism's ability to attribute meaning to objects and events and to anticipate future happenings, thereby adapting to its environment.

Although Piaget's theory can thus explain the phenomena studied by behaviorists, the converse is not the case. Let us take as an example the quantification of class inclusion. No behaviorist can explain why all children begin by saying that there are more dogs than animals. Neither can behaviorists explain why, without any teaching whatsoever, children later come to say that there are more animals than dogs. Furthermore, in the quantification of class inclusion, there is no extinction. Once the child believes that there are more animals than dogs, there is no way of convincing him that he should go back to his earlier belief.

Let us take another example from the realm of moral development to explain Fig. 15.1(b). In *The Moral Judgment of the Child,* Piaget (1932) spoke of sanctions, which the translator unfortunately changed to "punishment." In this book, Piaget stated that adults use sanctions to get children to behave in certain ways, and that in life it is often impossible to avoid sanctions (for example, when we don't want children to touch knobs on the television or stereo set). Although he thus acknowledged the inevitability of sanctions, he also insisted that sanctions have the effect of prolonging the child's heteronomy by preventing the development of autonomy. Autonomy, it will be recalled, is a political term that means "governing oneself." Heteronomy, by contrast, means "being governed by somebody else." Heteronomy can be seen in the example of the seven-year-old who answered the question "Would it be bad to tell lies if you were not punished?" with a straightforward "No" [p. 168]. Autonomy, on the other hand, can be seen in the example of the 12-year-old who said, "Sometimes you almost have to tell lies to a grown-up, but it's rotten to do it to another fellow [p. 173]." Heteronomy can be explained by behaviorism, but autonomy can be explained only by a broader theory.

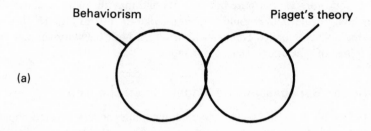

(a)

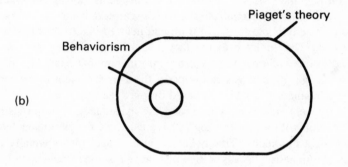

(b)

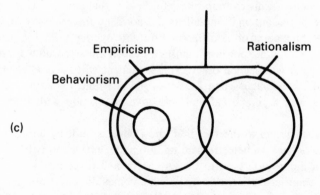

(c)

FIG. 15.1. The relationship between Piaget's theory and behaviorism, empiricism, and rationalism.

Most educators are not pure behaviorists and may dismiss the above discussion as being irrelevant. I would, therefore, like to shift to Fig. 15.1(c), which shows the epistemological context within which both behaviorism and various philosophies of education came into being.

Empiricism, Rationalism, and Piaget's Interactionism

Long before the birth of modern psychology, philosophers debated about how truth, or knowledge, is attained. Two main epistemological currents developed in answer to this question—the empiricist and rationalist currents.

Empiricists (such as Locke, Berkeley, & Hume) insisted that knowledge must rely primarily on sensory information which comes from outside the individual to the inside through the senses. They viewed the inside as a blank slate on which experiences are written. Rationalists (such as Descartes & Kant) rejected sensory information as the ultimate source of truth and insisted that truth is best guaranteed by reason. They pointed to the fact that our senses often deceive us in perceptual illusions and argued that sensory information thus cannot be trusted to give us knowledge. Rationalists saw support for their argument in the certainty and clarity of mathematics which is based on pure reason.

Piaget's frequent statements concerning the inadequacy of empiricism, and his preoccupation with the role of logic, have led some people to conclude that Piaget must be a rationalist. This belief is false. Piaget insists equally on the inadequacy of rationalism because rationalists have assumed innate knowledge or concepts that unfold as a function of maturation. Piaget is not a maturationist. He is an interactionist who believes in the *construction* of knowledge by the indissociable interaction between sensory experience and reason.

Piaget's interactionism can best be explained by comparing the outer oval of Fig. 15.1(c) with the overlap between the two circles inside that represent empiricism and rationalism. This overlap refers to the fact that empiricists recognized the importance of reason, and rationalists did not deny the necessity of sensory input. Piaget's interactionism is different from this overlap in that it states that observation and reason are not just important in such a juxtaposed way, but that one cannot happen without the other. This statement will become clear in the second part of this chapter when I discuss physical and logico-mathematical knowledge, as well as empirical and reflective abstraction with reference to Table 15.1.

Constructivism refers to the fact that knowledge is built by an active child from the inside rather than being transmitted from the outside through the senses. This view is in opposition both to the empiricist and rationalist views. Piaget disproved the empiricist belief that knowledge comes directly from the outside like light that reaches the film in a camera. He also disproved the rationalist view of maturation as stated above. The clearest examples of constructivism can be found in *The Moral Judgment of the Child*. No child is taught that it is bad to tell

TABLE 15.1
Child-Development Curriculum Activities Reconceptualized
with Piaget's Theory

Child-development curriculum activities	Physical knowledge	Social knowledge	Logico-arithmetical knowledge			Knowledge of space and time		Representation		
			Classification	Seriation	Number	Spatial reasoning	Temporal reasoning	Index	Symbol	Sign
Dramatic play		X					X		X	X
Block building	X					X			X	
Painting	X					X			X	
Other arts and crafts activities	X					X			X	
Caring for animals and plants	X						X			
Cooking	X						X			
Singing and playing musical instruments	X	X					X			X
Movement						X			X	
Listening to stories		X				X	X	X		X
Sand and water play	X									
Playing with playground equipment	X					X				
Table games (such as puzzles)							X		X	
Group games (such as Musical Chairs)		X								

lies only if one is punished for it. Yet children come to hold this belief by constructing an interpretation of what they are told. Later, as a result of interactions with others, they construct a different theory about lies and come to believe that a lie is bad regardless of whether or not one is punished for it. This construction even leads to the belief cited earlier that "Sometimes you almost have to tell lies to a grown-up, but it's rotten to do it to another fellow."[2]

As an educator, the most fundamental point I get out of the books by Piaget is that of constructivism by equilibration. The view that development takes place from within by constructing one level after another of being "wrong" is funda-

---

[2]The only example of constructivism I give in this paper deals with moral judgment. However, *all* knowledge is constructed according to Piaget, and I do not imply that construction is limited to knowledge that has sources in the external world.

mentally opposed to the empiricist assumptions on which education has been based for centuries.

Empiricist assumptions are reflected almost everywhere in education. For example, by considering the learner to be analogous to an empty glass, educators have arranged the classroom into neat rows like rows of empty glasses to be filled and passed on from one grade level to the next. In each grade, the teacher tries to fill all the glasses up to a certain level before giving them to the next teacher. This pouring of knowledge implies that the teacher is like a giant funnel that has collected all the wisdom of the past and selects out of her repertoire what to teach, with what organization, and in what sequence.

Interactionism, by contrast, has manifested itself in education in the form of protests against these traditional ways. For example, Rousseau (1780) opposed excessive verbal instruction. Froebel (1885) likewise insisted that the goal of education cannot be imposed on the student because each person is like a plant that unfolds. Dewey (1902) opposed the compartmentalization of the curriculum into subjects and lessons and argued that the curriculum should be rooted in each student's interests. More recently, we have seen a rash of protests from authors such as Dennison (1969), Goodman (1962), Herndon (1968), Holt (1964), Kohl (1967), and Silberman (1970). These authors based their psychological and pedagogical notions on personal observation and opinion rather than on a scientific theory. Their philosophy can nevertheless be recognized as belonging unmistakably to an interactionist current.

Most reformers including the followers of Dewey have run small, marginal schools, which have not lasted very long. The reason for this failure can be found in the fact that when a movement is small and based on personal convictions that go counter to all the forces of established tradition, it depends on a charismatic leader to keep it strong and united. When the leader is gone and the movement does not have a scientific base, each practitioner is left free to interpret a philosophy in his own way until the movement sooner or later dies. A school that uses Piaget's theory seems different in that Piaget's theory is scientific, and, therefore, both the theory itself and its application to education can be evaluated with theoretical rigor.

The difficulty with Piaget's theory today is that it is not only a scientific theory but also a revolutionary theory, and the psychology of learning is in the midst of what Kuhn (1962) called a scientific revolution. Kuhn points out that each scientific revolution grows out of the inadequacy of the previous theory. For example, the Copernican revolution came after a long period of dissatisfaction with the inaccuracies obtained in calculating the positions of planets and in trying to make the old calendar work. Astronomers kept making corrections for these inaccuracies until the geocentric theory became hopelessly incoherent and complex. What Copernicus did was to create a new conceptual framework through which he looked at the same planets, thereby increasing the accuracy, simplicity, and coherence of astronomy.

The first reaction to any revolutionary theory, according to Kuhn, is resistance. Since all scientists are trained to think about and study nature in a way that fits the conceptual framework supplied by their education, it is natural for them to resist a new framework that subverts the old rules of how to go about trying to get at the truth.

What happens after the initial resistance is competition between two groups—the one committed to the old framework and the one committed to the new one. According to Kuhn, competition between segments of the scientific community is the only process that has historically resulted in the rejection of a previously accepted theory.

If there is a tendency today to view behaviorism and Piaget's theory as mutually exclusive as shown in Fig. 15.1(a), this is so because we are in the midst of a revolution, when two segments of the scientific community are in competition. The mutually exclusive relationship implies that educators must choose one and reject the other. Fig. 15.1(b) shows that Piaget's theory leads not to the rejection of behaviorism but to its inclusion in a larger, more adequate theory.[3] This evolution of theories is similar to the evolution of the child's thought from one level to the next. For example, when he becomes a conserver, the conserver does not reject his previous way of thinking. He still thinks that the liquid in the taller, thinner glass is "more" in a certain sense, but he has a very different way of apprehending this "fact" when he can coordinate a host of relationships and assimilate the old "fact" into a new system of relationships. Just as preoperational relationships become incorporated into later relationships, behaviorism becomes incorporated into a more complete theory that eliminates the contradictions found in the previous theory.

The revolutionary nature of Piaget's theory was previously discussed to show that the validity of an educational program can be determined by the validity of the theory on which the program is based. To the extent that a theory is scientific, it can be subjected to the same scrutiny as any other scientific theory. I think, therefore, that the competition between behaviorism and Piaget's theory will eventually be resolved. What worries me more is the fact that most educational practices are based not on tightly conceptualized scientific theories but on diffuse, implicit beliefs which are not subjected to rigorous examination. I would like to show how Piaget's theory as shown in Fig. 15.1(c) makes it possible to evaluate the implicit theories underlying some programs.

---

[3]It is important for educators to remember that although Piaget's theory proved behaviorism inadequate, behaviorism can still be useful to solve certain problems within certain limits. For example, the logic of multiplication cannot be taught by programmed instruction, but once this logic is constructed by the child, memorization is the only way to learn the multiplication tables. Behaviorism can be useful within certain limits because immediate feedback is very useful in this kind of memorization.

Evaluating the Implicit Theories Underlying Educational Practices

In evaluating all the practices invented to date in early education, in light of the above reflection, I think the best developed so far is the child-development approach.[4] This conclusion is based on the fact that early-education programs can be considered on a continuum from the behaviorist to the interactionist end, and that the theory underlying the child-development approach is more interactionist than the theory on which any other program is based.

The Montessori method is an example of a program that can be located between the behaviorist and interactionist end of the continuum. Montessori insisted that children should not be forced to sit still on benches waiting for knowledge to be transmitted, but that they should be allowed to move about and choose their activities. Although she thus had a strong interactionist belief, which was revolutionary in her day, she remained a strong empiricist in her method and materials. In *The Montessori Method* (1912), she spoke of the "education of the senses" with her didactic materials and went on to advocate "intellectual education," which boiled down to the teaching of words that bears a remarkable resemblance to the DISTAR method (Engelmann, Osborn, & Engelmann, 1969) as can be seen in the following quote:[5]

> ... touching the smooth and rough cards in the first tactile exercise, she (the teacher) should say, "This is smooth. This is rough," repeating the words with varying modulations of the voice, always letting the tones be clear and the enunciation very distinct. "Smooth, smooth, smooth. Rough, rough, rough [p. 225]."

In the realm of moral education, too, Montessori made contradictory statements. Although she advocated the child's individual liberty and the abolition of prizes and punishment, she also said, ". . . loving the child, we should point out to him that obedience is the law of life [p. 364]." She thus favored autonomy and heteronomy at the same time, as well as active learning and passive associations. In a scientific theory, such contradictions become hard to defend.

---

[4]The term "approach" is used in this paper because this is neither a method nor a model but a certain philosophy which is shared by many teachers of young children. When I criticize certain statements made in books written within this tradition, however, I am sometimes told that that is not part of the child-development philosophy. Classification depends on one's point of view, and I see enough similarity among authors such as Biber (1977), Cohen (1972), Hildebrand (1976), Leeper et al. (1974), Read (1971), and Todd and Heffernan (1977) to consider them as belonging to the child-development approach. Although these authors may not agree with my classification, I think that they share certain beliefs that are very different from those on which DISTAR and behavior-analysis models are based.

[5]Some practitioners of the Montessori method do not agree with some of its parts such as this one. I am aware of this disagreement but wanted to discuss the method as presented by its founder.

THE USE OF PIAGET'S THEORY TO GO BEYOND THE BEST PRACTICE DEVELOPED TO DATE

In order to discuss good practice, we must be clear about the objectives we are trying to achieve. I will, therefore, begin with a clarification of objectives before discussing classroom practice. The chapter will conclude with the question of policy, since this seems to be the greatest obstacle to progress in the future.

The Definition of Objectives

Empiricism and Piaget's interactionism lead to very different ways of defining educational objectives. When we believe as empiricists do that knowledge and values are learned by internalization from sources external to the child, we define objectives according to the values that we hold for our pupils. Kohlberg and Mayer (1972) called this approach to defining objectives the "bag-of-virtues" approach. In the bag-of-virtues approach, if we value reading, writing, arithmetic, a good self concept, ability to get along with others, and critical, creative thinking, these are the objectives we define for our pupils. If, on the other hand, we believe that knowledge and values are constructed by the pupil from the inside in interaction with the environment, we define objectives as whatever supports and meshes with this process of construction.

The objectives of early education must be conceptualized in the context of long-range objectives, going up to early adulthood, shown in Fig. 15.2. The circle representing "development as long as development is possible" refers to the set of objectives that can be derived from Piaget's theory.[6] Piaget (1948) stated that it is a rare adult who is capable of critical, logical thinking and moral autonomy. This view was confirmed in part by recent research in the United States by McKinnon and Renner (1971) and Schwebel (1975), who studied the ability of college freshmen to engage in formal operations. The percentages they found to be capable of solid formal operations were 25 and 20 respectively. It must be recalled that these students were the "cream" of our school population who were successful enough to get into colleges (the circle to the right in Fig. 15.2). As far as the moral development of the average adult is concerned, we do not need any research evidence to tell us how underdeveloped adults are. We have only to open a newspaper to be reminded of corruption in public life and low-level behavior in private life. Most adults stopped growing at a low developmental level, both intellectually and morally.

The other circle in Fig. 15.2 indicates the long-range objective of "success in school." The part that does not overlap with the circle to the left refers to the "right" answers children learn only to satisfy teachers and get through exam-

---

[6]The original conceptualization of development as the aim of education was done by Kohlberg and Mayer (1972).

Development as long   Success in
as development   school
is possible

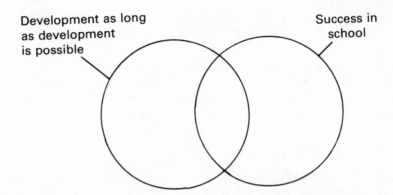

FIG. 15.2.   The relationship between two objectives: success in school and development as long as development is possible.

inations. The result of success in school is the findings reported by McKinnon
and Renner and by Schwebel about the "cream" of our school population mentioned above. (The reader must certainly remember being successful in school by
memorizing "right" answers to satisfy the teacher in class and get through
examinations.)

    The overlap between the two circles in Fig. 15.2 refers to things that are
taught in school that mesh well with and support development. Reading, writing,
and arithmetic can be personally meaningful and useful for our adaptation to the
environment. The study of physics, history, geography, and every other subject
can likewise be part of our development and adaptation to the world. I am not
against academic standards. I am all for them. However, the overlap between the
two circles should become larger.

    Within the context of the long-range objectives discussed above, we can
conceptualize the short-range objectives for early education. If development
takes place by construction from within, whatever fosters the constructive process is a valid objective for early education. More specifically, objectives derived
from Piaget's constructivism can be articulated in the following way:

1. In relation to adults
   we would like children to develop their autonomy through relationships in
   which adult power is reduced to a minimum.[7]
2. In relation to peers
   we would like children to develop their ability to decenter and coordinate
   different points of view.
3. In relation to learning
   we would like children to be alert, curious, confident in their ability to

---

[7]Power is exercised especially when adults use positive and negative sanctions to control children's behavior.

figure things out, and say what they honestly think. We would also like them to have initiative, come up with interesting ideas, problems, and questions, and put things into relationships.

This is a short and general list compared to my earlier conceptualizations (Kamii, 1971, 1972a, 1972b, 1973a, 1973b; Kamii and Radin, 1967, 1970; Sonquist and Kamii, 1967; Sonquist, Kamii, and Derman, 1970). If young children have all these qualities, I believe that the rest will naturally develop. For example, language development is absent from the above list. But when adult power is reduced to a minimum, the first thing that emerges is negotiation. When children participate in the decision-making process, they have to talk a great deal and articulate their ideas as logically and convincingly as they possibly can. It is meaningful use which encourages language development. By negotiating compromises with adults and peers and by expressing their ideas and listening to others, children develop their language in the best and most natural way. Socioemotional objectives, such as trust and a positive self concept, are likewise absent from the above list. But if children are respected and their autonomy is taken seriously, trust and a positive self concept are bound to develop.

To be sure, the above list is not free of all values. However, it is not a list arbitrarily drawn from a bag of virtues. The objectives were derived from Piaget's constructivism—a scientific theory based on research that showed how human beings develop as individuals and in history.

The first objective, autonomy, is both social and intellectual. Not telling lies and not breaking promises are examples of social (moral) rules. There is a big difference between being made to follow ready-made rules and constructing one's own convictions about these rules. The child who is asked, "Do you think I will be able to believe you next time?" is given room to construct his own rule autonomously. Autonomy as an educational objective is thus different from a long list of specific virtues and bits of knowledge. If children want to be believed, they *will* construct their own rules about honesty and keeping promises. If they are encouraged to think autonomously and to express and defend their ideas, they will likewise construct knowledge more solidly than when it is transmitted to them. For example, if a child believes that the way to make playdough firmer is to add water to it, he should be encouraged to go ahead and try his idea.

The second objective, the child's relationships with peers, is again different from the same objective drawn out of a bag of virtues. According to Piaget (1932, 1947), children can construct neither their logic nor their moral values without confronting points of view with their peers. Extending the work of Inhelder, Sinclair, and Bovet (1974), which showed, among other things, that children do not have to have the "right" answer taught to develop their logic, Perret-Clermont (1980) studied the effects of exchange of ideas among children in small groups. She found that when children are already close to a certain level of development, the confrontation of points of view is often enough to produce a higher level of logic. In the moral realm, likewise, children cannot construct the rule of sharing, honesty, or fair play if they do not have many opportunities to relate to their peers and negotiate agreements in conflict situations. We thus believe in developing peer relationships not because we value them by personal taste, but because a scientific theory shows that peer relationships are indispensable for children's moral and intellectual development.

The third objective dealing with learning is also derived from Piaget's constructivism. If children are encouraged to come up with their own problems and games, they are usually committed to working surprisingly hard at what they initiated. If they are alert and curious, they even raise questions about how to spell or read certain words. When they are encouraged to say what they honestly think, they sometimes tell the teacher that her idea is too easy and no fun. While playing board games with dice, alert children construct and memorize the addition table up to six. The third objective thus reflects the difference between teaching conceived as *in*struction and teaching conceived as the fostering of the child's own *con*struction of knowledge.

In conclusion, the implications of Piaget's theory are not just a different way of arriving at the same traditional goal of success in school. The pedagogical objectives of most Head Start and Follow Through programs are defined as success in school. An early education program that uses Piaget's theory must deviate in fundamental ways from this objective. Paradoxically, however, the product coming out of a Piagetian school will be more like the old American ideal of an intelligent, critical thinker who is well educated, morally incorruptible, and independent in his judgments.

What to Do in the Classroom

Piaget's recent twin books (1974), *The Grasp of Consciousness* and *Success and Understanding,* are on the relationship between what children *do* in practical intelligence and how they conceptualize what they do. These books shed much light on the relationship between what practitioners actually do in education and how they conceptualize their practice. Society has always had a need to educate at least some of its young, and education as a profession grew out of this practical need. Although education has thus attained a certain level of development, the only way it can go beyond its present level is by conceptualizing its practice in a more rigorous, scientific way.[8]

In *The Grasp of Consciousness,* Piaget gave many examples of children's ability to produce desired effects in relatively easy tasks, such as walking on all fours and twirling an object attached to a string and letting go of the string at the right moment to make it land in a box. Although children often succeeded in producing desired effects at a surprisingly young age, when asked *how* they produced the desired effect, they gave descriptions that differed from what they

---

[8]Agriculture and medicine are other examples of occupations which developed out of society's practical needs and later advanced through scientific research.

had done. For example, no 4 year olds had trouble walking on all fours. When asked how they walked on all fours, they said that they moved in a "Z" pattern, by moving the left and right hand first, and then the left and right leg. At level II, around ages 5 and 6, children reported that they walked in an "N" pattern. They said, for example, that they advanced the left leg and left hand first, and then the right leg and right hand. It was around ages 7 or 8 that they finally gave the level III description, which was the same as what they were in fact doing (i.e., an "X" pattern).

A similar phenomenon can be seen among practitioners in education. When we ask a teacher how s/he gets children to clean up the room so quickly, for example, we often get a description that differs from what s/he seems to be doing. Sometimes, teachers simply say they don't know how they produce the desired effect and add, "I do what *feels* right." Early education as a profession seems to be at this level of development. Many teachers intuitively do many things well in the classroom, but they do not observe their own behavior with precision. This inability to observe oneself reflects the absence of a theoretical framework in their mind. Without a theoretical framework, teachers cannot observe or reflect on what they do, or know the reason for what they do.

Success and Understanding shows that children can often succeed in getting certain desired effects, but that they cannot go beyond a low level of success when they cannot understand what they are doing. For example, children at the preoperational level can often make a balance beam stay horizontally by putting two equal weights on both sides of the balance in a symmetrical way. When they thus achieve success intuitively without understanding the mutual influence of the two weights, they often believe that the equilibrium will be destroyed if two equal weights are added to the two that are already holding the beam in balance. The rest of the story is easy to imagine on the basis of Chapter 11 of *The Growth of Logical Thinking from Childhood to Adolescence* (Inhelder and Piaget, 1955).

The child-development approach has similarly evolved mostly by trial and error and observation of what seems to "work." Just as a good theory is what children need to solve practical problems of balance, it seems to me that a scientific theory is what the child-development tradition needs to go beyond its present level.

If we had to start developing a curriculum from scratch with Piaget's theory, instead of starting with what already exists, we would have to go through the same path of trial and error that child-development teachers have already traversed. Piaget's theory is a descriptive and explanatory one, and its application to education cannot be direct. Knowing that young children at home like to engage in certain activities that are good for their development, we would experiment first by providing the materials and atmosphere necessary for symbolic play, painting, block building, collages, board games, sand and water play, etc. We would then observe children in these activities to determine which ones capture their interest, as interest indicates mental activity and construction. This is precisely what child-development teachers have already done as they experimented by modifying materials, the schedule, the room arrangement, and adult interventions.

Before discussing how Piaget's theory can be used to move the child-development approach beyond its present level, the strengths and weaknesses of the child-development approach will be mentioned.

The Strengths and Weaknesses of the Child-Development Approach

The greatest strength of the child-development approach is that its practitioners know children well, are particularly sensitive to children's emotional needs, and emphasize the context of trust and affection in adult-child relationships. They also emphasize the development of children's relationships with other children and are skillful in handling such problems as those involving aggression and jealously.

Although this tradition is consistent and strong in the socioemotional realm, it leaves much to be desired in the intellectual realm. First, in spite of its interactionist philosophy expressed in the belief in play, the child-development approach is still based on empiricist assumptions about how children learn. Second, there is an absence of theoretical rigor in early-education texts. The third shortcoming of the child-development approach is that since it developed before Piaget's theory became known, it does not have the benefit of scientific knowledge about preoperational thought. The first two of these points are elaborated below. The third one will be clarified in my discussion of how Piaget's theory can be used to build on the child-development approach.

Empiricist assumptions are reflected first of all in how learning is believed to take place in the child-development tradition. All early-education texts I have read state that young children begin by learning through their senses. Below is an example of such a statement (Read, 1971): "The child learns about the world around him through his senses, seeing, hearing, feeling, tasting, and smelling, and through his kinesthetic sense. The greater the input of sensory impressions, the more material he has out of which to build concepts of what the world is like [p. 197]." As it will be shown shortly in connection with the relationship between physical and logico-mathematical knowledge (Table 15.1), this interpretation of "the input of sensory impressions" is inadequate. According to Piaget's interactionism, sensory experience cannot have meaning without interpretation through a logical and spatio-temporal framework.

The second weakness of the child-development approach is a lack of theoretical rigor. Early-education texts are characterized by slogans, theoretical gaps, and contradictions. Below is an example quoted from Leeper, Dales, Skipper, and Witherspoon (1974) in a discussion of science education.

> In science education today the processes of learning are emphasized. The "process approach" offers opportunities for the child to participate in the processes of

science as inquiry, as exploration, and as discovery, and to begin development of skills in observation, description, problem solving, classification, seeing relationships, logical reasoning, and inferring [p. 302].

"Process approach," "discovery," "problem solving," and "logical reasoning" are all slogans which are now in vogue. Four pages later, we find the following list of "facts" and "concepts" to be learned with suggested activities that are either in contradiction or only remotely related to the general ideals:

Examples of Facts and Concepts to be Learned	Some Activities and Learning Encounters That Can Contribute to Concept Development
Air is around us.	. . . .
Air fills space.	
Wind moves many things. . . .	Observe things that are being moved by the wind.
We breathe air.	Blow up toy balloons.
Fire needs air to burn.	
Air has water in it.	[p. 306].

Since air is not observable, it is impossible for 3-to-5-year-olds to understand by "the process approach," "discovery," "problem solving," or "logical reasoning" the fact that air is around us, that it fills space, that fire needs it to burn, and that it has water in it. The only way we can *try* to transmit this knowledge is by talking, which means pouring words that children cannot understand.

How Piaget's Theory Can Be Used to Build on the Child-Development Approach

As stated earlier, the child-development approach is particularly strong in understanding children's socioemotional needs and fostering development in this area. I do not think Piaget's theory can add much in this realm in a practical way except for the implications of what he has to say about the development of autonomy. Teachers trained in the child-development tradition usually intervene in conflict situations by doing the same thing that teachers do after being trained to apply Piaget's theory—by explaining reasons, clarifying feelings, negotiating solutions, offering choices, and distracting. However, child-development teachers can sometimes be observed telling children to share their toys. This kind of "teaching" is in opposition to what a teacher would do on the basis of constructivism. It is not by having ready-made values taught that children come to believe that it is better to share toys than to fight over them. A better approach for the development of autonomy is to let children resolve their own conflicts, but this is often impossible for young children.[9]

Piaget, as discussed earlier, is realistic enough to say that sanctions are sometimes unavoidable. He points out, however, that when sanctions must be used, it is important to choose those that encourage children to construct rules of conduct for themselves. Spanking and depriving children of dessert are examples of sanctions that do not encourage the child to construct a rule, since there is no relationship between the act committed and the punishment.[10] Six examples of sanctions that are more conducive to the child's construction of rules can be found in *The Moral Judgment of the Child* (Piaget, 1932, Chapter 3). Since these were discussed in some detail elsewhere (Kamii & DeVries, 1977), they were omitted from the original version of this chapter.

One way of thinking about how to build on the child-development curriculum consists of the following: (1) by keeping certain activities and modifying them, (2) by eliminating some, and (3) by adding some. Each one of these is elaborated below.

1. *Keeping certain activities and modifying them.* The activities we keep are listed in the first column of Table 15.1, which shows a Piagetian conceptualization of child-development activities. As can be seen in this table, we keep almost all the activities including dramatic play, block building, painting, other art activities, caring for animals and plants, cooking, singing, playing musical instruments, movement, listening to stories, sand and water play, play with playground equipment, table games, and group games. The Piagetian reasons for believing in the value of these activities are indicated in this table with X's. As can be seen in the column headings across the top of this table, the Piagetian rationale is generally not the same as those found in early-education texts.

Let us examine the column headings referring to Piaget's conceptualization of knowledge.[11] One of the fundamental distinctions he makes is between physical knowledge and logico-mathematical knowledge.[12] Physical knowledge refers to

---

[9] Some teachers encourage children to resolve their own conflicts by saying, for example, "What do you think we should do about this? . . . I think the best thing to do is to put the toy up on the shelf while *you* decide what you want to do. You let me know when you decide, and I'll take the toy down." The important principle to keep in mind here is to reduce adult authority as much as possible so that children can construct a rule for themselves to deal with similar situations in the future.

[10] This kind of punishment results in three types of outcome: repetition of the act with calculation of risks, blind conformity (as it simplifies life when one conforms), and revolt (usually in adolescence, after a period of conformity).

[11] These columns do not indicate mutually exclusive categories. For example, names of objects belong to social knowledge as well as to representation with signs.

[12] The difference between "logico-mathematical knowledge" and "logico-arithmetical knowledge" is that the former includes geometry, which deals with space. The fundamental distinction Piaget usually writes about is between physical and logico-mathematical knowledge. In Table 15.1, however, it seemed best to refer to logico-arithmetical knowledge because knowledge of space and time appears separately in this table.

knowledge of objects which are "out there" in external reality. The source of physical knowledge is mainly in objects. The only way the child can find out the physical properties of objects is by acting on them materially and mentally and finding out how objects react to his actions. For example, by dropping a ball and a glass on the floor, the child finds out how the objects react differently to the same action. Since it is with his senses that the child observes the reactions of objects, physical knowledge is partly empirical knowledge.[13]

Whereas the source of physical knowledge is at least partly *in objects,* the source of logico-mathematical knowledge is *in the child.* I would like to clarify this statement by taking the example of the simplest relationship between two objects, such as a red bead and a green one of the same size, both made of wood. The two beads can be considered "different." In this situation, the relationship "different" exists neither in the red bead nor in the green one, nor anywhere else in external reality. This relationship exists in the head of the person who puts the objects into relationship, and if he did not put the objects into this relationship, the difference would not exist for that person. It is in this sense that the source of logico-mathematical knowledge is in each child. The same beads can also be considered "the same." In this case, the sameness exists neither in one bead nor in the other, but in the head of the person who puts the objects into this relationship. Another example of a relationship created by the child is "two." In this situation, the two-ness again exists nowhere in external reality but in the head of the person who puts the objects into this relationship. Logico-mathematical knowledge is constructed by coordinating these relationships that have their origins in the mental actions of the child. In the quantification of class inclusion with red and green beads, children coordinate the relationships of "same," "different," and "more," which *they* create and impose on the beads. In the conservation of elementary number task, likewise, children coordinate the numerical relationship that *they* created. Logico-mathematical knowledge in Piaget's theory thus represents the rationalist current, in which truth is decided by reason.

The above dichotomy is actually an oversimplification of Piaget's theory because, according to him, physical knowledge cannot be constructed outside a logico-mathematical framework, and conversely the logico-mathematical framework could not be constructed if there were no objects in the child's environment to put into relationship. To recognize a bead as being red, for example, the child needs a classificatory scheme of "red" as opposed to "all other colors." To recognize a bead as a bead, likewise, the child needs a classificatory scheme of "beads" as opposed to "all other objects (that are not

---

[13] "Partly" refers to the fact that, to draw conclusions about perceived regularities, or even to decide which action on certain objects will be particularly informative, the child needs a logico-mathematical framework. This statement will become clearer in the next five paragraphs.

beads).'' If the child did not have this logico-mathematical framework, every fact would be an isolated fact, unrelated to the rest of his knowledge.

When we speak of classification, seriation, and number with reference to children at the preoperational level, we have in mind only logico-mathematical actions that precede and lead to classification, seriation, and number.[14] When we say "classification," therefore, we are referring only to the mental (and physical) grouping of things that are the same and the separation of things that are different. For example, upon noticing that cylindrical blocks make a better tower than other blocks, the child may systematically look for the kind he likes. When we say "seriation," we are likewise referring only to the mental (and physical) action of comparing differences. For example, the child may look for a block that is long enough to bridge a certain space, and, having found one that is too short and one that is too long, he may look for a middle-sized one. Similarly, when we say "number," we are referring only to comparisons and numerical reasoning involving small quantities.

There is a third aspect of knowledge which Piaget did not study in depth that can be called "social (conventional) knowledge.'"[15] Examples are knowing that December 25 is Christmas Day, that there is no school on Saturdays and Sundays, that one is not supposed to jump on tables, that we eat meat and vegetables before dessert, and that a glass is called "glass." The characteristic of social knowledge is its conventional and arbitrary nature. Unlike physical and logico-mathematical knowledge, social knowledge is arbitrary in the sense that there is no physical or logical reason why December 25, for example, should be the most exciting holiday of the year. It is not in every culture that December 25 is such a special day.[16]

Physical and social knowledge are similar in that they involve information from sources external to the child. It is with the same logico-mathematical framework that the child organizes his physical and social knowledge. I hope it is clear now why Piaget cannot agree with the empiricist belief that knowledge merely comes from the outside through the senses. The senses are necessary for

---

[14]In Piaget's theory, the criterion of "classification" is the quantification of class inclusion, and the criterion of "seriation" is transitivity. The number system (as distinguished from small, elementary numbers) involves the synthesis of the class-inclusion structure and the structure of seriation.

[15]We say "social (conventional) knowledge" because people too often confuse "social knowledge" with social, moral, or socioemotional development or with socialization. Social (conventional) knowledge is simply a kind of knowledge, whereas moral and socioemotional development refers to feelings and behavior which include social (conventional) knowledge. For example, socialization involves learning the social (conventional) knowledge that tables are not to stand on. How the child feels about this rule and whether or not he abides by it belong to socialization and moral development.

[16]While some conventions are completely arbitrary, others are based on practical or physical considerations. Part of the convention of celebrating Christmas with presents and gay decorations, for example, is related to the fact that winter is a dreary time of the year in Europe, where Christmas originated. Eating dessert at the end of a meal and not using the spoon someone else has used are likewise not entirely arbitrary. The length of women's skirts, on the other hand, is completely arbitrary (except for the economic value of changing fashions).

observation, but, without a logico-mathematical framework, no observation can be interpreted.

Knowledge of space and time, too, is closely related to physical and social knowledge in that objects exist in space and time, and, therefore, no event can be understood outside a conceptual framework of space and time. According to Piaget, space and time are not mere containers of objects but frameworks, or systems of relationships, that are created by each individual in a way similar to the creation of the logical framework.

The task requiring the child to locate a point on a sheet of paper illustrates his construction of a system of spatial relationships. In this task (Piaget, Inhelder, & Szeminska, 1948, Chapter 7), the child is given two white sheets, one with a dot as shown in Fig. 15.3(a). He is also given a variety of instruments such as a ruler, stick, strips of paper, and bits of string and is asked to make a point on the blank sheet so that it will look exactly like the other sheet. Four-year-olds (level I), it will be recalled, drew the point by visual estimation of the position, without measuring anything. At level II, children began to use the ruler but made only one diagonal measurement, usually from the closest corner as shown in Fig. 15.3(b)! At level IIIB, around age 9, they finally became able to draw the point at the correct spot by making two measurements as can be seen in Fig. 15.3(c). This behavior is a manifestation of the fact that the child has constructed a system of coordinates and knows that this system is necessary to accurately locate the point on the second sheet.

Time for Piaget is likewise not a mere container of events but a framework, or a system of relationships, created by each child. In *The Child's Conception of Time,* for example, Piaget (1946) reports what he found out by asking 4-year-olds, ''Who will be the older of you two when you grow up, you or your baby sister?'' The answer was ''I don't know.'' The rest of the conversation went as follows: ''Is your Granny older than you mother? *No.* Are they the same age?

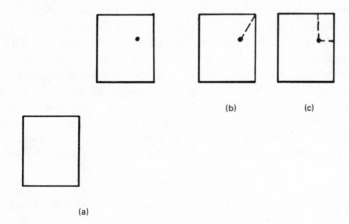

(b)   (c)

(a)

FIG. 15.3.   Three different ways of locating a point on a sheet of paper.

I think so. Isn't she older than your mother? *Oh no.* Does your Granny grow older every year? *She stays the same.* And your mother? *She stays the same as well.* And you? *No, I get older.* And your little sister? *Yes!* [p. 221]." This example shows how the child relies on observable "facts" when he does not yet have a coherent temporal framework. Everything this child says has a coherence based on what is observable. According to this child, the mother and grandmother are the same age because they look about the same size. Neither grows older because both adults look the same while children get bigger. Although the child thus believes that the two children grow older, she cannot know which one of the two will be older when they grow up. It is when the child has constructed an operatory framework of time that she will become able to deduce that the age difference between any two individuals always remains the same.

Before discussing representation, the last three columns of Table 15.1, it is necessary to clarify what Piaget means by "representation" as distinguished from "abstraction." For empiricist educators, "abstract" means "in representational form, in the absence of concrete objects." In early education, it is further believed that words are more "abstract" than pictures, and that pictures are more "abstract" than objects. When Piaget speaks of "abstraction," he means something quite different from "representation." I would like to discuss briefly what Piaget means by "abstraction" before discussing his view of representation.

Piaget distinguishes between two types of abstraction: empirical abstraction and reflective abstraction. In empirical abstraction, abstraction is from objects. When the child abstracts color or weight from an object, for example, he is focusing on color or weight while ignoring all the other properties of that object. In reflective abstraction, on the other hand, abstraction is from the (mental) action of the child, i.e., the action of putting objects into relationships. The creation of relationships such as "same," "different," and "two" are examples of reflective abstraction. As discussed earlier, these relationships do not exist in the observable, external world. They exist only in the mind of each individual who puts objects into relationships. The logico-arithmetical framework, as well as the framework of space and time are constructed by each individual by reflective abstraction. Physical and social knowledge, on the other hand, are constructed to a large extent by empirical abstraction from external reality.[17]

I hope this discussion clarifies Piaget's interactionism, which was discussed at the beginning of this chapter. For Piaget, there is no "fact" that can simply be read from reality without interpretation and relationships. Just as a grandmother is one thing to a 4-year-old and quite another thing to an 8-year-old, all other "facts" are not mere, empirical, objective "stimuli." The teacher who is aware

---

[17]I say, "to a large extent," because empirical abstraction, too, is an activity of the subject as I reiterate in the following paragraph.

of Piaget's interactionism can be sensitive to the way in which children learn by making new connections and systems of relationships.

Let us now consider representation. According to Piaget, the child represents his knowledge by using the following three types of signifiers: the index, the symbol, and the sign. The index is either part of the object or is causally related to it. For example, the sound we hear from a jet and the trace it leaves in the sky are indices of a jet. When we hear the sound, we know that there is a jet up there even if we cannot see it.

Symbols and signs are different from indices in that they are distinct from the object. Below are examples of symbols.

Imitation: the use of the body to represent an object, e.g., zooming around stretching one's arms out like the wings of a jet

Make-believe: the use of an object to represent another object, e.g., nailing two boards together in the form of an airplane and calling it a "jet"

Pictures: making or recognizing the picture of a jet.

The characteristics of symbols are that they bear a figurative resemblance to the real object or event, and they are often personal creations that may not signify the same thing to other people. For example, a child may draw a big circle and declare, "It's me."

Signs, such as words, do not resemble the object at all and are part of conventional systems used in communication among people. The word "jet," for example, does not bear any resemblance to a jet. Other examples of signs are the Morse code and mathematical signs. The example of make-believe given above, in which the child nailed two boards together and called it a "jet," illustrates the fact that, in reality, signs and symbols develop together in a mutually supportive way. The child's saying "It's me" about the circle he drew is also an example of the rich symbolic life of the child in which symbols and signs develop together.

It is important to remember that, according to Piaget, it is not the index, symbol, or sign itself that represents an object. Representing is what the person does when he gives meaning (significance) to indices, symbols, and signs (signifiers). Words, for example, are only as good as the knowledge the individual has when he uses them. The child who does not have elementary number concepts can often *count* eight objects in each of two rows and still say that there are *more* in one row than in the other. Number is constructed by reflective abstraction. If the child does not have number concepts, therefore, no amount of language (number names) will transmit to him the *idea* of "eight."

Let us now turn to an analysis of some child-development curriculum activities in relation to the above discussion. The "X's" in Table 15.1 indicate the aspects of knowledge each activity especially stimulates. Most activities received more than one "X." Because, in reality, all aspects of knowledge are present in all activities, I could have put an "X" everywhere in the matrix. However, the "X's" were used sparingly to indicate the aspects of knowledge the activity particularly encourages. The three columns in the logico-arithmetical realm are shaded because the logico-arithmetical framework is always involved in all activities.

In some activities the difference between the child-development and Piagetian interpretation is considerable. The first activity in Table 15.1, dramatic play, is an example of such an activity. As the term "dramatic play" implies, this activity is viewed in the child-development tradition as being related in some way to drama, and the emphasis is on the child's emotional life. Below is an example of this view according to Biber (1966):

> (In dramatic play, the child) is tasting and re-tasting life in his own terms and finding it full of delight and interest. He projects his own pattern of the world into the play and in so doing, brings the real world closer to himself. He is building the feeling that the world is his, to understand, to interpret, to puzzle about, to make over. For the future, we need citizens in whom these attitudes are deeply ingrained [p. 3].

For Piaget, pretend play is not *dramatic* play but *symbolic* play. As can be seen in *Play, Dreams, and Imitation in Childhood,* in symbolic play, the child uses his body to represent his knowledge of *his* reality, thereby assimilating it. Symbolic play also helps the child develop his ability to represent reality with mental images.

The "X" indicating social knowledge refers to the fact that a great deal of symbolic play is the representation of social situations. When young children accept invitations to birthday parties before being invited, they show the indissociable way in which temporal sequence, language, and social knowledge are involved in symbolic play.

Returning to the quote from Biber on dramatic play, we can now say that Piaget's theory puts symbolic activity in a larger context than the child-development view. For Piaget, symbolic play is the representation and assimilation of reality, which is both cognitive and affective. As the child assimilates reality and masters it, he constructs it in representation, and the resultant mental images eventually become tools in his thought. Part of this thought becomes tightly logical and part of it remains affective as in dreams.

The second activity in Table 15.1, block building, is an example of an activity which is similar in the child-development and Piagetian views. In both views, block building is considered a symbolic activity, which is good also for spatial reasoning. Piagetians, however, would go on to more precision. We would see the prominence of physical knowledge as children act on objects and observe the objects' reactions. As discussed earlier, we also see a great deal of comparison of sameness and differences as children look for cylindrical blocks, for example, to achieve balance, symmetry, or height. These comparisons and coordination of relationships are precisely what is involved in the development of logico-mathematical knowledge. As children build hospitals, roads, and gas stations with blocks, they represent their social knowledge, and block building flows into symbolic play.

The third activity in Table 15.1, painting, is understood as a symbolic activity both by child-development teachers and by Piagetians. When the child begins to paint for the first time, however, Piagetians see painting mainly as a physical-knowledge activity. As the child puts paint on a brush, moves it across a piece of paper, and observes the result of this action, he can be said to be constructing knowledge of these objects. As he drips paint or watches it dry, and as he compares what he gets by painting on dry paint and on wet paint, he also elaborates his physical knowledge. Putting the brush in any jar of any color, not washing it, and having to soak it the next day are also examples of his elaboration of physical knowledge, with all the comparison and creation of relationships these actions entail.

The Piagetian view of how children's ability to paint and draw develops differs from the child-development view. For example, Hildebrand (1976) explains this development as the result of the opportunities the child has had to "observe and create [p. 147]." For Piaget, ability to observe and know an object on the sensorimotor level is one thing, and ability to represent the object is quite another thing. As can be seen in *The Child's Conception of Space* (Piaget & Inhelder, 1948), young children's inability to draw human figures, for example, is due not to insufficient observation but to the fact that their ability to structure all spatial relationships at the representational level has not yet developed. This development at the representational level, too, takes place by a constructive process of differentiation and coordination. Thus, the body shown in Fig. 15.4(b) differentiates out of the structure shown in Fig. 15.4(a). In Fig. 15.4(a), the arms and legs come out of the head in spite of the fact that children know that arms and legs are not attached to the head. (The proof is that when given a choice between this picture and a more accurate representation, these children can explain why they think the latter is better.) Fig. 15.4(c) shows a further differentiation—that of the neck, hands, and feet. In Fig. 15.4(d), we see the elaboration of clothes as well as the further differentiation of facial features and fingers and better coordination of the parts which can be seen in proportional size.

In early-education texts, the fourth item of Table 15.1, "other arts and crafts activities," are always considered in terms of art alone. The following description of what a child did in a wood "sculpture" activity is in contrast to this concception. The child was trying to glue a "mast" onto his "boat" by putting glue at the end of a stick and holding it on a piece of wood for a while. When he removed his hand, the mast fell over; so he put more glue on the same spot and

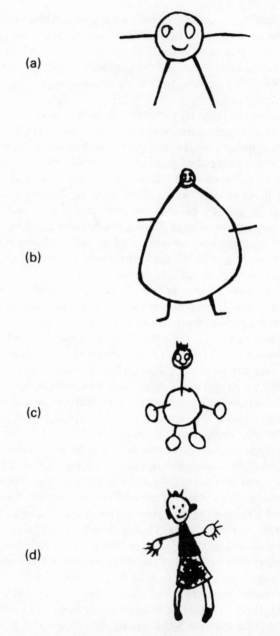

(a)

(b)

(c)

(d)

FIG. 15.4.   The evolution of a child's drawing by progressive differentiation and coordination.

repeated the same action. When he removed his hand, the mast again fell over. This time, the child put gobs of glue on the end of the stick and pressed it down with more force than before. The glue only spread around the mast, making no difference to the contact between the two pieces of wood. For this child, however, the relevant factors seemed to be the amount of glue and the force applied.

The reader must have recognized this activity as a physical-knowledge activity involving balance and the circumstances under which glue does not work. During the activity, the child also put many things into relationships by comparing, for example, the effects of the first two actions with those of the third action. The representation of boats, airplanes, Easter baskets, etc., is also an important part of these art activities.

Group games, the last item in Table 15.1, are used very differently in the child-development tradition and Piagetian approach. In the child-development tradition, group games are generally considered inappropriate before kindergarten, and some early-education texts do not mention group games at all. When they are recommended, group games appear in a variety of conceptual places such as a chapter on music (Hildebrand, 1976) and one entitled "play activities," apart from other more "serious" chapters on language arts, mathematics, social studies, science, and art and music (Leeper et al., 1974).

In a Piagetian framework, group games are considered in light of what Piaget says about the evolution of play in *Play, Dreams and Imitation* (1946) and his discussion of the game of marbles in *The Moral Judgment of the Child* (1932). In these books, we can see how games with rules become possible only when the child's intelligence has developed sufficiently to coordinate actions and points of view with other people. In *The Moral Judgment of the Child,* we can see that the ability to make rules, play by the rules, change rules, and negotiate agreements is a part of the child's development of autonomy. I will not go into many details, since Rheta DeVries and I have written a book on group games (Kamii & DeVries, 1980). Suffice it to say here that we believe strongly in the value of group games because they are particularly good for the attainment of the three objectives for education discussed earlier (the child's relationship to adults and to peers and his construction of knowledge). Let us take Musical Chairs as an example to illustrate how a teacher can use a group game employing Piaget's theory.

Piaget's theory makes the teacher accutely aware of the fact that children in the preoperational period think very differently from adults. In Musical Chairs, when the rule is modified so that there are enough chairs for all the children, 4-year-olds run just as fast to get a chair as when there is one chair fewer than the number of children. If this modification is introduced after the children have played the game in the usual way for some time (by having one chair fewer than the number of children and removing one of each at the end of every round), and we ask four-year-olds which of the two ways they prefer, they reply that they like the new way better. Why? Because, in the new way, each child can be sure of getting a chair and of being able to continue playing without fear of being put out. When the point of the game is to have fun marching to music, running, and sitting down with others, it is more fun to be able to continue doing this ritual for a long time. If we want children to participate actively in a game, we must be ready to modify the rules to fit *their* way of thinking.

Many child-development teachers prepare the room for Musical Chairs by setting up the chairs. The teacher who thus does the work for children is depriving them of an educational part of this game. It is the process of deciding how many chairs to put out that is the most valuable part for the children's development of numerical reasoning and their autonomy. When they have to agree on whether to play the game with enough chairs for everybody or with one chair fewer, children have to exchange views to come to an agreement. When they then have to put out the right number of chairs, they quantify objects for a reason rather than doing an exercise to do an exercise.

In addition to stimulating the development of autonomy and numerical reasoning, Musical Chairs can encourage children to think in other ways. When a record player is used and there are not enough chairs for all the children, 5-year-olds may think of watching the teacher to know when she is about to stop the music. They may also watch what other children are doing to figure out which chair(s) they are likely to try to get. Sometimes, it is better to try to get a chair that is far away but not likely to be desired by anybody else. This kind of thinking generally does not develop before five or six years of age. Most 4-year-olds do not even think of the desirability of marching close to the chairs.

Many child-development teachers have intuitively sensed the desirability of playing Musical Chairs with 3 and 4-year-olds with enough chairs for all the children. While many of them thus do the right thing, they cannot explain their practice on the basis of a scientific theory. Usually, they say that it is upsetting for children not to get a chair. Although I agree completely with this statement, I think the field needs to go beyond this level of explanation.

Although it is useful from a practical point of view to think about activities as they are presented in the first column of Table 15.1 entitled "Child-Development Curriculum Activities," the Piagetian conceptualization seems superior for the advancement of early education for two reasons: (1) It corresponds more closely to the way in which the child constructs his knowledge, and (2) it points to certain principles of teaching that are in line with this constructive process. Each one of these points will be discussed later.

As has already been pointed out, it is more productive to say that the child engages in symbolic play than to say that he engages in dramatic play. Likewise, it is sometimes more accurate to say that the child is building his physical and logico-mathematical knowledge than it is to say that he is learning about art. With respect to caring for animals and plants, too, it is more helpful for the teacher to know more broadly that learning about animals and plants is part of the child's building of his knowledge of objects by putting things into relationships.[18] In cooking, too, the child does not merely learn how to cook. He constructs knowledge of objects (ingredients), and learns what he has to do first, second, and third (temporal sequence) as well as the duration he has to wait to get the desired effect. While playing on the playground with swings, see-saws, and slides, the child builds a great deal of physical knowledge about pendulums, balances, and inclines. In other words, Piaget's theory provides an epistemological framework that helps the teacher understand how the child is building his knowledge as an organized whole.

Piaget's framework points to certain principles of teaching based on the ultimate sources of physical, social, logico-arithmetical, and spatio-temporal knowledge. When physical knowledge is involved, the best principle of teaching is to encourage the child to act on the object and find out how the object reacts. For example, the teacher who knows that cooking is a physical-knowledge activity will not set up an activity in which eight children sit around a table taking turns to stir the Jell-O that does not need stirring. When social knowledge is involved, on the other hand, the best intervention might be direct teaching, because social knowledge can come only from people. For example, if a child tells the teacher he wants to spend the night with him/her at school, the teacher might say, "I don't sleep at school. I go home just like everybody else, but after all the children go home."

Because logico-arithmetical and spatio-temporal knowledge are built by reflective abstraction, the principle of teaching here is "whatever encourages reflective abstraction." One of the effective ways of doing this is by exchange of points of view. For example, if a child complains in a card game that the dealer gave more cards to others than to him, the best intervention is to ask all the other children what they think. In logico-arithmetical knowledge, however, the teacher must be aware that it is pointless to try too hard. In "Go Fish" (Ed-U-Cards, 1951), for example, children use a deck of 32 cards which come in eight different colors, each in a set of four cards. The object of the game is to make pairs of the same color by asking for one that matches one that they have in their hand. While playing this game, we have tried to explain to some 5-year-olds that there is no point in asking for a green card when all four of the green cards are already down, face up. Such an explanation, even with empirical proof, does not necessarily stop children from asking for a green card when their turn comes again![19]

---

[18]Knowledge of objects is built by putting things into relationships with previous knowledge. For example, animals are like us in that they get hungry, eat, eliminate, walk around, sleep, and/or get scared, but they are different in that they have fur, walk on all fours, or live in water, etc. Young children often create relationships that adults do not think of. For example, when asked how animals are different from people, one child replied, "Animals don't laugh." Another put a cover on a cocoon to keep it from getting cold.

[19]This observation was made by Nancy Fineberg and Kathleen Harper.

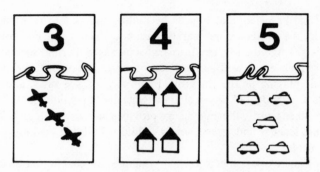

FIG. 15.5.   A puzzle based on associationism (empiricism) to teach number concepts.

2. *Eliminating certain activities.* Examples of "facts" and "concepts" about air that should not be taught to young children were already given previously. Other examples of contents that are beyond the ability of young children to understand are electricity, magnetism, and temperature, which are recommended by Hildebrand (1976, p. 207).

Many activities to "explore" time, space, and numbers should also be eliminated. Time, space, and number are constructed by reflective abstraction and, therefore, cannot be "explored" as if they were "out there" in observable reality. Following is an example of an activity which should be eliminated.[20] "Four and five-year-old children are able to imagine a world existing in another geologic era. . . . With *Dinny and Danny* (Slobodkin, 1951), . . . the teacher helps them to create an understanding of what life may have been like for a prehistoric child living among the reptiles of the Age of Reptiles (Todd & Heffernan, 1977, p. 376)."

Many activities intended for the teaching of number should also be eliminated. The toy shown in Fig. 15.5 is an example frequently found in classrooms. If children succeed in matching the correct pieces of these puzzles, they learn only that the pieces fit spatially, and such spatial relationships have nothing to do with number.

Piaget's theory makes it possible to understand that number can be constructed only by reflective abstraction and, therefore, it cannot be taught directly. Numerals and counting, on the other hand, are social knowledge and can, therefore, be taught. But there are better ways to learn numerals than with these puzzles or worksheets. One of the ways children learn numerals at Circle Children's Center is in a card game called "Card Dominoes."[21] For this game we

---

[20]I hasten to add that young children enjoy stories about prehistoric animals, in the same way that they enjoy monsters, ghosts, and cartoons. It may, therefore, be more productive to say that the thing to eliminate is the adult's illusion about what is being learned, rather than the activity itself.

[21]Credit goes to Nancy Fineberg and Kathleen Harper for experimenting with this game. Al-

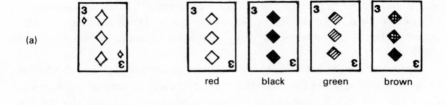

(a)

red   black   green   brown

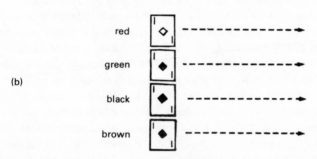

(b)

red

green

black

brown

FIG. 15.6.   Playing cards modified for use by young children.

made up 40 cards by modifying regular playing cards in the following way. We changed the Aces to "1's" and used numbers only up to ten. Instead of having four suits, we used four different colors as can be seen in Fig. 15.6(a).[22]

"Card Dominoes" begins by dealing all the cards to the players. When the cards are distributed, each player looks through his hand and puts down all the "1's" that he finds. All the "1's" are thus arranged in a column as shown in Fig. 15.6(b), and the game is played by taking turns putting down one card at a time to complete the matrix. For example, if the first player puts down a red "2" next to the red "1," the second player can put down a red "3" or a "2" of any other color, and so on. If a player does not have any card to put down, he passes. The winner is the first one to get rid of all his cards.

This game is a favorite that is often chosen at Circle Children's Center by children of kindergarten age. This is a far better way to learn numerals than with

---

though this activity does not belong to the category under discussion now (i.e., the activities we eliminate from the child-development curriculum), I permit myself to discuss it here, because it pertains to the teaching of numerals.

[22]This modification was made for the following reason: With the regular card shown on the left-hand side of Fig. 15.6(a), for example, some children were counting all the diamonds and learning that "3" stood for "five." By writing each numeral in four colors instead of four suits in two colors, we were able to overcome this problem because when the "suit" is contained in the numeral, there is no longer any need to draw a small diamond under each "3." (Without a small diamond under the "3," a player cannot know whether the red "3" is a diamond or a heart when he holds many cards in a fan-like arrangement.)

the puzzles shown in Fig. 15.5 because, in this game, children are motivated to learn numerals to have the fun of playing the game. When they cannot read a numeral, they either ask someone or figure it out by counting the squares on the card.

This game is good not only for the children to learn numerals but also for him to develop his logic. At first, children hold their cards in random order and put down any card they happen to find that can be played. It is much later that they think of the advantage of sorting their cards by color and ordering them within each suit. This way, they realize, they can not only find more easily the cards that can be played, but also know which ones to put down first to be able to play others that are in their hand. In this connection, it is interesting to note that some kindergarten children group their cards in ways that I never thought of: They make a dichotomy between big and little numbers—an organization which makes perfect sense according to *their* way of playing, which is without strategy.[23]

After playing this game for a few months, many 6-year-olds, each independently, come up with the following modification: "When it's your turn, you put down all the cards you can put down." This evolution is in accordance with the development of what Piaget calls "functions," i.e., the creation of relationships between two elements at a time in a unidirectional way. In the original way of playing "Card Dominoes," children put only two cards at a time into relationship. For example, if they see a series of red cards going up to "4," they know that the one they can put down next to it is a red "5." In the modified way of playing, by contrast, they think about all the possible cards they can put into this two-by-two relationship. They are no longer satisfied just to find one card to put down as they come to see many other possibilities all at the same time.

Card Dominoes is an excellent game also in light of the social objectives discussed earlier in this paper. The adult becomes one player just like any other player in this game, and the child's possibility of developing his autonomy increases as adult power is reduced. The adult is thus not the all-knowing teacher who corrects children. It is the children who correct each other, and if no child notices an error, the game can go on as long as no one is bothered by it. For example, if soneone places an "8" next to a "6," it is up to the children to object if they feel a need to do so. When the teacher thus refrains from correcting children in a game that is important to them, children become more alert and develop initiative.

---

[23]At the risk of repeating myself, I would like to summarize some advantages of this game because they illustrate principles that can be generalized to other activities. This game is good because children do not learn numerals just to learn numerals as they do in lessons and worksheets. They do not sort cards just to sort them as they often do in classification exercises. They do not seriate the cards just to seriate things as they do with Montessori materials. The making of a matrix, too, is not an empty exercise of merely placing the right object in the right place. From the child's point of view, all this learning is part of playing a game that *he* chose to play.

3. *Adding certain activities.* As stated earlier, the main contribution of Piaget's theory is in the reconceptualization and modification of what is already being done. However, the theory has made it possible for us to invent some new activities which we call "physical-knowledge activities" for short. This is discussed further in Kamii & DeVries (1978).

THE PROBLEM OF POLICY

The focus of the foregoing discussion has been on the relationship between the child-development tradition and Piaget's theory. In concluding this chapter, I would like to turn to the larger picture, namely the application of Piaget's theory in the early grades in the public schools. Historically, the child-development tradition developed in nursery schools and kindergartens independently of public school systems. This explains why the child-development tradition is basically interactionist in spite of the empiricist remnants discussed above. Public school practices, in contrast, have developed mostly on empiricist assumptions about how children learn. In recent years, these assumptions have been intensified with the use of machines, kits, behavioral objectives, and psychometric tests, a return to the three R's, and accountability defined in terms of test scores.

I used to think that the most important element in bringing Piaget's theory into the classroom was teachers who understood autonomy and the constructive process. Although I still think that no change is possible without well-trained teachers, I now agree with Almy (1978), who recently emphasized the need for policy change. I would like to explain why I came to this conclusion.

Many teachers change in fundamental ways after studying Piaget's theory. For example, they reduce their authority to make room for children to construct their own rules rather than demanding obedience from them. They begin to encourage children to exchange opinions and stop giving group lessons. Instead of teaching "right" answers, they come to encourage curiosity, initiative, and the expression of honest opinions. These changes that Piagetian teaching requires are very difficult because it is threatening to give up one's authority as the powerful adult.

Although change is thus difficult for many teachers, what is even more difficult is the disapproval of fellow teachers and the coercion by supervisors to go back to authoritarian teaching even to the point of being forced to use the DISTAR method. The result is that some of these teachers end up leaving public schools. Others stay but with a torn conscience. These teachers poignantly remind us of the revolutionary nature of Piaget's theory. Once they become Piagetian, they cannot go back to empiricism. But teachers cannot fight the revolution alone.

In education, the Establishment is conservative partly because supervisors, principals, and superintendents have reached the top of the hierarchy and have little reason to study a new and difficult theory. The only pressure they feel is from parents, community groups, and those who control funds and power, who also hold empiricist beliefs. In academic circles, too, the old and powerful do not even try to understand Piaget's theory. A few facts about the Copernican revolution warn us that opposition to Piagetian ideas can be expected for many years to come. Copernicus was laughed off the stage by his fellow scholars when he made his views public. The ridicule was so intense that for at least 16 years Galileo felt the need to pretend not to agree with Copernicus (Koestler, 1959).

Interestingly, some supervisors and principals are staunch supporters of Piagetian principles. One of their problems, however, is the fact that public schools are rigid systems in which the first grade is dictated by the second grade, the second grade by the third, and so on all the way up to the twelfth grade and university. Because each person is thus part of a system, individuals cannot change without a change in policy for the entire system. Parents rightfully worry about their children's survival the following year when teachers cannot say, for example, that the second and third grade teachers, too, will encourage children to want to learn how to read. But policy is controlled by Superintendents, who are in turn controlled by boards of education, community groups, state departments of education, and legislators, all of whom are traditional in their view about education. The prospect for change is, therefore, indeed dim.

In the midst of these pessimistic reflections, I recently received a request from the Superintendent of a school district to conduct a two-day workshop on Piaget's theory for all the elementary and secondary school principals of the district. When I asked why he advocated Piaget's theory, his reply was that Piaget's theory has a sound scientific base! With this kind of leadership from the administrative top, supported by principals, teachers can change and try out better ways from day to day.

Almy cautions us that change along Piagetian lines cannot be achieved quickly, and that large-scale research of the Head Start and Follow Through type is not what is needed. I agree completely with this position and believe that we must experiment with teachers in specific activities at specific grade levels to analyze what is good and bad in each activity and what principle of teaching to follow at different levels. Like all sciences and all children, experimental pedagogy can develop only by going through one level after another of being wrong. With a scientific theory, we can now formulate precise hypotheses, test them, and go on to formulate higher-level hypotheses. The application of Piaget's theory to education has a long way to go before finding the right balance between instruction on the one hand and the child's construction of knowledge on the other. It is only by carefully studying children in the classroom with teachers that we will some day know how to teach children so that they will develop more fully and become adults who go on developing.

ACKNOWLEDGMENT

The preparation of this paper was supported by the Urban Education Research Program, College of Education, University of Illinois at Chicago Circle. I would like to express appreciation to Marianne Denis, Kathleen Gruber, Bärbel Inhelder, Lucinda Lee-Katz, Hermina Sinclair, Mieko Kamii, Neal Gordon, and Elizabeth Hurtig for critically reading this paper. I am also grateful to the staff of Circle Children's Center, University of Illinois at Chicago Circle, who contributed to the research referred to in this paper.

REFERENCES

Almy, M. *Piaget and educational policy*. In *Piagetian theory and the helping professions, 7th annual conference*, Vol. II, G. I. Lubin, M. K. Poulsen, J. F. Magary, & M. Soto-McAlister (Eds.). Los Angeles: University of Southern California, 1978.

Biber, B. *Play as a growth process*. New York: Bank Street College of Education Publication No. 4, 1966.

Biber, B. A developmental-interactionist approach: Bank Street College of Education. In M. C. Day & R. K. Parker (Eds.), *The preschool in action* (2nd ed.) Boston: Allyn & Bacon, 1977.

Cohen, D. *The learning child*. New York: Vintage Books, 1972.

Dennison, G. *The lives of children*. New York: Vintage Books, 1969.

Dewey, J. *The child and the curriculum* (originally published in 1902) and *the school and society*. Chicago: University of Chicago Press, 1956.

Englemann, S., Osborn, J., & Engelmann, T. *DISTAR language I teacher's guide*. Chicago: Science Research Associates, 1969.

Froebel, F. *The education of man*. New York: Appleton-Century, 1885.

Goodman, P. *Compulsory-mis-education* and *the community of scholars*. New York: Vintage Books, 1962.

Herndon, J. *The way it spozed to be*. New York: Simon and Schuster, 1968.

Hildebrand, V. *Introduction to early childhood education* (2nd ed.). New York: Macmillan, 1976.

Holt, J. *How children fail*. New York: Pitman, 1964.

Hull, C. L. *A behavior system*. New Haven: Yale University Press, 1952.

Inhelder, B., & Piaget, J. *The growth of logic from childhood to adolescence*. New York: Basic Books, 1958 (originally published in 1955).

Inhelder, B., Sinclair, H., & Bovet, M. *Learning and the development of cognition*. Cambridge, Mass.: Harvard University Press, 1974.

Kamii, C. Evaluation of learning in preschool education: Socio-emotional, perceptual-motor, cognitive development. In B. Bloom, J. Hastings, & G. Madaus (Eds.), *Handbook on formative and summative evaluation of student learning*. New York: McGraw-Hill, 1971.

Kamii, C. An application of Piaget's theory to the conceptualization of a preschool curriculum. In R. Parker (Ed.), *The preschool in action*. Boston: Allyn and Bacon, 1972. (a)

Kamii, C. A sketch of the Piaget-derived preschool curriculum developed by the Ypsilanti Early Education Program. In S. Braun and E. Edwards, *History and theory of early childhood education*. Worthington, Ohio: Charles A. Jones, 1972. (b)

Kamii, C. A sketch of the Piaget-derived preschool curriculum developed by the Ypsilanti Early Education Program. In J. Frost (Ed.), *Revisiting early childhood education: Readings*. New York: Holt, Rinehart & Winston, 1973. (a)

Kamii, C. A sketch of the Piaget-derived preschool curriculum developed by the Ypsilanti Early Education Program. In B. Spodek (Ed.), *Early childhood education*. Englewood Cliffs, N. J.: Prentice-Hall, 1973. (b)

Kamii, C., & DeVries, R. Piaget for early education. In M. C. Day & R. K. Parker (Eds.), *The preschool in action* (2nd ed.) Boston: Allyn and Bacon, 1977.

Kamii, C., & DeVries, R. *Physical knowledge in preschool education.* Englewood Cliffs, N. J.: Prentice-Hall, 1978.

Kamii, C., & DeVries, R. *Group games in early education.* Washington, D.C.: National Association for the Education of Young Children, 1980.

Kamii, C., & Radin, N. A framework for a preschool curriculum based on some Piagetian concepts. *Journal of Creative Behavior,* 1967, *1,* 314-324.

Kamii, C., & Radin, N. A framework for a preschool curriculum based on some Piagetian concepts. In I. Athey and D. Rubadeau (Eds.), *Educational implications of Piaget's theory.* Waltham, Mass.: Xerox College Publishers, 1970.

Koestler, A. *The sleepwalkers.* London: Hutchinson, 1959.

Kohl, H. *36 children.* New York: New American Library, 1967.

Kohlberg, L., & Mayer, R. Development as the aim of education. *Harvard Educational Review,* 1972, *42,* 449-498.

Kuhn, T. S. *The structure of scientific revolutions.* Chicago: University of Chicago Press, 1962.

Leeper, S. H., Dales, R., Skipper, D. S., & Witherspoon, R. L. *Good schools for young children.* New York: Macmillan, 1974.

McKinnon, J. W., & Renner, J. W. Are colleges concerned with intellectual development? *American Journal of Physics,* 1971, *39,* 1047-1052.

Montessori, M. *The Montessori method.* New York: Schocken, 1964 (originally published in English in 1912).

Perret-Clermont, A.-N. *Social interaction and cognitive development in children.* New York: Academic Press, 1980.

Piaget, J. *The moral judgment of the child.* New York: Free Press, 1965 (originally published in 1932).

Piaget, J. *Play, dreams, and imitation in childhood.* New York: Norton, 1962 (originally published in 1946).

Piaget, J. *The child's conception of time.* London: Routledge and Kegan Paul, 1969 (originally published in 1946).

Piaget, J. *The psychology of intelligence.* Paterson, N. J.: Littlefield, Adams & Co., 1963 (originally published in 1947).

Piaget, J. *To understand is to invent.* New York: Viking, 1973 (originally published in 1948).

Piaget, J. *Biology and knowledge.* Chicago: University of Chicago Press, 1971 (originally published in 1967).

Piaget, J. *The grasp of consciousness.* Cambridge, Mass.: Harvard University Press, 1976 (originally published in 1974).

Piaget, J. *Success and understanding.* Cambridge, Mass.: Harvard University Press, 1978 (originally published in 1974).

Piaget, J., & Inhelder, B. *The child's conception of space.* New York: Norton, 1967 (first published in 1948).

Piaget, J., & Inhelder, B. *The psychology of the child.* New York: Basic Books, 1969 (originally published in 1966).

Piaget, J., & Inhelder, B. The gaps in empiricism. In A. Koestler & J. R. Smythies (Eds.), *Beyond reductionism.* London: Hutchinson, 1969.

Piaget, J., Inhelder, B., & Szeminska, A. *The child's conception of geometry.* London: Routledge and Kegan Paul, 1960 (originally published in 1948).

Piaget, J., & Szeminska, A. *The child's conception of number.* New York: Norton, 1965 (originally published in 1941).

Read, K. *The nursery school.* Philadelphia: Saunders, 1971.

Rousseau, J.-J. *Emile.* New York: Appleton, 1914 (originally published in 1780).

Schwebel, M. Formal operations in first-year college students. *Journal of Psychology*, 1975, *91*, 133-141.

Silberman, C. *Crisis in the classroom*. New York: Random House, 1970.

Slobodkin, L. *Dinny and Danny*. New York: Macmillan, 1951.

Sonquist, H., & Kamii, C. Applying some Piagetian concepts in the classroom for the disadvantaged. *Young Children*, 1967, *22*, 231-246.

Sonquist, H., Kamii, C., & Derman, L. A Piaget-derived preschool curriculum. In I. Athey and D. Rubadeau (Eds.), *Educational implications of Piaget's theory*. Waltham, Mass.: Xerox College Publishers, 1970.

Todd, V. E., & Heffernan, H. *The years before school* (3rd ed.). New York: Macmillan, 1977.

16 Stages in the Development of Reading

David Elkind
*Eliot-Pearson Department
of Child Study
Tufts University*

The study of reading is a very large problem that can be approached from many different theoretical perspectives. What I would like to do in this chapter is to look at reading from the standpoint of the cognitive developmental theory of Jean Piaget. It is important to say, however, that Piaget has not dealt with the issue of reading, nor with other practical educational issues, in detail. Accordingly what I am going to present is my interpretation of a cognitive developmental approach to reading. The presentation is in two sections. The first section deals with methodological issues, and second describes the stages in the attainment of reading derived from a developmental analysis of the skill.

SOME PRELIMINARY CONCEPTS

The cognitive developmental approach to reading starts from some basic concepts about learning in general. These concepts dictate the way any particular type of learning is to be approached. It is necessary then to deal with these concepts before we proceed to an actual analysis of learning to read. The concepts we will deal with are externalization and automatization, the intellective unconscious, and the logical substructure of the task.

Externalization and Automatization. From a Piagetian perspective our knowlege about the world is neither innate nor learned but is always *constructed* as a consequence of our interactions with the environment. All human knowlededge, whether of the simplest objects about us to the most abstract physical elements, such as quarks, are constructions. They are, in fact, unique creations which derive from the activity of the subject and the stimulation of the environment but cannot be reduced to either one.

Although Piaget has demonstrated the constructive nature of knowledge by showing how children, in the course of development, recreate a wide variety of concepts, of space, time, causality, number and so on, the idea that knowledge is a construction is still not widely accepted. For example, many of the attempts to show that children have quantity conservation (the understanding that a quantity remains the same despite a change in its appearance), at an age earlier than Piaget reports it occurs, stem from the belief that conservation is not a construction but rather a simple reading of experiential givens.

The reason that we have difficulty accepting the constructive nature of knowledge has to do with the processes of automatization and externalization. Once we construct a concept or acquire a skill, the constructive process becomes automatic (that is unconscious) and the product is externalized (seen as independent of the self). Consider a simple analogy. When a house is in the blueprint stage, it is clear that the proposed house is a matter of intelligence and imagination since it does not yet exist in fact. Likewise, as the house is being built, the constructive process is clearly in evidence. Once the house is completed, however, neither the plans nor the constructive process are any longer in evidence and the house is treated as an external reality and not primarily as a product of human intelligence and imagination.

A similar process occurs as we construct concepts of the world. A student who begins a foreign language, for example, is painfully aware of his or her ineptness in pronounciation, grammer and vocabulary. At that stage, the psychological complexities of learning a language are very much in the student's mind. Likewise the constructive process, the memorizing, listening, speaking and so on are quite conscious activities. But once the student masters the language, it becomes automatized and externalized. In using the language, whether in speaking or in reading, the student is no longer aware of the constructive process he or she underwent. And the meaning of the language is also externalized. Words in the new language, whether heard or read, have an immediate meaning that seems to reside in them and not in the student's head.

The same is true, of course, with one's native language. To an advanced reader of English, the meaning of words seems to rest on the page and not in the head. It is not unlike watching a film in the classroom. The voices seem to come from the people on the screen when in fact the sound comes from the projector in the back of the room. In these circumstances we are not conscious of our own part in joining sound and picture and see them as both emanating from the screen. The processes involved are automatic and externalized.

The Intellective Unconscious.   As the preceding discussion has suggested, much of the constructive activity of knowing becomes unconscious and makes up what Piaget calls the "intellective unconscious." Unlike the affective unconsious of Freud, however, the intellective unconscious does not consist of re-pressed ideas and wishes pushing for discharge. Rather, as we have seen, it consists of processes which have become automatized. This means that the ways in which these two types of unconscious spontaneously reveal themselves and the means by which they can be reached are different also.

The affective unconscious of Freud is revealed spontaneously through slips of the tongue and pen, in dreams, acts of forgetting, and so on. Such errors are symbolic of unconscious motives and have to be interpreted to be correctly understood. The intellective unconscious is revealed by errors too, but of a different sort. If you are typing and suddenly focus attention upon your fingers, you begin to make mistakes—or more mistakes. The same is true for any skilled action that has become automatic, including reading. If you are an advanced reader and try to sound out letters as you read you find yourself making errors of pronunciation. In short, the intellective unconscious is revealed by errors of skilled action caused by attention to the action rather than to its result. That is to say, we know that a skill has become part of the intellective unconsious when any attempt to focus attention upon the mechanics of the skill results in disruption of the skilled action. In other words, skilled action *requires* automatization and externalization.

Getting at the intellective unconscious, however, presents a very difficult problem. Once a person becomes truly skilled in a particular action, there is no way to get back to the intellective unconscious. The processes have become so rapid and automatic that it is impossible to become conscious of them to any great extent. Errors of skilled action reveal the *presence* of automatization and externalization, but they reveal nothing about the *structure* of the intellective unconscious. It is simply a fact that, once we become skilled in a particular domain, there is no longer any way that we can discover, by reflection or attention to our own behavior, either the underlying structure of the skill or how we acquired it.

What this means is that to learn the intellectual and/or motoric components of a particular skill and how these components are put together, we cannot rely upon the introspections of those who are adept in that skill. It is for this reason that many people who are skilled in a particular area, whether it be playing the piano or doing research or therapy, may nonetheless, be poor teachers. Being skilled does not imply knowledge of how we became skilled. Contrariwise, many people who are not the best performers can nonetheless be good teachers. A voice coach or piano teacher will be able to train individuals who are much above her or his own level of proficiency.

This puts a whole new meaning upon the old adage "those who can do; those who can't teach." It is not, as the adage suggests, that teaching is a kind of second choice, but rather that good teaching requires different skills and abilities than does performance. To be sure, the teacher must be able to perform the skill to be taught because this ensures that the teacher can assess the learner's progress. But it does not ensure that the performer can teach the skill in question. Basically, the good teacher in any field has learned the cardinal rule about the intellective unconscious, namely, that it cannot be gotten by reflection. The good teacher knows that to understand the structure of a skill (its components and their organization) and the process of acquiring it, you have to observe the skill being acquired. *The good teacher watches the learner.* Whether it be a ski, or tennis, or piano teacher, the person who wants to demonstrate is less effective than the teacher who observes carefully. It is only through the careful observation of others that we can ever arrive at the unconscious processes that we ourselves employ.

This, in effect, is the central lesson Piaget has been trying to teach us. What each of his books, filled with studies of how children acquire various ideas, tells us is that if you want to know how children acquire concepts of space, of time, number, and so on, you must study how children acquire those concepts. It is only by observing children's struggles to learn that the underlying structure of the task and its particular mode of acquisition are revealed.

The same is true for reading. If we really wish to know the underlying structure of reading and how this structure is acquired, we have to study children who are learning to read. I am afraid that, too often in the past and in the present as well, investigations have made the assumption that a reflective analysis would reveal something about the nature of reading. Information processing models are a case in point. Although these models may be suggestive, they often seem to be spoken of as if they truly represented what goes on in the child's head. But because these models were not derived from a careful observation of children who were learning to read, this assumption is very suspect. What we must avoid, and what Piaget constantly cautions us against, is the substitution of reflective analysis for careful observation. Reflective analysis is most useful when it is applied to collected observations not to the *a priori* reconstruction of our past acquisitions.

The idea that the best teaching derives from careful observation of the learner is an old maxim which is given fresh support with the concept of the intellective unconscious. It challenges again the assumption that one can arrive at learning sequences by a priori logical analyses and reflection rather than by empirical observation. With respect to reading it means that any description of the stages of reading must be in accord with what we know about how children actually go about acquiring the skill. But insightful observation of children requires knowledge about the task as well. It is for that reason that we turn now to the logical substructure of the task.

The Logical Substructure of the Task.   In the last section I argued that we cannot learn about learning by reflection on our own past learning experiences. We can, however, employ the knowledge arrived at by the observation of children in some learning contexts to their performance in others. Indeed, Piaget's empirically derived stages of cognitive development provide us with powerful tools for analyzing various tasks and for guessing at the intellectual operations required to attain them. This analytic process does not guarantee success, however, but provides a much better chance than if we analyze the task from some model which is far removed from the ways in which children think. Using an understanding of children's mental structures to analyze task structures is what I have called finding the "logical substructure of the task."

It is perhaps important to differentiate this approach to task analyses from other approaches. This is a useful exercise because it is at the point of task analysis that the different theories of learning can best be differentiated. I will use the analysis of reading as an example because it has perhaps been the most analyzed of all curriculum subjects.

One approach to reading is that of information processing. In this approach computer terms and technology are employed to analyze the reading process. An important concept is that of *redundancy,* the extent to which the same information is given in different ways. The difficulty with the information processing analysis, from a developmental perspective, is its lack of a base in the logic of the child. That is to say, an analysis of a task in terms of redundancy still ignores the child's capacity to deal with redundancy. It may be, too, that what is redundant on the basis of formal analysis may not be for the child. That is to say, redundancy may not exist at the time the child is constructing letters and words but only after they are fully attained. The use of concepts derived from the analysis of written language as a total system, with the child who has not yet constructed this system, is an example of the dangers of externalization—it presupposes that which is to be constructed.

Task analysis has also been approached from the standpoint of behavior modification. Looked at in this way, reading involves a set of visual stimuli (letters and words) to be discriminated and a set of responses (verbal) to which they must become associated. Correct discriminations and responses are rewarded or reinforced while wrong discriminations and responses are not. The advantage of this type of task analysis is its simplicity. But that is also its difficulty. The adult who is deciding what the stimulus is has already constructed and externalized it. Hence what the adult sees as the stimulus may not be what the child sees. Fortunately adjustments are made because it is an empirical system, but the complexity of the child's task in learning to read is badly oversimplified.

In the second section of this chapter, I will present a detailed illustration of how one might go about arriving at the logical substructure of a particular skill, namely, reading. From a developmental perspective, reading has a complex logical substructure that must be understood before we can really understand the processeses by which children acquire that skill. As we shall see, structure and process are reciprocal and interwoven. Once we know what the underlying structure is, the required processes of acquisition become quickly evident.

STAGES IN THE DEVELOPMENT OF READING

In this section I suggest some stages in the development of reading derived from analyzing the logical substructure of the task. Unfortunately, not all facets of this analysis have been verified experimentally. On the other hand, classroom observations lend considerable support to the analysis and give evidence that it is an approach that is worth pursuing more systematically. For each stage we begin with a brief discussion of children's intellectual powers and then look at how these powers interface with adapting to the printed letter and word.

The Global Undifferentiated Stage. Children at this stage, usually 3- to 4-years of-age, have acquired some grammar and a limited vocabulary. They also have limited conceptual ability and utilize what Piaget calls *preconcepts.* At this stage a child may have, say, a concept of a dog so that he or she says dog whenever such an animal appears. It is not clear, however, whether when the child says dog, he or she means "the dog" in a particular sense (the same dog I saw yesterday) or in a general sense (another dog). At this stage each dog is both an individual dog but also the prototype of all dogs. There is a confusion between the one and the many. When a child calls a stranger "daddy" we see the same confusion between Daddy as an individual and daddy as a generic man.

Children at this stage are also preserial. To be sure some children can stack a series of size graded plastic donuts on a stick, but this is not a true series, anymore than calling a dog at this stage is indicative of a true dog concept. That is to say, the donuts on the stick form a kind of picture of a tower, and it is that picture of a tower that the child recreates. This is easy to demonstrate. Take the donuts off the stick and lay them on the table in a nonsequential pattern. Then ask the child to arrange them from biggest to smallest. Many children who could stack the donuts on the stick cannot seriate them on the table.

I have emphasized the young child's difficulties with classification and seriation because these processes are crucial to the construction of letters and words and later, to comprehension. A letter, as I suggested earlier, is really a class concept and effective reading means that the child must understand that A's are alike in some ways (they are all a's) but different in others (context, size, print, script). Reading also requires seriation in the sense that children must learn to scan from left to right which is in effect a seriation. A before B, B before C and so on.

Accordingly, a child's acquaintance with letters and words at this stage is global and undifferentiated. A child may learn the names of some letters but his or her knowledge is not conceptual. The child will know an A in one context and not in another. In the same way, the child may learn a few letters of the alphabetic order but this is rote learning and not a true seriation. For example, the child cannot say the letters backwards, which is the test of a truly operational seriation. Sight words learned at this stage are of the same order. Because they are learned as discrete stimuli, not really as concepts, the child may not recognize a word that he or she knows in a new context. Even at older age levels such errors are frequent in children who have learned by the "whole word" method because the child has not really learned the word as a class with many different exemplars.

At the global undifferentiated stage, therefore, children have a beginning acquaintance with letters and words. But because children do not yet know these as concepts, letters are global conglomerates of the class and the individual. Sight words have the same status and cannot be recognized in all contexts. They are more like pictures than true symbols. Seriation is also global and children cannot seriate more than a couple of items at a time.

Identity Decoding.   From about the age of 4½ to 6½ children make significant progress in classification, seriation and the understanding of transformations. By the age of 6, for example, most children understand that there are more children than boys or girls in their class. That is, they understand that a particular boy or girl can also be a member of the larger class of children. Likewise, in seriation, children from about the age of 5½ are pretty good at seriating as many as seven or eight size-graded elements. By this age, too, most children appreciate that a row of pennies transformed into a longer one does not change in number.

The development of all of these new abilities can facilitate progress in reading. But it must be emphasized that this facilitation does not occur in any automatic way. Rather the attainment of these abilities will facilitate reading only if children have the opportunity to practice them on language materials. Manipulating blocks with letters, or plastic letters, for example, enables the child to recognize a particular letter whether it is sideways or upside down. Such manipulation gradually gives the child a general sense of the letter quite apart from any single presentation of it. In other words, manipulation of such material facilitates letter conceptualization.

Learning to print letters has the same facilitative effect. After a child has printed the same letter many times, he or she begin to see how each is different yet still the same in a certain way. Moreover, printing simple words gives children practice in seriation of letters from left to right. In short, from a cognitive developmental perspective, printing and writing are important reading readiness activities. This is far from being a novel idea, however, and both Montessori and Fernald recognized the value of writing before reading. What has to be emphasized is that such activities facilitate concept formation not rote learning.

Listening to stories is another important way in which the child can apply his or her new cognitive abilities to language. In addition to the pleasure of the story, and the language enrichment it provides, listening to stories has another benefit. When children observe an adult reading a story, they are in effect watching the adult transform printed marks into sounds. Remember that this is the age when children are beginning to deal with transformations, and to recognize, for example, that six pennies are still six whether bunched together or spaced apart. In the same way, the adult reading a story is transforming printed marks into sounds without changing those marks. In both the case of the pennies and the reading something is transformed in one way but left unchanged in another.

Manipulating and naming letters, writing and listening to stories, thus help children to conceptualize and seriate letters and to begin to understand transformations. Clearly the understanding that letters and words can be transformed into sounds is what we usually mean by decoding. The understanding of physical transformations thus parallels the concept of language decoding. Unfortunately, however, this is still a limited concept of transformation and of decoding which is really not sufficient to deal with the complexity of English phonics.

To make this point clear I would like to distinguish between two levels of decoding, *identity decoding* and *equivalence decoding*. The difference between identity and equivalence is comparable to the distinction I have made between identity and equivalence conservation (Elkind, 1967; Elkind, & Schoenfield, 1972). So it might be easiest to introduce the distinction between the two types of decoding by way of this distinction between the two types of conservation.

It will be recalled that the standard conservation task presents the subject with two quantities (two clay balls, two rows of pennies, and so on) and requires the subject to judge their equality. After the subject makes this judgment, one of the quantities is transformed in appearance (one of the clay balls is made into a "sausage" or the row of pennies is spaced out). After the transformation the subject is asked to judge whether the two quantities (the unchanged quantity and the transformed one) are still the same in amount. A child who says that the two quantities are no longer equal is said to lack conservation, whereas the child who says that the two quantities are the same, despite a transformation in the appearance of one, is said to have attained conservation.

The typical conservation task can, therefore be diagrammed in the following way, letting t_1, t_2 etc. be the time dimension and A and B the quantities of whatever type. Then

t_1 examiner asks $\qquad\qquad\qquad\qquad$ A = B?
t_2 examiner performs transformation $\qquad$ B => B'
t_3 examiner asks $\qquad\qquad\qquad\qquad$ A = B'?

According to this paradigm it becomes clear that the standard conservation task deals with the quantitative *relation* between two quantities and this is what I have called equivalence conservation.

But the paradigm also makes clear that the final equivalence judgment rests upon a prior judgment, namely, that B $\Rightarrow$ B', that a quantity changed in appearance remains equal to itself. This understanding, the understanding that a single quantity remains the same across transformation in its appearance, is what I have called identity conservation. Unlike equivalence conservation, identity conservation does not involve logical deduction. Rather, it depends upon the child's past experience and manipulation of the materials. There is now considerable research (e.g., Brainerd & Hooper, 1975; Elkind & Schoenfeld, 1972), which supports the distinction between identity and equivalence conservation and the hypothesis that identity conservation is attained prior to equivalence conservation.

In terms of underlying mental processes, identity conservation requires primarily imagery and anticipation and not the mental abilities that Piaget calls *concrete operations*. Concrete operations appear at about the age of 6 to 7 and are essentially a system of internalized actions which permits children to do in their heads what before they had to do on the plane of action. Concrete operations also enable children to engage in transitive reasoning. Accordingly, as is apparent from the foregoing paradigm, equivalence conservation but not identity conservation requires the attainment of concrete operations.

After this long digression we can return to reading. When children recognize that letters can be translated into sounds and that combinations of letters can be transformed into words, this is essentially identity decoding. In the conservation problem identity conservation has to do with the recognition that a single quantity transformed remains equal to itself. Likewise identity decoding involves the recognition that a single letter or combination of letters transformed (i.e., spoken) nonetheless remains the same as before. In identity decoding the child knows only a single sound for each letter and only a single word for each combination of letters. As in the case of identity conservation, such decoding involves only the understanding of transformations and this can be acquired on the basis of experience and without the direct intervention of logic.

With English, identity decoding takes the child into reading, but not very far. As soon as the child encounters the complexities of English phonics, identity decoding will no longer suffice. In working with a group of children who had learned the identity decoding of the hard c, I tried to teach them the word *city* and the soft c. Their eyes either crossed or went heavenward and it was clear that they did not understand what I was trying to communicate. I had crossed the boundary between identity and equivalence decoding. We need now to look at this next stage of equivalence decoding in more detail.

Equivalence Decoding.   The next stage in the development of reading might be called the stage of equivalence decoding. As I suggested earlier, this stage coincides with the attainment of concrete operations. Just as these operations make possible deductive reasoning and equivalence conservation with respect to physical quantities, so they make possible equivalence decoding in the realm of reading. It remains to demonstrate what equivalence decoding actually means in the acquisition of English phonics.

To do that we have first to talk about logical addition and logical multiplication, both of which are also made possible by concrete operations. Logical addition has to do with combining two classes to form a higher order class which includes them both. For example, collies and spaniels are both dogs; roses and pansies are both flowers, and so on. Clearly there can be more than two sub-classes and the general formula for logical addition is that $a + b + c + d \ldots = A$.

Concrete operations also make possible logical multiplication. In logical multiplication two or more classes are brought together to form a third intersecting class of those individuals who belong to both of the multiplied classes. For example, the class of red headed persons × the class of boys produces: the class of red headed persons, the class of boys, and the class of persons who are both red headed and boys. In logical terminology this would by symbolized R × B = R$\bar{\text{B}}$ + $\bar{\text{B}}$R + BR where the dash signifies which persons are excluded from the class (i.e., R$\bar{\text{B}}$ = the redheads who are not boys).

Logical addition and logical multiplication are a subset of the operations made possible by concrete operations. They parallel the transitive operations that make equivalence conservation possible. Transitive reasoning allows the child to understand that a quantity remains the same despite a change in its appearance. Logical addition and logical multiplication permit the child to grasp that a class of people or things remains the same despite being combined with or ordered under other classes. In general logical addition and logical multiplication have to do with classes whereas transitive reasoning has to do with class membership. All three types of reasoning depend upon the logic of classes and relations made possible by concrete operations.

But what do logical addition and logical multiplication have to do with reading? Recall that identity decoding dealt only with single transformations, with letters that were transformed only into a single sound and words that were translated into single words. But in English phonics there are 44 phonemes that are represented by 26 letters in some 250 combinations. To deal with the complexities of English phonics, therefore, the child must deal with the fact that the same letter can represent different sounds while the same sounds can be represented by different letters. To appreciate these combinations the child must engage in equivalence decoding which is analagous o logical addition and logical multiplication.

Perhaps some examples will help to make the distinction between identity decoding and equivalence decoding concrete. Suppose the child, via identity decoding, learns the short /a/ as in bat. This can be symbolized as a $\Rightarrow$ a (a transformed into the short sound a). Suppose now that the child has to learn the long sounds of /a/, namely /ā/. He or she now not only has to learn the two identity decodings but, in addition, these two have to be coordinated. That is, the child must learn that a = a + ā. Put differently, the child must learn that in the class of /a's/, /a/ can be decoded as /a/ or as /ā/. This coordination of two or more identity decodings is a kind of logical addition. It is the logical addition of letters and sounds that constitutes one form of equivalence decoding.

Consider another example. Suppose the child learns, via identity decoding, the long sound for o = ō and the hard sound for w = w. Now suppose the child is taught the dipthong /ow/ which is a new sound to a combination of the familiar letters. To learn this dipthong the child has to coordinate the two identity decodings in a way that is essentially a logical multiplication. That is, the logical multiplication of o and w is o × w = ow + ow + ow (the class of letters that are pronounced /o/, the class of letters that are pronounced /w/ and the class of letters that are pronounced /ow/). The logical multiplication of letters and sounds is another type of equivalence decoding.

It is clear, then, that as soon as the child moves from single letter naming and sight words to phonics proper, the child must also move from identity decoding to equivalence decoding. It is for this reason that I have advocated (e.g., Elkind, 1975a, 1975b) that children not be introduced to equivalence decoding until they attain concrete operations. Until then, there is much children can learn in the way of identity decoding that will prepare them for equivalence decoding.

As children progress in reading and equivalence decoding the same processes are applied to higher level reading skills. Word combinations are a case in point. A child may learn the word "fall" and the word "water" and then the combination "waterfall." This is a logical multiplication directly analogous to the logical multiplication of /o/ and /w/ to make /ow/. In a recent study (Elkind & Waxman, 1978) we demonstrated that it was not until children had attained concrete operations that they understood that a compound word was one thing and not two. So word combinations like letter combinations are mastered thanks to equivalence decoding, which in turn derives from the progressive mastery of concrete operations. Again, it has to be emphasized that none of this occurs automatically; the child learns equivalence decoding by virtue of practicing it upon printed material and is not able to do it simply by virtue of possessing concrete operations.

Before leaving the stage of equivalence decoding one point needs to be emphasized. I have argued that identity decoding depends primarily on experience whereas equivalence decoding depends primarily on reasoning. Learning to read, from this perspective, requires both experience and mental development. Too often in the past, or so it seems to me, we have tried to teach reading as if it were dependent only upon experience or only upon development or maturation. What I hope the identity-equivalence distinction will do is emphasize the fact that learning to read requires both language experience and cognitive development.

Automatization and Externalization. The age from 9 to about 12 is the period in which equivalence decoding becomes more automatic and the results increasingly externalized. What this means is that children are progressively less conscious of the decoding process and that it becomes ever more rapid and efficient. A behavioral evidence of this progress is decreased visual fixations as a consequence of increasingly automatized decoding. Another consequence is enhanced comprehension as the decoding process becomes externalized and the child's attention is more and more given over to the interpretive as opposed to the decoding function.

It is important to remember, however, that automatization and externalization do no proceed at the same rate in all children any more than identity and equivalence decoding do. Too often, it seems to me, teachers assume that because a child has reached the fourth grade, reading is at the automatized, externalization stage. Many children, however, are still struggling with equivalence decoding and need much more practice in this domain before automatization and externalization can be taken for granted.

Lexical Egocentrism and Receptive Discipline. Once reading has become fully automatized and externalized, usually by early adolescence, a new cognitive problem emerges. By early adolescence many young people have attained a new set of mental abilities, which Piaget calls formal operations, that takes them well beyond what they could do with concrete operations. They can now hold many ideas in mind at the same time, grasp metaphor and simile, think in terms of historical time and celestial space, grasp contrary to fact conditions, and much more.

But this new mode of thinking entails new problems as well. At this stage in reading, the reader is communicating almost directly with the writer. This means that the reader must be willing to take the writer's perspective and to follow his or her train of thought. Although young people are capable of doing this, they are also quite egocentric as far as thinking is concerned and are obsessed with their own thoughts and concerns. This amounts to a kind of *lexical egocentrism* wherein the young person reads but does not get the author's drift because he or she is too busy answering, or too engaged in parallel fantasy activity, to listen. The situation is exactly analogous to talking with someone who is not listening but only waiting for his or her turn to talk.

What young people have to acquire, then, is a *receptive* discipline. They must learn to listen to a writer much as they had to learn to listen to a speaker. This is a difficult achievement and requires the highest form of what Piaget calls equilibration. In intellectual equilibration we take in new information, organize it within our existing knowlege without distorting the information or the system of existing knowledge. Receptive discipline, then, means learning to listen carefully to what the writer is saying and put it into our own intellectual framework without at the same time changing the writer's message.

The discussion of lexical egocentrism and receptive discipline brings us to the adult reader. It is really not possible to discuss adult reading and its cognitive vicissitudes here. But it might be well to say that the problems of lexical eogcentrism and receptive discipline are always with us as adult readers. This is true because receptive discipline takes effort and because lexical egocentrism is easily aroused by strong emotions.

CONCLUSION

In this chapter I first described some concepts—automatization and externalization, the intellective unconscious and the logical substructure of the task, that are essential to a developmental analysis of any task. Then I outlined five stages in the development of reading that roughly parallel stages in the cognitive development of the child. Of particular importance is the distinction between identity decoding which allows children to learn single sounds for single letters, and words and equivalence decoding, which permits children to grasp that the same letter can represent different sounds while the same sound can be represented by different letters. Equivalence, but not identity decoding requires what Piaget has called concrete operations that develop by age 6½.

What I have presented here is far from a complete analysis of the development of reading. Rather what I have tried to do is provide an illustration of how a cognitive developmental analysis of the reading process might go. What such an analysis does, and what I have tried to emphasize here, is to take both the child's thinking and the structure of the language into account. It seems to me that any viable theory of reading must always look at the fit between the child and the skill or material to be learned.

This raises the final point that I want to make in this chapter. Throughout the discussion I have emphasized that the attainment of intellectual operations is not enough to move children into reading. In every domain, whether it be space, time, mathematics or reading, effective application of cognitive abilities presupposes a strong experiential base. Children will learn equivalence decoding much more easily when they have already acquired a sound sense of identity decoding than when they have not. In advocating a cognitive developmental approach to reading, I am advocating a language enrichment approach as well. Effective reading grows out of cognitive development in interaction with abundant language experience.

REFERENCES

Brainerd, C. J., & Hooper, F. H. A methodological analysis of developmental studies of identity conservation and equivalence conservation. *Psychological Bulletin,* 1975, *82,* 725–37.
Elkind, D. Piaget's conservation problems. *Child Development,* 1967, *38,* 15–27.
Elkind, D. Perceptual development in children. *American Scientist,* 1975, *63,* 5, 535–541. (a)
Elkind, D. We can teach reading better. *Today's Education,* 1975, *64,* 4, 34–38. (b)
Elkind, D., & Schoenfeld, E. Identity and equivalence conservation at two age levels. *Developmental Psychology,* 1972, *6,* 529–533.
Elkind, D., & Waxman, B. *Age related changes in children's understanding of compound words.* Unpublished manuscript, University of Rochester, 1978.

Commentary on David Elkind: Stages in the Development of Reading

Herbert Zimiles
Bank Street College of Education

David Elkind's chapter aroused conflicting reactions within me. On the one hand, it showed the relevance and the wisdom of Piagetian constructs and values to a complex applied problem in cognitive development. On the other, it reminded me of my old professors, who were devoted to Hullian learning theory, and their penchant for stretching what was basically a very restricted theoretical framework based largely on laboratory studies of rats to account for all manner of complex human behavior. Their exercises in expounding the breadth and utility of the theory were always made after the fact—in response to questions or challenges. I came to the conclusion that there were no limits to the facts that could be accounted for by any given psychological theory and that, when evaluating a theory, I should be concerned with its generative quality and not with its capacity to be dragged along on a post hoc basis after others have discovered the phenomena and defined the key issues.

I do not feel nearly as strongly about Elkind's discussion of the relevance of Piagetian theory to reading, but as you will see I have some concerns on that score. At the same time, in his presentation Elkind has helped to clarify how landmarks in the child's increasing capacity for conceptual functioning define the stages of mastering the task of reading. When he speaks of the need to identify with and understand the conceptual level of the child who is being taught, I am in strong agreement with him. When he cautions us against developing teaching strategies on the basis of an abstract conceptual analysis of the task at hand, he makes an important point. Ruddell (1977) has recently raised the same issue in reviewing Gibson and Levin's volume on reading. While acknowledging the value of these authors' enumeration of the cognitive demands of reading—abstracting relationships, ignoring irrelevant information, locating high potential information areas and using distinctive features—Ruddell wonders how these elements can be worked into a viable strategy of instruction, and winds up questioning the ecological validity of laboratory research.

Like Elkind, my colleagues at Bank Street who are concerned with the teaching of reading to children tend to emphasize the multiple strands of skill building and conceptual functioning that are entailed in learning to read. In their analysis of the basic elements of learning to read, they emphasize: learning to express oneself orally, understanding written material as recorded language, and realizing that reading is getting meaning from the written symbols. Similarly, Frank Smith (1977), in a recent paper aptly entitled "Making Sense of Reading," emphasizes the salience of two cognitive insights: (1) that print is meaningful, and (2) that written language is different from speech. Unlike more traditional approaches that are preoccupied with the perceptual demands of decoding—the child's ability to learn to discriminate the distinctive features of letters and the sounds associated with them—Elkind focuses on the conceptual aspects of the task of learning to read.

There are various other aspects of the cognitive-developmental theory that support a solid approach to the teaching of reading—encouraging children to explore and discover on their own, relying heavily on observation of children in free activities or in loosely structured experimental situations to assess conceptual functioning, observing the qualitatively different features of thought processes associated with different developmental stages, and anticipating the wide degree of variation in which children pace their passage through the fixed stages of cognitive development, and so forth.

On the other hand, in his necessarily skeletal characterization of the process of learning to read, I think that Elkind overextends the application of Piagetian constructs. For example, the left to right scanning required in reading that Elkind cites as an instance of seriation seems to me to represent, instead, an arbitrarily set convention that has little to do with seriation. Nor do I understand how true seriation is involved in learning the alphabet, a task which must, of necessity, entail rote learning. Further, I doubt that a child finds it noteworthy that an adult who reads a story is transforming printed marks into sounds without changing those marks. I do not see how that event has any more to do with conservation than a child recognizing that the act of looking at an object does not bring about a change in its appearance.

In many ways, the child who is learning to read must deal with transformations in a manner that is at variance with the patterns learned in perceptual constancy and in conservation. When the small letters "p" and "b" are rotated 180°, they lose their identity and are called something else. On the other hand, a letter does not change its identity according to its position in a word, but if it is a vowel, and sometimes even if it is not, how it is pronounced varies. In effect, learning to read requires the child to follow an elaborate set of rules that have little correspondence to the way in which other aspects of his world behave.

This brings me to one of Dave Elkind's main points—his distinction between identity and equivalence decoding. I have had a hard time wrestling with his ideas on this issue, and they do not wash. If I understand him correctly, the reason that much of the teaching of reading cannot proceed smoothly until the child is older is that the task of having the child associate the same letter to multiple sounds entails multiplicative reasoning, and this form of reasoning occurs only at the level of concrete operations. Again, if I understand Elkind, he is thinking of the different sounds associated with a given letter as *attributes* of the letter and he reminds us that preoperational children cannot deal with multiple attributes *at the same time*.

My understanding of the process of decoding is different. I view the different sounds associated with the same letter *not* as attributes but as functions. Decoding calls for the child to learn the rules—defined in terms of letter combinations, position in the word, and other contextual cues—that dictate which function (i.e., sound) is called for by the appearance of a letter. As I see it, the difficulty of this task stems from several factors none of which have to do with multiplicative reasoning. First, the child is being asked to deal with the idea of a function of a *symbol,* and I am suggesting that the idea that a letter functions to evoke a sound (irrespective of whether it is many sounds or one sound) is complicated. Further, because there are so many different letters and so many more rules associated with their functions, the child is being overloaded cognitively. This overload is worsened by the fact that the contextual rules that define the functions are intricate and require quite fine perceptual discriminations. Thus the task of decoding calls for an integration of several different intellectual accomplishments—absorbing and putting into use the idea of the function of a symbol, learning a very large set of intricate rules, and making a set of very fine perceptual discriminations among stimuli that are relatively novel and whose distinctive features are not so apparent. It is, indeed, a difficult task, but one that does not seem to me to involve multiplicative reasoning or to be described by the defining properties of Piagetian stages of cognitive development. I think that Dave Elkind is correct in emphasizing that it is the child as a conceptualizer that must be taken into account in the teaching of reading. But whether the conceptual demands made by learning to read correspond so closely to the attributes of conceptual functioning that have been used to define the Piagetian stages is another matter.

I want to make two points in concluding this discussion. The first is that I am impressed with the fact that it is the formal aspects of the Piagetian approach and not the specific content of the theory that I tend to cite in considering its relevance to the learning of reading. Maybe it is time to distinguish between the secular trends in Piagetian thought and those that are an integral part of the dogma. There are a host of methodological and theoretical values and perspectives that owe their widespread currency to the Piagetian movement. They have been incorporated into the conceptual and methodological frameworks of many developmental psychologists who are not necessarily committed to the substantive details of the Piagetian framework. The situation is not unlike the large number of people influenced by the Judeo-Christian ethical code who do not however adhere to the specific theology. In the case of learning to read, it is the Piagetian surround, the ways of thinking about children's cognition, and not the specific theoretical constructs that seem to be helpful. Perhaps we need to think about ordering the various patterns of selective application of the theory.

My second point has to do with the substance of the theory, but not really—rather, with the methods for assessing children's cognitive functioning that provide indices of the theoretical constructs. The well-established techniques for assessing conservation, transitivity, and class inclusion serve the theory well, but they do not encompass the full diversity of conceptual functioning in children. When confronted with the task of analyzing the cognitive demands of a particular process, instead of seeking always to demonstrate that these demands are isomorphic with the elements of the Piagetian system, I think it would be more constructive to use such as occasions for expanding the framework. In effect, I am calling for greater accommodation of the theory to the diverse phenomena of cognitive development and less assimilation of the phenomena to the framework as it now stands.

ACKNOWLEDGMENT

I would like to acknowledge the very helpful observations of Mari Endreweit of the Bank Street Follow Through Program in preparing this discussion.

REFERENCES

Ruddell, R. B. Review of "The Psychology of Reading," by E. J. Gibson & H. Levin. *Harvard Educational Review*, August 1977, *47*(3), 442–444.
Smith, F. Making sense of reading—and of reading instruction. *Harvard Educational Review*, August 1977, *47*(3), 386–395.

17 Education and Formal Thought—A Modest Proposal

Robert Karplus
Group in Science and Mathematics Education
and
Lawrence Hall of Science
University of California, Berkeley

INTRODUCTION

How do you deal with absurdities? How do you deal with the following story (ADAPT, 1975)? Identify your sources of concern.

A Nice March Day

On a nice March day our club organized a day's outing. Although it had been raining all night, the roads were quite wet and muddy in the morning; but this did not spoil our pleasure. We came through a woods consisting entirely of fir trees. Unfortunately, there were no leaves on the trees as it was still early in the season; how lovely this woods must be in summer time when the trees with their shade protect us against the sun. Then we saw in the distance a rabbit. I ran after it, but as it ran faster than I did, I could overtake it only slowly and finally caught it. I did not hurt it, but let it go again shortly. . . .

With many games the afternoon passed quickly. We hardly noticed that the shadows grew shorter and shorter and we were suprised when we saw that the sun was setting. We sat down for a while on the shores of a lake. All of a sudden, a dense fog came up from the lake, but it did not spread over a large area; it just covered us and all the things close to us disappeared but all the objects in the distance remained distinctly visible. Tired, but well satisfied, we reached home after complete darkness had fallen.

After finding some errors, you might explain why you took them as mistakes and how you would "correct" them. You might also classify the errors, grouping similar mistakes together.

It is not unusual to find secondary school and college students who critique the article's grammar and writing style, fixing up the punctuation, placement of modifiers, transition words between sentences, sentence length, and paragraphing, without noting any of the logical problems in the meaning of the story. Other students approach the task on a sentence by sentence basis, correcting the sense of a single statement without paying attention to the contradictions that result when two sentences are considered together (ADAPT, 1975).

A successful analysis of *A Nice March Day* depends on some factual knowledge—the foliage of fir trees and the geometrical relations of sun, obstacles, and shadows. Yet this and other knowledge must be applied in light of the conjunctions used in the presentation and the time sequence of events. These considerations require logical reasoning, or hypotheticodeductive reasoning, to use a term frequently employed by Piaget. The reader must tentatively accept statements in the story as hypotheses, make certain inferences from them, and then compare these with common knowledge or other events in the story. If the trees in the woods are really fir trees, then they have leaves year-round; if the rabbit runs faster than the narrator, he can never catch it.

This chapter is concerned with educational implications of the demands for reasoning. The developmental research of Jean Piaget has much to offer, but his theory presents some obstacles because it is not easily compared with observations of student behavior on intellectual tasks. Most importantly, we shall apply Piaget's idea that knowledge, to be useful for reasoning, must be constructed to a large extent by the individual, often with the assistance of teachers, parents, and peers. At the same time, we find that the narrow concept of a developmental stage is not useful for educational applications because the observable behavior of students does not show the consistency that a simplistic interpretation of stage theory would imply (Wohlwill, 1973).

Yet we believe that a notion of levels can be used roughly to characterize the reasoning required for success on an individual task and to classify student behavior on that task. Thus, successful critical analysis of *A Nice March Day* requires formal level reasoning. Individuals who overlook the logical problems but correct the punctuation and other grammatical details are exhibiting concrete level reasoning by their application of simple learned rules. Persons who do not approach the story with any consistent point of view or do not understand the assignment could be termed preoperational with respect to this particular task.

Critical reading therefore requires formal level reasoning. Effective participation in social studies, English, science, and other curriculum areas in seconday school and college depends heavily on critical reading and also on the direct application of formal level reasoning to mathematical problems, scientific phenomena, and social occurrences. It is becoming increasingly evident that many high school graduates and college students do not apply formal reasoning consistently in their academic work, employment, needs as consumers, or responsibilities as citizens (McKinnon & Renner, 1971).

A large number of tasks have been invented and used during the last 10 years to assess the reasoning of secondary school students. These tasks resemble Piaget's clinical interviews in some ways, but differ in that they permit group administration and require written rather than oral responses. There are advantages and disadvantages to these differences. The latter stem from the facts that group administration virtually eliminates probing beyond a subject's first reply, handicaps individuals who do not comprehend the task or have difficulty articulating their thoughts in writing, and permits various forms of "cheating."

Advantages of the group approach are a very large saving in time, the elimination of need for a very skillful interviewer, an increase in the reproducibility of task administration, and a greater similarity of the task to ordinary school assignments. It is essential to interview some subjects when a new group task in being developed in order to determine whether the intended population does, in fact, reveal its reasoning adequately on the proposed task; if not, then the task must be revised or replaced. Because this chapter depends heavily on data gathered through group-administered tasks, it is important for the reader to recognize these pros and cons.

In the next section of this chapter we introduce the notion of reasoning patterns, which we have found more useful for the analysis and improvement of teaching than the stage concept. The subsequent section illustrates what can be learned from research of one particular reasoning pattern, proportional reasoning. The learning cycle approach to teaching that allows students to construct knowledge actively is described in the last major section, before brief concluding remarks.

REASONING PATTERNS

Jean Piaget created his developmental theory from the sequence and relationship in which he and his associates observed subjects of various ages using logical operations such as conservation, class inclusion, proportions, and propositional logic. He introduced the notion of developmental stage as a period when a person's reasoning and behavior show certain consistent and distinctive features that have been described in many publications (Flavell, 1973; Ginsburg & Opper, 1960; Gorman, 1972; Inhelder & Piaget, 1958; Piaget, 1968; Wohlwill, 1973).

The stage concept has attracted particular attention to Piaget's work because it emphasized the very different nature of adults' and children's thinking. To understand the implications of Piaget's work, however, one must realize that the stages of development are not as clearly defined or sharply distinguished as the steps of a staircase. In fact, Flavell (1971) has pointed out that each stage develops gradually rather than abruptly, and that certain stage-specific operations such as conservation of number, quantity, length, and area need not appear simultaneously. Karplus (1977) raised questions about the adequacy of viewing formal thought as a developmental stage. Wohlwill (1973, p. 236) asserts that the usefulness of the stage concept is an open question and tries to identify ways in which the concept might be given significance. Munby (1978) and Bady (1978) have pointed out the difficulties inherent in the stage concept and how teachers might respond. Even though the stage concept may be reinterpreted, modified, or discarded, the difference between children's and adults' reasoning certainly exists but cannot be described in as simple terms as concrete and formal operational thought.

As a way of describing the difference more effectively and charting individual students' developmental progress, we have found it useful to introduce the notion of a *reasoning pattern*. A reasoning pattern, such as seriation, conservation, or control of variables, is an identifiable and reproducible thought process directed at a type of task. Thus, ordering a set of beakers of water according to their fullness would be one behavior giving evidence of seriation reasoning; ordering sandpapers according to grit or stretched rubber bands according to their pitch when plucked would be other behaviors giving evidence of the same reasoning pattern.

Reasoning patterns may be compared with the logical and logicalmathematical operations introduced by Jean Piaget and his collaborators to interpret the thought processes of their subjects. Some of these operations, such as conservation, appear to be fairly easily identifiable in a subject's words and actions, whereas others require detailed analysis of extensive protocols. By contrast, reasoning patterns as defined above, are intended to allow teachers to classify their students' thought processes on the basis of classroom conversations, observations, and written work without requiring the resources of the psychological researcher.

Some reasoning patterns that are used frequently are conservation reasoning, additive reasoning, serial ordering, control of variables, proportional reasoning, functional reasoning, propositional reasoning, and analogical reasoning. This list is not intended to be exhaustive. An important characteristic of all reasoning patterns is that they do not refer to specific content, experiences, or relationships, but that they are concerned with certain recurring relationships. Thus, conservation or serial ordering may be applied to coins, quantities of liquid, energy, or economic assets; theoretical reasoning may be applied to plane geometry, the propagation of light, or the development of intelligence.

It is clear that the reasoning patterns listed above are not completely independent. Thus, functional reasoning includes additive, proportional, and conservation reasoning, at least when these are concerned with numerically measurable quantities. The addition of more reasoning patterns may lead to more such overlapping relationships. At the present time we do not envisage a "fundamental" set of reasoning patterns that combine in various ways to make up more complicated reasoning processes—empirical research will have to reveal whether and how different reasoning patterns are related.

By merely listing the reasoning patterns in a more or less equivalent way, it appears that all developmental significance has been lost. To restore order or sequence, we shall add a developmental dimension to each reasoning pattern. Consider conservation, for instance. It is well known that many 5 to 6 year-old children apply conservation reasoning successfully to number and continuous quantity. Conservation of length and area are achieved only two or three years later and conservation of displaced volume later still. Conservation reasoning applied to energy, angular momentum, or still more esoteric variables has not been investigated extensively, but presumably requires more knowledge and understanding than most adolescents can muster.

Proportional reasoning also exhibits a progression, from situations involving small whole numbers such as 2/1 or 3/1 that are mastered by relatively young children (Lunzer & Pumfrey, 1966), to fractional ratios such as 6/4 or 5/3 that are not applied reliably by many secondary school students (Lovell & Butterworth, 1966; Wollman & Karplus, 1974). With respect to many of the other reasoning patterns, data are not now available regarding such a developmental sequence, but one can hypothesize that analogical reasoning with familiar objects (hand:arm as foot:_____arm, head, leg, bones?) is achieved earlier than with less evident relationships (boy:sugar as tree:_____ water, sunlight, soil, fertilizer?) The developmental sequence may also involve several distinct reasoning patterns, as when additive reasoning appears as a precursor to proportional reasoning (Wollman & Karplus, 1974), and the concept of "fair test" appears as a precursor to controlling variables (Wollman, 1977).

In fact, it seems possible to distinguish between broadly defined concrete level and formal level applications of reasoning patterns. The concrete level applications involve real objects, directly observable properties, and simple relationships. The formal level applications could involve hypothesized or idealized objects with postulated properties; logical, mathematical or other complex relationships; an individual's own thought processes making use of reasoning patterns; and assertions that are contrary to experience. We intend to establish distinct levels by these criteria but do not expect that all possible applications of reasoning patterns will be included. In other words, a gray area of intermediate applications will not fall clearly into either of the two levels.

The reader may wonder how the above classification scheme differs from Piaget's stage theory. *The difference lies in the fact that we propose classifying the applications of a reasoning pattern rather than the developmental level of an individual.* By means of this change, all concern with decalage is eliminated, since the expectation of closely comparable performance by the same person on many tasks no longer exists. At the same time, of course, the integrative features of the developmental stages, such as mental structures like the INRC group, are sacrificed. *The hypotheses proposed here are much weaker than Piaget's theory, but they may accord better with teachers' observations.*

Since levels of reasoning are being distinguished, the contributions of many scholars who have attempted to define the concrete and/or formal levels of reasoning are directly applicable to the suggestions made above. In particular, Lunzer's (1978) extensive analysis of formal reasoning presented to this Society in 1973 is very pertinent. Lunzer pointed out that no single criterion can be used to characterize formal thought. Instead, he referred to second-order relations (Lunzer, 1965), acceptance of lack of closure (Collis, 1972), and multiple interacting systems. Fischer (1980) has formulated an approach to classifying the complexity of a relationship in order to determine whether its understanding requires concrete or formal reasoning. Lovell (1971) has used the idea of a second-order operation to identify formal thought.

All of these criteria share in the notion that formal reasoning can cope with tasks that require an indirect approach, analogous to making a right turn from a freeway by taking a left off-ramp and then looping through 270°. Yet it is clear that identification of formal reasoning has not been reduced to an algorithm, because all of the criteria taken together do not result in an unambiguous conclusion in all cases. A certain amount of professional judgment is necessary to assess the degree of complexity of a relationship and decide whether it justifies the label formal or concrete, as suggested by Neimark (1975). Here are a few of the reasoning patterns mentioned earlier, classified by the author according to their level of application:

Classification

(concrete level) Separating a group of objects into several groups according to an observable property (e.g., distinguishing consistently between acids and bases according to the color of litmus paper).

(formal level) Arranging a group of items (objects or abstractions) into a multilevel hierarchy according to observable or intangible properties (e.g., classifying the member states of the United Nations according to their form of government, economic system, and standard of living).

Conservation

(concrete level) Realizing that an observable quantity remains the same if nothing is added or taken away, even though it may appear different (e.g., when all the water in a glass is poured into an empty bottle, the amount originally in the glass equals the amount finally in the bottle—unless some was spilled).

(formal level) Realizing that certain properties of a system remain the same if nothing is added or taken away, but that this reasoning cannot be applied to all properties (e.g., the total angular momentum of an isolated system is constant, but some students can gain knowledge without depriving others of knowledge).

Proportional Reasoning

(concrete level) Making inferences from data under conditions of a constant ratio equal to a small whole number (e.g., if two pieces of candy cost $.25, four pieces cost 50¢).

(formal level) Making inferences from the data under conditions of a constant ratio not equal to a small whole number (e.g., if 12 pieces of candy cost 16¢, then 15 pieces cost 20¢).

Interactional Reasoning

(concrete level) Attributing an easily observable change to interaction among a set of objects (e.g., magnet picking up nail, rubber band stretching when it is pulled).

Correlational Reasoning

(formal level) Recognizing relationships among variables in spite of unpredictable fluctuations that mask them (e.g., drunk driving is associated with increased accidents even though sober drivers also have accidents, and many intoxicated people do not have accidents).

Propositional Reasoning

(concrete level) Making correct inferences when simple given premises are fulfilled, but not clearly distinguishing between sufficient and necessary conditions (e.g., given the promise, "If the weather is good, we will go to the beach," expects to go to the beach in good weather).

(formal level) Using postulates or axioms of a theory to derive consequences without regard to the factual basis of the postulates; distinguishing clearly between sufficient and necessary condition (e.g., making inferences from the theory according to which the earth's crust consists of rigid plates moving in relation to one another).

One very important behavior usually associated with formal thought is the conscious direction of one's own reasoning. As a result, the individual looks for inconsistencies among conclusions, checks the appropriateness of an approximation, or compares the outcome of a procedure with rough estimates made at the beginning. According to the present hypotheses, this behavior is a formal level application of reasoning patterns as was stated earlier. At the same time, it has some aspects of a personality characteristic, like impulsiveness and reflectivity.

Several important consequences follow for the educator who wishes to take the students' reasoning into account when planning instruction. In the next section, we shall take up the formation of new reasoning patterns. Here we shall only refer to the need for matching subject matter and assignments to the students' reasoning. To do so, the teacher has to analyze the course content according to its demands for reasoning and survey the students' ability with respect to those demands. Because many studies have indicated that a large fraction of secondary school students and also many college students use important reasoning patterns successfully only at the concrete level, one can predict learning difficulties in courses that require extensive formal level reasoning. Because course content is often specified in terms of concepts such as temperature (science), point (geometry), market (economics), plot (literature), and cell (biology), it is worthwhile to identify the reasoning patterns and the levels that are necessary to understand them.

Look first at "point." A mathematical point is a dot with zero dimensions. Though a pencil or chalk dot is often used to represent a point, a point is really the limit of conceiving a succession of smaller and smaller dots without end. A point, therefore, is not an object and cannot be represented by an object, but is an idealized entity that can only be defined through certain postulated properties. From this description, it is clear that theoretical reasoning at the formal level is needed to understand this concept. A common mistake of students who do not distinguish a point from the pencil dot used to represent it is to connect two dots by means of two or three lines drawn with a straight edge. Depending on the dots' size, this may be easy, but it certainly makes for difficulty in "proving" that only one straight line can connect two points.

Temperature can be defined in terms of sensations (hot/cold) or thermometer readings. When this is done, temperature can be understood in terms of reasoning patterns at the concrete level because it is based on easily observable criteria and seriation along a pre-established scale. Temperature, however, can also be defined as a measure of the average molecular kinetic energy. When this is done, temperature becomes a "formal" concept that can be understood only in terms of other concepts (molecule, kinetic energy, random motion), the kinetic molecular theory (theoretical reasoning), and the mathematical relationships connecting these quantities.

This example illustrates the fact that a particular concept can be either "concrete"—understandable in terms of concrete level reasoning patterns—or "formal"—understandable in terms of formal level reasoning patterns, depending on the meaning used. To identify the reasoning required of the students in a course, the instructor has to be clear about the definition of the concepts that are introduced. Special care must be taken to use a concept always with the meaning that was explained to the students and not to expect that temperature or another concept introduced as "concrete," can be applied automatically with formal significance.

Of the other concepts listed above, market and cell can be given definitions and meaning in terms of familiar actions and examples and can therefore be introduced as "concrete" concepts. A market can be a grocery store, and a cell can be observed when tissue is examined under a microscope. Yet these meanings do not exhaust the significance of the concepts by any means. Both of them can also be defined as "formal" concepts by generalizing their interpretation to include the market's role in balancing supply and demand, and the cell's functioning as a unit in various life processes.

The remaining concept, plot, can in our opinion only be defined as a "formal" concept, in terms of other concepts and abstract properties such as the separation of the basic story line from the details of all happenings.

PROPORTIONAL REASONING

Proportions are the most widely-used mathematical relationship in beginning science courses. Many important scientific concepts such as speed, concentration, density, specific heat, and electrical resistance are defined as ratios of more directly observable quantities. Proportions also are a special case of linear functions, the simplest mathematical functions that relate continous variables and can be represented easily in algebraic form (Suarez, 1977). Consumer mathematics depends on an understanding of ratios for comparison of grocery prices, evaluation of gasoline consumption of automobiles, and recognition of hidden costs in the form of interest charges or taxes. Kitchen recipes often require adaptation of the total amount and corresponding adjustment of the ingredients. It would seem, therefore, that proportional reasoning is a subject of great importance to the mathematics, science, and home economics teachers in secondary school, as well as to instructors concerned with quantitative applications in the social sciences. Though mathematics books have included chapters on ratio and proportions for decades, the application of these concepts to word problems— that is, outside the drill-and-practice format involving pure numbers—has always been difficult for many students.

Inhelder and Piaget (1958) investigated proportional reasoning as applied to two physical phenomena, the equilibrium of a balance and the projection of shadows. They identified the proportionality scheme as an element of formal thought used for quantitative comparisons and predictions. They observed that preadolescents tended to employ qualitative seriations and correspondences or additive compensations. Extension of these investigations by Lovell and Butterworth (1966), who used a variety of ratio and proportion tasks, revealed that fewer than 50% of even 15-year-old subjects applied proportional reasoning sucessfully. Lunzer and Pumfrey (1966) had similar results on several tasks that employed mechanical aids such as rods of various lengths and a pantograph for enlarging diagrams. These researchers also discovered that many students proceeded to solve their tasks by iterating a common multiple rather than using proportional reasoning directly.

In 1969, the present author became interested in proportional reasoning while engaged in the planning for a motion picture that would illustrate formal thought. The balance and shadows tasks were considered too complicated because they required knowledge of certain physical principles (moments about the fulcrum for the balance, rectilinear propagation of light for the projection of shadows) and familiarity with several variables in addition to the proportionality schema. Out of this need, the Paper Clips Task—Form A was created (see Appendix), and a brief research study surveyed the use of proportional reasoning as identified by this task (Karplus & Peterson, 1970).

Table 17.1 presents the results obtained with urban low income and upper middle class population samples, classified according to the response categories described with the task in the Appendix, by Karplus and Peterson (1970) and Karplus, Karplus, and Wollman (1974). All samples except the upper-middle class eleventh and twelfth graders have high percentages of responses in Category I (intuitive), which includes the procedures that do not use all the given data systematically. Many of these students gave answers that depended on their estimates of the appearance of the diagrams and paper clips or on illogical combinations of the numerical values associated with the task. Only a relatively small percentage of subjects in all samples except the advanced upper-middle class students used proportional reasoning to combine the data, and larger fractions of them used additive reasoning instead.

In an effort to reduce the number of responses that depended on visual estimates, the Paper Clips Task—Form B was introduced (see Appendix and Karplus, Karplus, & Wollman, 1974). As can be seen in Table 17.2, the effort was successful and resulted in more additive, transitional, and ratio responses at the expense of intuitive responses. In other words, the more abstract presentation of the task stimulated more advanced performance rather than confusing the

TABLE 17.1
Response Distributions on Paper Clips Task—Form A by
Socioeconomic Level and Grade (percent)

Category	Upper Middle Class				Urban Low Income		
	4^a	6^a	8^a	$11-12^a$	6^b	$8-10^b$	$11-12^b$
I	73	60	45	10	74	62	48
A	22	31	29	10	23	33	43
Tr	3	3	8	15	1	2	3
R	2	7	18	65	2	3	6
(number)	(51)	(161)	(156)	(153)	(95)	(123)	(67)

[a]San Francisco Bay Area,
[b]Northeast and North Central United States
I = Intuitive, A = Additive, Tr = Transitional, R = Ratio

TABLE 17.2
Response Distributions on Paper Clips Task—Form B
by Socio-Economic Level and Grade (percent)

Category	Upper Middle Class					Middle Class		Urban Low Income	
	4^a	6^a	8^a	8^b	$11-12^b$	8^b	$11-12^b$	8^b	$11-12^b$
I	28	30	14	11	7	18	8	53	24
A	55	33	38	47	10	41	34	43	54
Tr	12	15	20	8	8	16	9	3	6
R	4	21	28	34	75	25	48	2	16
(number)	(63)	(73)	(403)	(157)	(145)	(514)	(308)	(182)	(110)

[a]San Francisco Bay Area,
[b]Northeast and North Central United States
I = Intuitive, A = Additive, Tr = Transitional, R = Ratio

subjects and leading to reduced performance. One has the impression that many students respond according to the easiest way available: perceptual estimates if these can be made, abstract reasoning if necessary.

The data in Table 17.2 are divided according to three socioeconomic levels, judged according to housing and parental education in the community in which a particular school was located. The upper middle class samples showed steady progress in proportional reasoning, from 4% in grade four to 75% in grades 11 and 12. Regional differences between the San Francisco Bay area and the Northeast/North Central regions were minor at the eighth grade level, where a comparison could be made. San Francisco Bay area students used transitional responses more extensively, whereas the Northeastern students responded more frequently in the additive and ratio categories. At the eighth grade level, the middle class subjects' distribution was close to that of the upper-middle class, but by the eleventh and twelfth grades more of a difference was noticeable: whereas 75% of the upper-middle class high school juniors and seniors responded in Category R, this was true for only 48% of the middle class students.

The urban low income students used very little proportional reasoning at either the eighth or eleventh/twelfth grade levels—much less than the two other groups. In this respect the results obtained with Form B of the task were quite similar to those obtained with Form A (Table 17.1). In fact, the lack of proportional reasoning by the urban high school students would appear to be a serious and tragic obstacle to their education in science and mathematics.

The survey of proportional reasoning using Paper Clips Task—Form B was extended to six Western European countries in 1974 in an effort to determine whether: (1)the same four response categories would be adequate to classify the student responses; and (2) the frequency distributions might shed some light on the variability in progress on proportional reasoning that might be ascribed to educational influences. The survey used the two-item Paper Clips Task—Form C (see Appendix, #3), which includes Form B as the first item, but then requires the subjects to apply the inverse ratio, to predict the size of Mr. Tall's car in buttons when it is given in paper clips. This form of the Paper Clips Task was intended to be more demanding than Form B in that the second item involved more thoughtful manipulation of the data.

Three of the European countries, Austria, Germany, and Great Britain, had selective school systems with populations stratified according to academic ability while the three others, Denmark, Sweden, and Italy, had comprehensive school systems. The task was translated and administered with the help of science educators native to the countries visited. More details of the study and the participating school systems have been given elsewhere (Karplus, Karplus, Formisano, & Paulsen, 1979).

Analysis of the responses of more than 2000 eighth and ninth grade students in these countries revealed that the same four major categories used for subjects in the United States were adequate. The similarities of individual explanations for the predicted height of Mr. Tall were striking and could be recognized clearly regardless of the language used. This observation suggests that the development of proportional reasoning proceeds through similar stages in all these countries. Such a conclusion is not really surprising, since all the countries are culturally and technologically alike.

The European frequency distributions on the first item (identical to Form B) are presented in Tables 17.3 and 17.4. The individual population samples were

TABLE 17.3
Response Distributions on Paper Clips Task—Form B
in Three Countries with Selective School Systems (percent)

Category	Austria (Vienna)[a]			Germany (Göttingen)[b]			Great Britain (London)[a]		
	(Top Group)[x]	(Middle Group)[y]	(Low Group)[y]	(Top Group)[x]	(Middle Group)[x]	(Low Group)[y]	(Top Group)[x]	(Middle Group)[x]	(Low Group[z]
I	5	6	8	4	1	25	2	9	19
A	6	26	52	2	17	25	3	11	44
Tr	14	16	6	4	16	8	5	10	9
R	74	52	35	89	66	41	90	70	29
(number)	(298)	(189)	(104)	(92)	(119)	(107)	(87)	(117)	(172)
percent of age group	50	30	20	20	30	50	10	10	80
(average age)	(14.3)	(14.3)	(14.5)	(14.8)	(15.2)	(14.9)	(14.3)	(14.3)	(14.3)

[a]eighth grade,
[b]ninth grade (no eighth grades in session because of a school calendar change)
[x]segregated by sex,
[y]coeducational,
[z]coeducational or segregated by sex
I = Intuitive, A = Additive, Tr = Transitional, R = Ratio

TABLE 17.4
Response Distributions on Paper Clips Task—Form B
in Three Countries with Comprehensive School Systems (percent)

Category	Italy (Rome)[a] (Upper Middle)[z]	(Middle Class)[z]	(Working Class)[x]	Denmark[b] (Middle Class)[y]	Sweden (Göteborg)[c] (Middle Class)[y]	(Working Class)[x]
I	7	12	26	18	13	13
A	19	37	26	21	16	42
Tr	5	8	18	25	16	20
R	70	43	31	37	54	25
(number)	(161)	(110)	(196)	(397)	(98)	(179)
(average age)	(13.2)	(13.3)	(13.7)	(14.0)	(14.5)	(14.0)

[a]eighth grade,
[b]seventh grade, corresponding to eighth in U.S.,
[c]seventh and eighth grades, corresponding to eighth and ninth in U.S.
[x]segregated by sex,
[y]coeducational,
[z]coeducational or segregated by sex
I = Intuitive, A = Additive, Tr = Transitional, R = Ratio

classified socioeconomically in countries with comprehensive educational systems, but according to ability level in countries with selective educational systems. Also indicated in the tables are the localities within a country where the participating schools were located, the average ages, and the percentage of an age group enrolled in a particular school type in this locality in Austria, Germany, and Great Britain. Because the educational systems in Germany and Great Britain are changing toward more comprehensive and coeducational schools, the situation as it existed during the study in 1974 may not continue.

It is clear from Table 17.3 that the academic stratification in the three countries with selective school systems selects significantly for proportional reasoning. The top groups exhibited a preponderance of responses in Category R. The middle groups, however, also showed strength in Category R, but the low groups' modal response was additive, as it had been for the eighth grade students in the United States. Particularly noteworthy is the achievement of the top group of Austrian students, which includes about 50% of the age group and is therefore not nearly as highly selected as the top groups in Germany and Great Britain. The middle group in Austria, of course, did not achieve as well as the middle groups in the other countries—the latter represented a higher ability range.

In the countries with comprehensive shcool systems, the upper middle class Italian students distinguished themselves. Their frequency distribution was close to that of the top ability group in Austria; in fact, many of these students attended a private school. Performance of the middle and working class samples resembled that of the Austrian middle and lower achievement groups.

It is remarkable and disappointing that the response distribution of the upper middle and middle class students in the United States was rather close to the distributions of the lowest European ability or soioeconomic samples. The relatively low percentage of proportional reasoning used by adolescents in the United States therefore does not seem to be determined by developmental factors but rather by educational experiences. This conclusion gives promise that new course materials dealing with proportional reasoning might be very effective when used with the large numbers of high school students who do not develop proportional reasoning under present programs.

The reader may at this time raise the question as to whether perhaps the research results obtained with an instrument consisting of a single test item have not been overinterpreted. Two steps were taken to determine the reliability of the results. First, the two-item Form C of the Paper Clips Task was used in the international study mentioned earlier (Karplus et al., 1977 and 1979). Second, several completely different tasks for assessing proportional reasoning were used to compare the performance of several student samples with the performance of similar samples on Paper Clips Task—Form B. As expected, the second item of Form C in the international study was substantially more difficult than the first in that about 30% of all subjects gave a response of lower category to this item. Most of these changed from additive to intuitive or from ratio to transitional (Karplus et al., 1979).

What is significant in this observation is that the large changes quite clearly separate the four categories into two groups: I and A on the one hand, Tr and R on the other. The latter two may therefore be considered as giving evidence of proportional reasoning with varying degrees of competence; the former two give clear evidence of the absence of proportional reasoning, again manifested in a more or less consistent way.

It is of some interest to know what percentages of students in the population samples have the firm grasp of proportional reasoning to respond in Category R on both items of Paper Clips Task—Form C. These are given in Table 17.5 where the difficulty of Item 2 can be judged by comparing the figures with the Category R rows repeated from Tables 17.2, 17.3, 17.4. Though the relative performance of the several populations is largely unchanged, it is clear that there is substantial variation in the consistency with which proportional reasoning was applied. The similarity of the United States samples and the working class or low-ability European samples can also be seen again.

Additional evidence regarding the reliability of the distributions was obtained from surveying populations similar to those described above with other tasks requiring proportional reasoning. The distributions in Table 17.6, which presents data obtained with the Cylinder Puzzle (Suarez & Rhonheimer, 1974) and Candy Task (Wollman & Karplus, 1974) in upper-middle class schools in the San Francisco Bay Area, show high frequencies of sixth and eighth graders in Category A and a gradual increase in ratio responses from rather low frequencies in

TABLE 17.5
Responses in Category R on the Paper Clips Task—Form C (percent)

Population Sample	Category R Item 1	Category R Items 1 and 2	Population Sample	Category R Item 1	Category R Items 1 and 2
United States 8th Grade			Austria 8th Grade		
Upper Middle	34	20	Top Group	74	49
Middle Class	25	15	Middle Group	52	33
Urban Low Income	2	0	Low Group	35	16
United States 11th–12th Grades			Germany 9th Grade		
Upper Middle	75	53	Top Group	89	64
Middle Class	48	31	Middle Group	66	39
Urban Low Income	16	11	Low Group	41	7
Italy 8th Grade			Great Britain 8th Grade		
Upper Middle	70	40	Top Group	90	75
Middle Class	43	25	Middle Group	70	45
Working Class	31	18	Low Group	29	13
Denmark					
7th Grade	37	16			
Sweden 7th–8th Grades					
Middle Class	54	29			
Working Class	25	11			

grade six to the great majority of students in grade 12 (Karplus, Adi & Lawson, 1980; Wollman & Karplus, 1974). These results are generally similar to the Paper Clips Task—Form B distributions reported in Table 17.2. The Cylinder Puzzle elicited perhaps somewhat more additive and somewhat fewer transitional responses than the Paper Clips Task. Because the transitional approaches to the Paper Clips Task cannot be used so easily with either the Cylinder or Candy Tasks, these shifts in the frequencies are plausible.

Even though the distributions of responses obtained with the differing tasks are similar, it is true that a particular subject frequently gives responses classified into different categories when responding to different tasks. In that sense, the single item tasks have only a fair reliability of permitting individual student assessment with predictive power, something the teacher who wishes to use these tasks for diagnosis must keep in mind.

It is of some interest to compare the progress of boys and girls on proportional reasoning, because secondary school mathematics has been described as a barrier that discourages girls from planning for careers in science and engineering. The separate response frequency distributions of boys and girls in the 31 population samples whose proportional reasoning was described in Tables 17.1, 17.2, 17.3,

TABLE 17.6
Response Distributions of Upper Middle Class Population
Samples on the Cylinder Puzzle and Candy Task (percent)

		Cylinder Puzzle			Candy Task (Item 1)
Category	Grade 6	Grade 8	Grade 10	Grade 12	Grade 8
I	17	13	5	6	24
A	65	49	26	16	50
Tr	11	9	10	10	3
R	7	29	59	68	23
(number)	(188)	(193)	(213)	(212)	(238)

and 17.4 has therefore been examined. In 25 of the samples, the distributions were quite similar, with girls registering a slight advantage in some and boys in others. For six of the samples, however, there were substantial and statistically significant differences in favor of the boys. The individual distributions and the statistical evaluation by means of a chi square test with Yates continuity correction are presented in Table 17.7.

It can be seen that substantially more girls used additive reasoning, whereas an excess of boys used proportional reasoning (Category R). The United States and Austrian samples were enrolled in coeducational classes, whereas the German and Italian working class students were enrolled in segregated classes. The Italian upper middle and middle class samples were from coeducational and from segregated classes. Distinct educational programs experienced by girls and boys could therefore account for the differences in only two of the six samples.

TABLE 17.7
Response Distributions on Paper Clips Task—Form B for Boys and Girls
in Six Population Samples That Showed Significant Differences (percent)

	United States Grades 11–12		Italy Grade 8				Austria Grade 8		Germany Grade 9	
	Middle Class		Upper Middle		Middle		Working Class		Middle Group		Middle Group	
Category	Girls	Boys	Girls	Boys	Girls	Boys	Girls	Boys	Girls	Boys	Girls	Boys
I	9	7	4	9	9	16	19	32	6	7	2	0
A	45	19	33	9	54	18	41	10	43	11	29	5
Tr	7	13	4	2	5	12	21	16	17	15	20	12
R	40	61	58	77	32	55	20	41	34	67	49	83
(number)	(185)	(123)	(69)	(92)	(59)	(51)	(97)	(99)	(88)	(101)	(59)	(60)
df	3		3		3		3		3		3	
X^2	23.1		13.6		13.1		27.8		27.1		14.3	
p	0.001		0.005		0.005		0.001		0.001		0.003	

In Germany, for instance, the segregated middle group schools (Real schule) had quite differently oriented programs before World War II, but the curricula had been made very similar during the last 15 years. Nevertheless, according to the director of the girls' school, differences in approach and point of view among the teachers persisted and could easily have an antimathematics impact on many girls. Beginning in 1971, however, the schools were changing to partial coeducation at the rate of one grade a year, so that the differences reported for German students in Table 17.3 may not persist.

In Italy, one of the working class boys' classes was taught by a particularly outstanding teacher. Because it is the custom in the European countries visited to have the same teacher work with a particular classroom group of students for several years, the impact of an exceptional teacher at the end of a three-year program can be substantial. In fact, the responses from this one class included a specially large number of boys who used proportional reasoning.

The differences in proportional reasoning observed in coeducational classes is much more difficult to explain. And why these differences occurred in the middle groups in the United States, Austria, and Germany, and not in the upper or lower groups, is also hard to understand.

Let us summarize this section. Surveys of proportional reasoning using several tasks in several countries, geographical regions, and socioeconomic samples, have shown conclusively that a very substantial fraction of secondary school students applies inappropriate additive strategies to problems that require proportional reasoning. In some low ability or working class populations an additional smaller but substantial percentage uses no systematic procedure that takes the given data into account. At the same time, the variability in the frequency distributions with which various response categories occur suggests that there are significant cultural and educational influences on proportional reasoning. Hence there is promise that effective teaching programs might be developed to increase proportional reasoning substantially among student populations that are not proficient in this reasoning pattern at the present time.

THE LEARNING CYCLE

For the educator who accepts the hypotheses proposed here, teaching of concepts and the formation of new reasoning patterns become very important, linked concerns. Consider the concept of density, for example. Density is a ratio of mass to volume—understanding it requires proportional reasoning at the formal level, because the masses and volumes may have any integral or nonintegral relationship. Thus, meaningful understanding of density requires applying proportional reasoning in a new way. This will be relatively easy for a student who has applied proportional reasoning to geometrical scale changes, exchanges of money from one currency to another, or concentrations of salt in water, but it will be difficult for a student who has not applied proportional reasoning except when simple integral ratios were used.

At the core of concept learning, therefore, is the Piagetian notion that an individual constructs new reasoning patterns or new applications of reasoning patterns through an active process. Piaget has described four factors that contribute to the development from one stage to another: (1) maturation; (2) experience with the physical environment; (3) social transmission; and (4) equilibration. In the scheme of educational applications, we hypothesize that the same four elements contribute to the formation of new reasoning patterns and to concept learning that requires new applications or adaptation of existing reasoning patterns. In other words, development or learning, which we do not distinguish as sharply as Piaget (1964), proceeds through these same four factors within individual reasoning patterns one by one. Over a period of time, of course, an individual may form or extend so many reasoning patterns, may acquire meaningful understanding of so many new concepts, that a substantial transformation of his or her reasoning becomes manifest.

Before describing how teachers can carry out instruction to facilitate the development of reasoning, we shall cite a few additional investigations that provide evidence to the effect that this can be done. The formation of conservation reasoning with concrete level applications was the focus of Karplus and Siegelman (1966), who conducted a formative evaluation of the *Systems* unit produced in a trial edition by the Science Curriculum Improvement Study (Kagayama & Karplus, 1966). Note the intimate relation between the systems concept—closed systems—and conservation reasoning. One cannot distinguish clearly between meaningful concept learning and the development of reasoning.

Control of variables reasoning has been investigated extensively, with documentation of effective teaching in several reports (Lawson & Wollman, 1976; Linn, 1980, and Linn, Chen, & Thier, 1975, 1977). Here the concept of variable played a key role. Proportional reasoning at the formal level also has been taught successfully to secondary school students (Kurtz, 1976; Kurtz & Karplus, 1979; Wollman & Lawson, 1978). The concepts contributing here are ratio, constant of proportionality, and linear function.

We have chosen to use the term *self-regulation* for the active internal mental process involved in the formation or adaptation of reasoning patterns. The term is intended to suggest the learner's taking initiative and then adjusting to the feedback received from the environment in response to this initiative. An analogy in physical actions is the experience of driving an unfamiliar car with a brake of differing stiffness than one is accustomed to. One first uses the habitual foot pressure on the pedal, only to discover that the brake responds too much and the car jerks, or too little and the car does not slow down. After trying variations that attempt to correct the error, the driver gradually discovers how to apply pressure that brings the car to a smooth stop. One's first encounter with an unexpected power brake, which responds greatly to a very light touch, can lead to near disaster!

Self-regulation involves the student in a feedback loop with the environment. He or she analyzes a problem situation, considers tentative solutions, evaluates their effectiveness, and uses new approaches when the initial trials do not produce the desired results. Self-regulation that leads to formal level reasoning patterns generally requires the student's awareness of his or her reasoning. Intuitive trial and error procedures may lead to self-regulation with respect to reasoning patterns at the concrete level, which we are not concerned with in this chapter.

As another and very different example, consider the relationship of pizza price to pizza size. A child using concrete level reasoning in a pizza parlor may decide that the 8-inch pizza costing $1.40 is too small and orders a 16-inch pizza without looking at the price, expecting that it would cost $2.80, "Because it's twice as big." Imagine the dismay when the gigantic pizza arrives, together with a check for about $5.50! Is the pizza parlor operated by an extortioner? Here is a surprise that may trigger the search for more successful reasoning to cope with the relation of pizza size to pizza price, a mathematical relationship requiring formal reasoning. In other words, the concept of area when circles are being compared is much more demanding than when squares with simple edge ratios are compared, because a large square can be assembled from many small squares set side by side, but the same cannot be done for circles. Applying the memorized formula for the area of a circle is different from the understanding of length and area comparisons needed to derive the formula for the area of a circle.

Whatever one's specific way of coping with a challenge, when the changes required are not too great, one is likely to reorganize one's reasoning patterns appropriately. One may realize that doubling the edge of a square pizza increases the size four-fold, and that doubling the diameter of circular pizza is likely to have a similar outcome. Confirmation of a new reasoning pattern through applications to further similar experiences will stabilize it and will lead to its more frequent use.

If the required changes in reasoning are great, however, an individual may need the help of peers, parents, or teachers to suggest more appropriate reasoning, more effective new concepts. They may suggest, "It's the area of the pizza that determines the price, and the area varies as the square of the diameter." Such direct teaching is not effective, however, unless the learner has had previous experience with length, area, circles, or the other ideas needed, and can subsequently test them against his or her own observations. Reinforcing feedback from the environment is neressary to make sure that the interplay of thought and action, an essential part of self-regulation and the learner's construction of knowledge, continues until the new reasoning patterns are firmly established.

The classroom is a place where experience with the physical environment, social transmission, and self-regulation can occur if the teaching program allows for autonomous activities by the students as well as explanations and suggestions from the teacher. Put more concisely, the teaching program should allow for (1) autonomous activities by the students as they seek challenges, test their ideas, evaluate the feedback from the environment, and then formulate a new hypothesis or other initiative; and (2) conceptual input from the teacher who may provide a definition, model a classification scheme, suggest similarities and differences, or explain an event in terms of familiar experiences. The learning cycle approach introduced as part of the Science Curriculum Improvement Study (1970–1974) combines autonomous student activities and conceptual teacher input in a form of inquiry teaching that has been effective at the elementary school level for the formation of concrete level reasoning patterns. More recent evidence indicates that it is also effective with older students and formal reasoning (Lawson, Blake, & Nordland, 1975; Lawson & Wollman, 1976; Wollman & Lawson, 1978).

What is the learning cycle? Consider the following approaches to teaching the density concept. Here are several activities that appear to be suitable:

a. Viewing a film in which (1) one cubic decimeter blocks of aluminum, paraffin, styrofoam, iron, and other solid materials are carefully weighed and (2) the volumes of one kilogram blocks of the same materials are calculated from the dimensions. These presentations allow two density determinations of each material to be compared.

b. Having a laboratory session in which the students can use rulers, calipers, graduated cylinders, and balances to determine the volumes and masses of objects of widely differing shapes and various materials for plotting on graphs of volume vs. mass.

c. Holding a discussion in which the students can tell of their experiences with floating and sinking objects, including themselves when they swim or play in the water.

d. Presenting an explanation accompanied by demonstrations in which the teacher weighs various specimens of certain materials, finds their volume by appropriate means, and finally computes the density of each material.

e. Having a laboratory session in which the students make accurate measurements of the masses and dimensions of carefully machined blocks and rods whose volume can be calculated easily from their linear dimensions.

Note that the laboratory alternatives (b) and (e) allow for physical experiences, that options (a) and (d) provide social transmission with illustrations, and that (c) draws on the students' past experience and allows for social transmission. All five approaches, therefore, include elements we have identified as important for concept learning and the formation of reasoning patterns.

To differentiate among the approaches, we return to Piaget's notion that an individual constructs new knowledge actively. Option (b) above fits this requirement most closely. In this laboratory session, the students have a great deal of freedom to use their own judgment, try out their own ideas, and learn from their own mistakes as they gain practical experience with materials specimen and instruments that will be used in the definition of density later. The teacher can circulate among the students and diagnose any learning problems they might have, as well as identify the reasoning patterns they use.

After the laboratory experience (b), the concept of density might be introduced by means of the film (a) or the lecture-demonstration (d). Both of these expository procedures employ materials similar to the ones used earlier by the students, so that they will be more easily able to participate in the presentations vicariously. Following this introduction of the density concept by the teacher or film, the discussion of floating and sinking objects (c) and the more careful density measurements in laboratory (e) can allow for applications of the new concept and an informal assessment of the students' understanding.

We have introduced the term "learning cycle" for the three-phase procedure we have just described (Eakin & Karplus, 1976; Karplus & Lawson, 1974; Karplus & Thier, 1967). The three phases are called *exploration, concept introduction*, and *concept application*.

During exploration, the students learn through their own actions and reactions in a new situation. In this phase they explore new materials, ideas, and relationships with minimal guidance or expectation of accomplishments. Besides encouraging the students to apply their previous learning, develop their interest, aand satisfy their curiosity, the open-ended conditions of the exploration phase permit the teacher to assess the students' initial understanding and their preconceptions. Through questions and suggestions, the teacher can help students relate the new experience to their existing knowledge.

The new experiences in exploration should raise questions that the students cannot answer with their accustomed patterns of reasoning—relating mass and volume of irregularly-shaped specimens might serve this purpose for the density and ratio concepts. Individual investigations and small group work are important. These two approaches encourage each student to become aware of his or her own ideas as well as providing a supportive social environment with a multiplicity of questions and viewpoints. Students who are not very inventive or thoughtful can learn through sharing the ideas and suggestions of their classmates.

The second phase of the learning cycle, concept introduction, starts with the introduction of a new concept or principle—ratio, density—that leads the students to apply new reasoning patterns to their experiences. The concept may be introduced by the teacher, a textbook, a film, or another medium. This phase, which aids in self-regulation, should always follow exploration and relate directly to the exploration activities. The film in approach (a) above or the demonstration lecture in (d) could well serve as concept introduction sessions following the laboratory activity (b). Students should be encouraged to develop or adapt as much of a reasoning pattern as possible before it is explained to the class, but expecting students to introduce complex ideas completely by themselves is unrealistic.

In the last phase of the learning cycle, concept application, the students apply the new concept and/or reasoning pattern to additional examples. The accurate measurement of densities in laboratory (e) would be an appropriate application activity following the introduction of the density concept. Other application activities might involve the densities of liquids and solutions, floating and sinking, and possibly the densities of gases.

The application phase is necessary to extend the range of applicability of the new concept or principle. Concept application provides additional class time and experiences for self-regulation and the stabilizing of a new reasoning pattern. Group discussions of everyday applications, posing of related problems by members of the class, and comparison of differing interpretations furnish a social setting that helps many individuals refine their thinking.

Without numerous varied applications, the new concept's meaning might remain restricted to the particular examples used to illustrate the definition. Many students may fail to generalize it to other situations, since the concept introduction activity is necessarily limited to a few special cases—often only four or five can be included for lack of time and space.

In addition, application activities aid students whose conceptual reorganization takes place more slowly than average, or who did not adequately relate the teacher's explanation during the introduction phase to their previous experiences. Teachers can observe students during the application phase to evaluate their understanding. If necessary, individual conferences with these students can help resolve the difficulties. Small group discussions where students can compare their ideas can also help individuals reduce their misunderstanding.

Teaching procedures very similar to the learning cycle have been described by others concerned with teacher education (Biggs, 1973). It has so many appealing qualities that good teachers may often use it instinctively without articulating their procedures or relating them explicitly to pedagogical and psychological principles.

The learning cycle approach has been applied by Kurtz (1976; Kurtz & Karplus, 1979) to the teaching of proportional reasoning in high school prealgebra classes. In view of the commonly occurring confusion of constant ratio and constant difference relationships, Kurtz provided instruction in constant ratio, constant difference, and constant sum problems in his 12 hour course entitled *Numerical Relationships* (Kurtz, 1976). His intent, accomplished successfully, was to enable more students to discriminate among situations where one or the other relationship would be appropriate.

Eight features distinguish the Numerical Relationships (NR) program from the usual textbook approach to proportions:

1. It is conceptually organized to challege students to distinguish among constant ratio, constant difference, and constant sum problems.
2. Teaching provides for student autonomy and teacher input through learning cycles.
3. *NR* directs the student' attention at the variables necessary to describe a relationship.

4. Graphical means are employed to help students identify the corresponding changes of variables for each constant ratio relationship.
5. NR makes use of laboratory activities.
6. NR avoids algorithmic techniques such as equating the products of means and extremes in a proportion.
7. NR often requires descriptive answers and explanations rather then exclusively numerical solutions to exercises.
8. Word problem situations are used to generate sets of closely related numerical questions.

Here is an example of the learning cycle applied to the NR activity concerned with introducing the constant connection between the situational context and the appropriate mathematical numerical relationship. As exploration, the teacher presents a two variables table with the entries

$$X = 4 \quad 6$$
$$Y = 8 \quad ?$$

The students are challenged to propose values for the missing entry and to justify their suggestions with reference to illustrative examples. Many possibilities exist, of course, and at least three numerical values may be derived from the examples studied earlier in the NR program. These are $Y = 12$ (constant ratio, 4 books cost $8, 6 books cost $12), $Y = 10$ (constant difference), and $Y = 6$ (constant sum). Students who are more creative may propose $Y = 5.33$ (constant product) or $Y = 14$ ($Y = 3X - 4$), but these are unlikely unless students have been encouraged previously to be inventive.

Concept introduction in this activity presents the idea that the numerical data by themselves are insufficient to determine the answer uniquely, and that other information—the situational context of the numerical data—must be taken into account to determine just which numerical relationship is most appropriate.

The following is an example of an application exercise that requires a descriptive answer and justification but no numerical solution:

Two parachutists, Bill and Karen, are falling towards the ground with the same velocity. Bill jumped out of the plane later than Karen, so he is originally above her. Both Bill and Karen measure their altitude above ground. The two variables in this situation are _____ and _____. The relationship between these variables is _____ because (please justify your answer) _____

The reader may object at this point that the concept introduction phase of the learning cycle is in conflict with Piaget's notion that the individual must construct knowledge for him- or herself. We believe that there is no contradiction; that when concept introduction follows exploration, as we have stated above, then concept introduction serves as a social transmission contribution to development. Self-regulation then takes place as the student relates the new concept or principle to previous experiences gathered in an open-ended situation in which he or she could function with high autonomy.

It is clear, therefore, that beginning instruction with exploration is a key aspect of the learning cycle. It differs from either of two more traditional approaches to rule-learning of (1) providing a rule and then giving examples or (2) giving examples and then summarizing their common properties by the rule. Both of these strategies lack the high degree of autonomy of students during the exploration phase.

For the learning cycle to become widely used, effective exploration activities have to be designed. Not many such activities are available at present because student autonomy in most secondary and college teaching programs has been low. The ADAPT project at the University of Nebraska, Lincoln (ADAPT, 1977) has described a few examples that were developed by the participating faculty. One of these, in anthropology, requires a pair of students to look for the conditions under which a stranger walking in the opposite direction can be made to smile at one of them, while the other observes. Investigating this process prepares the students for introduction of the concepts of social customs and rituals. In an economics class, student exploration of the cost-of-living concept involves them in making an inventory of their own purchases and expenses so as to create a personal "cost of living" before introducing this idea as a composite index for an entire population. In trigonometry, the students have a laboratory activity in which they measure the sides and angles of many cardboard triangles and look for patterns in the ratios of corresponding sides.

Though based primarily on developmental principles, the learning cycle has aspects compatible with other learning theories. Because educational theories are not rigorous deductive systems, the fact that similar outcomes can follow from differing starting points is not surprising. Thus, the exploration phase permits learning by discovery, concept introduction taken together with exploration provides "guided discovery," and concept application provides for repetition and practice. The approach is even close to Ausubel's Assimilation Theory, whose central ideas are (1) that learning depends on what the learner already knows and (2) that meaningful learning involves a conscious effort on the part of the learner to relate new and existing knowledge in substantive ways (Novak, 1977). The first of these corresponds to the importance of prior experience and existing reasoning patterns emphasized in the present article, while the second is not far from Piaget's view that knowledge is constructed actively by the individual. We therefore see the Ausubelian and Piagetian approaches as variations on a theme rather than as the mutually exclusive alternatives described by Novak (1977). There is this difference, however: The awareness of one's own reasoning required by Ausubel for meaningful learning (Novak, 1977, p. 456) would limit success of Ausubel's approach to students who use formal level reasoning patterns extensively. In our opinion, the learner's connecting new and old knowledge need not be conscious, and is unlikely to be conscious for individuals using primarily concrete level reasoning patterns. The combination of autonomy and input provided by the learning cycle has been designed to further self-regulation. Assembling a larger teaching program out of many learning cycles is a task we have not described here; the sequence might well take into account the learning hierarchy approach of Gagné (1977) and the structure of the discipline emphasized by Bruner (1960).

In addition to its direct contribution to learning, autonomy during exploration and concept application has great motivational value. Doing something because you want to do it, and doing it the way you want to do it, are powerful incentives. After a research visit to an eighth grade by the author, one of the students who had responded to Paper Clips Task—Form C (Appendix, #3) wrote this comment: "I, . . . have really enjoyed you here today. And I have really learned how to say and write what I and only I think, with no one else to try and tell me." The autonomy enjoyed by this student was merely that of explaining how she had arrived at the prediction of the height of Mr. Tall!

CONCLUSION

This chapter presents a pragmatic point of view aimed at the improvement of education. Because Piaget's developmental theory is concerned with concepts such as stages and structures, which do not manifest themselves clearly in the learning behavior of students, this theory is of only limited direct value to the classroom teacher. Two aspects of Piaget's research are, however, very valuable: (1) the focus on student reasoning as it is manifested by students' explanations or justifications; (2) the recognition that knowledge is constructed actively by the learner.

We have applied the first of these aspects by identifying certain reasoning patterns and describing research results that indicate the prevalence of proportional reasoning among various population samples. The second aspect led to the formulation of the learning cycle approach to teaching. The learning cycle provides for active participation by the learners during exploration and application phases, supplemented with instruction by the teacher during the concept introduction phase. More extended descriptions of these approaches have been published elsewhere in a format especially intended for teacher education (Karplus, Lawson, Wollman, Appel, Bernoff, Howe, Rusch, & Sullivan, 1977).

This chapter also has an implication for research on the development of reasoning. In our opinion, developmental research could be much more useful over the long term if data interpretation were not so thoroughly dependent on Piagetian theory. Investigators might well be somewhat more cautious about interpreting subjects' performances on one or two Piagetian tasks as implying achievement of a stage of formal thought. Also, the "averaging" of performance by a subject on several tasks, so as to identify an "average" level of thought, would seem to be suspect if the tasks demand application of differing reasoning patterns.

ACKNOWLEDGMENT

I am indebted to Marilyn Appel, Richard Bady, Anton Lawson, Steven Pulos, Irving Sigel, and Barbara Strawitz for reading a draft of this chapter and suggesting improvements.

REFERENCES

ADAPT, *College teaching and the development of reasoning.* Lincoln, Nebraska: University of Nebraska, 1975.

ADAPT, *Multidisciplinary Piagetian-based programs for college freshmen.* Lincoln, Nebraska: University of Nebraska, 1977.

Bady, R. Comment on "current uses of Piaget's concept of stage." *Journal of Research in Science Teaching,* 1978, *15,* 573-574.

Biggs, E. Investigations and problem-solving in mathematical education. In A. G. Howson (Ed.), *Proceedings of the second international congress on mathematical education.* London: Cambridge University Press, 1973.

Bruner, J. *The process of education.* Cambridge, Mass: Harvard University Press, 1960.

Collis, K. A study of concrete and formal operations in school mathematics. Ph.D. thesis, University of Newcastle, New South Wales, 1972.

Eakin, J., & Karplus, R. *SCIS final report.* Berkeley, CA: University of California, 1976.

Fischer, K. A theory of cognitive development: The control and construction of hierarchies of skills, *Psychological Review,* 1980, *87,* 477-531.

Flavell, J. H. "Stage related properties of cognitive development," *Cognitive Psychology,* 1971, *2,* 421-453.

Flavell, J. H. *The developmental theory of Jean Piaget.* New York: Van Nostrand, 1973.

Gagne, R. *The conditions of learning.* New York: Holt, Rinehart, and Winston, 1977.

Ginsburg, H., & Opper, S. *Piaget's theory of intellectual development* Englewood Cliffs, New Jersey: Prentice-Hall, 1969.

Gorman, R. M. *Discovering Piaget.* Columbus, Ohio: Charles E. Merrill, 1972.

Inhelder, B., & Piaget, J. *The growth of logical thinking from childhood to adolescence.* New York: Basic Books, 1958.

Kageyama, C., & Karplus, R. *Systems.* Berkeley, CA: University of California, 1966.

Karplus, E. F., Karplus, R., and Wollman, W. Intellectual development beyond elementary school IV: Ratio, the influence of cognitive style. *School Science and Mathematics,* 1974, *74,* 476-482.

Karplus, E. F., & Siegelman, E. *Systems feedback testing.* Berkeley, CA: University of California, 1966.

Karplus, R. "Science teaching and the development of reasoning." *Journal of Research in Science Teaching,* 1977, *14,* 169-175.

Karplus, R., Adi, H., & Lawson, A. E. Intellectual development beyond elementary school VIII: Proportional, probabilistic, and correlational reasoning. *School Science and Mathematics* 1980, *80,* 673-683.

Karplus, R., Karplus, E. F., Formisano, M., & Paulsen, A-C. Proportional reasoning and control of variables in seven countries. In J. Lochhead & J. Clements (Eds.), *Cognitive Process Instruction*, Philadelphia: The Franklin Institute Press, 1979.

Karplus, R., Karplus, E. F., Formisano, M. & Paulsen, A-C. A study of proportional reasoning and control of variables in seven countries. *Journal of Research in Science Teaching*, 1977, *14*, 411–417.

Karplus, R., Lawson, A. E., Wollman, W. T., Appel, M., Bernoff, R., Howe, A., Rusch, J. J., & Sullivan, F. *Science teaching and the development of reasoning*. Berkeley, CA: University of California, 1977.

Karplus, R., & Lawson, C. A. *SCIS teacher's handbook*. Berkeley, CA: University of California, 1974.

Karplus, R., & Peterson, R. W. Intellectual development beyond elementary school II: Ratio, a survey. *School science and Mathematics*, 1970, *70*, 813–820.

Karplus, R., & Thier, H. D. *A new look at elementary school science*. Chicago, IL: Rand McNally, 1967.

Kurtz, B. *A study of teaching for proportional reasoning*. Doctoral dissertation, University of California, Berkeley, 1976. Ann Arbor, MI: Xerox University Microfilms, 77-15,747.

Kurtz, B., & Karplus, R. Intellectual development beyond elementary school VII: Teaching for proportional reasoning. *School Science and Mathematics*, 1979, *79*, 387–398.

Lawson, A. E., Blake, A. J. D., & Nordland, F. H. Training effects and generalization of the ability to control variables in high school biology students. *Science Education*, 1975, *59*, 387–396.

Lawson, A. E., & Wollman, W. T. Encouraging the transition from concrete to formal cognitive functioning—An experiment. *Journal of Research in Science Teaching*, 1976, *13*, 413–430.

Linn, M. Teaching students to control variables: Some investigations using free-choice experiences. In S. Modgil & C. Modgil (Eds.), *Toward a Theory of Psychological Development Within the Piagetian Framework*. London: The National Foundation for Educational Research, 1980.

Linn, M., Chen, B., & Thier, H. D. Personalization in science: Preliminary investigation at the middle school level. *Instructional Science*, 1976, *5*, 227–252.

Linn, M., Chen, B., & Thier, H. D. Teaching children to control variables: Investigation of a free-choice environment. *Journal of Research in Science Teaching*, 1977, *14*, 249–255.

Lovell, K. Some aspects of the growth of the concept of a function. In M. Rosskopf, L. Steffe, & S. Tabac, (Eds.), *Piagetian Cognitive Development Research and Mathematical Education*. Reston, VA: National Council of Teachers of Mathematics, 1971.

Lovell, K., & Butterworth, I. B. "Abilities underlying the understanding of proportionality." *Mathematics Teaching*, 1966, *37*, 5–9.

Lunzer, E. A. Problems of formal reasoning in test situations. In P. H. Mussen (Ed.), European research in cognitive development. *Monographs of the Society for Research in Child Development*, 1965, (2, Whole No. 100), 18–46.

Lunzer, E.A. "Formal Reasoning: A reappraisal." In B. Z. Presseisen, D. Goldstein, & M. H. Appel (Eds.), *Topics in cognitive development, Vol. 2*. New York: Plenum Publishing Co., 1978.

Lunzer, E. A., & Pumfrey, P. D. "Understanding proportionality." *Mathematics Teaching*, 1966, *34*, 7–12.

McKinnon, J. W., & Renner, J. W. Are colleges concerned with intellectual development? *American Journal of Physics*, 1971, *39*, 1047.

Munby, H. "Piagetian research in science: Some misgivings about its potential to improve practice." Paper presented to the National Association for Research in Science Teaching, Toronto, April 1978.

Neimark, E. D. Intellectual development during adolescence. In F. D. Horowitz (Ed.), *Review of child development research* (Vol. 4). Chicago: The University of Chicago Press, 1975.

Novak, J. D. An alternative to Piagetian psychology for science and mathematics education. *Science Education*, 1977, *61*, 453–477.

Piaget, J. Cognitive development in children: Development and learning. *Journal of Research in Science Teaching*, 1964, *2*, 170-186.

Piaget, J. *The Psychology of Intelligence*. Paterson, N. J.: Littlefield, Adams, and Co., 1968.

Science Curriculum Improvement Study. Chicago, IL: Rand McNally, 1970-1974.

Suarez, A. *Formales Denken and Funktionsbegriff bei Jugendlichen*. Bern: Hans Huber, 1977.

Suarez, A., & Rhonheimer, M. *Lineare Funktion*. Zurich: Limmat Stiftung, 1974.

Wohlwill, J. R. The study of behavioral development. New York: Academic Press, 1973.

Wollman, W. T. Controlling variables: A neo-Piagetian sequence. *Science Education*, 1977, *61*, 385-391.

Wollman, W. T., & Karplus, R. Intellectual development beyond elementary school V: Using ratio in differing tasks. *School Science and Mathematics*, 1974, *74*, 593-613.

Wollman, W. T., & Lawson, A. E. The influence of instruction on proportional reasoning of seventh graders. *Journal of Research on Science Teaching*, 1978, 15(3), 227-232.

APPENDIX: PAPER CLIPS TASKS

Three tasks used to assess proportional reasoning have been mentioned in this article. For convenience they are collected in this appendix.

1. *Paper Clips Task-Form A* (Proportional Reasoning, Karplus and Peterson, 1970)

Materials: 8-10 #1 gem paper clips for each student
8 large paper clips hooked to form a chain
1 picture of Mr. Tall (equal in height to 6 large paper clips)—a stick man
1 answer page with a picture of Mr. Short (equal in height to 4 large paper clips)—a smaller stick man similar to Mr. Tall

Directions: Tell the students that this problem concerns Mr. Short on their answer pages and Mr. Tall on your paper. Show them that when you measure Mr. Short with your large paper clips, he has a height of four, and that when you measure Mr. Tall, he has a height of six. Write this data on the chalkboard and then put away the picture of Mr. Tall and the large paper clips.

Ask: Direct the students to the items on their answer pages and read these to them (see below).

Answer page:

Diagram (Mr. Short)
What is the height of Mr. Short, measured with *your* paper clips?
What is the height of Mr. Tall, measured with *your* paper clips?
Please explain carefully how you found this answer.

Response Categories:

Category I (intuitive)—The explanation does not use all the data, or it uses the data in a haphazard and illogical way; e.g. "12—I got Mr. Tall is 12 because I doubled the six big paper clips;" or, "(no prediction)—I have no big paper clips to work with, so I can't tell."

Category A (additive)—The explanation focuses on the difference in heights of the two men; e.g. "8—Mr. Short went from four big clips to six smalls, so Mr. Tall will also go up by two;" or, "Mr. Tall was two more big ones than Mr. Short, so he'll be two more small ones."

Category Tr (transitional)—The explanation makes reference to concrete comparisons or iterations, or only partial proportional reasoning; e.g. "9½—I guessed at the middle of Mr. Short and then quarters (there were marks in the picture) to find how long the big clips were, and then I marked off and measured for six of the big ones with my paper clips;" or, "7½—first I divided four into six and got 1½, and then I added six, the big clips in Mr. Tall, to 1½ and got 7½."

Category R (ratio)—The explanation uses a proportion or derives the exact scale ratio from the data available; e.g. "9—I put their heights in big clips into a fraction (4/6) and by putting their height in small clips into a fraction (6/x) put them equal and found x to be 9."

2. *Paper Clips Task-Form B* (Proportional Reasoning; Karplus, Karplus, & Wollman, 1974)

Materials: 8–10 #1 gem paper clips for each student
1 answer page with picture of Mr. Short (equal in height
to about 6½ paper clips)—a stick man

Directions: Tell the students that this problem concerns Mr. Short, pictured on their papers, and his friend Mr. Tall, also pictured on a piece of paper but not available in the classroom. When measured by large round buttons placed side-by-side, the two figures were found respectively, to be four, and six buttons high. Write the data on the chalkboard.

Ask: Direct the students to the answer page and read these items to them (see below).

Answer page:
(Same as for Paper Clips Task-Form A)
Response Categories:
(Same as for Paper Clips Task-Form A)

3. *Paper Clips Task-Form C* (Proportional Reasoning; Karplus & others, 1977 and 1979)

Materials: (Same as for Form B)
Directions: (Same as for Form B)
Ask: Direct the students to the items on the answer page and read these to

them (see below). Have them wait to begin until you have finished the presentation.

Answer page:

Diagram (Mr. Short)
What is the height of Mr. Short measured with your paper clips?
What is the height of Mr. Tall measured with your paper clips?
1. Please explain carefully how you found this answer.

Mr. Tall's car is 14 paper clips wide. How wide is Mr. Tall's car measured in buttons?
2. Please explain carefully how you found this answer.

Response Categories:

Item 1 (Same as for Form A)
Item 2 (Similar to Form A)
Category I (intuitive)—E.g. "7—because you say, what's half of fourteen."
Category A (additive)—E.g. "12—as in the first example, there are two more clips than buttons, so I subtracted 2 and got 12 buttons."
Category Tr (transitional)—E.g. "21—since 6 paper clips = 4 buttons, 14 paper clips is N buttons. 6/4 is N/14. Cross multiply, $6 \times 14 = 84 \div 4 = 21$."
Category R (ratio)—E.g. "9⅓—I put his height in paper clips over the width of the car (9/14), then put his height in buttons over the car width in buttons (6/x), $6/x = 9/14$, $84 = 9x$, $x = 9⅓$."

18 Piaget and Education: the Contributions and Limits of Genetic Epistemology

Herbert P. Ginsburg
University of Rochester

Piaget's theory of genetic epistemology has been extended beyond its intended domain to deal with problems of education. At first many of these applications involved the *direct teaching* of Piagetian concepts like conservation. An example is provided by Kohlberg and Mayer (1972) who believe that the very aim of education is the promotion of the Piagetian stages and that therefore the curriculum should focus on them. Subsequently, other applications have taken a different form, involving the use of general principles derived from Piaget's theory to guide educational practice. As Sinclair (1976) puts it:

> I'm not sure that much can be done with applications of Piaget's theory in a detailed way by the Piagetian psychologist. . . . As you know there are absolutely no practical applications in the work of Piaget with respect to education. All one can do is to talk about some general principles, some hints and some cautions. . . . Piaget has very little to say with respect to specific problems such as how to teach reading and writing, and various other educational techniques [p. 1].

Hence, it is necessary to limit oneself to a consideration of general principles derived from Piaget.

In all attempts at applying a theory to practical concerns and at extending its principles from one domain to another, there may arise problems of legitimacy and validity. Can the principles discovered in one area be used to provide a valid explanation of phenomena in another? Is the application a legitimate one? With respect to the extension of Piaget's theory to education, issues of this sort need to be examined most closely for several reasons. One is that the applications have concrete effects on the lives of many children; we need to be sure that the interventions are helpful. Another is that the Piagetian approach to education has

315

become something of a faddish movement; clear analysis of the issues is especially warranted so as to avoid dogmatism. Piaget himself has taken a cautious attitude towards educational applications of his theory.

The aim of this chapter is therefore to achieve a clearer understanding of the relations between Piaget's theory and educational practice. The goals are to describe the theory's contributions and limits, to identify misapplications of the theory, and to outline important educational issues which remain to be solved. I shall argue that the literal approach to applying Piaget—e.g., the direct teaching of Piagetian concepts—is a mistake. A more reasonable strategy involves a focus on Piagetian principles which can furnish overall guidance for educational practice. But this approach also has its limits: the Piagetian principles are of a general nature, can be misapplied, and are not easily extrapolated to the classroom context. And there is a more serious difficulty: the very nature of Piaget's theory sets strong limits on its potential contribution to education. In particular, the theory has little to say about cultural knowledge, individual differences, the social context of education, and certain modes of learning prevalent in the classroom. This of course is no criticism of Piaget's theory itself. Although it already deals with an incredibly wide range of phenomena, the theory cannot be expected to concern itself with everything. Given the limits of the theory, a truly Piagetian approach to education requires innovative research going beyond Piaget's particular focus on genetic epistemology.

To develop these arguments, we shall review a number of commonly held propositions concerning the applications of Piaget's theory to educational practice. These propositions are grouped into several categories. First, we consider two relatively literal applications of Piaget's theory: I. Curriculum development, and II. Testing. Next we consider somewhat broader applications in the areas of: III. Learning and IV. Limits and opportunities. Finally we consider areas where the theory has fundamental limitations with respect to education, namely V. Individual differences and VI. Academic knowledge.

I. Curricula

One major approach involves the derivation of curricula from Piagetian theory. Kohlberg and Mayer (1972) propose essentially that school curricula can be derived directly from the Piagetian stages. According to Kohlberg and Mayer, the aim of education is to promote the kind of development described by Piaget. What better way to do this than to teach the Piagetian stages? Taking this approach, Kamii (who has subsequently changed her position) has developed a "program of preschool intervention related to each of the chapter headings of Piaget's books: space, time, causality, number... [p. 488]."

This approach is misguided for several reasons. First, in the vast majority of children, at least in Western cultures, the preoperational and concrete-operational stages develop in a spontaneous fashion, and therefore, do not need to be taught.

There is some debate about whether this is true of formal operational thought as well. Our view is that there is no clear evidence indicating the lack of spontaneous development of formal operations in Western adolescents (Ginsburg & Koslowski, 1976; see also Piaget, 1972). Whatever may be true of adolescents, it seems clear that for Western elementary school children, instruction in Piagetian subject matter is likely to be unnecessary. Second, it makes little sense to provide instruction in a topic like conservation since it is intended only as an index for tapping deeper thought structures. The training programs may inculcate only the surface manifestations and not the underlying structure. As Sinclair (1971) puts it: "Piaget's tasks are like the core samples a geologist takes from a fertile area and from which he can infer the general structure of a fertile soil; but it is absurd to hope that transplanting these samples to a field of nonfertile soil will make the whole area fertile [p. 1]." Third, the aims of education should not be limited to—and perhaps should not at all include—the promotion of the Piagetian thought structures. Surely education must stress the transmission of the cultural wisdom and basic social values. It is not at all clear that Piaget himself would endorse Kohlberg and Mayer's "Piagetian" model.

It is therefore necessary to take a more modest approach in which one attempts to adjust particular curricular materials in line with the child's understanding as described by Piaget. Thus, if a physics curriculum is to be introduced, it behooves the curriculum developer to take into account the child's informal knowledge of physics and his related thought processes. Although rare, work of this type, as for example conducted by Shayer (1972), has great potential for education. A curriculum at least partially based on the psychology of the child is apt to be more effective than one which is not. On the other hand, there is some danger in this approach as well. One must not allow the Piagetian conception of thought in a given area fully to determine one's approach to it. For example, Piaget's view of scientific reasoning in adolescence places heavy stress on the hypothetico-deductive method. Although useful, that is not all there is to science. A curriculum based entirely on such an approach would ignore a good deal that characterizes the essence of scientific activity, for example, exploration, the formation of hypotheses by analogy and intuition, the role of luck and serendipity. Obviously, future research should concentrate on expanding our knowledge of the child's spontaneous understanding of the various subject matter areas— science, mathematics, etc. The more we know about the child's informal reasoning in these areas, the better are we able to design effective curricula in them. We shall return to this topic later when we consider *academic knowledge*.

In brief, an attempt to base education on the teaching of the Piagetian stages is an unfortunate misapplication of the theory. A more useful approach is the modification of the curriculum in line with knowledge of the Piagetian stages, without, however, placing undue emphasis on them and without allowing them to circumscribe one's approach. More research is needed on the nature of the child's informal knowledge of the various subject matter areas.

II. Testing

There seem to have been two major approaches to applying Piaget's theory to the question of testing. One approach is to standardize the various Piagetian tests in order to be able to administer them to large numbers of children. The purpose of this is of course not to measure academic accomplishment—the achievement tests are intended for that—but to obtain a psychometrically reliable portrait of the child's cognitive structures, in Piagetian terms. This approach is misguided for two reasons. One is that it is not clear that knowledge of the Piagetian thought structures helps us a great deal in understanding the child's academic work. If one is going to test children in the schools, it would seem more relevant to find out how they go about doing addition than whether they conserve number. A second reason is that, even if one has an interest in measuring the Piagetian thought structures, standardized testing is an inferior method for assessing them. Piaget's clinical method is deliberately unstandardized since that is a superior way to explore the subtleties of the child's cognitive structure. The rationale for the clinical method (for an early account see Piaget, 1929) is straightforward and sensible. Tapping the child's competence requires subtle and sensitive procedures, tailored to the peculiarities of each individual child. Pursuing the idiosyncracies of the child's solution processes requires flexibility in approach. The clinical method, used properly, accomplishes these purposes well; standardizing the procedure only serves to vitiate its power. Perhaps the major gain for standardization is a false sense of scientific respectibility.

A second application of Piaget to testing involves retaining both the clinical method and the Piagetian content as well. Sometimes teachers are encouraged to use the clinical method as applied to problems like the conservation of number. Such demonstrations may make an important impression on teachers, showing them that the child's thought can be distinctive. At the same time, the contribution of orthodox clinical interviewing is limited because of its failure to go beyond the Piagetian content, and to address itself directly to the teachers' concerns.

In brief, the standardization of Piagetian tests is not beneficial as it focuses too narrowly on Piagetian phenomena and because it deliberately abandons the strengths of the clinical method. The demonstration of Piagetian phenomena via the clinical method may be of some utility to teachers in illustrating the distinctiveness of the child's thought, but it does not speak directly to their needs. In education, we do not need more standard tests, nor even clinical interviews concerning Piagetian subject matter. Instead we need to exploit the great advantages of the clinical method in order to engage in the direct exploration of children's academic knowledge. It may be helpful for teachers to appreciate children's distinctive reasoning on the conservation tasks: but it would be even more useful for them to observe, via the richness of the clinical method, the unusual patterns of reasoning displayed by young children as they grapple with ordinary school arithmetic. Future work on testing needs to explore the uses of the clinical interview procedure with respect to uncovering the structure of academic knowledge.

III. Learning

One can derive from Piaget's theory several principles concerning children's learning and understanding.

1. Learning and understanding as active processes. According to Piaget, learning is not simply imposed by environmental forces. Learning is not shaping. The child takes an active role in his own learning. He assimilates environmental events into his own cognitive structures. The result is an active system of knowing. Knowledge is constructed by the child: "to understand is to invent."

These psychological principles have been extended to the educational setting. Piaget's theory provides a general rationale for active approaches which have existed for many years, stemming from Rousseau, Pestalozzi, and Froebel. The logic is simply that to know something in depth requires that one rediscover the matter for oneself. The teacher may guide the student in the direction of rediscovery, but the active learning involved in the rediscovery is itself crucial. If knowledge is active reconstruction, then active methods of education are required. We see then that in this case Piaget's contribution is to provide a psychological rationale for an already existing educational approach which is certainly a useful alternative to traditional education, with its heavy stress on passive learning.

At the same time, the educator must recognize that the Piagetian rationale is a general exhortation, itself solving no educational problems. It needs to be supplemented by specific techniques deriving from the art of the teacher. Further, there are possibilities for mischief in the application of the Piagetian ideas. One involves the misinterpretation of Piaget's notion of active learning. For example, some writers place undue stress on the role of concrete activity. Ginsburg and Opper (1969) maintain that: "Children, especially young ones . . . learn best from concrete activities [p. 221]." Further, "The teacher should not teach, but should encourage the child to learn by manipulating things [p. 221]." These undoubtedly well-meaning authors exaggerate. The important Piagetian idea is activity, not necessarily physical, concrete activity. Important for learning are active engagement and commitment, not necessarily actions on things. As Piaget (1970) puts it: ". . . it has finally been understood that an active school is not necessarily a school of manual labor. . . . The most authentic research activity may take place in the spheres of reflection, of the most advanced abstraction, and of verbal manipulations (provided they are spontaneous and not imposed on the child . . .) [p. 68]."

More important than simply misinterpretation is a limitation in Piaget's theory. It fails to provide an adequate account of receptive learning. We should not forget that education has a *legitimate* receptive side as well. Indeed Piaget

(1970) feels that: "Memory, passive obedience, imitation of the adult, and the receptive factors in general are all as natural to the child as spontaneous activity [pp. 137-138]." One of the many legitimate aims of education is to promote receptive learning. By necessity, students must engage in some "rote learning," such as learning the names of the states, memorizing addition facts, learning the chemical elements, acquiring foreign vocabulary, etc. All this is not the only aim of education, or even the most important one: but receptive learning cannot be avoided. Further, Piaget points out that for learning of this type, the teaching machine and various forms of programmed instruction may be extremely efficient and useful. Yet, while receptive learning or "learning in the narrow sense" is a basic part of education, Piaget has no good theory of it. He simply has not been interested in this type of learning, so that if you wish to understand the teaching of vocabulary or some other aspect of receptive learning you must go to other theorists.[1]

In brief, Piaget's theory provides the theoretical underpinnings for an active approach to education. But it suggests no specific techniques, is liable to misinterpretation, and does not provide much understanding of receptive learning which is basic for education.

2. *Cognitive conflict and equilibration.*   Another proposition derived from Piaget's theory is that cognitive development is promoted when there is a moderate degree of discrepancy between the child's cognitive structure and some new event which he encounters. This notion has been expressed in various forms within Piagetian theory. Piaget's early work on infancy proposed that moderate novelty tends to attract the infant's interest and hence promotes learning. In later work, Piaget has stressed cognitive conflict as promoting the equilibration process. Certainly Piaget's notion of the role of cognitive conflict gives a different perspective from behaviorists' approaches to learning. The strategy of deliberately jarring the student's cognitive structure and thereby enhancing active learning is an important idea for education.

At the same time, there may be a number of difficulties with the notions of cognitive conflict and equilibration as applied to education. First, the Genevans would be the first to admit that equilibration theory is itself not yet fully developed. It has only been in the past decade that Genevan research has extensively focused on problems of cognitive conflict and equilibration. Equilibration theory itself requires further elaboration.

Second, the proper applications of equilibration theory to school learning are unclear. No doubt, the informed pursuit of cognitive conflict is at least on some occasions a useful model for education. But we do not really know for which

---

[1]The irony is that modern experimental psychology views receptive learning as very much an active process. For example, memory of nonsense syllables involves active organizational strategies. Even rote learning is no longer seen as the stamping in of associations onto a passive learner.

circumstances this model is most appropriate and for which circumstances other models are required: Does all school learning involve cognitive conflict? Is equilibration theory a useful approach to reading, for example, which involves some memorization of whole words, and some abstraction of orthographic rules? In other words, while the notion of equilibration may be informative with respect to the development of those cognitive structures of concern to Piaget, it is not clear to which aspects of school learning the notion of cognitive conflict might apply.

Third, and even more fundamentally, whereas the notion of cognitive conflict may be a key notion for educators in many areas, identification of the precise nature of educational conflicts is hardly guaranteed by knowledge of the Piagetian structures. Thus, a student's cognitive conflict in the area of history, for example, may in no way involve the concrete operations or any other Piagetian cognitive structure. If this is so, identification of the precise nature of the conflict requires a theory of the cognitive structures which in fact are involved in school learning. Unfortunately, as we shall see later, such a theory is almost entirely lacking, and Piaget's theory of cognitive structures is not an adequate substitute for such a theory.

In brief, Piaget's principle of cognitive conflict offers a useful educational alternative to receptive teaching procedures. But the theory of equilibration is only in its formative stages; the areas of application of the model to academic knowledge are unknown; and identification of the precise nature of educational conflict is not guaranteed by knowledge of Piagetian structures.

3. Self-directed learning. Piaget's theory proposes that sensorimotor and cognitive structures develop in a spontaneous, and self-directed fashion. The child takes a major role in directing the course of cognitive development: the latter does not depend on instruction. No doubt, self-directed learning is a real phenomenon. As Piaget has demonstrated most convincingly in the case of infancy, children *can* learn on their own. The coordination of schemes, for example, is not taught; it is learned spontaneously and parents are often quite oblivious of it.

Piaget's theory of spontaneous, self-directed development of cognitive structures has often been generalized to education in the form of an exhortation to allow children to engage in extensive self-directed learning. For example, Ginsburg and Opper (1969) state that children "... should be allowed considerable freedom for their own learning [p. 224]." They state further that, "If left to himself the normal child does not remain immobile; he is eager to learn. Consequently it is quite safe to permit the child to structure his own learning [p. 225]." In arguing against adult controlled teaching, writers sometimes point out an analogy with speech. Without instruction, children in all cultures learn to speak. If such natural learning were replaced by formal instruction in school, there would no doubt be disastrous results. Arguments of this sort have been used to justify some long-standing practices of progressive education. Thus Piagetians often support the "open classroom" approach, popularized in the British infant school, in which children are assumed to control a good deal of their own learning.

Although Piaget's theory demonstrates that self-directed learning *can* take place in the natural environment—and indeed in that setting may be the prevalent mode of learning—there is once again a problem of goodness of fit when the psychological principle is applied to the educational setting. The model of self-directed learning was originally designed to explain such phenomena as the development of cognitive structures or sensorimotor schemes. We cannot know a priori whether self-directed learning does indeed characterize some or all academic situations. This is an empirical matter. Unfortunately, little evidence exists concerning the issue. Informal observation of open classrooms suggests that under some circumstances self-directed learning can take place in school and indeed can predominate there. At the same time, it is also obvious that self-directed learning does not always occur and that other forms of learning appear to be successful in some situations. For example, some forms of receptive learning may have to be imposed on children and it may be that only after such an imposition takes place that self-directed learning is possible. Music teachers often report that young children have to be *forced* to play an instrument before they can spontaneously appreciate it. Another example involves minority education. In the 1960s, it was reported that some poor black inner-city children who failed miserably in ordinary public schools achieved a high degree of success when they attended extremely structured and indeed militaristic, authoritarian schools run by Black Muslim groups. Presumably these children benefited from the discipline and structure.[2]

All this is to say that the freedom to learn principle may be effective in some cases and may even be an ideal to which education should aspire. Yet, common experience teaches us that the principle does not apply under all circumstances. And Piagetian theory does not concern itself with the nature of these circumstances. The theory does not attempt to disentangle the social, ecological, and political factors which seem to play a major role in determining whether self-directed learning is possible in a given school situation. Those who attempt to apply Piagetian theory must become aware of the realities of the schools; but to learn about these realities, they must look beyond Piaget's theory.

4. Factors influencing development. Piaget proposes that several factors influence development: maturation, physical experience, logicomathematical experience, social experience, and equilibration. We have already dealt with

---

[2]Perhaps an open school environment could work for these children under very special circumstances with very special teachers (for example, Herbert Kohl who had enormous success with his *36 children* [1967]).

equilibration, and there is nothing much to say about the role of physical maturation, except that it is important but poorly understood. Now we consider the other factors, physical experience, logicomathematical experience, and social experience.

In the case of *physical experience,* Piaget points out that individuals sometimes obtain knowledge of the world through direct perceptual experience with external objects and the consequent abstraction of properties from them. This is usually classified as perceptual learning, as in the theory of J. J. Gibson (1966). Piaget (1971) further points out that physical experience involves "a vast category of knowledge [p. 266]." Surely, in schools, physical experience may be very important in some areas. In the case of science, for example, it is often important for children to "mess around" with objects (to use David Hawkins', 1974, phrase) in order to obtain through physical experience—through perceptual learning—a "feel" for objects' properties. In mathematics, it is important for children to observe the behavior of numbers. Yet, while perceptual experience is both extensive and important for education, Piaget's theory has tended to slight it. His theory focuses on thought, not perception, and has been unsuccessful in offering an explanation of the means by which individuals manage to abstract knowledge directly from the real world. As a result, Piaget's theory has virtually nothing to say about this aspect of education, just as it has little to offer concerning the mechanisms of receptive learning.

The notion of *logicomathematical experience* is a unique, and I think very valuable notion in Piaget's theory. The idea that the individual learns from reflecting on his own actions on the world gives a new perspective to learning. In the case of mathematics, for example, the child may, after considerable activity, learn something about *his own actions* with respect to number, and this may be an important acquisition. The perspective afforded by the notion of logicomathematical experience seems to be an extremely useful one for teachers. The only problem with it is that it is so unique that we have little insight concerning the aspects of educational activity to which it applies.

Social experience can have several senses in Piaget's theory. It may refer to the role of language, to the effect of peers, and to that of adults. Consider each in turn.

For Piaget, *language* generally plays a secondary role to thought. Because the child's thought is distinctive, his language therefore bears distinctive meaning. Such an emphasis is extremely useful for education, since it prods teachers to listen with the "third ear" to what children say, and to go beyond teaching by mere verbalisms, in accordance with the mistaken belief that children simply learn by listening.

From his early work in the 1920s and 1930s on egocentrism and moral judgment, Piaget has stressed the facilitating effect of *peer interaction* on cognitive development. In general, the view is that the conflict of opinions generated through peer interaction is instrumental in promoting decentration, and hence development in general. The recent experimental work of Murray (1972) supports this view, showing that peer disagreements seem to promote development in reasoning concerning conservation.

In general, the Piagetian view on peer interaction seems to have some value. Surely it is wasteful for children to spend a good portion of their time in school observing a vow of silence. Surely debate, the exchange of ideas, and intellectual conflict is all to the good in many classroom situations. At the same time, we must recognize the obvious fact that peer interaction has many dimensions, and does not always promote intellectual growth. Peers interact with one another in many ways, and sometimes this interaction involves the transmission of values which are antithetical both to genuine intellectual activity and to school learning (the two do not always coincide!). On some occasions, the promotion of learning among teenagers may require less peer interaction and more contact with appropriate adult models. All this is to say that in the context of education the social psychology of peer interaction must obviously go far beyond the Piagetian analysis.

With respect to *adult influence*, Piaget feels that it has an important role in the promotion of intellectual development. The adult can help to structure a situation so that the child is able to assimilate it effectively. The adult can intervene in the course of events so as to produce a moderate degree of intellectual conflict within the child. Piaget's position is similar to that of John Dewey who felt that the adult has a distinctive responsibility in the educational process, mainly to devise situations in which the child can engage in active learning. In this regard, Piaget (1970) reports a visit he paid to an open school run by Susan Isaacs. Piaget found the school interesting but somewhat undisciplined and felt that the adults should have taken a more active role in structuring the situation for the children.

The principle of adult influence is a most useful emphasis for the teacher. Yet Piaget does not go beyond a very general and well-meaning position. Piaget has nothing further to say on the role of the teacher; he has no theory of instruction. Indeed in Piaget's enormous corpus of writing on child development, one can find virtually no mention of the role of the adult. One exception to this is in the case of moral judgment, where Piaget reports, somewhat plaintively, that as a parent he was unable despite his best efforts to advance his daughter beyond a primitive stage of moral judgment. Because Piaget's almost exclusive emphasis has been on the child, he has virtually nothing to say about teaching.

In brief, a number of factors influence development, among them physical experience, logicomathematical experience, and social experience. Although Piaget acknowledges the importance of physical experience, his theory has little to say concerning the perceptual learning it entails and hence can contribute little to the understanding of vast areas of education. The notion of logicomathematical experience is promising, but its sphere of application is uncertain. In the area of social experience, Piaget's view of language encourages in teachers a sensitivity to the unique meanings of children's speech; his conception of the beneficial effects of peer interaction is useful but limited; because of his almost exclusive concentration on children, Piaget has little to say concerning teaching.

IV. Limits on Learning and Opportunities

To some extent Piaget's theory has a pessimistic side with respect to education. One principle states that because of the nature of his current stage of intellectual development, the child is limited in what he can learn. Thus, in the stage of concrete operations, he may not be able to engage in certain forms of scientific reasoning. Or, in the preoperational stage, he may not be able to understand certain basic mathematical concepts. In general, this must be true. Everyone knows that you cannot teach a baby to speak or a young child to do the calculus. It is certainly useful for the teacher to be alert to aspects of the child's thought processes which might make it difficult for him to assimilate a certain body of material.

Yet there is a serious danger in the Piagetian position. Some Piagetians have adopted too zealous a view of the child's limitations. It is a common belief, for example, that the preoperational child cannot engage in "abstract thought" or that he cannot perform any useful scientific activity. These are misconceptions. The young child is capable of mental representation from the age of about 18 months, and indeed sometimes thinks *too* abstractly, as when he overgeneralizes the meaning of words. Piaget himself is careful to point out intellectual strengths in the preoperational child, as in the case of the early understanding of functional relations. Similarly, there is a good deal that the young child can do with respect to science, whose scope should not be limited to the kind of hypothetical reasoning Piaget attributes to adolescents. It is even more incorrect to suppose that the preoperational child or even the concrete operational child is not yet "ready" for reading since his thought structures are so primitive. Obviously 3 and 4 year old children can learn to read—this is a common observation—and it is by no means clear that the structures of preoperational or concrete operational thought set any kinds of limits on basic reading. In brief, there is some validity to the Piagetian principle that the nature of the young child's thought limits his learning. But this principle has been applied indiscriminately, with the unfortunate effect of restricting the range of educational experiences for the young child.

Piagetian theory displays an optimistic side as well. According to Piaget, the spontaneously developed thought structures existing at various stages make it possible for the child to assimilate various aspects of school material. These thought structures form the cognitive basis for academic knowledge. Because the child approaches many areas of academic study with spontaneously developed and relatively powerful "intuitions", the task for education is to make connections among the child's intuitions and the formalizations which are taught in school. As Piaget (1970) puts it; "The pedagogic problem . . . still subsists in its entirety: that of finding the most adequate methods for bridging the transition between these natural but nonreflective structures [that is, the child's spontaneously developed but unaware intuitions] to conscious reflection upon such structures and to a theoretical formulation of them [p. 47].'' There is thus a particularly Piagetian form of consciousness raising: in presenting formalizations, the teacher must make an effort to exploit the child's intuitions. As Freud put it in a somewhat different context, ''Where id was there ego shall be.''

Pursuing this analysis, Piaget claims that children should not have as much difficulty as they do with school mathematics, since it is more or less an elaboration of what they already know. As Piaget (1970) puts it: ''. . . it is difficult to conceive how students who are well-endowed when it comes to elaboration and utilization of the spontaneous logicomathematical structures of intelligence can find themselves handicapped in the comprehension of a branch of teaching that bears exclusively upon what is to be derived from such structures [p. 44].''

The notion of drawing on the child's spontaneous intuitions and relating them to what is taught in school is a key idea for education.[3] Piaget makes an important contribution in stressing that a basic strategy for education should consist in bridging the gap between spontaneous and cultural knowledge. Yet the Piagetian analysis cannot carry us very far in this direction because the theory pays scant attention to two areas which we shall consider next, namely *individual differences* and *academic knowledge*.

V. Individual Differences

In many of his works, Piaget takes pains to point out that there exist individual differences in children's rate of attainment of the various cognitive structures. In the Piagetian scheme such individual differences may result from variations in any of the factors promoting development—maturation, physical experience, etc. Such differences may also appear in the rates of development displayed by entire cultures.

Although the theory acknowledges the existence of individual differences—how could it not?—Piaget has little interest in them. His concern is with the ''general human mind'' of Wundt, with the development of common structures of knowledge. Hence Genevan theory and research have paid scant attention to individual differences in rate of attainment of the various stages. Moreover, the theory has virtually ignored other individual differences. The theory does not concern itself with such variables as impulsiveness, intellectual conscientiousness, persistence, commitment, creativity. These are all individual difference characteristics at the heart of intellectual activity. To observe that Piaget's theory fails to deal with them is no criticism, merely a statement of fact: the theory cannot be expected to solve all psychological problems.

---

[3]Of course, the idea is not completely unique to Piaget. For example, Vygotsky (1962) made a similar distinction between spontaneous and scientific knowledge.

At the same time, this gap in Piaget's theory limits its relevance for the classroom. Individual differences are at the heart of education. To a large degree, education is or should be concerned with developing meaningful forms of learning for individuals who differ in important ways. To some extent, these important characteristics may include individual differences in rates of attainment of the Piagetian stages. Perhaps some topics in mathematics will come easier to the 7 year old who is in the period of concrete operations than to one who is preoperational. But it is likely that other individual differences—those not discussed by Piaget—are at least equally important for education, and may well be more important than rate of attainment of the Piagetian stages. For real children in classrooms, what matters is creativity, intelligence, cognitive style, and intellectual motivation. A deep understanding of these factors is vital for the effective conduct of everyday education. Yet these are factors concerning which Piaget's theory has virtually nothing to say.

VI. Piagetian Thought Structures and School Knowledge

It is usually assumed that educators should be sensitive to the child's intellectual status as described in terms of Piagetian thought structures. There is some validity to this notion. A teacher should be aware of the concrete operational child's one-to-one correspondence or of the formal operational child's capacity for hypothetico-deductive reasoning. To some extent, the structures described by Piaget are informal intuitions which can serve as a foundation for formal instruction and hence the teacher can profit from knowledge of them. The open question, however, is this: In what ways do the Piagetian structures *account for* the nature of academic cognition? To what extent can the concrete operations *explain in detail* the child's performance in algebra or in reading?

It is becoming evident that the explanatory power of the Piagetian structures with respect to academic knowledge is weak. For example, in the case of adolescent science, as we have pointed out below, the Piagetian theory deals with the details of hypothetico-deductive reasoning. Yet this is only one part of the scientific enterprise. Similarly in the case of mathematics, Piagetian theory deals with some fundamental notions of one-to-one correspondence and equivalence, but does not have a great deal to say about the child's uses of counting or the details of his problem solving techniques in algebra. In particular, Piaget's theory does not deal with knowledge which is symbolized and codified. Thus, it does not seem very productive to use Piagetian notions in developing models for reading, either at the level of "decoding" (the technical aspect of reading), or at the level of comprehension. In brief, although Piaget's theory may explicate some fundamental structures of thought, it does not concern itself with, and therefore cannot be directly applied to, basic aspects of academic knowledge in particular, and culturally derived thought in general. Whereas the theory gives insight into such informal "intuitions" as one-to-one correspondence, it does not deal explicitly with the cultural elaborations of these intuitions. Hence the effort to bridge the gap between intuition and formalization is hindered.

Why does Piaget's theory not pay more attention to cultural forms of knowledge? Piaget (1970) sees education as a dialectic process involving interaction between child and society. "To educate is to adapt the child to an adult social environment, in other words, to change the individual's psycho-biological constitution in terms of the totality of collective realities to which the community consciously attributes a certain value [p. 137]." The culture attempts to transmit to the child its wisdom, its modes of thought, knowledge, and values. On his part, the child attempts to assimilate the cultural wisdom and eventually to contribute to it, to modify it. In the case of mathematics, for example, over the course of centuries the culture has developed codified, written procedures and explicit, symbolized principles, a cumulative legacy which the educational system attempts to inculcate in the child. This accumulated wisdom is powerful and can serve the child well once it is assimilated into his cognitive structures. This having been done, the child is then in a position to make original contributions to the culturally derived body of knowledge.

Although apparently recognizing the central role of the "collective realities"—the cultural wisdom—Piaget's theory does not contribute a great deal to understanding them. As a genetic epistemologist, Piaget has been concerned mainly with the development of fundamental but noncultural forms of knowledge. Thus he is interested in the notion of one-to-one correspondence, not with written algebra. Piaget focuses on ideas and modes of thought operating outside the school context, not within it. Another way of putting it is to say that Piaget is interested in biologically based forms of knowledge, not socially based forms: Piaget (1971) maintains that:

> We are omitting [from consideration] the modes of metaphysical and ideological knowledge because they are not kinds of knowledge in the strict sense but forms of wisdom or value coordinations, so that they represent a reflection of social life and cultural super-structures rather than any extension of biological adaptation. By this we do not mean to dispute their human importance; it simply means that the problems are quite different and are no longer the direct province of biological epistemology [p. 268].

Thus, Piaget's theory has focused on "biological epistemology," on the basic Kantian categories of thought, and has slighted social knowledge.

If education is in good measure concerned with acculturation—the transmission of the accumulated wisdom of a culture—then Piaget's theory is limited in its explanatory power with respect to academic knowledge. At the very least we can say that it is not clear that there is a strong relation between the Piagetian structures and the kinds of thought processes involved in school learning. To a large extent the question is an empirical one, since we have very little knowledge concerning the thought processes actually employed in academic learning. A productive approach, I think, is for those with a Piagetian orientation to undertake direct investigations of academic cognition in order to determine whether the Piagetian notions are indeed useful, or whether new accounts need to be developed. For education, knowledge of the Piagetian thought structures is only a preliminary first step.

CONCLUSIONS

Piaget's theory yields several principles providing both deep understanding of children and general guidance for the educational enterprise. The principles serve as a basis for a progressive approach to education. At the same time, we must recognize that the theory may be misinterpreted: sometimes this results in too literal and rigid an application of Piaget's views. Much more importantly, we must also understand that Piaget's is a specialized theory, failing to consider many issues crucial for education. In particular, because Piaget is a genetic epistemologist, whose theory focuses on the development of what he considers to be the basic categories of the general human mind—on biologically based, Kantian categories—he has little to say about the acquisition and nature of culturally-based forms of knowledge, the forms inculcated by schooling.

Considering these limitations in Piaget's theory, it seems fair to say that we sometimes rely too much on Piaget, and the result is detrimental to the understanding and practice of education. Too often, we say to teachers that Piaget wants us to look at the child, but then all we show them is what Piaget has seen. We demonstrate the child's distinctiveness through his inability to conserve, but we cannot describe his unique approach to addition. While preaching a child-centered view, Piagetians too often assume a Piaget-centered view.

An effective contribution to education requires utilizing the Piagetian framework to go beyond Piaget. Such an approach requires, among other things, attempts to understand self-directed learning within the social context of the classroom and the ecological setting of the school in the larger society. It requires a direct focus on the structures of academic knowledge in particular and cultural knowledge in general. It requires the use of flexible methods to investigate cognitive structures of direct relevance to education. In these ways can we begin to understand the education of the child.

ACKNOWLEDGMENT

The writer wishes to thank the following colleagues for their helpful comments on the paper: Kathy Hebbeler, Jane Knitzer, Leon Levy, Barbara Means, Ellin Scholnick, Marilyn Wang.

REFERENCES

Gibson, J. J. *The senses considered as perceptual systems*. Boston: Houghton Mifflin, 1966.

Ginsburg, H., & Koslowski, B. Cognitive development. *Annual Review of Psychology*, 1976, *27*, 29-61.

Ginsburg, H., & Opper, S. *Piaget's theory of intellectual development: an introduction*. Englewood Cliffs, N.J.: Prentice-Hall, 1969.

Hawkins, D. *The informed vision*. N.Y.: Agathon Press, 1974.

Kohl, H. *36 children*. New York: New American Library, 1967.

Kohlberg, L., & Mayer, R. Development as the aim of education. *Harvard Educational Review*, 1972, *42*, 449-96.

Murray, F. B. Acquisition of conservation through social interaction. *Developmental Psychology*, 1972, *6*, 1-6.

Piaget, J. *The child's conception of the world*. London: Routledge & Kegan Paul, 1929.

Piaget, J. *The science of education and the psychology of the child*. N.Y.: Orion Press, 1970.

Piaget, J. *Biology and knowledge*. Chicago: University of Chicago Press, 1971.

Piaget, J. Intellectual evolution from adolescence to adulthood. *Human Development*, 1972, *15*, 1-12.

Shayer, M. Conceptual demands in the Nuffield 0-level physics course. *School Science Review*, 1972, *186*, 26-34.

Sinclair, H. "Piaget's theory of development: The main stages" In M. F. Rosskopf, L. P. Steffe, & S. Taback. *Piagetian cognitive-developmental research and mathematical education*. Washington, D.C.: National Council of Teachers of Mathematics, 1971.

Sinclair, H. In T. C. O'Brien, *Implications of Piagetian research for education: Interview with E. M. Hitchfield*. St. Louis: Teacher's Center, 1976.

Vygotsky, L. S. *Thought and language*. Cambridge, Mass.: MIT Press, 1962.

V

MECHANISMS OF LEARNING: A SYMPOSIUM ORGANIZED

by George E. Forman

Chapter 19 differs from the preceding chapters in that it contains a set of papers addressing the common topic of the mechanisms of learning. The commonality of the theme, however, does not result in a singular theoretical, methodological perspective. Rather, once the writers acknowledge the significance of the issue, each proceeds to focus on his/her particular area. The diversity may be exhilarating to some and disconcerting to others. The exhilarating aspect is the challenge the authors pose regarding how to conceptualize the problem, how to study the problem, and what to make of what is learned. On the other hand, diversity can be viewed as chaos and chaos breeds discouragement.

For us, the polarity of exhilaration and despair in the context of a need to come to terms with just what the problem of study is and how we elect to approach that problem provide perhaps the needed stimulus for theoretical growth. Is that not an expression of the equilibration principle functioning in our own theoretical development?

Each paper contributes a constructive note by providing new perspectives or theoretical constructs. Gallagher contends that the time is ripe to attack the mechanisms of learning issues in the context of the classroom, moving away from the stage concepts as the educator's point of departure or Forman's suggestion of the negation of negation as a developmental construct by which to gain further insight into not only the mechanisms of learning, but also the conditions which activate these mechanisms.

Reid demonstrates the variability in learning patterns and in levels of cognitive achievements among exceptional children. Finally, Kuhn presents an experimental approach to the study of the learning mechanisms that perhaps approximate what a classroom can do.

It is Duckworth who sharpens the issue in her closing paragraph where she says, "Piaget has no answers to the question of *what* it is that children ought to learn. But once, as educators, we have some sense of what we would like children to learn, then I think that Piaget has a great deal to say about *how* we can go about doing that [p. 363]."

The authors, however, have also something to say about *how* we can go about understanding the mechanisms of learning. In the end, the reader will construct his/her own agenda as to how to answer the question posed directly and implicity in these papers. As with all development, we shall then have to wait and see the directions, the detours, the delays and the delights our search will take. At least we know now that we have exciting options which in the long run will provide the basis for a more rational, productive educative system.

19a Knowing How a Child Knows: Phase Three of Piaget and the Learning Process

Jeanette McCarthy Gallagher
Temple University

A few years ago, Sigel (1974) asked in a provocative essay; "When do we know what a child knows?" The title highlighted Sigel's concern that the context of the testing situation and the test items themselves prevented psychologists from obtaining accurate evaluations of competence. Thus, a child may know something in one context (concept of *one* cookie) but not in another (concept of *one* block upon demand in a testing situation). Sigel, in part, answered his own question "When do we know when the child knows" by suggesting that the child's knowledge is contingent upon the interaction of environmental events and unassessed cognitive processes. The theme of this essay is that investigation of cognitive processes, in the Piagetian sense, assists us not only in "what" of the child's knowledge, but more importantly, in the "how." It is through this concentration upon the "how" that phase three in the application of Piaget to education may prosper.

Piaget's (1970) theory is essentially the development of knowing: the movement ". . . from a state of less sufficient knowledge to a state of higher knowledge [pp. 12-13]." This movement, the development of knowing, is learning in the widest sense defined by Piaget (1959) as an adaptive process unfolding in time as a function of responses given to a group of prior and present stimuli. Learning in the strict sense, according to Piaget, is reserved for those results (knowledge or performance) acquired as a function of experience (See Gallagher & Reid, 1981).

It is easier to *say* that Piaget's notions on learning, whether in the broad or strict sense, have rich meaning for educators than it is to *spell out* just what this meaning may be. Phase one of such attempts centered upon direct application, such as "teaching the tasks" or "teaching exercises in logic." We are now hopefully at the end of Phase Two: concentration upon stages as limiters of what should or should not be introduced into the classroom.

Phase Three is the promising one, the search for the mechanisms of learning. Stages are no longer perceived as stairsteps for the struggling child but as a continuous, dynamic spiral of knowing based upon the overriding mechanism of equilibration. Current research of the Genevan School is centered upon the test of the new equilibration model, especially in the subareas of reflexive abstraction and contradiction (Piaget, 1974a, 1974b, 1974c, 1975, 1977, 1978). Fortunately, for educators, these two areas of reflexive abstraction and contradiction directly relate to the process of learning (Gallagher, 1978b, 1979). Research, however, precedes effective application.

Unfortunately, the classical behaviorist approach in learning studies, which places emphasis upon response and not process variables, does not capture the subtle changes which are the basis for studies in reflexive abstraction and contradiction. According to Piaget (1977), reflexive abstraction involves projection to a higher level of understanding and reordering at that higher level. States of contradiction are "caught" not only by explanations, but also by expressions of puzzlement. The slow, involved method of critical exploration (Inhelder, Sinclair, & Bovet, 1974) used by Genevans trained for at least one year, has not seemed practical to American investigators. Voyat (1977) summarized the essence of the problem of adapting Genevan problems to traditional paradigms of learning research: ". . . it is hard to find any common measure between, say, the data produced by administering a five-minute questionnaire to a hundred children and that obtained by conducting a hundred-minute experiment with just five children [p. 344]."

So we are faced with a dilemma. On one hand two theoretical areas, reflexive abstraction and contradiction, seem ripe for testing and application to learning in the classroom. On the other hand, an ongoing body of learning studies with sophisticated analysis based upon relatively large samples, seem far removed from any step-by-step interview method.

If research precedes application, then investigators need to be convinced that some aspects of the Genevan method of critical exploration are not beyond implementation. In other words, the time is ripe for an era of experimentation based upon the premise that explanations are not just "nice" to add to data but are absolutely essential. Some recent research efforts point in this direction.

The key problem before us is the merger of the method of critical exploration with the traditional experimental method in psychology. How is it possible to retain objectivity and, at the same time, insure that probing questions are not altering the context of the experimental session? Striking evidence that questioning does not have to be disruptive was supplied by a recent study of the cognitive bases of children's moral judgments (Gottlieb, Taylor, & Ruderman, 1977). In the fourth experiment of a series, children were asked a standard set of questions at preplanned intervals so as to determine whether they were using motive, outcome, or both to make moral judgments. In fact, according to the findings, the answers to the interjected questions revealed what items of information from a single story were being processed. Three different strategies of moral reasoning were identified which were not isolated in previous massive research efforts in the study of moral reasoning.

What is evident from the findings of Gottlieb and his coworkers is that judgments in moral reasoning studies have little meaning apart from close and careful questioning which reveals the strategies, the bases for the judgments. Far from disruptive, such questioning proved to be the core of the study and source of the suggestions for further research.

Evidence that explanations are essential in cognitive studies is further supplied by our studies (Gallagher & Reid, 1975, 1978) in which children were asked to solve Piagetian-type problems based upon conservation of continuous quantity. Kindergarten, first and second-grade children were given water problems with a built-in solution of equal containers. A key research question of the studies was whether or not the pouring of water into equal containers was related to judgment and/or to explanation criteria. That is, what additional insight into processing was gained by asking children for an explanation of their solutions over and beyond the simple scoring of right and wrong answers?

For the third problem of the series, in which children had to cope with double relationships of equal water and equal containers, the addition of the explanation criterion contributed significantly to the variance in the conservation scores. For all problems, the use of equal containers was significantly associated with both judgment *and* explanation criteria, but more closely with the explanation criteria. Our findings support the view of Reese and Schack (1974) that explanations are important in eliminating irrelevant hypotheses.

What was striking about our research was the frequency of correct judgments followed by incorrect explanations. Even though the explanation question was far from simple ("How do you know *now* for certain") it was evident that the children grasped that we were asking for the "why" of their attempted solutions. Thus, it seems too risky to eliminate the probing for the "why" on the false assumption that such methods will lead to a higher rate of error (Brainerd, 1973, 1974, 1977) or that children will fail to grasp the question.

A third area of research which emphasizes the need for probing beyond the judgment level is that of verbal analogies. In a series of studies Achenbach (1969, 1970a, 1970b, 1975) claimed to separate children who responded on an associative level to analogy items from those who responded on a higher, relational level. Of the several thousand children studied by Achenbach, there is no evidence that he asked children *why* they selected one item instead of another. The question arises, due to the very structure of the items: were the children, whose "style" was associative, only attending to the last part (C:D) of the analogy?

Following the lead of Piaget (1977) who studied solution of analogies from the perspective of reflexive abstraction, we planned a series of studies (Gallagher, 1978; Gallagher & Wright, 1977, 1979) to investigate both form and content of analogies. Children, ages 9 to 12, were asked to select an answer from four alternatives and to write a reason for each of the answers: "Why do you think your choice is the best answer?" Initially it was expected that such a simple question would give us limited but fruitful insight into the process of analogy solution.

With the refinement of scoring procedures, some important findings emerged. It was possible to predict performance level from structural analysis of written reasons. At the earlier ages, associative reasons predominated with little awareness of total form (A:B as C:D). There were indications that older children manifested a freedom of form by stating true inversions (A:C as B:D) with concomitant statement of a higher-order rule as in Sternberg's (1977) analysis.

Brief mention may be made of other studies which demonstrated the value of asking for justifications or explanations: Moore's (1977, 1979) assessment of seriation problems; Jusczyk's (1977) addition of questionnaire items to a developmental study of poetry; Strauss' (1977) investigation of structural reversion of conservation; and Powell's (1977) probing for the reason for wrong answers in a proverbs test. In each of these studies, as in those previously reviewed, the addition of the probing "why" questions significantly changed the interpretation of the results. Thus, without such questioning, not only would valuable data be lost, but more importantly, the conclusions of the studies would be incomplete or even inaccurate.

Let us return to a point made earlier: the functional importance of reflexive abstraction and contradiction to learning in the wide and narrow sense. In the research of the Genevan School (Inhelder et al., 1974; Piaget, 1974a, 1974b, 1977) on reflexive abstraction and contradiction, the study of strategies involving judgments *and* explanations is basic. For example, how do we know if a child is aware of a built-in contradiction? How do we know if a child has reorganized his/her thinking, that is, the idea that reflexive abstraction may lead to contradiction? Obviously, both educators and researchers need to rely heavily upon the child's explanations.

If we are in Phase Three of applying Piaget to education, that is, the phase of mechanisms, then the method of critical exploration in both traditional and modified forms holds center stage. To discard this method or to throw out explanations may be incorrectly labeled "neo-Piagetian." However, such loss of valuable data and consequent opportunities to refine studies is hardly Piagetian, let alone neo-Piagetian. The challenge then for researchers is to attempt experimental procedures which will facilitate use of the method of critical exploration. A related challenge is to seek the implications of the research findings for the improvement of educational methods.

Sigel's question "When do we know what a child knows?" needs, therefore, to be expanded: "When will we *trust* a child to tell us *how* he/she comes to know?"

REFERENCES

Achenbach, T. M. Cue learning, associative responding, and school performance in children. *Developmental Psychology*, 1969, *1*, 717–725.

Achenbach, T. M. Standardization of a research instrument for identifying associative responding in children. *Developmental Psychology*, 1970, *2*, 283–291. (a)

Achenbach, T. M. The children's associative responding test: A possible alternative to group IQ tests. *Journal of Educational Psychology*, 1970, *5*, 340–348. (b)

Achenbach, T. M. A longitudinal study of relations between associative responding, IQ changes, and school performance from grades 3 to 12. *Developmental Psychology*, 1975, *11*, 653–654.

Brainerd, C. J. Judgments and explanations as criteria for the presence of cognitive structures. *Psychological Bulletin*, 1973, *79*, 172–179.

Brainerd, C. J. Postmortem on judgments, explanations, and Piagetian cognitive structures. *Psychological Bulletin*, 1974, *81*, 70–71.

Brainerd, C. J. Response criteria in concept development research. *Child Development*, 1977, *48*, 365–366.

Gallagher, J. M. Equilibration—the central concept of Piaget's theory. *The Behavioral and Brain Sciences*, 1979, *2*, 141.

Gallagher, J. M. The future of formal thought research: The study of analogy and metaphor. In B. Z. Presseisen, D. Goldstein, & M. H. Appel (Eds.), *Topics in cognitive development* (Vol. 2); *Language and Operational Thought*. New York: Plenum, 1978. (a)

Gallagher, J. M. Reflexive abstraction and education: The meaning of activity in Piaget's theory. In J. M. Gallagher & J. A. Easley (Eds.), *Knowledge and development* (Vol. II): *Piaget and Education*. New York: Plenum, 1978. (b)

Gallagher, J. M., & Reid, D. K. *To relate or to discriminate; that is the question*. Paper presented at the Fifth Annual Symposium of the Jean Piaget Society, Philadelphia, 1975.

Gallagher, J. M., & Reid, D. K. An empirical test of judgments and explanations in Piagetian-type problems of conservation of continuous quantity. *Perceptual and Motor Skills*, 1978, *46*, 363–368.

Gallagher, J. M., & Wright, R. J. *Children's solution of verbal analogies; Extension of Piaget's concept of reflexive abstraction*. Paper presented in the symposium: "Thinking with the left hand; children's understanding of analogy and metaphor." Society for Research in Child Development, New Orleans, 1977.

Gallagher, J. M., & Wright, R. J. Piaget and the study of analogy; structural analysis of items. In M. K. Poulsen & G. I. Lubin (Eds.), *Piagetian theory and the helping professions*. Los Angeles: University of Southern California, 1979.

Gallagher, J. M., & Reid, D. K. *The learning theory of Piaget and Inhelder*. Monterey, California; Brooks/Cole, 1981.

Gottlieb, D. E., Taylor, S. E., & Ruderman, A. Cognitive bases of children's moral judgments. *Developmental Psychology*, 1977, *13*, 547–556.

Inhelder, B., Sinclair, H., & Bovet, M. *Learning and the development of cognition*. Cambridge: Harvard University Press, 1974.

Jusczyk, P. W. Rhymes and reasons: Some aspects of the child's appreciation of poetic form. *Developmental Psychology*, 1977, *13*, 359–363.

Moore, G. W. The developmental analysis of strategies, explanations, and judgments within seriation problems. *Dissertation Abstracts International,* 1977, *37,* 7644A-7645A. (University Microfilms No. 77-13, 597).

Moore, G. W. Transitive inferences within seriation problems assessed by explanations, judgments, and strategies. *Child Development,* 1979, *50,* 1164-1172.

Piaget, J. Apprentissage et connaissance (première partie). In P. Greco & Piaget (Eds.), *Étudies de épistémologies génétique.* Vol. 7 *Apprentissage et connaissance.* Paris: Presses Universitaires de France, 1959, 21-67.

Piaget, J. *Genetic epistemology.* Columbia University Press, 1970.

Piaget, J. *Recherches sur la contradiction* (Vol. 1). *Les differentes formes de la contradiction. Études d'épistémologie génétique.* (Vol. XXXI). Paris: Presses Universitaires de France, 1974. (a)

Piaget, J. *Recherches sur la contradiction.* (Vol. 2). *Les relations entre affirmations et négations. Études d'épistémologie génétique.* (Vol. XXXII). Paris: Presses Universitaires de France, 1974. (b)

Piaget, J. *Adaptation vitale et psychologies de l'intelligence; Sélection organique et phenocopie,* Herman, Paris, 1974. (c)

Piaget, J. *L'équilibration des structures cognitives. Problème central du développement.* Paris: Presses Universitaires France, 1975.

Piaget, J. (avec J. Montangero et J. Billeter). Les correlats. In *Recherches sur l'abstraction refléchissante* (Vol. 1). Paris: Presses Universitaires de France, 1977.

Piaget, J. *Behavior—and evolution.* New York: Random House, 1978.

Powell, J. C. The developmental sequence of cognition as revealed by wrong answers. *Alberta Journal of Educational Research,* 1977, *23,* 43-51.

Reese, H. W., & Schack, M. L. Comment on Brainerd's criteria for cognitive structures. *Psychological Bulletin,* 1974, *81,* 67-69.

Sigel, I. E. When do we know what a child knows? *Human Development,* 1974, *17,* 201-217.

Sternberg, R. J. *Intelligence, information processing and analogical reasoning.* Hillside, N.J.: Lawrence Erlbaum Associates, 1977.

Strauss, S., Danziger, J., & Ramati, T. University students' understanding of nonconservation: Implications for structural reversion. *Developmental Psychology,* 1977, *13,* 359-363.

Voyat, G. In tribute to Piaget: A look at his scientific impact in the United States. In R. W. Rieber & K. Salzinger (Eds.), *The roots of American psychology: Historical influences and implications for the future.* New York: Annals of the New York Academy of Sciences, Vol. 291, 1977.

19b

Learning and Development from a Piagetian Perspective: The Exceptional Child

D. Kim Reid
The University of Texas at Dallas

Piaget (1975a) is fond of likening the adaptive mechanisms of cognitive development in children to those he has observed in herbs and snails. When a *limnaea stagnalis*, for example, is transported from still to turbulent waters, a hereditarily stable change occurs in its form. Piaget argues that this modification is the result of the snail's increasing its motor activity in order to avoid being washed off the rocks. Conviction that it is the snail's *activity*, rather than heredity or environmental pressure, which is responsible for the adaptation has led Piaget to approach the study of cognitive development in children by examining their interaction with their environments, their integration of novel elements into previous cognitive structures, and their gradual elaboration of new cognitive structures (Inhelder, Sinclair, & Bovet, 1974).

A large and steadily increasing literature relating Piagetian theory to exceptional children, however, seems to be asking two kinds of questions: What happens when something is wrong with the snail? What happens when the environmental pressures are varied? The first line of questioning led to research designed to discover whether children with various constitutional disorders progressed through the same stages of cognitive development and in the same order as Piaget had described for his "epistemic" subject. The second question focused on an analysis of the effects variation of environmental factors had on such children (Reid, 1978). These lines of research have contributed to our understanding of exceptionality by confirming that handicapped children (except the psychotic) do conform to normal patterns of stage development, although sometimes at a slower pace and sometimes with limitations on the ultimate level achieved. Further, some research has indicated that specific performances are alterable by the manipulation of task variables. Nevertheless, most research has

339

failed to ask questions concerned with how the activity of the snail might account for the observed variations. What Piaget's biological model offers researchers interested in developmental deviancy is the opportunity to extend investigations with normal children to an examination of the interaction between the deficient organism and its environment, the methods by which exceptional children intergrate new elements into existing structures, and the procedures these children use to gradually elaborate new structures.

At least two approaches appear fruitful in answering such questions about the cognitive development of exceptional children. The first is the use of the method of critical exploration to elucidate processes children use to solve problems. Because of Piaget's emphasis on interaction and the process of equilibration (1975b), researchers attempt to understand the synergistic relations between observable cues (Which properties of objects do children notice? What do they learn from the manipulation of objects?) and the children's subjective and logical coordinations (What kinds of inferences do children draw about how and why events occur? What kinds of correspondences do they make?). A second strategy would be to pursue learning studies of the type designed by Inhelder, Sinclair, and Bovet (1974). These studies were designed to activate cognitive schemes and to encourage children to search for new coordinations. Most included the presentation of activities in which the transformational aspect of the operations was made as apparent as possible. Children were asked to make predictions about the outcomes of various activities and then to observe the results when the activities were actually carried out. By heightening sensitivity to contradiction between prediction and outcome and between subschemes, such studies enable the researcher to observe the mechanisms that assure transition between and among stages (Piaget, 1974).

Studies that have attempted to analyze regulatory mechanisms in exceptional children are few and have been limited to three areas of disability: mental retardation, emotional disturbance, and a more general category that might best be described as learning disability.

The first such study was conducted by Inhelder (English edition, 1968) who reported that the thought structures of retarded children were essentially analogous to those of younger, normal children. Retarded children took particular notice of concrete properties and irrelevant cues and oscillated between higher and lower levels of functioning in a way which Inhelder (1966) later characterized as indicating attainment of a "pseudo-equilibrium."

Schmidt-Kitsikis (1976) conducted experiments with mentally retarded and prepsychotic children that both examined responses to a variety of cognitive tasks and introduced "control" tasks (roughly analogous to the learning tasks of Inhelder, Sinclair, & Bovet) to observe these children's ability to develop new coordinations in a modified situation. The mentally retarded children displayed the ability to respond adequately to both the demands of the experimental tasks and of questioning techniques. Although their deductive processes appeared limited, they were able to regulate their activities in terms of successive discoveries and a fixed goal and to thereby achieve low-level, but nevertheless stable constructions. Quite different results were found for the prepsychotic children. These children considered each action as independent and were tied to spatial and temporal considerations. They, therefore, did not evidence any sense of logical necessity and failed to establish a definite logical, structural level.

Voyat (1978) obtained similar findings with psychotic children. He reported a general lack of operational reasoning characterized by an absence of reversibility, discrepancies between modes of functioning, explanations dependent on actions rather than observations of objects, lack of order among cognitive tasks, lack of learning during the experiments, and egocentrism in justifications. Both he and Schmidt-Kitsikis concluded that the equilibrium of the psychotic child is *structurally different* from that of the normal child. Voyat postulates that this difference results from organization without adaptation to an external world and suggests the possibility of a structural relation between affect and cognition.

Our own research (Reid, Brill, Weiserbs, & Hresko, 1978) substantiates these earlier findings. We studied children who were sufficiently seriously emotionally disturbed that they could not be maintained in either regular or special classes in the public schools and were consequently attending a special day school at public expense. Of these 50 lower-middle class children ranging in age from 8 to 14 years, 32 had been previously diagnosed as having emotional disturbances related to environmental causes and the other 18 had diagnoses of organicity, especially minimal brain dysfunction. Because children with organic symptoms are typically resistant to change and most often unable to self-correct even simple errors, we were eager to see whether they would be capable of attaining the cognitive operations so dependent on self-regulation and whether their approaches to problems would differ from the nonorganic group. It must be remembered, however, that all of these children were severely disturbed.

We used three sets of tasks, which included two variants of a cognitive task, followed for those children who did not display operational reasoning by a learning task, and ending with a third variation of the original task. Conservation of substance was examined by transforming clay balls into pancakes and sausages and finally by removing clay from one side of a clay ball and resting in on another side (Piaget, 1976). This last task is usually achieved 2 years earlier than the traditional tasks. The learning task, adopted from the Schmidt-Kitsikis study, required the children to make slow and continual deformations in one of the clay balls while constantly making comparisons to the standard and then to make predictions about what would happen if the deformation were reversed. A second set of tasks required the children to seriate sets of ten pencils, straws, and cusinaire rods. The learning task involved building a staircase of blocks, with error introduced by the examiner (Inhelder, Sinclair, & Bovet, 1974). Finally, the class-inclusion tasks were all drawn from the work of Inhelder, Sinclair, and Bovet because previous research (Smith-Burke, Reid, & Nicolich, 1977) had indicated that transitional and compromise solutions were undetectable with the traditional tasks. The children were required to put into their baskets more of one type of fruit than the experimenter had in her basket, while maintaining a constant total. The learning task consisted of using a single collection to construct subordinate and superordinate classes (Inhelder, Sinclair, & Bovet, 1974).

We found little vascillation in response levels. Children most often gave a response and then maintained it across a given set of tasks. Justifications were usually based on egocentric arguments, for example, "It's bigger because I know it is," or "It's right because I did it," without recourse to the objects for proof. It was often difficult, therefore, to determine whether the children couldn't or simply wouldn't give more adequate explanations.

Although the children were grouped according to initial substage level (Inhelder, Sinclair, & Bovet, 1974), neither group at any level was able to benefit from the learning tasks. The continuous transformation in the conservation task was not sufficient to foster a sense of contradiction in any of these children. They generally watched closely, but some argued that the quantity changed immediately, while others suggested that it changed after two or three rolls. In the seriation task, even those who were able to build a staircase with each step one block higher than the previous one tended to fill in the form to make a complete rectangle or square. In the class-inclusion task, the children argued that the three apples were fruit and that each of the other items they put in the basket were also pieces of fruit. With equal certainty, counting, manipulation, and even countersuggestion, they concluded that there were more apples than pieces of fruit. None of the children performed better on the third variant of the cognitive task, which followed the learning segment. This was particularly surprising in the case of conservation, since the third task is easier than the earlier two for normal children.

In general, the so-called environmentally emotionally disturbed group tended not to try to adapt to task demands. They showed annoyance at repeated questioning, were easily distracted by irrelevant detail, and even indulged occasionally in bizarre avoidance behaviors (e.g., bird calls and echolalic responses). These behaviors were strikingly absent among the emotionally disturbed children previously diagnosed as organically impaired. They seemed to attempt to structure the tasks and their own actions, but to do so inappropriately. These children counted in the seriation task, talked to themselves and to the task materials, fidgeted, and touched objects in the room, such as the walls and the chairs. Organically impaired children did much better on the class-inclusion problems in which the children themselves introduce organization, rather than the conservation problems in which children cannot introduce or exclude properties of objects at will (Inhelder, Sinclair, & Bovet, 1974, p. 263).

The final group of children who have been studied from the point of view of the analysis of regulatory mechanisms is the learning disabled. Those with language disorders tend to compensate for their deficit by recourse to real or imagined action (deAjuriaguerra, 1963); disturbed figurative functioning becomes subordinated to cognitive operations (Inhelder & Schmidt-Kitsikis, 1963); and dyspraxia appears to affect cognitive functioning only when concrete manipulations are involved (Schmidt-Kitsikis, 1969, 1972).

Our research (Knight-Arest & Reid, 1980) was conducted within a learning paradigm and used peer interaction rather than the method of critical exploration as a means of helping children become aware of contradiction. We compared groups of normal and learning disabled children who were invited, three classmates at a time, to a party. One conserver was given a glass identical to that of the nonconserver, while the second conserver was given a taller, thinner glass. The nonconserver was asked to pour the juice until all were satisfied the portions were fair (Doise, Mugny, & Perret-Clermont, 1975; Murray, 1972).

Although most learning disabled children were able to give conservation responses after the party, none could offer justifications they had not heard from their peers. Their learnings appeared not to be integrated into their assimilative schemes. Instead, they were able to recognize correspondences between the experimental and posttest tasks and to apply a learned, specific response, but one which did not alter developmental level. As Piaget has pointed out, however, recognition of correspondences between states and transformations is an important aspect of cognitive development and may precede the acquisition of operations (1976). We were able to observe a number of compensatory strategies developed by these children: moving the glasses together to compare levels, using fingers as markers of contrasting levels, and finally of physical movements such as kneeling on the floor or moving to the side and looking up at or through the glasses. Learning disabled children resisted making inferences about their own actions. They expected to find answers in the empirical aspects of the objects, if only they could perceive them accurately!

In summary, these analyses of regulatory mechanisms have begun to facilitate understanding of how the exceptional child's *activity* (or lack of it) might account for some of the variations: The mentally retarded display adequate regulation of activity, but poor deductive reasoning, which leads to stable, but low-level constructions. The severely emotionally disturbed exhibit erratic and egocentric behaviors. They tend to assimilate the world to their own subjective needs rather than to attempt to adapt to reality and thereby resist accommodation of assimilative schemes. Although children of postulated organic etiology appeared to be attempting to structure their behaviors in accordance with task demands, their procedures for elaborating new structures were often inappropriate to the task. Finally, the learning disabled appeared most capable of developing compensatory strategies. Although they were able to establish correspondences between and among tasks, they attempted to rely almost exclusively on empirical abstraction as a learning mechanism. They concentrated, as do very young children, on affirmations, seemingly without the ability to construct negations. Actions and states of objects were adequately perceived, but the links between the actions and states were lost to these children. One cannot help but wonder whether this resistance to thinking about their activity, that is the reflexive aspects of abstraction, is not in some way related to the emphasis on perceptual stimuli so common in the education of learning disabled children. Perhaps, as Piaget (1974) has suggested, it becomes difficult for those who passively receive information from adults to learn anything without such help. If this is the case, educators could also learn a great deal from the snail!

REFERENCES

de Ajuriaguerra, J., Jaeggi, E., Guinard, F., Kocher, F., Maquard, M., Paunier, A., Quinodoz, D., & Siotis, E. Organisation psychologique et troubles de development du language. (Etudes d'un groupe d'enfants dysphasiques). *Problems de psycholinguistiques.* Paris: Presses Universitaires de France, 1963.

Doise, W., Mugny, G., & Perret-Clermont, A. Social interaction and the development of cognitive operations. European Journal of Social Psychology, 1975, *5*, 160-174.

Inhelder, B. Cognitive development and its contribution to the diagnosis of some phenomena of mental deficiency. *Merrill-Palmer Quarterly*, 1966, *12*, 299-321.

Inhelder, B. *The diagnosis of reasoning in the mentally retarded.* New York: John Day, 1968.

Inhelder, B., & Schmidt-Kitsikis, E. Observations sur les aspects operatifs et figuratifs des enfants dysphasiques. In *Problems de psycholinguistiques.* Presses Universitaires de France, 1963.

Inhelder, B., Sinclair, H., & Bovet, M. *Learning and the development of cognition.* Cambridge, Mass.: Harvard University Press, 1974.

Knight-Arest, I., & Reid, D. K. Peer interaction as a catalyst for conservation acquisition in normal and learning disabled children. *Proceedings of the 9th Interdisciplinary International Conference on Piagetian Theory and the Helping Professions, 1980.*

Murray, F. B. Acquisition of conservation through social interaction. *Developmental Psychology*, 1972, *6*, 1-6.

Piaget, J. Forward. In B. Inhelder, H. Sinclair, & M. Bovet, *Learning and the development of cognition.* Cambridge, Mass.: Harvard University Press, 1974.

Piaget, J. From noise to order: The psychological development of knowledge and phenocopy in biology. *The Urban Review*, 1975, *8*, 209-218. (a)

Piaget, J. *L'equilibration des structures cognitives: Probleme central du development.* Paris: Presses Universitaires de France, 1975. (b)

Piaget, J. On correspondences and morphisms. *Genetic Epistemologist*, 1976, *5*, 8-10.

Reid, D. K. Genevan theory and the education of exceptional children. In J. M. Gallagher & J. Easley (Eds.), *Knowledge and development Volume II: Piaget and education.* New York: Plenum, 1978.

Reid, D. K., Brill, M., Weiserbs, B., & Hresko, W. P. *The relations among seriation, class inclusion, conservation, and academic achievement in emotionally disturbed and learning disabled children.* Unpublished manuscript, 1978.

Schmidt-Kitsikis, E. The cognitive mechanisms underlying problem-solving in psychotic and mentally retarded children. In B. Inhelder & H. H. Chipman (Eds.), *Piaget and his school: A reader in developmental psychology.* New York: Springer-Verlag, 1976, 234-255.

Smith-Burke, M., Reid, D. K., & Nicolich, M. *Cognitive prerequisites of reading comprehension.* Final report to the Spencer Foundation, August, 1977.

Voyat, G. *Psychosis: A cognitive and psychodynamic perspective.* Paper presented at the 8th Annual Interdisciplinary Conference on Piagetian Theory and the Helping Professions, Los Angeles, February 1978.

19c The Power of Negative Thinking: Equilibration in the Preschool

George E. Forman
University of Massachusetts, Amherst

Piaget's theory of equilibration, recently revised and expanded (Piaget, 1977), plays heavily on the concept of negation. The child, when meeting an obstacle, compensates by actively negating something. The construction of the appropriate negation defines the child as an active learner. This constructivistic view can be contrasted with the view that learning occurs by remembering affirmations, commonly called positive reinforcements. To the constructivist, however, even positive reinforcement is the child's negation of a negation, the removal of a deficit or a gap. To Piaget there is a power to negative thinking. I would like to define this power and trace its implications for preschool education.

First, allow me to apply the binary language of negation to a case of continuous change—that old standby—the ball of clay rolled into a sausage. At a very young age the child negates the ball altogether. The sausage is a new object. Identity is not conserved. Call this the level of *ABSOLUTE DIFFERENCES*. Once the child can think about object qualities, like tall, the identity of that object can be conserved across these transformations. The ball rolled into a sausage is the same clay, but it is no longer tall. The initial state is tall, the transformed state is not-tall. Call this form of negation the level of *OPPOSITION*.

But how is the child to call intermediate states? It seems contradictory to call the same object both tall and not-tall. So the child invents the middle term "a little tall." The child has negated the "not" in the term "not-tall." You might say the child undoes the knot. Here we have three ordered categories. Call this the level of *DISCRETE DEGREES*.

At this level the child has qualified a qualification, but she is still thinking predicatively instead of relationally. A "little tall" is not yet "less tall" on a continuum. But as the discrete categories continue to multiply by forming new

345

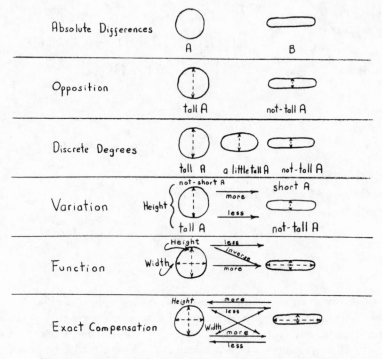

Fig. 19.1.   Six levels of cognitive development between years 1 to 6.

middle terms the differences are eventually negated and the idea of continuous change is constructed. Call this the level of *VARIATION*. At this level the child understands that tall approaches not-tall at the same time that not-short approaches short. *VARIATION* is the coordination of two series of *DISCRETE DEGREES*.

The rest of the story you probably know. The child constructs other VARIATIONS, like a change in width. At first these two VARIATIONS, changes in height and changes in width, remain separate from each other. A change in height is not seen as a function of the change in width. But this separation causes disturbances which must be negated. The child feels the contradiction when someone suggests that the rolled out ball gains in both height and width. She can see that the ball loses height. At the same time the child negates the gain-gain possibility, she, in essence, has constructed a functional relation between height and width, which is, in this case, a gain-lose relations. Call this the level of *FUNCTIONS*.

This takes us to the end of preoperational intelligence, about age 6. The next higher level, the level of *EXACT COMPENSATION* occurs when the child knows with logical certainty that the variation in height exactly compensates the variation in width, a case of operative negation. But my concern is for younger children.

So there you have it. Negated differences form opposites, negated opposites form degrees, and so forth to the level of variations and functions.

We now leave the oscillating clay and enter the any-day world of the preschooler. I will describe two activities that we have tried at the School for Constructive Play, a Piaget based preschool at Amherst for 2 to 4 year olds (see Forman & Kuschner, 1977). The first activity consists of a pair of swing seats on opposite ends of a nylon rope that passes through two pulleys attached to the ceiling. I will describe the children's free play with the swings using the language of negation.

Tanika sits in one of the swing seats, call it seat A. The teacher pushes down on seat B raising Tanika, lowers her, and repeats again. After several seconds of being at rest, Tanika jiggles in her seat in an attempt to make it go up. She obviously knew that her seat was "not up." She was beyond the level of absolute differences. In fact none of our children treated a swing seat up as a different object than that same seat down. But Tanika's attempt to negate the down seat did not work. So she stands up, turns to the seat and commands it with an emphatic "up, up." This verbal negation of down worked no better than her jiggle. A slightly older and heavier girl named Jake wants to play. The teacher places Jake in seat B. Now Tanika goes up and Jake remains on the ground. Jake looks enviously at Tanika swinging freely in midair. Jake gets out of her seat and

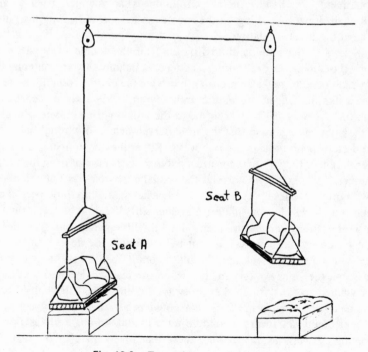

Fig. 19.2. Two swings on a single rope.

Tanika drops to the cushion below. Jake then issues a command to Tanika "I want the up swing." Evidently Jake understood that seat A was variable, but did not understand the functional relation between the two seats. Her negation of her own down position was to exchange seats with Tanika.

On another day Aaron was at these swings by himself. He pushes on seat A to make it go down. Rather by accident he notices that swing B is up. So he turns around and pushes this one down. Now seat A is up. So he turns and pushes that one down again. He repeats this alternation a good 10 or 12 times. Then he does a curious thing. He turns sideways, stands midway between the two seats and pushes down on both seats at the same time. He knew that both seats could be reversed to their respective opposites, but his attempt to simultaneously negate their up position suggests that he was not aware of the precise functional relation between the two seats. He was progressing toward the synthesis of the two variations because in some global sense he knew that seat B's movement had something to do with the position of seat A.

Loren, a 3½ year old, apparently had reached the level of functions. When he was in seat A he would tease a lighter playmate in the opposite seat by alternately pushing his feet against the floor and then relaxing his legs. His awareness of the inverse function was even more apparent when he hoisted a vacant seat to the ceiling using down pulls on the rope and let it return to the floor by pushing the rope out hand over hand. Another child, one year younger, tried to get the hoisted chair down by pulling on the rope even harder, indicating his failure to understand the inverse relation.

Consider a second activity quite different from the double swing. This simple task turned out to be very revealing. The teacher balances two rectangular blocks against each other to make an arch. To motivate the child to rebuild the arch the teacher walks his fingers under the arch saying, "My little person can walk through the doorway." The teacher takes the arch apart and invites the child to make the doorway again so that the little person can walk through it.

Children respond basically in two ways. Either they try to reconstruct a static spatial relation or they try to reconstruct a dynamic relation of one block supporting another. The next figure portrays the spatial approach. Tristan's first attempt was two upright blocks spaced apart. The teacher said, "my little person can go between the blocks, but not under." Tristan shifted to the half-T formation as shown in this slide. The teacher then said, "the little person can go under, but I want to go under and between, I want to go through the doorway." With that Tristan stands a single block upright and pivots it open on an imaginary hinge. Loren began the same as Tristan, but when the teacher declared that the little person wanted to go through the doorway, Loren rotated the half-T until an approximate arch was formed. Tristan could negate *between* by constructing *under*, but could not form the middle term as did Loren. Perhaps Loren, by anticipating *between* as *not-under*, knew that to go back to *between* would destroy the requirement to go *under*.

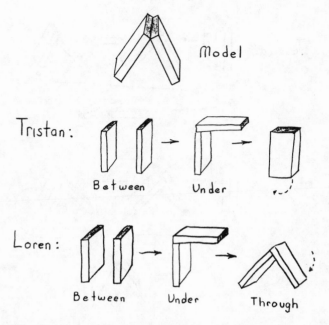

Fig. 19.3.   Two attempts to make a two-block arch. Tristan ends by making a
solid block the doors. Loren ends by tilting his half-T over.

In other cases the children began immediately with attempts to support one of
the blocks with the other. Jessica first places the two blocks together so that they
both stand alone but touching. Then she alternates, first resting block A on block
B, then resting block B on block A. Her attempts are rather discrete alternations
between these two relations. She concludes with block B resting at an incline on
block A laying flat. Loren, now shifting from his attempts to reconcile *between*
and *under* as I mentioned earlier, attempts to support the two blocks. He begins
this sequence the same as Jessica, alternating between A on B and B on A. But
his alternations seem less discrete and he eventually constructs the middle term
making valiant attempts to rest A and B on each other. Loren seems to understand that the support of A is a direct function of the support of B. Jessica, on the
other hand does not. She can, however, convert not-support into support within
each block separately. She is, at least, at the level of *OPPOSITION*. But her
failure to construct the middle term of not-not-supported, i.e., a little supported,
maintains her rather discrete alternations and failure to progress further.

So what have we learned that will help us teach young children? These
observations, and many more, suggest that certain forms of negation are preferred at different ages. During the ages from two to three children usually negate
by *exchanging* one object for another. Jake's seat did not go up so she negotiates
an exchange with Tanika. One of Jessica's blocks keeps falling so she tries the

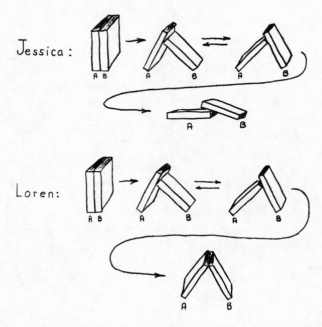

Fig. 19.4.   Two additional attempts to make a two-block arch. Jessica ends with a small hole, but not a well supported arch. Loren ends with a discovery of the mutual support between both blocks.

other block. At the play dough table, Kevin grabs the teacher's plastic spool because his identical plastic spool was not, at the moment, making the type of imprints that the teacher was making. Children make an exchange *between objects* when a change *within* their own object would do as well. At the School for Constructive Play there is a slogan: *Change Without Exchange.* Games are designed to encourage children to make within-object changes. In other words, games are designed which use the identity of a single object to help children relate successive states to each other. Instead of two bowling balls, one light and one heavy, a single hollow bowling ball is used to which children can add or subtract weight. Instead of two outdoor structures, one a tunnel, the other a well, a single tube is used that can pivot forming now a tunnel, now a well. Instead of two halloween masks, one frowning, one smiling, we use one mask with the mouth made of pipe cleaners so children can negate the smile into a frown by bending the pipe cleaners. Negations which occur within an object provide more continuity and will also help the child construct continua between discrete objects later. For after all, the within-object negation of opposites is more likely to take children through the middle term and the construction of the middle term increases the likelihood that children will progress to the level of *VARIATION*.

Of course young children must deal with between object comparisons from time to time. But even here we maintain our emphasis on the middle term. For between object comparisons the slogan: *Down with Dichotomies* is used. This means that we cause children to compare two opposites to a middle object: a three object series. The middle object should induce the conflict necessary for the child first to construct DISCRETE DEGREES and then a VARIATION that runs the range of the opposites. For example, a sphere rolls, a cube does not roll, and the elipse does a little bit of both. Add conflict to these Froebelian gifts and you have Piaget.

But it is not clear that all forms of discontinuity are bridged by this digital process of multiplying static elements. What about an analogical process like kinetic imagery? Roger Shepard (1978) suggests that the mental image can be a continuous analogue of motion. Does this in any way challenge Piaget's view that the kinetic image is initially a series of static stills, a "cinematographic" display (Piaget & Inhelder, 1971, p. 177)? Perhaps the kinetic image is cinematographic only because most objects move too fast or move without a tangible trace of motion.

With this view in mind we are trying some new games with the children. The games are called freezing motion and digitalizing motion. A child drives a tricycle through a water puddle and the tracks beyond are a trace of his continued motion. A child swings a pendulum made of a bottle that continuously drains sand as it swings. The continuity of the action is frozen by the trace that remains behind. The child can digitalize motion by rolling a spool with only a spot of paint on its rim, or by rolling a plastic gear across a layer of clay. These games may help the child convert a continuous motion into segments without losing sight of their continuity. But these games assume that the discontinuities are assimilated to a prior scheme of continuous motion. The basic question involved is as follows: is continuity conserved by an analogical process of assimilating the discrete elements to the continuous image or by a digital process of multiplying the discrete elements until overlap results. Although the child's understanding of EXACT COMPENSATIONS most certainly requires a digital logic, does progress up to the level of VARIATION also require a digital process of negating opposites? The interplay between the analogical and digital modes of thought during the preoperational period needs further research. This research should give us a more realistic understanding of the power of negative thinking.

REFERENCES

Forman, G. E., & Kuschner, D. S. *The child's construction of knowledge: Piaget for teaching children*. Monterey: Brooks/Cole, 1977.

Piaget, J. *The development of thought, Equilibration of cognitive structures*. New York: The Viking Press, 1977.

Piaget, J., & Inhelder, B. *Mental imagery in the child*. New York: Basic Books, 1971.

Shepard, R. N. The mental image, *American Psychologist,* 1978, *33*(2), 125–137.

19d The Role of Self-Directed Activity in Cognitive Development

Deanna Kuhn
Laboratory of Human Development
Graduate School of Education, Harvard University

The *constructivist* concept—the idea that more advanced forms of cognition are constructed anew by each individual through a process of "self-directed," or "self-regulated," activity—is the foundation of Piaget's developmental theory. As interesting and valuable as Piaget's stage descriptions may be, it is still his account of the processes underlying their construction that is of critical importance in terms of developmental theory. In a parallel way in the brief history of application of Piagetian theory to education, while it was initially Piaget's stages that were adopted as curriculum goals, it was soon recognized that it is Piaget's account of the constructive process underlying learning and development that provides the critical rational for the application of Piagetian theory to education.

Yet despite its fundamental role both within the theory itself and in application of the theory to education, it can be argued that remarkably little knowledge exists regarding this constructive process and that this is a critical direction in which our work must turn. In what follows I shall briefly describe a piece of research by Kuhn and Ho that was designed to begin to remedy our lack of knowledge about the constructive process. Very briefly, our objectives in this research were: (1) to monitor closely the child's self-directed activity in the process of constructing formal operational reasoning strategies in a problem-solving situation; and (2) to isolate through experimental manipulations components of this process that occupy a critical role.

This particular study is part of a larger one which has as its purpose an examination of the mechanisms underlying the transition from a concrete operational to a formal operational mode of thought. Subjects in this larger study are individuals of varying chronological ages from preadolescence through old age who show no reasoning above the concrete operational level. They participate in a several-month-long program, the purpose of which is not to teach or otherwise expose subjects to formal reasoning strategies, but rather simply to provide a rich problem environment which gives subjects considerable opportunity to exercise, and in so doing perhaps revise, their existing reasoning strategies. Our objective is close observation of the natural developmental process by means of which individuals construct new reasoning strategies.

In the particular phase of this research to be described here, subjects were preadolescents and our focus was on the critical role that "self-directed" activity has been alleged to play in the constructive process. Our intent was to examine critically this alleged role by designing two identical intervention situations with the exception that in one subjects selected the particular information-seeking activities they would engage in while in the other they did not. This was accomplished by pairing each experimental subject with a yoked-control subject, who engaged in exactly the same activities as had been chosen by his or her experimental partner. Thus, each subject of the pair was "active," each carried out an identical set of activities and hence was exposed to identical information stemming from those activities, but only the experimental subject selected the activities to engage in.

Subjects were 45 fourth and fifth graders who showed no ability to isolate variables on Kuhn and Brannock's (1977) simple plant problem. They were assigned to one of three conditions: experimental, yoked-control, and simple control. Subjects were also administered two other pretest problems: (1) the complex plant problem (Kuhn & Ho, 1977), also designed to assess the isolation-of-variables scheme; and (2) a version of the combinations problem.

The program lasted for 11 weeks. Each subject met individually with the interviewer once a week for a 20 to 30 minute session, yoked-control subjects immediately following their experimental partners. Subjects in the simple control condition received only pre- and posttests. Inhelder and Piaget's chemicals problem was used as a point of departure in constructing the series of problems. The problems were designed to require application of a combinatorial scheme and an isolation-of-variables scheme for effective mastery. The materials consisted of (1) five clear liquids labelled B, C, D, E, and F; (2) a large reagent bottle labelled A and referred to by the experimenter as "mixing liquid"; (3) a supply of beakers for mixing.

In the initial problem one of the liquids (B) was sufficient when combined with the "mixing liquid" to produce a chemical reaction, either a color change or a precipitate. The interviewer demonstrated the reaction by adding the mixing liquid to a mixture of B, C, and D, and to another mixture of D, E, and F. Only the mixture in the first beaker turned red (or cloudy). The subject was then asked the following questions: (1). What do you think makes a difference in whether it turns red [cloudy] or not? (2). How do you know? (3). Can you be sure what makes a difference? Why? (Why not?) (4). Do the others have anything to do with it? Which ones? How do you know?

Subjects in the experimental condition were then asked: Are there any other ways of doing it you'd like us to try to find out for sure? Let's set up the ones you'd like us to try.

The subject was then encouraged to plan as many experiments as he or she wished, by setting up small vials of the appropriate elements next to a beaker. The following questions were then asked, before the actual mixing began: (5). What do you think you will find out by trying it these ways? (6). How do you think it's going to come out? Why?

The interviewer then assisted the subject in mixing the chemicals, following which she asked: (7). What do you think about how it's turned out? (8). What did we find out? Questions 1–4 were then repeated.

For yoked-control subjects the procedure was identical except that in place of the invitation to experiment the interviewer substituted: Watch. I'm going to set up some other ways we can try doing it. She then set up exactly those experiments that had been constructed by the subject's experimental partner. The remainder of the interview was identical.

There were seven problem types in the series, the first being the "single-operative-variable" problem just described. The remaining problems were more complex ones in which any of two or more elements were sufficient to produce the reaction or in which a combination of elements was required. The subject's own performance determined the rate of progress through the sequence. A subject was considered to have mastered a given problem type only when, in response to Questions 1–4, the subject isolated the effective variable, or combination of variables, and correctly specified the remaining variables as inoperative. Each problem type was presented on successive occasions until the subject achieved mastery. The pretest problems were readministered during the week following the final session and again 4 months later.

As explained earlier, our major interest in the larger project we have described is the nature of the process of construction of new thinking strategies, as it may be observed during the intervention sessions themselves. Thus, our major analytic effort will consist of a detailed study of the intervention protocols of subjects in the experimental condition. In the analysis to be described here, we shall concentrate on a comparison of subjects in the experimental and yoked-control conditions, in an effort to isolate the role that "self-directed" experimentation may play in the construction process. This comparison can take two forms: (1) a comparison of the highest problem in the intervention sequence mastered by subjects in the two conditions; (2) a comparison of the posttest performances of subjects in the two conditions, as well as the simple control condition.

As would be predicted from their pretest performance, subjects initially showed little formal reasoning ability. They typically, for example, upon observing that B + C + D produced the reaction, concluded ". . . you need all three to make it turn red" (false inclusion). The majority of subjects, however, developed new reasoning schemes during the course of the intervention, despite the fact these were never modeled or suggested to them. Furthermore, experimental subjects made significantly greater progress than their yoked-control partners. In 7 of the 15 pairs, the two subjects were at the same level at the final intervention session, in five pairs the experimental subject was one problem ahead, in two pairs the experimental subject was two problems ahead, and in one pair the experimental subject was four problems ahead. In no pairs was the yoked-control subject more advanced.

Posttest data were analyzed in terms of pretest-posttest difference scores. There were significant effects of experimental condition for the simple plant problem at Posttest 1, the complex plant problem at both posttests, and the combinations problem at Posttest 1. A series of individual comparisons indicated that experimental subjects showed significant advancement over yoked-control subjects only on the complex plant problem. There is some logic to this finding. The complex problem assesses complex isolation-of-variables schemes of the type entailed in the latter problems of the intervention series. Thus, experimental subjects, who achieved mastery of the advanced problems in the intervention series to a greater extent than did yoked-control subjects, could display their more advanced competence only in the complex plant problem. There is some logic, as well, in terms of structure of the problems, to the fact that change was least on the combinations problem and only the experimental group showed significant change. Only Problems 4-7 of the series require any complex usage of a combinatorial scheme; Problems 1-3 can be mastered simply by constructing an experimental scheme in which each of the five liquids occurs in isolation. Only six subjects progressed beyond Problem 3 in the intervention series, and the majority of these were experimental subjects. Thus, the majority of subjects did not progress far enough in the problem series to necessitate their use of sophisticated combinatorial strategies.

The present results substantiate Kuhn and Angelev's (1976) finding that concrete operational preadolescents make significant progress in the construction of new thinking strategies when they are simply exposed to a rich problem-solving environment over a period of months. With respect to the comparison of experimental and yoked-control conditions that is of concern here, it should be emphasized first that yoked-control subjects did show progress during intervention. This finding in and of itself is supportive of a point often made in connection with application of Piagetian concepts in educational contexts: There is no simple definition of what it means to be "active" in a learning situation. Clearly the definition does not pertain simply to the physical manipulation of materials; children can be mentally active without using their hands, just as they can "mindlessly" manipulate physical materials. But, similarly, neither is there a simple definition of what it means to be "mentally active": Subjects in the yoked-control condition in the present study were able to make some progress in the development of new reasoning strategies based only on their observations of experimental outcomes presented to them by an adult.

Experimental subjects did make greater progress than their yoked-controls, however, and we must ask what implications are to be drawn from this fact. First, we must avoid indulging in what we have come to call the "training study fallacy." If training method A produces greater change than training method B, it does not follow that the processes involved in A more closely approximate the natural process of development of the structures in question than do the processes involved in B; nor, for that matter is it proven that either method in any way resembles the natural developmental process, simply because the methods are capable of producing the change in an experimental situation. Indeed, in relation to the present two conditions, Kuhn and Brannock (1977) argue that the situation in which an individual attempts to interpret the results of an experiment he or she has played no role in designing (the present yoked-control condition) is more common (or "natural") than the situation in which the individual constructs the experiment.

The point, rather, in conducting the sort of study we have here, is that if a difference emerges between the two methods it may perhaps provide some clues as to the nature of the natural developmental process. The experience of experimental subjects in the present study differed from that of their yoked-controls in that the experimental subjects were required to "direct" their own activity, in the sense of planning the specific activities they would carry out. Both groups were physically active (in manipulating the materials) to an equal extent, and experimental subjects did not overall appear more "interested" or "motivated" because of their additional role in designing the experiments.

The critical difference, in our view, is rather that the experimental subjects were encouraged to develop an *anticipatory scheme* with respect to possible experimental outcomes, simply because of the fact that they had to design the set of experiments that would yield one of these outcomes. The interviewer's questions ("What do you think you will find out by trying it these ways?") may have facilitated development of such schemes, but recall that yoked-control subjects were asked the identical questions. It is our hypothesis that experimental subjects, because of these anticipatory schemes, were better able to "make use of," in the cognitive sense—in other words, assimilate into a theoretical framework—the data yielded by the experiments, and thus they gained more from their experience. And thus our results lead us to the hypothesis that the natural process of development of new reasoning strategies involves an individual's attempted reconciling of an observed set of events with a "theory" that he or she has constructed to account for those events. The discrepancies that inevitably occurred between anticipated and actual outcomes may have played a major role in the constructive development that took place in the present study, or perhaps not. We are hopeful that our detailed analysis of the intervention protocols will provide some insight regarding important questions such as these.

REFERENCES

Kuhn, D., & Angelev, J. An experimental study of the development of formal operational thought. *Child Development*, 1976, *47*, 697–706.

Kuhn, D., & Brannock, J. Development of the isolation of variables scheme in experimental and "natural experiment" contexts. *Developmental Psychology*, 1977, *13*, 9–14.

Kuhn, D., & Ho, V. The development of schemes for recognizing additive and alternative effects in a "natural experiment" context. *Developmental Psychology*, 1977, *13*, 515–516.

19e Learning Symposium: A Commentary

Eleanor Duckworth[1]
Massachusetts Institute of Technology

The general theme of this volume strikes me as an extremely significant one. The emphasis is on *how* knowledge develops, rather than on the fixed stages of development, and I believe this is a much more fruitful pursuit for educators.

Just to emphasize the difficulties that educators can encounter by focusing on stages, I would like to mention some work by Christiane Gillieron (1976) in Geneva. Classically, the seriation of length is mastered at about 7 years of age, and the seriation of weight at about 9 years of age, and these two events are often taken as indicators of stage level. Piaget's explanation of this age difference is that weight is a more complex notion than length, and that therefore any operations relating to weight are developmentally later than the same operations relating to length. Gillieron, however, points out that in their classical forms, the seriation of length is logically simpler than the seriation of weights. Lengths are arrayed simultaneously, and can all be seen at once. There is no comparable way, however to size up all the weights at once. They can only be compared two by two, and inferences must be made from these pair-relationships. There is a difference in the logic required in the two cases.

Gillieron studied the seriation of lengths with a technique logically parallel to the technique used in the seriation of weights. The sticks were behind a screen, and the children had to ask for two-by-two comparisons, and from these to construct the whole series—just as they are required to do with weights. Using comparable techniques, age differences between seriation of length and seriation of weight disappear.

---

[1]These comments were prepared while the author was visiting lecturer at the University of Massachusetts, Amherst.

With this kind of doubt cast upon some of the foundations of stage-related data, I think educators do well to draw other sorts of lessons from Piaget.

One of the reasons educators are so strongly drawn to the tasks themselves is that the relationship between child and adult, in much of the Genevan research, *looks* like the relationship between a pupil and a teacher: an adult and a child are having a profitable conversation that has to do with what the child does or does not know. It is very tempting, then, to think that the pedagogical "implication" is simply to do the same thing—to do, as a teacher, exactly what Piaget did as an experimenter. There are still residues of this tendency in the chapters in this section. The work described is, on the whole, psychological research, not classroom research. What takes place between adult and child is not necessarily what ought to take place in education. *Perhaps* the specific activities researchers do with children are pedagogically appropriate. But then again, perhaps not. Perhaps the pertinence for education, once assimilated by educators, would lead to adult-child activities that are in fact quite different from the ones these researchers have done. Not all the chapters draw attention to that distinction, and I may at times fail to do so, but the reader should keep them in mind.

I would like to start with a few remarks addressed to the psychological research discussed in these papers. The first point is that I was astonished that Gallagher's paper was necessary. That one should listen to why children are saying what they are saying, rather than just to the rightness or wrongness of their answer, was Piaget's starting point 60 years ago. It is clear that the only thing of interest is *why* children give the answers that they do. This is certainly the only thing of interest to psychologists and I would argue that it is also the only thing of interest to educators, although some might want to debate this latter point. In so many of the Piaget tasks there are intermediate levels where *more* advanced thinking is reflected in a *less* good final answer; and it is only by looking at the reasoning behind the answer that we can have any idea of the level of thinking. That is only the simplest of the many reasons to urge that the reasoning and not just the right answers be the subject of psychological investigation.

My second point about psychological research is the importance of the children's interest in what they are being asked to do. Reid raised the question about her own research. When children did not respond, was it because they could not, or because they did not want to? She also referred to a number of children who were angry, or showed avoidance behaviour. Children's whole-hearted participation is really the *sine qua non* of this kind of research. Unless we are reasonably certain that the problems we are raising mean something to the children—both in the sense that they understand them, and in the sense that they find them worth thinking about—we can really draw no conclusions at all. Especially in the case of exceptional children, I think a great deal of imaginative effort must yet go into finding the kind of problem and the kind of research situation which more nearly assures that children are interested in what they are being asked to do. Let me offer, by way of suggestion, two examples from recent Genevan work.

Working with very young children can be just as difficult as working with exceptional children. How can you tell whether 2, 3, or 4-year-olds know or care what you are asking them to do? In working with very young children, Robert and Sinclair (1974) gave half the children a specific problem, but the other half were given the same material and allowed to do what they wished. A large majority of this second half happened upon the same problem by themselves. This allowed the researchers to feel fairly confident that the problem they set was a legitimate one for children of that age, and that the children's participation was genuine.

Christiane Gillieron (1978)—in a light-hearted, small-scale probe of the same question—attempted to see whether the classical problem of the conservation of weight was a comprehensible one for children from 6 to 10. She told the children that, once she had shown them the materials, she would ask them a question but that she would ask it in Finnish. She pointed out that they would certainly not understand what she was asking, but asked them to try to guess what she might have asked and then to answer that question. (The children—well socialized to school—found that a reasonable thing to be asked to do!) She showed the children the balance, established two balls of clay that weighed the same, changed the shape of one ball, and then, in Finnish, asked if the clay still weighed the same. The response was always something to the effect of, "Oh, you're asking me if they weigh the same." Six-year-olds went on to say that they did not weigh the same, of course, because one was longer now; 10-year-olds said they did, of course, because she had not added anything and she had not taken anything away.

This was nothing more than a pilot study, carried out with too few children to warrant any definitive conclusion, but indications were that the problem of the conservation of weight is indeed legitimate at those ages; more importantly, the technique for establishing whether a problem is legitimate is a suggestive one.

My third point about psychological research is more conceptual. Kuhn points out the ambiguities in the notion of what it means for a child to be "active," and the research she describes contributes some interesting analysis of this notion. Her interpretation that children who developed anticipatory schemes were better able to " 'make use of' the data," or in other words, to assimilate it into a theoretical framework, seems quite plausible. Her study complements the Karmiloff-Smith and Inhelder (1975) study described in a paper entitled, "If you want to get ahead, get a theory." This study had no control group, but in looking developmentally at children solving a practical problem, the authors documented the importance of having a "theory," a general set of reasons for why some ways worked and others did not. Only to the extent that they had a "theory" that enabled them to anticipate the outcome of any given trial were children surprised by unexpected outcomes, and, subsequently, led to modify that theory into a more adequate one. Without anticipations, there are no surprises, and without surprises, there is no reason to modify ways of thinking about the phenomenon.

I would like to turn now from the psychological research described in these papers to some of the pedagogical implications drawn, because I could not agree more with Gallagher when she says, "It is easier to *say* that Piaget's notions on learning . . . have much meaning for educators than it is to *spell out* just what this meaning may be." I would insist again that the most direct route—redoing as educators the activities that Genevans have done as psychological researchers—is probably not the most fruitful one.

Reid made one point that I find deserving of close attention. In her closing paragraph, she wonders "whether this resistance to thinking about their activity . . . is not in some way related to the emphasis on perceptual stimuli so rampant in the education of learning disabled children." This is precisely the level at which I think psychological theory can be brought to bear on educational practice. It is, moreover, an exceedingly significant question, and I very much hope that it will be pursued.

George Forman's work in designing educational activities also has the merit of drawing back from specific psychological experiments, thinking through the theoretical points, and working through from there to different activities that are specifically pedagogical.

Is there not still a step missing, however, at least in his summary account? The account would make us think that once an activity was justified through its analysis in cognitive terms, it had all necessary qualifications for a pedagogical activity. But that is clearly not the whole story. The pedagogical question is how to get children to stop and reflect. There is something about the swings which invites children's participation and intellectual struggles, and this is not simply the fact that their understanding can be analyzed in terms of levels of negation. I would even parry that Forman's invention of the swings preceded his analysis in terms of negation. Does it matter, pedagogically, whether the children's thinking about the swings is analyzed in terms of negation, or in terms of functions (Piaget, Grize, Szeminska, & Vinh Bang, 1968), or in terms of contradictions (Piaget et al., 1975)? What matters, pedagogically, is that the children are thinking.

The activities outlined earlier—the games called freezing motion and digitalizing motion—raise theoretical issues for the psychologist, and Forman has put those issues in a stimulating way. But I would also parry that the trace-leaving activities do not yet work pedagogically—that given a tricycle and a puddle, for example, few preschoolers become intellectually engaged with the trace left by the wheels. What is the difference between the swings and the tricycle?

The recent Genevan work can suggest some lines of thought for the development of pedagogical activities that encourage children to stop and reflect. One current emphasis—and the Karmiloff-Smith and Inhelder paper is an example of it—is the interplay between understanding and solving practical problems. Three recent books by Piaget all develop this theme—*Understanding Casuality* (1974), *The Grasp of Consciousness* (1976) and *Success and Understanding* (1978). Inhelder's current research also deals with this theme (see Duckworth, 1978.)

With Forman's swings, the children are trying to arrange things so they can be seated in a swing and swinging—not seated on the ground. It took a lot of varied effort for them to pull this off, and the pedagogical value would be in the thought that went into those efforts. The trace-making activities, I would guess, lack that element. Put in Kuhn's terms, there is little reason for children to anticipate a trace, or no trace, or a particular kind of trace; none of the traces is likely to surprise them, or push them to think in new ways. Wanting to accomplish some practical aim is one sure way of having anticipation in mind.

In summary, for some time I have agreed with the position put forward on the platform today, that it is not fixed points of development that should be of interest to educators, but rather the way knowledge develops. Piaget has no answer to the question of *what* it is that children ought to learn. But once, as educators, we have some sense of what we would like children to learn, then I think that Piaget has a great deal to say about *how* we can go about doing that.

REFERENCES

Duckworth, E. Either we're too soon and they can't learn it, or we're too late and they know it already: The dilemma of "applying Piaget." *The Genetic Epistemologist, VII,* 3,4, 1978.

Gilliéron, C. *Le Role de la Situation et de l'Objet Experimental dans l'Interpretation des Conduites Logiques. Les Decalages et la Seriation.* Universite de Geneve, 1976.

Gillieron, C. Personal communication, 1978.

Karmiloff-Smith, A., & Inhelder, B. "If you want to get ahead, get a theory," *Cognition,* 1975, *3,* 195-212.

Piaget, J. *The grasp of consciousness.* Cambridge: Harvard University Press, 1976.

Piaget, J. *Success and understanding.* Cambridge: Harvard University Press, 1978.

Piaget, J., et al., *Recherches sur la contradiction.* Paris: Presses Universitaires de France, 1974.

Piaget, J., & Garcia, R. *Understanding causality.* New York: W. W. Norton, 1974.

Piaget, J., Grize, J.-B., Szeminska, A., & Vinh Bang. *Epistemologie et psycholgie de la fonction.* Paris: Presses Universitaires de France, 1968.

Robert, M., & Sinclair, H. Reglages actifs et actions de transformations Etude de l'enchainement des conduites d'un groupe d'enfants de trois a cinq ans a propos de taches d'ajustement de grandeur et/ou de forme: *Archives de Psychologie,* 1974, *XLII,* 425-456.

Author Index

Numbers in italic indicate the page on which the complete reference appears.

A

Abeles, F., 54, *68*
Abelson, R. P., 224, *228*
Achenbach, T. M., 332, *337*
Adcock, C., 17, *25* , 64, *69*
Adi, H., 180, *189* , 299, *310*
Alford, G. S., 44, *48*
Allen, A., 41, *48*
Allen, T., 170, *171*
Almy, M., 261, *263*
Ames, G., 165, *173*
Anderson, R. B., 65, *69*
Angelev, J., 356, *357*
Anglin, J. M., 10, *24*
Anisfeld, M., 80, *85*
Appel, K. J., 36, *37*
Appel, M., 309, *311*
Armstrong, S., 148, *173*
Asch, S., 154, *171*
Ault, R. L., 30, *37*
Austin, G. A., 223, 224, *227*
Austin, J. L., 128, *140*

B

Bady, R., 228, *310*
Bandura, A., 6, *24* , 40, 41, 42,
    45, 46, *48*
Banet, B., 54, *68*
Barlow, J., 80, *85*
Bates, E., 129, 130, 132, 133, 136, *140, 141*
Bateson, G., 90, *94*
Beilin, H., 10, *24* , 76, 83, 84, *85* 120,
    123, 124, *125* 127, *141* , 170, *171*
Bellugi-Klima, U., 77, *86*
Bem, D. J., 41, *48*
Benigni, L., 129, 130, 132, 133, 136, *140, 141*
Bentler, P., 145, 152, 162, *172*
Bernoff, R., 309, *311*
Berzonsky, M. D., 144, *171*
Bever, T., 147, *171* , *173*
Biber, B., 237, 252, *263*
Biggs, E., 306, *310*
Bizzi, E., 108, *113*
Blake, A. J. D., 304, *311*
Blasi, A., 13, *24* , 177, 178, *187*
Bliss, J., 106, *114*
Bloom, L., 79, *86*
Botkin, P. T., 128, *141*
Botvin, G., 165, *173*

365

Subject Index

A

Abstraction
  defined, 250
  empirical abstraction, 250
  reflective (reflexive) abstraction, 54, 250,
    257–258, 334, 336
Accommodation, 55, 59
Adaptation, 55
  vs. viability in constructivism, 87–94
Assessment (*see also* Education, Piagetian
    theory applied to)
  of conservation of continuous quantity, 335
  of moral judgment, 334–335
  of verbal analogy solving, 336
Assimilation, 55, 59
  function of, 82
  theories, 71
  types of assimilation processes
    generalizing assimilation, 82
    recognitory assimilation, 82
    reproducing assimilation, 82

C

Classification (class inclusion), 143, 247, 248,
    290
  cross-cultural research, 221–224
  in exceptional children, 341–342
Communication (*see also* Language)

communicative competence, development of,
    115–116, 128
  defined, 129
  discrimination of potential agents, 139
  intentional communication, development of,
    128–140
    and object permanence, 137–138
    parental style, role of, 139
    prerequisites, 130–133
    and representational abilities, 138
Concrete operational thought (*see also* Oper-
    ational thought)
  logical addition, logical multiplication and
    reading, 275–276
  transition to formal operational thought,
    353–357
  transitivity and conservation, 276
Conservation
  criteria for conservation competence, 146–
    147, 162
  in exceptional children, 341–343
  logic of conservation and nonconservation
    competence, 147–150
  nonstructural paradigm factors, 150–167
    animate vs. inanimate materials, 154
    concrete-abstract dimension in materials,
      152–154
    discontinuity-continuity dimension in mate-
      rials, 151–152

DATE DUE
REMINDER

MAI 24 '99

DEC 15 2004

Please do not remove
this date due slip.